CINEMA & COUNTER-HISTORY

CINEMA & COUNTER-HISTORY

MARCIA LANDY

INDIANA UNIVERSITY PRESS
Bloomington & Indianapolis

This book is a publication of

Indiana University Press
Office of Scholarly Publishing
Herman B Wells Library 350
1320 East 10th Street
Bloomington, Indiana 47405 USA

iupress.indiana.edu

© 2015 by Marcia Landy

All rights reserved

No part of this book may be reproduced or utilized in any form or by any means, electronic or mechanical, including photocopying and recording, or by any information storage and retrieval system, without permission in writing from the publisher. The Association of American University Presses' Resolution on Permissions constitutes the only exception to this prohibition.

♾ The paper used in this publication meets the minimum requirements of the American National Standard for Information Sciences—Permanence of Paper for Printed Library Materials, ANSI Z39.48–1992.

*Manufactured in the
United States of America*

Library of Congress
Cataloging-in-Publication Data

Landy, Marcia, [date]
  Cinema and counter-history / Marcia Landy.
    pages cm
  Includes bibliographical references and index.
  ISBN 978-0-253-01612-6 (cloth : alk. paper) — ISBN 978-0-253-01616-4 (pbk. : alk. paper) — ISBN 978-0-253-01619-5 (ebook)
  1. Motion pictures and history. I. Title.
  PN1995.2L36 1996
  791.43'658—dc23
                                    2014036942

1 2 3 4 5   20 19 18 17 16 15

CONTENTS

Acknowledgments   vii
Introduction   ix

1. A Crisis of the Movement-Image and Counter-History   1
2. History Growling at the Door: Horror and Naturalism   32
3. Comedy, Theatricality, and Counter-History   70
4. Minoritarian Cinematic Forms as Counter-History   123
5. Memory, the Powers of the False, and Becoming   185

   Epilogue   247

   Bibliography   253
   Index   271

ACKNOWLEDGMENTS

MORE THAN ANY BOOK I have written, this book is vastly indebted to colleagues and friends. To begin with, I express my gratitude to Adam Lowenstein, who, after reading my draft of a proposal for publication, encouraged me to pursue the work. I hope that, after reading the completed volume, he feels I have not disappointed his expectations. Daniel Morgan generously read the manuscript and offered many helpful comments on it. I am grateful for the time he took from his busy schedule to devote to my thinking and for his encouraging responses. I also want to thank David Martin-Jones for his early support of the project and for his wonderful studies of cinema that are mindful of the significance of the writings of Deleuze. My thanks go also to an unidentified reader who perused the manuscript not only in terms of copy-editing but also with an eye rigorously and critically trained on the positions expressed. Similarly, I thank Robert Burgoyne for his extremely helpful critical observations on and suggestions for improvement of the text. I acknowledge the support of the Richard D. and Mary Jane Edwards Endowed Publication Fund in the publication of this book.

I owe a huge debt to N. John Cooper, dean of the Dietrich School of Arts and Sciences at the University of Pittsburgh, who has, over the years, been supportive of my work. Thanks as well to my colleagues in the French and Italian Department at the University of Pittsburgh, Francesca Savoia and Lina Insana, who were instrumental in selecting me to give the keynote address at the American Association of Italian Studies conference in

2011, where I was able to test ideas for the book. Along the same lines, I am grateful to the Italian Department at the University of Texas at Austin and to the graduate students and faculty, especially Professors Daniela Bini and Paola Bonifazio, for giving me the opportunity to present my paper "Biography, Spectacle, and Counter-History."

By way of print that facilitated my thinking on aspects of the present volume, I mention three published essays of mine that are relevant to my book; sections are included herein with permission from the presses. I am grateful to the editors for their inclusion of my works in their anthologies and for their permission to incorporate parts of them into *Cinema and Counter-History*:

"Comedy and Counter-History." In *Historical Comedy on Screen: Subverting History with Humour*, edited by Hannu Salmi, 175–98. London: Intellect Press, 2011.

"The Hollywood Western, the Movement-Image, and Making History." In *Hollywood and the American Historical Film*, edited by J. E. Smyth, 26–48. London: Palgrave Macmillan, 2011. Reproduced with permission of Palgrave Macmillian.

"Horror and Counter History: *Deep Crimson*." In *Transnational Horror across Visual Media: Fragmented Bodies*, edited by Dana Och and Kirsten Strayer, 228–42. New York: Routledge, 2013. Reproduced by permission of Taylor and Francis Group, LLC, a division of Informa pic.

My thanks to colleagues in film studies whose thinking has been influential in my thinking, writing, and teaching: Paul Bové, Nancy Condee, Colin MacCabe, Adam Lowenstein, Dan Morgan, Lucy Fischer, Lina Insana, Francesca Savoia, and Jane Feuer. And a special thanks to the editors at Indiana University Press: to Jane Kupersmith, a former editor, for her initial encouragement of the project, and to Raina Nadine Polivka, present editor, for her ongoing help in every aspect of the publishing process. I am also indebted to the friendship and ongoing technical help and intellectual support of Dr. Kirsten Strayer. I have also been extremely grateful for the indefatigable efforts on my behalf of Jen Florian, film studies secretary and mainstay; Joe Kluchurosky, my administrative assistant; and graduate student assistants Jacob Spears and Kelly Andrews. Above all, I am grateful to my dear friend Stanley Shostak for his incisive critical intelligence, humor, intellectual generosity, and companionship.

INTRODUCTION

> To me History is, so to speak, the work of works; it contains all of them. History is the family name, there are parents and children, literature, painting, philosophy .... let's say History is the whole lot. So a work of art, if well made, is a part of History, if intended as such and if this is artistically apparent. You can get a feeling through it because it is worked artistically. Science doesn't have to do that, and other disciplines haven't done it. It seemed to me that History could be a work of art, something not generally admitted except perhaps by Michelet.
>
> —Jean-Luc Godard, in *Cinema* (Godard and Ishaghpour 2005, 28)

CINEMA, TELEVISION, and the Internet have become major sources for access to historical events despite declarations of the end of history and of cinema. Nonetheless, historians, social critics, and film scholars continue to debate what constitutes an accurate and realistic version of past events in relation to cinema and in light of new visual technologies. Although the media's predilection for fiction and entertainment has often been judged antithetical to truthful and legitimate presentations of history, a growing number of critics and artists regard the cinema as a significant medium for reevaluating the nature and status of the image as a guide to the uses, and particularly the disadvantages, of history for the present and future. *Cinema and Counter-History,* as its title suggests, proposes that, in the late twentieth and early twenty-first centuries, visual media have contributed to, and continue to contribute to, an expanded and altered understanding of what constitutes historical thinking.

My book does not claim that written and visual histories are identical, but it takes seriously how visual and aural technologies "contribute to historical thinking" (Rosenstone 2006, 12). Thus, *Cinema and Counter-History* closely examines select critical writings and visual media texts that offer versions of the past and future that run *counter* to received views about historicizing. My book pays specific attention to various, often conflicting theories, forms, and styles in order to identify the philosophic, aesthetic, and political stakes in thinking through media. I focus on both dominant and marginalized or neglected forms of visual history that are implicitly or explicitly illustrative of different conceptions of space and time, of bodies and places. In identifying counter-historical thinking, I am attentive to the existence of different popular and experimental film forms and their uses of the cinematic medium in relation to camera movement, continuity and discontinuity, framing, montage, and real and virtual bodies. My discussion of film theory and historical narration is directed toward a transnational context, with major attention paid to European, Asian, and African films.

My object in thinking counter-historically is to locate it in the role of invention, artifice, theatricality, and conjecture as allowing for and enlarging on an active engagement with feeling and thought as expressed through cinema. *Counter-history* assumes an active and irreverent position for the reader and viewer in relation to the disciplines of history and popular culture in their predilection for memorializing in terms of the past, and it regards thinking on visual media as complicit with this position. This book is not antihistorical: however, it is committed to escaping history through expanding our thinking on what constitutes historical thought. To think counter-historically does not mean condescendingly admitting visual media into considerations of the past, but rather investigating and challenging the character and quality of affective investments in them as expressed through cinema.

A RATIONALE FOR COUNTER-HISTORY THROUGH FILM

The idea of moving images existed before the invention of movie technology, through explorations in physics, biology, philosophy, and the visual arts concerning development and movement in relation to time and space.

However, the invention of the movie camera in the late nineteenth century challenged thinkers to find a language and methods to characterize the new technological medium—one that promised to cross the boundaries between popular and elite art forms and science—so as to explore the potential impact of the medium on the culture. Far-seeing cultural and political writers in the United States and transnationally, such as Vachel Lindsay, Hugo Münsterberg, Béla Balázs, Siegfried Kracauer, Walter Benjamin, Sergei Eisenstein, Dziga Vertov, and André Bazin accorded serious attention to characterizing and identifying cinema's potential impact on culture and society. The problems raised through their work were hardly antiquarian but still remain fundamental to an understanding of visual culture, in light of its increasing dominance, and for rethinking the body of film and the body in film. In addressing the implications of technological reproduction, their understanding of visual culture extended to considerations of the making and remaking of historical thinking.

Pedagogy was inherent in their discussions of the fate of the new medium, also expressed by individuals and social groups through religious and social organizations, popular scientific literature, inventors, and modest early attempts to establish courses on media in a few institutions (Polan 2007). The resistance to the academic study of film was conspicuous and contentious, ranging from indifference to media to fears of diluting established curricula. Aside from production-oriented film schools in Europe and Asia, it was not until the second half of the twentieth century that college and university programs dedicated to "film studies" courses designed to explore the history of the medium, relation to the other arts, theories of cinema, film grammar and form, and modes of production were legitimized. However, the issue of what was to legitimize their intellectual focus, parameters, and methodology became—and remains—a concern of cinema as art form involving both the history of cinema and the uses of history through film. The ongoing problem of what constitutes history through cinema has had to address two questions: "What is history" and "What is cinema"? This book seeks to link these questions under the rubric of counter-history, which I define as an escape from formal history to a world of affect, invention, memory, art, reflection, and action.

Contemporary challenges to historical thinking can be traced to early twentieth-century France through the Annales school, with its focus on geography, mentalities, and anthropology. These historians emphasized a social scientific and interdisciplinary methodology that privileged earlier historical eras but largely rejected Marxism and especially its considerations of social class. The European Annales historians in their various incarnations were concerned to emphasize social theories relating to everyday life and, thus, cautiously segmented the archive for historical analysis. They broadened the boundaries of historicizing. In the aftermath of World War II, at the onset of the Cold War, their reckoning with fascism and especially the Holocaust, with a focus on memorialization, was critical in exacerbating concerns about interpretation, uses of visual data, and questions of authenticity in the proliferation of media documents (photographs, newsreels, and documentaries). The growth and militancy of global social moments in the 1960s relating to the exclusion of racial, ethnic, classed, and gendered groups also engendered a rethinking of history making through memory and through visual documents. These texts questioned the effectiveness of traditional history and chose to include personal narratives, anecdotal material, and diaries. On the theoretical front, poststructuralism and postmodernism challenged the "sacred myths of order, exhaustiveness, and objective neutrality" (Amad 2010, 4).

In the European context, the rethinking of historicizing was exemplified in the prolific influential writings of Jacques Derrida on language and deconstruction, Michel de Certeau on the "practice of everyday life," and, if differently, in those of Michel Foucault on "effective history." The writings of Antonio Gramsci and of his interpreters and modifiers (for example, Louis Althusser, Ernesto Laclau, and Chantal Mouffe) played a critical role in the 1970s in reconfiguring conceptions of history, language, politics, and culture. Gramsci's thinking is evident in the postcolonialism writings of Edward Said, Gayatri Chakravorty Spivak, and the Subaltern Studies Group in the work of Ranajit Guha. The political and transnational character of postcolonial thought sought to create a form of historicizing critical of existing treatments of historiography, especially in relation to the character of archival sources and the means and ends of investigation. Carlo Ginzburg in *Il formaggio e i vermi* ([1976] *The Cheese and the Worms*, 1989) and *Miti, emblemi, spie: morfologia e storia* ([1986] *Clues, Myths, and the Historical Method*, 1992) reflected on the practices of historians, redefining their scope and methods, which resemble crime detection in their focus on symptoms, clues, and intuitive processes. As a microhistorian, he trained his attention on the cultural practices of dominant and subaltern groups.

Hayden White's writings offered a rethinking of history in *Metahistory* (1973), *Tropics of Discourse* (1978), and *The Content of the Form* (1987), sharing with Ginzburg a skepticism of history as a science and drawing on literary forms to elaborate a "poetics of history," narrativity in particular, to identify "What does it mean to think historically"? (1973, 1). His work, especially his distinction between historiography and what he called (visual) "historiophoty" (White 1988), influenced historians such as Robert Rosenstone by bringing a "contemporary sensibility" into twentieth- and now twenty-first-century history making (Rosenstone 2006, 3) by paying attention to rethinking the archive through film images (ibid., 23).

Coincidentally, film scholars have been mindful of the role that cinema plays in addressing the past and have incorporated many aspects of historical analysis into their discussions of cinema (Kracauer, Bazin, and more recently Charles Musser, Vivian Sobchack, Richard Abel, Miriam Hansen, and Philip Rosen). Another form of historical treatment is the everyday and the ceremonial associated with the writings of de Certeau (1988) and identified with writings on Indian cinema of the 1940s and 1950s (Kaarsholm 2007). The role of allegory is an unpredictable and often painful conjuncture for locating where the past and present collide and where tropes for history "remain disconcertingly close to the habitual surfaces and mundane realities of everyday life" (Shaviro 1993, 82; cf. Lowenstein 2005, 9). The treatment of history from the position of daily life in both documentary and fiction is a mode of "archiving the world anew and revealing the provisional, denaturalized, and open nature of history" (Amad 2010, 15).

In this reevaluation of historicizing, the earlier writings of Walter Benjamin became influential, especially his *Das Passagen-Werk* (*The Arcades Project*, 2002) and *Ursprung des deutschen Trauerspiels* ([1928] *The Origin of German Tragic Drama*, 1998) for insights on historical method through his conception of modern allegory. His work enabled a serious encounter with cinema and drama as purveyors of history by bringing into relief connections between material culture and the character of the work of art in the age of mechanical (now, electronic) forms of reproduction. Benjamin's work maps the changing contours of the past in relation to culture and politics. His conception of allegory, itself historically inflected, emphasizes the incompleteness and imperfection of "objects." In his words, "Allegories are, in the realm of thoughts, what ruins are in the realm of things.... The quintessence of these decaying objects is the polar opposite to the idea of transfigured nature.... But it is as something incomplete and imperfect that objects stare out from the allegorical structure" (Benjamin 1998, 178, 179, 186).

Benjamin's work became an invitation to document and explore the existence of new and transforming modes for recollecting the past in relation to the barbarism of power and the cinematic uses of the past. His writings are a gloss on the ruins of storytelling and the rise to power of cultural and political forms to which this world of "decaying objects" has given rise: his form of allegorizing "produces a history from nature and transforms history into nature in a world that no longer has its center" (Deleuze 1993, 125) and are thus helpful for thinking counter-historically, since one of the primary elements of counter-history is its decentering of narrativity through discontinuity or fragmentation in the interests of a different relation to bodies and movement. The writings of philosopher Gilles Deleuze have become important for reconsiderations of historicizing through cinema: especially influential are two written with Félix Guattari—*Kafka: Toward a Minor Literature* (1986) and *What Is Philosophy?* (1994)—and his solo works *Difference and Repetition* (1994), *The Logic of Sense* (1990), and the two cinema books, *Cinema 1: The Movement-Image* (1986) and *Cinema 2: The Time-Image* (1989a). These works are important for the light they shed on Deleuze's continuing preoccupation with historicizing through cinema along the lines suggested by Godard, that "history could be a work of art" (Godard and Ishaghpour 2005, 28).

The cinema books, linked to the other cited texts, are not a history of cinema in the conventional sense but an investigation of film as history—or, as I prefer to understand them, as counter-historicizing. Deleuze's observations on cinema, similar to his discussions of literature and painting, are committed to exploring the civilization of the image through changing technologies as a response to a crisis of the image (Deleuze 1986, 197) as it impacts on culture and politics. His project in his reflections on cinema is to examine the image at a moment when the entire culture seems to have gone visual. If the civilization of the image has produced a concerted organization of clichés, Deleuze ceaselessly explores whether it is possible to extract from this "misery" the possibility of thinking differently about the relation of cinema and thought through an expression of bodily sensation to delineate the conditions for counter-historical thinking.

Counter-history as I develop it from Deleuze's work involves conceiving of "thought without image," in which thought via sensation is "a new principle which does not allow itself to be represented" (Deleuze 1994, 147) but is, nonetheless, a form of thought. According to Deleuze:

> Artaud said that the problem (for him) was not to orientate his thought, or to perfect the expression of what he thought, or to acquire application and method or to perfect his poems, but simply to manage to think something. For him, this was the only conceivable "work": it presupposes an impulse, a compulsion to think which passes through all sorts of bifurcations, spreading from the nerves and being communicated to the soul in order to arrive at thought. Henceforth, thought is also forced to think its central collapse, its fracture, its own natural "powerlessness." (Ibid.)

The concept of the unthought or the powerlessness of thought in Deleuze's counter-historical thinking acknowledges the intolerable and banal character of the absurd world to "discover the identity of thought and life" (Deleuze 1989a, 170). Deleuze stresses that affect and sensation are requisite bases for thought as both material and as virtual. Of particular importance is the distinction he makes between surfaces and depths, the skin and the interior body parts. If sense is on the surface and incorporeal, the work of sensation emerges from the depths and plays a major role in responses to the world. In the case of the schizophrenic, the "surface has split open" and "the entire body is no longer anything but depth," in which the "body sieve, fragmented body, and dissociated body" are the three primary dimensions of the schizophrenic body. "In this collapse of surface, the entire world loses its meaning," but what is experienced is "in a hallucinatory form" (1990, 86–87) characteristic of cinematic modernism, if not of surrealism, and hence of thinking differently about time past, present, and future.

Counter-history involves direct encounters with fragmented time as in Proust's highly cinematic *À la recherche du temps perdu* (*In Search of Lost Time*, aka *Remembrance of Things Past*) to substantiate the prominence of forms expressed through fragments, "gaps that are affirmations, pieces of a puzzle belonging not to one puzzle but to many, pieces assembled by forcing them into a certain place where they may or may not belong" (Deleuze and Guattari 2009 43). Proust's work is an example of an emancipation of time inherent to modern cinema that enables a heretical or counterhistorical view. For Deleuze,

> [*In Search of Lost Time*] is nothing more than a part alongside other parts, though it has an effect on these other parts which it neither unifies nor totalizes, though it has an effect on these other parts simply because it establishes aberrant paths of communication between noncommunicating vessels. . . . There is never a totality of what is seen nor a unity of points of view, except along the transversal that the frantic passenger traces from one window to the other "in order to draw together, in order to reweave intermittent and opposite fragments." (Deleuze 1977, 43)

This process of writing is connected with "what Joyce called *re-embodying*" and is related to the conception of the Body without Organs that is "in its own particular place within the process of production, alongside the parts that it neither unifies nor totalizes" (ibid.), reminiscent of other modernist writers/thinkers, such as Samuel Beckett with his schizophrenic strollers and their scrambled codes and circular states. Deleuze's discussions of pre–World War II filmmakers in *Cinema 1* focus on Abel Gance, D. W. Griffith, Jean Renoir, F. W. Murnau, Fritz Lang, Sergei Eisenstein, John Ford, Luis Buñuel, and Alfred Hitchcock as exemplars of the movement-image and its relations to perception, affect, and action and its crisis in the post–World War II era.

The movement-image exemplifies a conception of historicizing reliant on a conception of time that is linear, organic, and universal: "Movements are represented as actions prolonging themselves in space as reactions, thus generating chains of narrative cause and effect in the form of linear succession. Ultimately, the sensorimotor schema implies a world apprehensible in an image of Truth as totality and identity" (Rodowick 1997, 84). The movement-image in its various affective connections between situation and action is one in which history is determined by a system of judgment based on the belief "that one party will ultimately—finally and teleologically—represent the side of the right and the true" (ibid., 85). This form of thinking about history was dominant in pre–World War II cinema and was to weaken in the postwar era, leading to what Deleuze refers to as the regime of the time-image.

Deleuze's observations on the time-image in *Cinema 2* are indebted to Friedrich Nietzsche, Henri Bergson, and Michel Foucault in addressing conceptions of space, time, and sensation to reveal heterogeneities and heterochrony, "discontinuous spatio-temporal structures operating at different scales" (DeLanda 2009, 122). Hence, style as technical and aesthetic composition unleashes "strange becomings" (Deleuze and Guattari 1994, 169) and provides clues to Deleuze's modes for identifying the multiple strategies and tactics of counter-historicizing dependent on chance and discontinuities, in an interplay between molar and molecular forms of analysis. Among the numerous filmmakers included in the second volume on cinema whose works are exemplary of the time-image are Michelangelo Antonioni, Orson Welles, Joseph Losey, Jean-Luc Godard, Roberto Rossellini, Pier Paolo Pasolini, Federico Fellini, and Hans-Jürgen Syberberg, whose works experiment with history, memory, and falsifying narration.

Foucault's essay on Nietzsche and history in *Language, Counter-Memory, Practice* (1977, 139–64) intersects with Deleuze's (and Guattari's) insistence on counter-historicizing (what Foucault termed "effective history"). In contrast to Foucault, Deleuze and Guattari replaced "power relations of knowledge and power in favour of desire" in which "power is merely the zero degree of desire" (Goodchild 1996, 135), expressed through lines of flight creating thought through "heterogenesis" (Deleuze and Guattari 1994, 199)—that is, to move beyond present history into a time of becoming of the virtual and of the incorporeal, manifest through the upsurge of time and through desire as becoming. Hence, conceptions of history are transformed. For them, "History is not experimentation, it is only the set of almost negative conditions that make possible the experimentation of something that escapes history" (ibid., 111). The conception of becoming, largely derived from Nietzsche, is an ethical intervention in conceptions of belief about the world and truth that becomes "the powers of the false" (Deleuze 1989a, chap. 6). While aware of the dominant forms of treating the past consonant with the Nietzschean critique of monumentalism, antiquarianism, and subjective forms of history, their form of history is that of emergence, a becoming that is

> born in History and falls back into it, but is not of it. In itself it has neither beginning nor end but only a milieu. It is thus more geographical than historical. Such are revolutions, societies of friends, societies of resistance, because to create is

> to resist: pure becomings, pure events on a plane of immanence. What History grasps of the event is its effectuation in states of affairs or in lived experience, but the event in its becoming, in its specific consistency, in its self-positing as concept, escapes History. (Deleuze and Guattari 1994, 110)

Deleuze's escape from history is neither nihilistic nor ahistorical. It is counter-historical. Deleuze is concerned with "the peculiar way in which we can be said to be 'in time,'" with "images that make visible or palpable this 'acentered' condition or that 'sensibilize' us to it" (Rajchman 2010, 287). Thinking counter-historically is expressive of viewing practices that resist linear, exegetical, and coherent conceptions of the world through considerations of time.

The present volume focuses on strategies to generate forms of thought that work in and through the body and brain via the cinema screen. Deleuze's version of historicizing is not cynical (in the pejorative sense raised by Carlo Ginzburg in *Threads and Traces,* his 2012 book critical of postmodern views on history) but focuses on "reasons to believe in this world" (Deleuze 1989a, 172). Deleuze's position on becoming is an affirmation of thought in relation to the world, since the principle of becoming entails change and differentiation, developed through his Nietzschean position on sameness and difference as articulated in *Difference and Repetition.*

Counter-history is an investigation of what escapes history in the name of the real. No amount of reiterating events and striving to reproduce and retain impressions of the real can counteract antiquarian images and their religious and teleological narratives, except through considerations of time. The injection of time exposes how the desire to animate and preserve the past "as it was" becomes impossible and counterproductive to acknowledging change as difference. Subtending Deleuze's work is the proposition that time puts all thought into the crisis of filming history that is bound to chronology, objectivity, and causality. Deleuze does not quarrel with forms of thinking that are bound to historicizing but focuses conceptual energies on thinking differently by generating propositions about new technologies and their impact concerning ethics, choice, and determinations directed toward the future rather than the past.

Although Benjamin and Deleuze remain major interlocutors on counter-history, a few other figures have also been instrumental in challenging disciplinary forms of historical thinking. Hayden White in *Metahistory,*

Tropics of Discourse, and *The Content of the Form* elaborated on different structural forms and ideological forms to provide a philosophical method for thinking about how historical meaning is created through imaginative modes of figuration. White made the vicissitudes of representation critical to reconfiguring the notion of history as really happened. White's "metahistory" was influential for locating the differentia and investments of discourses for history.

Jacques Rancière's writings have shed further light on the various "names of history" through a poetics of knowledge that is aesthetically and politically heretical. He is aware of the three elements that are critical to a "new history": a scientific contract, a narrative contract, and a political contract, all of which entail connections between "science and nonscience" (Rancière 1994, 9), literature and common language, and the "multiple paths ... by which one may apprehend the forms of experience of the visible and the utterable ... in the forms of writing that render it intelligible in the interlacing of its times, in the combination of numbers and images, of words and emblems" (ibid., 103). In his concern for exploring the relationship between aesthetics and politics, Rancière offers a more immediately engaged sense of obstacles and possibilities for thinking art as counter-historical that seem to echo concerns involving changing conceptions of art over time, the nature of spectatorship, and, most recently, of cinema. Similarly Vivian Sobchack's *Carnal Thoughts* (2004) has invoked phenomenological thinking to address ontological issues germane to thinking involving the role of bodily affection and sensation in the creation and reception of cinema's uses of the past, and more recent cinema scholars such as Patricia Pisters and Elena Del Río have pursued this form of analysis.

The growing scholarly literature on connections between popular film and historicizing reveals a rethinking of genre forms in relation to social and cinema histories regarding the role of spectatorship (Galt and Schoonover 2010). Rosenstone's *History on Film/Film on History* (2006) contests long-held positions that viewed historical films as, at best, mere entertainment or, at worst, as escapism, distortions, inaccuracies, and harmful fictions. In addition, film historians such as Adam Lowenstein, Robert Burgoyne, Amy Herzog, and Hannu Salmi have redeemed popular cinema from opprobrium when it comes to their treatments of history.

Lowenstein's *Shocking Representations* (2005) examines films that enact historical traumas in a manner that not only redeems these texts from trash aesthetics but demonstrates the power of cinema to create a strongly affective and critical encounter through allegorizing and surrealism.

In different fashion, Robert Burgoyne in his reconsiderations of Hollywood cinema's appropriations of the American past (2008, 2010b), as well as his edited anthology on the genealogy of the epic form (2010a), offers a reexamination of historical films from a historical and transnational perspective ranging from *Cabiria* (1914) to *Gladiator* (2000). Hannu Salmi's 2011 anthology of film comedy as history explores the power of humor and parody to unsettle classical versions of history. Amy Herzog in "Becoming-Fluid," her creative yoking of Tsai Ming-liang's *The Hole* and Esther Williams's aquatic world (2010, 154–201), conjoins contemporary transnational cinema, cinema history, and social history for rethinking the past in relation to affective treatments of bodies and catastrophe and of liberating clichés about representation. In these various forms for reconsidering history via media, cinema theory and history have returned to concerns about realism, artifice, animation, and intermediality, among a number of other theoretical and formal concerns. Digital media have become a challenge to cinema history, and texts that offer versions of history through cinema now take into account the effect of these technologies: the global reconfiguration of film production, an anastomosis of formerly experimental and popular forms through genre explorations of horror, science fiction, surrealism, and special effects.

The geopolitical character of machinic and electronic images has not only affected conceptions of genre production but has also challenged long-standing conceptions of the nature and fate of national media in such studies as David Martin-Jones's *Deleuze, Cinema and National Identity* (2008), as well his *Deleuze and World Cinemas* (2011). My discussion of counter-history is attentive to the dramatic alterations in conceptions of the national body, landscape, and language. In an interview, Godard claimed that "movie-making at the beginning was related to the identity of the nation and there have been very few 'national' cinemas ... Italian, German, American, and Russian. This is because when countries were inventing and using motion pictures, they needed an image of themselves." And, on the subject of a Euro-cinema, he added, "Today if you put all these people in one so-called 'Eurocountry,' you have nothing: since television is television, you only have America" (Petrie 1992, 98).

Godard's comments, contentious though they may be, are now one more compelling invitation to rethink cinema production and cinema history within and beyond the national boundaries and expressive forms pertinent for contemporary considerations of history making and unmaking. Godard's work on cinema, especially his *Histoire(s) du cinéma* documentaries (1988–98), projects a very different sense of cinematic memory, problematized through boundary crossings that complicate conceptions of national forms and their connections to both film and social history. He provides an alternative, pedagogical sense of the potential of the image in this cinematic essay series that is an intervention in the melancholy reflections on the death of cinema, one consonant with Paul Virilio's observations on the fate of the image in a regime of speed and acceleration, where "there is no more here and there, only the mental confusion of near and far, present and future, real and unreal—a mix of history, stories, and the hallucinatory utopia of communication technologies" (Virilio 1997, 35).

On these grounds, I examine counter-history as a form that contests deterministic, linear, and reductive thinking in order to situate media within a different cultural and political trajectory, one that acknowledges the dynamic and rhizomatic character of the cinematic image, with the assistance of the writings of Deleuze. His conceptions of the movement- and time-images are a major force for rethinking cinematic historicizing expressed as perception and affection that enable or frustrate conceptions of agency and action and, above all, unsettle certainty about events.

Changing events between the two world wars and fascism, among other world-historical transformations, contributed to a weakening of sensorimotor responses indicative of a crisis of the movement-image (Deleuze 1986a, 206–15). The time-image introduces a different dimension of cinematic form in relation to space and time, subjectivity and objectivity, and conceptions of the real and the imaginary. Critical to conceptions of counter-history is how characters become viewers through forms of seeing and hearing "what is no longer subject to the rules of a response or an action" (Deleuze 1986, 3). The body becomes central in a cinema in which "characters are constituted gesture by gesture and word by word ... less to tell a story than to develop and transform bodily attitudes" (ibid., 193).

Hence, the modernist political film will demand a greater attention to optical and sound situations than to narrative or to common sense. Deleuze's writings on the movement-image and time-image have moved film study further in the direction of historical and global issues, reconsiderations of mimesis and representation, and complex assessments of affect, sensation, and reception.

ORGANIZATION OF THE BOOK

The chapters of *Cinema and Counter-History* are particularly engaged with the philosophical import of thinking about repetition and difference: how these are expressed through various existing forms of cinema, conceptually and globally, that rethink movement and time through cinema (and related literary, dramatic, and musical forms) and are central to thinking differently about events, time, and space. Working against the tendency to focus on national cinema traditions to the exclusion of their connections to world media, I have selected visual texts (and critical discussions of them) from different parts of the world (for example, Europe, the United States, Russia, India, and Africa) to illustrate conflicting theoretical perspectives; differing narrative forms; styles, relations to other arts (painting, music, and architecture); uses of actors (professional and nonprofessional) and of landscape, imaginary and actual; metropolitan and rural spaces; and treatments of documentation. Among the diverse works that I select for discussion as contributing to historical thinking are films by John Ford, William Wellman, Dario Argento, Djibril Diop Mambéty, Satyajit Ray, Arturo Ripstein, Fernando Solanas, Sally Potter, Carlos Saura, Park Chan-wook, Sylvain Chomet, Aleksey Balabanov, Tsai Ming-liang, Michael Haneke, Jane Campion, and David Cronenberg. Each of the next five chapters concentrates on strategies used by these filmmakers that identify their works as suggesting a crisis in thinking historically, in relation both to media history and to conventional modes for conceptualizing agency, action, ethics, and spectatorship.

Chapter 1, "A Crisis of the Movement-Image and Counter-History," focuses primarily on the Hollywood western to discuss pre–World War II cinematic forms of history. Derived from nineteenth-century conceptions of history and modified by cinema, the film western is an instantiation of the power of the cinematic image to animate confidence in historical agency as well as symptomatic of a decline in the belief of agency. I situate my discussion in the light of Deleuze's conception of the movement-image as expressive of the body, faces, and spaces that engender affects organized around action in ways that allow for a sophisticated comprehension of the power of monumental, machinic, and organic forms in presenting the past. This chapter focuses on two silent films, James Cruze's *The Covered Wagon* (1923) and John Ford's *The Iron Horse* (1924), and three sound films, John Ford's *Stagecoach* (1939), George Marshall's *Destry Rides Again* (1939), and William Wellman's *The Ox-Bow Incident* (1943). I argue that these films offer changing cinematic versions of actual or fictional historical figures through affective images (faces, bodies, objects, landscapes) that dramatize a founding or refounding of the American nation.

The transformations in style between 1923 and 1943 exemplify changing attitudes toward history—attendant on the emergence of fascism, World War II, and ultimately the Cold War—that, in their form of narration, are revealing of counter-history. The commercial cinemas of Hollywood, as well as those internationally, revealed signs of the inadequacy of the movement-image as expressed through action and indicated the need for the creation of mental images to confront the loss of belief in historical and national destiny that Deleuze identifies as a crisis. Thus, the chapter also includes a discussion of Tonino Valerii's *My Name Is Nobody* (*Il mio nome è Nessuno*, 1973), as a self-reflexively critical and parodic exploration of the Italian western that memorializes the passing of the Hollywood western through its treatment of history as myth. This chapter concludes with a discussion of *Meek's Cutoff* (Kelly Reichardt, 2010), a revisionist western that focuses on uncertain knowledge to investigate history and myth.

Chapter 2, "History Growling at the Door: Horror and Naturalism," increases the value of the character and impact of filmmaking in light of this crisis of the movement-image by addressing "apparent characteristics of the new image" (Deleuze 1986, 210), as in neorealism and other forms of realism. However, as recent writers on postwar cinema have indicated, the cinematic newness, the "neo," was "stained" by the past and was attached to older forms of melodrama, reacting to the "inordinate pretension of a defeated country, an odious form of blackmail, a way of making the conquerors ashamed" (ibid., 212). Karl Schoonover, in his revaluation of the critical writings on the films identified with neorealism, also revises prevailing views of these films by focusing on their body politics (corporeality) in a sympathetic appeal to the global spectator. Neorealism's optical politics was to have an impact on subsequent cinema either as a "visual commodity" or as an attempt to undermine its appeal (2012, 229–30).

As defined by Deleuze, neorealism was set in motion, nationally and internationally, in fiction and nonfiction film. An elliptic form, the weakness of linkages among events, the adoption of a journey form, and attention to the detection of habitual formulas have become clichés characterizing this cinema. Neorealism and its historical interpreters claimed to abjure historical narratives to challenge the prefabricated roles identified with the characters and situations identified with the prior popular cinema, particularly under fascism, war, and reconstruction. While in commercial cinema there was evidence of "a negative or parodic critical consciousness," according to Deleuze, the crisis was how to create a cinema that would enable a "thinking image" (Deleuze 1986, 214–15) to challenge historicism and substitute a sense of history as "becoming."

This chapter, thus, examines films that are identified with the Deleuzian crisis of the movement-image in the direction of examining the body, violence, and sensation but that operate differently from neorealism through the surreal, grotesque, and horrific, revealing a different, though related conceptual, response to the crisis. The films selected for this chapter can be traced back in cinema history to surrealism, Artaud's theater of cruelty, and the aesthetics of the horrific. They exemplify a crisis of history and of the body in the movement-image, trapped in a form of naturalism that does not culminate in redemption or restoration but produces reflection, if allegorically, on thinking images of the world seen through violence to the body. Such films as Argento's *Deep Red* (1975) and *The Stendhal Syndrome* (1996), Ripstein's *Deep Crimson* (1996), and Park Chan-wook's *Thirst* (2009) invoke a theater of cruelty as confrontation with the intolerability of a world in which vision is imperiled. These films call attention to what Karl Schoonover has termed an "epistemological crisis" (2012, 220) and to what Deleuze regards as one expression of the crisis of the action-image where impulse, rather than affection, obstructs ethical action.

Chapter 3, "Comedy, Theatricality, and Counter-History," explores the role of humor as an alternative to the melodramatic for combating the ubiquity of the cliché. This chapter underscores the power of humor and parody to unsettle classical versions of history, if not always in the interests of counter-history. For Foucault, "effective history" is differentiated from traditional history by the parodic and the farcical, which expose its disguises and masquerades (Foucault 1977, 160), by the dissociation of identity "which we attempt to support and to unify under a mask" (161), and by a "sacrifice of the subject of knowledge" (162). Deleuze's comments on history and humor are central for clarifying my conception of counter-history. In addressing effective forms of historicizing, Deleuze introduces "a new value, that of humor" (1990, 141). Humor becomes for Deleuze an aesthetic expressing a "physical art of signals and signs determining the partial solutions or cases of solution" (1994, 245), in contrast to monumental and generalizing forms for narrating history—thereby evoking Foucault's comments on "effective history."

I focus on different forms of comedy in their invocation of the carnivalesque through their considerations of the body, the body politic, and biopolitics in the uses of parody, farce, and allegory as they relate directly to counter-historical investments. My focus is on previously marginalized films such as *Carry On Up the Khyber* (1968) and its farcical treatment of British imperialism, three films set in a medieval context: *Brancaleone's Army* (1966), *Brancaleone at the Crusades* (1970), and *Monty Python and the Holy Grail* (1975). Mario Monicelli's *The Great War* (1959) and *The Organizer* (1963) are not easily subsumed under the genre of comedy and its relation to laughter, but the chapter argues for a view of comedy, exemplified by the *commedia all'italiana*, that entails a tragicomic treatment form of historicizing in which the comedic is used to portray a version of counter-history.

Similarly, the films' engagement with history through the comic involves dancing and musical bodies in confrontation with natural or social history to become a form of Foucaultian "effective history." Their historical treatments of bodies puncture monumental conceptions of the past by regarding them not from superior heights but with a shortening of "vision to those things nearest it—the body, the nervous system, nutrition, digestion, and energies; it unearths the periods of decadence and if it chances upon lofty epochs, it is with the suspicion—not lofty, but joyous—of finding a barbarous and shameful confusion" (Foucault 1977, 155). Although the films might seem frivolous portraits of history in their emphasis on the body and on sexuality, they invite a rethinking of the mechanisms that underpin (literally as well as metaphorically) the exercise of political force and power, introducing disorder and confusion into a system of beliefs and practices that have consequences for counter-assessments of history.

Chapter 4, "Minoritarian Cinematic Forms as Counter-History," examines the politics and aesthetics of counter-historicizing in European and non-European literature and cinema. Postcolonialism and poststructuralism have immeasurably complicated questions of identity, subjectivity and objectivity, fact and fiction, space and time. The films selected for discussion offer versions of storytelling identified by Deleuze with the writings of Franz Kafka, with gendered sexual bodies, and located in other global spaces where minorities have been given voice spoken through the language of colonizers.

This form of counter-history, often identified with postcolonial narratives, involves the "invention of a people" through storytelling (Deleuze 1989a, 217), through radical "experiment[s] in modes of constructing historicity" (Rosen 2001, 289). These may focus on invention through song and dance, as in three films involving the tango as a medium to include the cinema of exile and repression in Argentina: *Tangos: The Exile of Gardel* (Solanas, 1985), *Tango* (Saura, 1998), and *The Tango Lesson* (Potter, 1997), a postfeminist drama of difference, of becoming. In this cinema of minorities, the people are "doubly colonized: colonized by stories that have come from elsewhere, but also by their own myths become impersonal entities at the service of the colonizer" (Deleuze 1989a, 222). In the case of Potter's film, the issue of women's access to language and power is addressed through a cinema of the body to transform bodily attitudes (ibid., 193).

In Ousmane Sembène's *The Camp at Thiaroye* (1988) and Djibril Diop Mambéty's *Hyenas* (1992), memory serves to highlight what has been forgotten or repressed by means of a self-conscious strategy for addressing storytelling through a conception of cinema as pedagogy. History and memory function critically, not to recover a lost moment in the past but to interrogate and repeat the past in pedagogical fashion, so as to allow difference to emerge—if not always for the characters, then at least for the viewers. According to Deleuze, this type of filmmaking seems most political among the "third world and minorities[, which] gave rise to authors who would be in a position, in relation to their nation and their personal situation in that nation, to say: the people are what is missing" (Deleuze 1989a, 217). The two African directors discussed are in the position of producing "collective utterances capable of raising misery to a strange positivity, the invention of a people" (ibid., 222).

Through myth and allegory, the spectator is challenged to confront a complex assemblage of elements that not only reconfigure the past but also place it in relation to the present and the future. Their languages and narrative styles are built on the ruins of the past and on the project of creating another past: one different from conventional narratives of homeland and monumental history and with an eye to the present and future. The style is intertextual and polylingual, drawing on forgotten fragments of social history, myths, folklore, and everyday events; on multiple and colliding languages; and on the changing geography and landscape integral to the counter-history they dramatize. I explore how in minoritarian cinema the viewer is given a distinct instance of counter-history inasmuch as it adopts this mode of minoritarian address. I end the chapter with a discussion of two films by Tsai Ming-liang, *The Hole* (1998) and *What Time Is It over There?* (2001), that offer multivalent responses to time, place, and bodies.

Chapter 5, "Memory, the Powers of the False, and Becoming," undertakes an analysis of Deleuze's complex elaborations on temporality and its relation to truth. What Deleuze calls "the powers of the false" (1989a, chap. 6) renounce reductive forms of judgment and unexamined belief through and about cinema that rethink conceptions of falsity as the expression of the inexpressible. Deleuze regards the cinema of the time-image as introducing uncertainty concerning the role of vision and sound central to the crisis in the movement-image, wherein the sensorimotor links between perception and affection are altered. The cinema of the time-image introduced characters that have become viewers, seeing and hearing "what is no longer subject to the rules of a response or an action" (Deleuze 1989a, 3). In this cinema, Deleuze writes,

> We run in fact into a principle of indeterminability, of indiscernibility: we no longer know what is imaginary or real, physical or mental, in the situation, not because they are confused, but because we do not have to know and there is no longer even a place from which to ask. It is as if the real and the imaginary were running after each other, as if each was being reflected in the other, around a point of indiscernibility. (Ibid., 7)

Deleuze's writings on cinema are concerned with history but from an ontological and ethical position involving temporality as a becoming that, "although it does not take place 'elsewhere' than in history, although it is born in history and always falls back into it, it nonetheless does not belong to history" (Marrati 2008, 85). The cinematic world of the time-image is not reducible to chronology, automatism, codified truth, or formula. Deleuze is arguing against a reductive conception of the image in terms of adequacy of representation and habitual response, substituting instead conceptions of the cinematic image that are dependent on the coexistence of different orders or levels of duration and change. The object is to examine the possibility of thought and, hence, of a form of cinema that introduces thinking into the process of image making through the insertion of time.

Direct images of time challenge habituation and shift attention onto philosophic issues through the potential of the cinematic apparatus to put the actual into crisis by intertwining it with the virtual. Cinematic history is thereby addressed as being incommensurable with "a teleological History: it is discontinuous, interstitial, and it serves to destabilize and falsify notions of identity and truth" (Herzog 2010, 156). When placed in the crystals of time, truth is constantly being modified and challenged, "not according to subjective variations, but as a consequence of disconnected places and de-chronologized moments" (Deleuze 1989a, 133). This is the powerful, non-organic life which grips the world" (ibid., 81). What we see in the crystal is the gushing forth of time through different facets of time and thereby "time itself ... as affector and affected, 'the affection of self by self'" (ibid., 83). Truth when placed in the regime of time renders absolute judgments false. Narration is, thus, constantly being modified and challenged, "not according to subjective variations, but as a consequence of disconnected places and de-chronologized moments" (ibid., 137).

Asking what takes the place of continuity, teleology, and eschatology, Deleuze answers, "bodies, which are forces, nothing but forces" (1989a, 139). This form of narration is aligned with Deleuze's "powers of the false" and a form of becoming. In the discussion of the powers of the false and their imbrication in time, Deleuze invokes Nietzsche to reinforce his own view of the necessity of challenging transcendental categories of belief. In a Nietzschean vein, "the new narration ... substitutes the power of the false for the form of the true, and resolves the crisis of truth ... in favour of the false and its artistic, creative power" (ibid., 131). In the Nietzschean world, "the truthful man ... wants nothing other than to judge life.... [H]e sees in life an evil, a fault which is to be atoned for: the moral origin of the notion of truth" (ibid., 137).

At stake in falsifying narration is indiscernibility between the real and the imaginary, the true and the false, as revealed through the crystal images of time. While "truthful narration is developed organically, according to legal connections in space and chronological relations in time," falsifying narration "shatters the system of judgement," since "the elements themselves are constantly changing with the relations of time into which they enter, and the terms with their connections" (Deleuze 1989a, 133). Among the characters that populate the power of the false are the forger, the confidence man, the hypnotist, the liar, and the artist; these figures dislodge universal claims to truth and instead expose that "even 'the truthful man ends up realizing that he has never stopped lying'" (Nietzsche quoted by Deleuze, ibid.). However, not all falsifiers are guarantors of escaping the will to truth. There are those who are indicative of the "impoverishment of the vital force [*élan vital*], of an already exhausted life" (ibid., 146) in the service of rage and *ressentiment*. They are exemplars of nihilism, of a negative will to power.

As introduction to forms of global neorealism that altered national and international filmmaking in the direction of thinking counter-historically, I examine Satyajit Ray's Apu trilogy, *Pather Panchali* (1955), *Aparajito* (1956), and *Apu Sansar* (*The World of Apu*, 1959). However, it is his Calcutta "city films" of the 1970s, *The Adversary* (1971), *Company Limited* (1974), and *The Middleman*, 1976), that enable profound and variant encounters with the powers of the false.

The films I have selected to probe counter-history from the position of the powers of the false include David Cronenberg's *A History of Violence* (2005), an expression of falsifying narration that challenges belief in righteous moral action as being based on claims to truth through its focus on a protagonist who is a liar. My discussion also considers *The Illusionist* (Chomet, 2010), a work of animation in which a magician, Tatischeff—the animated figure of filmmaker Jacques Tati as double—becomes the film's strategy for invoking time and memory through cinema to offer a philosophic confrontation with orders of time that "pose inexplicable differences to the present and alternatives which are undecidable between true and false to the past" (Deleuze 1989a, 131). Two films by Michael Haneke, *The Piano Teacher* (2001) and *The White Ribbon* (2009), are my opportunity to examine the filmmaker's treatments of violence and torture, in which the spectator is implicated in a form of falsifying narration reminiscent of Artaud's theater of cruelty. Finally, three films by Aleksey Balabanov—*Trofim* (1996), *Of Freaks and Men* (1998), and *Morphia* (2008)—are further examples of falsifying narration that question reigning truths and unsettle habitual modes for addressing recollection and memory regarding social history, the history of cinema, the role of spectatorship, addiction, violence, and history. They offer a form of biopolitics in relation to memory, space–time, the body, the real, and the imaginary that is critical to understanding the different registers of time and their crystalline expressions as constituting forms of counter-history.

In these films, allegorizing becomes a major mode for addressing uncertain relations among past, present, and future. According to John David Rhodes,

> Allegory makes use of an earlier text that is no longer sufficient but is nonetheless necessary—necessary for pointing out the text's insufficiency and the nature of that insufficiency. Furthermore, allegory is a mode of both transparency (seeing through to the earlier text) and transformation (taking what that text did and doing something else with it) and therefore is not about one-to-one correspondences. (Rhodes 2007, 69–70)

This form of allegorizing gives rise to a multilayered and often uncertain set of meanings that challenge positivist and univalent interpretations of events, personages, and their existence in space and time.

Walter Benjamin's *Arcades Project* and *The Origin of German Tragic Drama* and Gilles Deleuze's *The Fold* (1993b) focus on the allegorical and neobaroque character of films in which visual images of the past are scattered throughout the natural and social landscape, emblematic of past melodramas but also redolent of the possibility to blast open time's continuum. Benjamin wrote, "Allegories are, in the realm of thoughts, what ruins are in the realm of things. . . . The quintessence of these decaying objects is the polar opposite to the idea of transfigured nature. . . . But it is as something incomplete and imperfect that objects stare out from the allegorical structure" (1998, 178, 179, 186). An emphasis on the incompleteness and imperfection of allegorical "objects" enables new and different forms for rethinking the past in the present. Benjamin's writings are a gloss on the ruins of storytelling evident in the rise to power of cultural and psychic forms to which this world of "decaying objects" has given rise. Thus, Benjamin offers a different conception of historical thinking in which counter-history assumes a prominent position. The films discussed in chapter 5 emblematize the difficulty of thinking counter-historically through conceptions of time that appear disjointed, their images opaque, and their meanings indiscernible in terms of the relations between subject and object; and they challenge false expectations of transcendence through the selection of figures who are exhausted, immoral, and degenerate.

Cinema and Counter-History closes with a brief discussion of the fate of cinema, concerning its investments in history in the age of digital media. Deleuze's *Cinema 2*, both in relation to his comments on the time-image and his ambivalent explorations of future forms involving digital media, raises questions about the future of visual media in the light of past and recent formulations on the society of control. Against the threats of "informatics," Deleuze's work beckons toward an exploration of new projects that "respond to the virtual as an energetic field of what has yet to be thought or registered" (Murray 2010, 360) in which concerns with memory become a counter-history, a philosophy of the future, a kind of science fiction that "induces the impossible and unthought, and that refuses to be assimilated" (Flaxman 2012, 21).

CINEMA & COUNTER-HISTORY

1

A Crisis of the Movement-Image and Counter-History

A FORM OF history making, associated with the cinematic treatment of national history, involved monumental and antiquarian modes of filmmaking; these flourished in pre–World War II cinema and were described by Deleuze in *Cinema 1* as characteristic of the movement-image. In this chapter, I examine films that are representative of the movement-image as exemplified by the Hollywood western, a cinema where history and myth converge to express ethical leadership, the presence of a people, an organic relation to nature, and the performance of requisite action. Two westerns from the mid-silent era are addressed: James Cruze's *The Covered Wagon* (1923) and John Ford's *The Iron Horse* (1924). This form of filmmaking—much as with the earlier epics by D. W. Griffith, *The Birth of a Nation* (1915) and *Intolerance* (1916)—underwent a crisis in identity and belief in the post–World War II world, giving rise to forms that revealed altered modes of perception, affect, and action, as these effect thinking differently about historicizing. Hence, I also discuss three Hollywood films from the sound era that exemplify the crisis of the action-image from the interwar years up to World War II: John Ford's *Stagecoach* (1939), George Marshall's *Destry Rides Again* (1939), and William Wellman's *The Ox-Bow Incident* (1943).

Deleuze's discussion of the "crisis of the movement-image" (1989a, 43) extends his explorations of the cinematic image into a different type of image, the time-image, which he claims was initiated by Italian neorealism and further developed by the French New Wave as a cinema of thought. However, the movement-image did not disappear; instead, it accommodated to more self-reflexive and critical forms of narration evident in *Paths of Glory* (Kubrick 1957), a fictional treatment of World War I trench warfare. The film dissects the rules of war and visually identifies characters and milieu with the game of chess. Refusing to monumentalize, reinforce national identity, and elevate heroic action, this counter-historical film destabilizes revered styles of militarism and patriotism derived from official and popular history, photography, and cinema to stage a crisis of the movement-image and belief in action.

In writing on the movement-image and its realization of action, Deleuze engages with philosophical and aesthetic concepts that account for the power of the cinematic image both to animate confidence and belief in historical agency and to express symptoms of a loss or transformation in this belief. His is neither an archival nor an empirical study of history proper; nor is it a generic study of historical films, though his work speaks to the changing functions of film that are indeed historical. Rather, his is a taxonomy of cinema's expressive uses of the body, of faces, and of spaces that engender affects as sensations conducive to action on a milieu generated through "movement as physical reality in the external world, and the image, as psychic reality in consciousness" (Deleuze 1986, xiv). His emphasis is on "images and the signs which correspond to each type" of "pre-verbal intelligible content" (ibid., ix), involving a perception of images before they are consciously apprehended or acted on.

What engages Deleuze's attention in the exploration of the movement-image realized through perception is its mobilization of a sensorimotor response to constitute a delayed reaction "between a perception which is troubling in certain respects and a hesitant action" (Deleuze 1986, 65). This hesitancy is resolved, on the one side, through affects being "actualised in an individuated state of things, and in the corresponding *real connections* (with a particular space–time, *hic et nunc*, particular characters, particular roles, particular objects)" that are essential to realization of the action-image (ibid., 102; his italics). But there are perceptual responses not realized in affection and action. When the affection-image is idealist, spiritual, or even degenerate, perception points to an "'acentred'" state of things (Flaxman 2000, 97). This form of cinema is exemplary of a crisis of the movement-image and contributes to an understanding of what escapes history proper. What is distinctive is how the affection-image, contrary to the action-image, introduces the element of time—in terms of a choice for violence and destruction rather than the moral imperatives of the action-image.

In discussing the movement-image, Deleuze distinguishes among perception-, affection-, and action-images to designate bodily modes of response that transform movement to produce a new response to the images received (Rodowick 1997, 34). Hence, Deleuze creates a taxonomy, a classification, of the variety of images and signs "to present a world situation that is recognizable to the spectator and which can put coherent subjects to work to re-order that world" (Deamer 2009, 162). Following philosopher Henri Bergson's *Creative Evolution* (1998) and *Matter and Memory* (1988), Deleuze derives his conception of perception from the physical universe, in which images are matter in movement reliant on "the propagation of energy and force" (Rodowick 1997, 31). The images are "everything that appears" (Schwab 2000, 112) but are distinguishable from what they will become through the bodies, the sensory organs and mind that perceive them. The initial perception of images emerges as a *prehension* of things that "are incomplete and prejudiced, partial, subjective" (Deleuze 1989a, 64), since they entail a subtraction, an elimination of unwanted data.

Henri Bergson's conception of an acentered universe accords with Deleuze's conception of the universe "as a perfect *metacinema* but only when it has also given rise to 'living images' and to everything that our ordinary perception sees and names: actions, affects, bodies" (Marrati 2008, 32–33). Deleuze relies on a twofold character of the image as an origin of effects and as a reaction to the image in differential forms of expressivity that are both subjective and objective, involving both inside and outside. While perception is one side of the movement-image and its other is action (images to be acted on), affection conveys the emotional intensity that animates the "domain of the action-image" (Deleuze 1986, 97). Affection serves, on the one hand (as in close-ups), to "tear the image away from spatio-temporal coordinates in order to call forth the pure affect as the expressed" (ibid., 96). On the other hand, affect leading to action in a determinate space–time is "actualised in a state of things" (ibid., 106), producing real connections among objects, people, and events and, thus, conducive to historical films via movement as moral action.

The movement-image as conceived by Deleuze in *Cinema 1* is dependent on organic, dialectic, quantitative, or intensive forms of montage. This image involves the "people" or their representatives, who find themselves in situations where they must overcome a threatening milieu and establish (or restore) a moral order to the community. The generation of affect and forms of action differs among American, Soviet, German, and French pre–World War II filmmakers such as Griffith, Eisenstein, Gance, Renoir, Murnau, and Sternberg, though the impetus in each is toward "a true and a good world, that bestows order on life from a transcendent perspective" (Rodowick 1997, 135). These various forms of montage are composed of segmentations of space whose parts are commensurate with the whole of the film in producing universal, linear, and teleological conceptions of history. What connects the various kinds of montage that Deleuze identifies is their adherence to expressive organic or machinic forms that convey belief in the world via the combination of the senses via affection and realization through meaningful actions.

One expression of the movement-image in its action-oriented incarnation is conveyed in its large form, a form of universal or monumental cinema, in which actions are determined by heroic figures acting in the interest of the community to modify situations through action (Deleuze, 1986, 146–48). Following Nietzsche's discussion of monumental and antiquarian forms of history, the affect of monumentalism can be seen as a celebration of great figures and actions and that of antiquarianism as veneration of customs and artifacts from the past. The epic form—the large form, as Deleuze terms it—belongs to forms of historicizing that involve the vast natural landscape and address the hero's passionate commitment to contend with forces that lie in the way of realizing the ethical goals of overcoming or subduing natural and social obstacles that confront a community and its survival. But there are forms other than the large that are also characteristic of the action-image, discussed by Deleuze under the rubric of the "small form and burlesque" (ibid., 169–77), indicative of a critical or comic treatment; these too may be counter-historical, that is, critical of ways of seeing and, hence, thinking about events.

FRONTIER SPACES AND AFFECTION-IMAGES

The Hollywood western from the 1920s to the 1940s is a key genre for tracing the rise and transformation of a mode of cinematic history making tied to a project of nation building. These films convey a form of historicizing based on a nineteenth-century faith in the constancy and universality of truth, the efficacy of enlightened moral action, and chronological progress, invoking the telos of progress as the ultimate aim of history and the dynamic role of the people. The cinematic vision of the western frontier world was expressed through a form of montage meant to inspire awe and confidence in the imperative of collective moral purpose through progressive action on the natural and social environment. This cinema of the movement-image accomplished through the action-image offers a version of cinematic history making in such silent films as *The Birth of a Nation* (1915), *The Covered Wagon* (1923), and *The Iron Horse* (1924).

The "Large Form" of the American Western

Deleuze's conception of the American cinema in the Griffith model (for example, *The Birth of a Nation*) is as an archetypal epic—in Deleuze's terminology, "the birth of a nation-civilisation" (Deleuze 1986, 148). In relation to the movement-image in this epic, "the principal quality of the image is breath, respiration" involving the treatment of space: "It not only inspires the hero, but brings things together in a whole of organic representation and contracts or expands depending on the circumstances" (ibid., 145–46). The western in its incarnation as Cruze's *The Covered Wagon* was indebted to a form of representation in which the character is acted upon by the milieu, becomes equal to it, and, through a series of duels with the aid of the community, is able to "re-establish its accidentally or periodically endangered order." In the large or epic form "the hero ... does not modify the milieu, but re-establishes cyclic order in it" (ibid., 146).

The Covered Wagon was cast in a large form in its narration of the conquest of the American West, described in the intertitles as "empire building." The film solicits the viewer's perception of a series of duels between men, and battles with nature and with other hostile forces, to arouse sensations of curiosity, wonder, and admiration. In Kevin Brownlow's assessment of the film's treatment of spectacle, "the filming of the epic western ... was an epic in itself" (Brownlow 1997, 334). Even the intertitles are more than dialogue, description, or explanation: the language "gain[s] an almost epic poetry, exactly fitting the mood of the film" (ibid., 295). According to its publicity, the film employed the services of a thousand Native Americans from reservations in Wyoming and Mexico (under the direction of a military officer). Forty thousand feet of canvas was used for the Conestoga wagons. The numerous "wild" bison (five hundred) for the hunt were hired from a firm known as Buffalo Livestock Corporation. Cowboys managed the animals, including 150 steers and a thousand horses (*The Covered Wagon*, 1923).

The film bears comparison to the Wild West shows of the time, and the director, James Cruze, a former traveling actor in road shows, was the perfect impresario for this type of spectacle. Through the panoramas, the viewer perceives the vastness of the country and of the natural obstacles faced by the characters. The photography of the landscape is of high mountains, expansive space, and dangerous waterfalls. The movement through space is connected to the trials that the pioneers encounter in their westward movement, demonstrated by the various obstacles entailed in such a long and arduous trek: the dangerous and dramatic crossing of a deep river by the wagons, buffalo hunting, an attack by Native Americans, and fights among individuals and factions. Rather than focusing on a psychological treatment of the individuals, the film's epic style insists on situating its protagonists within long and difficult collective emotional ordeals: childbirth, death, shortages of food supplies, and dissension among groups, culminating in a split between those men who seek gold in California and the "men of the plow" who want to settle the land and create a community.

The choreography of the large cast filmed against this landscape also contributes to its epic character. Woodhull (Alan Hale) is the antagonistic and obstructionist figure who attempts to turn the journey into a personal duel between himself and Banion (J. Warren Kerrigan), the "natural" leader of the pioneers capable of bringing them to the "promised land." Cruze's casting of actors is consistent with the focus on the physical ordeals of the journey. The dominant figures are the pioneers and Kerrigan as their deliverer. While the film presents Banion as playing a critical role in the trek westward, he is less an individual hero distinguished from his men than a social type dependent on others for the realization of the collective good. Slight of figure and short, less athletic, and visibly older than many heroes, without benefit of low-angle shots, Banion is a nurturing figure, a chivalrous defender of women and children, a maligned hero fighting untrue reports about his military past, and a man of honor who refuses to use violence unjustly. What is significant about Kerrigan's unprepossessing physical appearance as Banion is that it does not eclipse the physical trials confronted by the pioneers. His physiognomy and bodily form distinguish him from the traditional wilderness scout exemplified by the portrayal of James Fenimore Cooper's Natty Bumppo and by the hunter-hero image of Theodore Roosevelt and his "Rough Riders," comprised of aristocrats and cowboys (Slotkin 1992, 56).

Unlike Tom Mix and Fred Thomson, who appear in other westerns of the time, Kerrigan lacks the distinctive physical appearance associated with later heroes of this action-oriented genre, such as John Wayne and Henry Fonda. Cruze's emphasis, however, is not on the actor's unique performance (a star quality) but on the character Banion in relation to the physical appearance and gestures of the other figures with whom he interacts. Banion is often grimy and disheveled, hardly a larger-than-life portrait. Moreover, the antagonism between him and Woodhull does not threaten to overwhelm the larger imperial mission but personalizes the drama, providing melodramatic affect. Both Tully Marshall's Bridger and Ernest Torrence's Jackson, who provide comic interludes, also overshadow Kerrigan's dominant role.

In a film that uses close-ups sparingly, Molly Wingate, a former schoolteacher played by Lois Wilson, receives the largest share. She is often framed by the arched front of the Conestoga wagon, akin to an iris-shot (*cum* halo) that situates her in the position of threatened femininity. Molly embodies the image of an attractive pioneer woman: not glamorous, exotic, or clinging but wholesome looking and adventurous—the Prairie Madonna. She is the object of contention between Banion and Woodhull, but the duels between the men involve not only possession of her person but also the political fate of the pioneers on their journey. Banion, cleared of false charges brought by Woodhull (and eventually rid of Woodhull, who is shot dead), becomes a wealthy man, thanks to his also having prospected for gold. The pioneers divide, one group to continue to prospect gold, the other to settle on the land. Banion is united with Molly to form the basis of a new society, and the plow that Banion and the other pioneers employ to break the plains becomes the sign of the coming civilization.

The Covered Wagon, then, encompasses the different persons and groups that undertake the journey to the promised lands of California or Oregon. The affective elements on which it draws are eclectic, involving adventure, romance, threats to the body, and antagonisms with natural forces that are reconciled through romance, marriage, and work. The film is prophetic, though, of the death of the "red man" (as articulated by the Native Americans in the film). However, despite showing Native Americans in scenes where they attack the encircled wagons, Cruze plays down images of bloodthirsty "Indians." Though presented in a comic vein, Bridger is "married" to two Indian women and serves as helper to Molly and Banion.

John Ford's *The Iron Horse* (1924) is also a monumental epic, offering another large form of the journey westward, in which the building of the railroad symbolizes the union of East and West. "What *The Covered Wagon* does for the wagon train," writes David Lusted, "*The Iron Horse* does for the locomotive by placing the railroad within the foundation myth" of the American nation (2003, 136)—a position commented on by Wolfgang Schivelbusch (1986, 89–112). From *The Great Train Robbery* (1903) to *Once Upon a Time in the West* (1968), the "iron horse" has played a role in establishing the large forms of the film western and contributed to versions of the action-image of realizing the nation form—or, as in the spaghetti western, of indicating its unsteadiness, if not demise. Aside from the film's choreography of the workers in the ordeal of constructing the railroad and its insertion of actual political figures (for example, President Lincoln, played by Charles Edward Bull), *The Iron Horse* emphasizes the importance of building the railroad from East to West as a symbol of national unity, attained through the concerted actions of its laborers.

In its multiple narrative lines (familial, romantic, and moral) and in the selection of its historical and fictional characters, *The Iron Horse* poses a range of potentially divisive elements to create binary conflicts involving racial groups and ethnicities (Easterners and Westerners; Native Americans; Irish, Italians, and Chinese workers). The conflicts also involve obstructive opportunists related to visible distinctions between a rural

Figure 1.1. Journey's end: Parting of the ways, *The Covered Wagon*, Cruze, 1923.

and a developing industrial society. Furthermore, a motif critical to many westerns (including Ford's *Stagecoach*) is that of the Civil War and its divisive aftereffects on national unity between the defeated South and the victorious North. In Ford's western, the Union Pacific Railroad becomes the sign of a promised unity between North and South as well as West and East, visualized through images of Abraham Lincoln expressing his dual priority of winning the war and of creating the railroad in the interests of a peaceful union.

The motif of national unity signified by the building of the railroad is also tied to domestic politics that involve obstacles to romance, reconciled at the end of the film in the marriage of Miriam Marsh (Madge Bellamy) to her childhood sweetheart (and the film's protagonist), Davy Brandon (George O'Brien). Their romance and wedding, consummated in the completion of the railroad, foregrounds the wedding of nature and technology, labor and industry, promising not merely continuity of the family but of national union and industrial productivity. What is striking about the epic is how the film interweaves multiple situations and characters to redeem the images from being didactic and polemic or a mere reflection of the historical literature on the winning of the West and the birth of the nation.

The differences between workers and bosses, scouts and entrepreneurs, politicians and lawmakers, fictional and historical characters, horses and machinery, tradition and the emergence of modern industrial life are all captured in what came to be Ford's visually encyclopedic style, exemplified in the style of this film. The awesome spectacle of the panoramic landscape, the filming of individual characters both in close-up and in relation to their groups, and especially the laborious advance of the building of the railroad are in the vein of Deleuze's description of the laws of organic composition. Through the perception of space contracted and expansive, the movement of the drive toward progress is animated by affection-images generated through an overcoming of large obstacles (internal and external, natural and social, organic and mechanical) so as to inspire heroic action in the protagonist, realized in the ultimate combat with the antagonists.

The trials of Davy Brandon consist not only in his battling natural obstacles but also in confronting and finally overwhelming Bauman (Fred Kohler), the scheming and unscrupulous capitalist (replete with mustache and ambiguous skin color). Audiences of the 1920s (recent and older immigrants) could be wooed not only by the scenes enacting the physical hardships of laborers but also by their bodily images, identified with struggles, incarnating the ethical dimensions of the threatening trials. The portrayal of Miriam belongs to a vision of romance that is pragmatic as well as chivalric. Her union with Davy links the epic to the mundane to create a vision of a history that underpins the reconciling of the different groups in the film: rural and urban, male and female, ethnic, working class, professional, and patriotic.

The narrative pays particular attention to minority groups and to a vision of the emerging United States as the "melting pot of minorities, that is, what brings them together, what reveals their correspondences even when they appear to be opposed, what already shows the fusion between them necessary for the birth of a nation" (Deleuze 1986, 146). The inspirational dimension of the film derives from the allusions to folk music, archival photographic inserts, and the awesome uses of space: the vastness of the land and the ubiquitous shots of the sky that rely on dramatic visual intercutting between vertical and horizontal planes, exemplified by the paintings of Albert Bierstadt (Mitchell 1996, 86–87). Monumentality is also captured through the mythic figures of Lincoln and Buffalo Bill (George Wagner). Antiquarianism is evident in the evocation of familiar folk music, referenced through the intertitles as well as in the tableaux of familiar historical and domestic scenes. The history of the nation in its expansion westward is thus dramatized in the organic sense of naturalness conveyed through the affect that animates the vast landscape, the ethical conflicts among the different nationalities, and, in their resolution through action, contributing to belief in the "healthy illusion as continuity of the nation" (Deleuze 1986, 148) and of the people.

Post–Civil War Forms of Chivalry: Ford's Stagecoach

After a period of waning interest in the late 1920s and early 1930s, the western again became again a popular form, and 1939 was a watershed year: Ford's *Stagecoach* appeared in March, Michael Curtiz's *Dodge City* in April, and DeMille's *Union Pacific* in May. The second half of the decade can be taken as a transformative time for the action-image. The film's focus is not only on the male protagonist but also on a distinctive cast of diverse characters played by recognizable performers: Claire Trevor, who was associated with comedy and fast-talking professional females; John Carradine, a versatile character actor identified with crime films; Andy Devine, a comic character actor; and Thomas Mitchell and Donald Meek, also established character actors. Their casting and the quality of their performances demonstrated the film's focus on the differentiated forces inherent to the western community.

Stagecoach creates a portrait of the West that contrasts with that of the monumental *Iron Horse*. It offers a different version of the epic, veering toward a "small form" in which it is not the situation that triggers the action but the action that "discloses the situation." Here, the action "advances blindly and the situation is disclosed in darkness, or in ambiguity" (Deleuze 1986, 160), suggesting signs of fissures in the social landscape, in which a different version of national history is growling at the periphery. The film unlinks the epic from its role as universal founding narrative; instead, it becomes a form of *re*founding in its focus on conceptions of justice in conflict with institutional morality and legality. It contrasts the cramped and ungenerous world of the town against the expansiveness of the social outcasts associated with an awesome vision of the natural landscape—still a vital element, signifying openness of space versus its closure in the settled towns. The film is not a celebration of the national community so much as an elevation of singular protagonists against the social-class constraints of the urban community. In contrast to *The Covered Wagon* and *The Iron Horse, Stagecoach* points to a shift in emphasis from traditional frontier/nation-making westerns, revealing a crisis of the action-image that will intensify with the coming of World War II.

Allegory in its modern incarnations seems a suitable form for describing *Stagecoach*'s uses of the past. The history portrayed in *Stagecoach* is not a sequential narration of the winning of the West and the establishment of civilization in the untamed world of the frontier; the film alters that narrative. The town of Lordsburg, from which the travelers either have been expelled, are escaping, or are leaving due to exigency, is integral to an allegory of the changing frontier world. The film, a fiction based on a short story, is designed for a 1939 audience. Its portrait of an earlier moment in time is not archival or antiquarian. It is intended not to reproduce how it "actually was" but to evoke a world poised between the circumscribed modern world and the breathing spaces of a West that is closing up (Sickels 2008). The film evokes the post-Depression changes in contemporary U.S. urban economic and social life of the 1930s.

Stagecoach still employs the narrative of the journey through space that is both material and figurative. The travelers include Ringo, Dallas, Doc, and Peacock, moral and legal reprobates who are exiled from the town to find themselves in the company of those who are leaving on the stagecoach in the company of the unscrupulous southerner Hatfield and the dishonest banker Gatewood. The prostitute Dallas and the genteel southern lady Lucy Mallory embody two different concepts of femininity in relation to class, sexuality, and maternal behavior—the prostitute emerging with the qualities of a lady. Dallas is a residue of an earlier vital frontier community (if not also an allusion to the censorious judgment of moral critics in the Hollywood of the late 1920s and 1930s). Condemned by the righteous, she is aligned with the Ringo Kid: an outlaw and the film's agent for affirming a democratic and humane form of respect for the beleaguered (white) outcasts of a settled world that has lost its ethical moorings. Ringo modifies Deleuze's notion of the hero as an "Encompasser": "a man who is larger than life" and conceives of an action that "is the only one capable of rivaling the milieu in its entirety" (Deleuze 1986, 184). Although an outlaw, his grievances are not such as to deter him from pursuing justice; yet he functions not as the agent for reestablishing the larger social order (ibid., 147), as in the epic form, but rather as an ethical figure to embody the integrity of the dispossessed community, if not of society more generally.

The history embedded in the film addresses the aftermath of the Civil War, the earlier open and spacious world dramatized in frontier epics of westward movement, and the morally and physically reduced world of the town—and perhaps that of contemporary America at the time of the film's production. The Ringo Kid's defiance of existing law to pursue his ethical quest of vengeance breathes affective life into the western cult of individualism, masculine honor, and even chivalry. His treatment of Dallas reinforces a conception of the frontier (if not of the nation) guided by an unwavering sense of social justice in which all (whites) are treated equally—a belief system fast fading but inherent in the foundational myths of the United States (Sickels 2008, 142–43).

John Wayne's portrayal of Ringo solidified his star identification with the western hero as it changed in the genre over time. He came to embody the new "westerner" through identification with the grandeur and solidity of the natural landscape: his physical movement, his chivalric demeanor and diffidence, his halting speech compensated by action, and an unwavering moral code derived from lived experience. Wayne's Ringo is an independent and self-reliant spirit, less committed to action in the interests of "saving society" than for personal individual mobility and freedom. He is the hinge of the narrative, a figure who, like the Virginian, lacks formal education; but he has preserved the frontier spirit and a form of law that transcends constraining hypocritical and corrupt practices identified with the narrow institutional (including sexual) morality characterized by the settled community.

Ringo has the sympathy of Marshall Curley (George Bancroft), who, while acknowledging the injustice done to Ringo by criminal factions, is compelled to reinforce the law and bring him back to the town. At the film's closure, and with Curley's sanction, Ringo and Dallas escape to the

Figure 1.2. Chivalry of the westerner, *Stagecoach*, Ford, 1939.

still untamed reaches of the West (Mexico)—but at the price of sacrificing an epic vision for one of a community that "has no illusions about itself" (Deleuze 1986, 148).

DELEUZE'S SMALL FORM AND BURLESQUE: A DIFFERENT HERO IN *DESTRY RIDES AGAIN*

Burlesque, though it relies on the action-image inherent to the western, can be more definitively described as a "small form" that presents a different version of affect and action. It pokes fun at the large and epic form, lending prominence to characters that are no longer larger than life but who appear weak, if not foolish, and reveal disparities between modes of action. In the case of the small form, the action, not the situation of the large form, "triggers off a new action" (Deleuze 1986, 160). Also appearing in 1939, *Destry Rides Again*, with its burlesque qualities, has been described as "a 'different' Western . . . but the differences made dyed-in-the-wool western devotees shudder, especially those who recalled with pleasure the old Tom Mix version" (Fenin and Everson 1962, 253).

Destry was a success in large part because of the performance of Marlene Dietrich in the role of Frenchy and of James Stewart in the starring role of Destry. Frenchy belongs to another, peripheral and alien, burlesque world. In contrast to other western heroines—for example, schoolmarm Molly Wood in the various versions of *The Virginian*—Frenchy is a disruptive force working against the domesticated portraits of femininity that are instrumental in the restoration of respectability. Whereas Molly serves as a convincing foil to the Virginian in the 1923 and 1929 films, Dietrich's Frenchy creates differences in the action that leads to a situation that becomes equivocal (Deleuze 1986, 160, 182) as in the transformations and inversions in character and action that ultimately become ethical.

Both Dietrich as Frenchy and Stewart as Destry seem to invert, if not undermine, expectations: he, of the western hero, she, of familiar forms of femininity. Together they deform gender through a functional reversal or "permutation of . . . opposites" (Deleuze 1986, 166). Frenchy is initially less abject than Dallas in *Stagecoach*, her sister from the margins, though she will finally pay for her feistiness and arrogance with her death. The character of Frenchy will become the Dietrich icon of the American West. As such, her foreign persona is significant for genre production in the 1930s, as well as for Hollywood history and its response to national and social changes during that decade.

Destry follows the trajectory of the western in its emphasis on the "attempts by the White frontier community to impose and establish a law-abiding settlement" through the agency of a male protagonist (Jacobowitz 1996, 88). To maintain this position, the film must eject Frenchy in behalf of restoring femininity to a "proper" role as a defender of civil society. Both Dietrich's own persona and her dancehall girl Frenchy evoke the decadent aura of her other films, her siren and *femme fatale*, but they also dramatize feminine vulnerability in her encounters with Destry. The burlesque portrait of an imperious, amoral, gender-bending, and disruptive Dietrich is converted to an abject and sacrificial figure of femininity.

A related burlesque feature centers on the initially "gunless," indeterminate masculinity of Destry. In his sermonizing and resistance to violence (based, as he recounts it, on the traumatic memory of his father having been shot in the back), he becomes an object of ridicule by the frequenters of the Last Chance Saloon. In contrast to Frenchy, Destry initially refuses to answer violence with violence. However, following the death of another father figure, "Wash" (Charles Winninger), Destry is finally moved to duel with the unscrupulous Kent (Brian Donlevy), whose character bears the burden of the community's ills: greed, gold, and violence. The film is riven by unresolved schisms in the conversion of the pacifist Destry to the gunman in his killing of Kent and in the elimination of Frenchy, who, although converted by Destry's moral guidance, nonetheless must yield to the domestic power of the town's wives.

The film reveals its divided strategies and its designs on the box office: on the one hand, by soliciting mixed generational and class audiences and confronting the changing times in its address of sexuality, morality, violence, and xenophobia (Stanfield 2001, 172); on the other, by first permitting the pleasures of viewing the excessive physical vitality and eroticism of Frenchy, then killing off that source of feminine pleasure, a renegade from domesticity and conventional morality. Her role places Frenchy uneasily between different conceptions of gendered and sexual performance. In its contradictory cinematic evocation of the American nation and changing national identity, the film gives further evidence of an emerging crisis of the action-image in relation to clear-cut moral imperatives identified with the former world of the West. The burlesque form, in its revelation of "the slight difference in the action which brings out an infinite difference between two situations," produces laughter but also pathos and incongruity (Deleuze 1986, 170). As such it constitutes a form of counter-history that removes monumental forms from their mythic comfort zones and aligns them to other cinematic forms that reveal history growling at the door.

VIGILANTE JUSTICE: *THE OX-BOW INCIDENT*

In keeping with the evolution of the western, William Wellman's *The Ox-Bow Incident* (1943) provides insight into the transformations of the genre in the war years, focusing on "the inability of the hero to right the wrongs of the West." The film "introduces a new social realism and an overt political liberalism to the genre" (Lusted 2003, 177) that undermines, if not dismantles, the western foundational narrative. *The Ox-Bow Incident* transforms the protagonist from a romantic conception of the outlaw to a tired cynic who is morally paralyzed. His bitterness is initially attributed to his being jilted by a woman whose painting hangs conspicuously in the saloon into which Gil Carter (Henry Fonda) and his sidekick, Croft (Harry Morgan), wander in the opening moments of the film. The painting comes to life later when Rose appears (Mary Beth Hughes), married to a wealthy rancher aligned to the negative members of the community. Her presence reinforces the motif of betrayal but links it to a psychological investigation of perverse connections between femininity and masculinity that is tied to violence.

Instead of being a man with a mission, Carter, as Dana Polan writes, is a wanderer, "occupying a place outside history" (1986a, 264–65). The treatment of Carter as nomadic is evocative of Deleuze's discussion of the crisis of the movement-image, where the "sensory-motor action or situation has been replaced by the stroll" (Deleuze 1986, 208) and where the situation in which the character finds himself "outstrips his motor capacities on all sides, and makes him see and hear what is no longer subject to the rules of a response or an action.... He is prey to a vision, pursued by it or pursuing it, rather than engaged in an action" (Deleuze 1989a, 3). Like a sleepwalker, Carter becomes more of a spectator than a major force to impede and overcome the destructive behaviors of a posse in pursuit of three alleged cattle rustlers and murderers. The men (and one woman) who have formed the posse are set on immediate justice, displaying indifference to trial by jury and the need of evidence to justify their charges. (The woman, the bellicose Ma Grier, is played by Jane Darwell, cast against her usual type of a benevolent grandmotherly figure.) The accused—eventually revealed as innocent—are a Mexican (Anthony Quinn); a young rancher, Donald Martin (Dana Andrews); and "Dad," a senile old man (Francis Ford).

The film presents the behavior of the posse as a nightmare of egregious vigilante justice and indicts the community for the murder of three men. Although identified with the emergent social problem films of the 1940s

(Landy 2005b, 238), *The Ox-Bow Incident* is still at pains to explore the motif of law specifically in relation to failed conceptions of masculinity and of community. The inhabitants of the town are vengeful and subservient to authority, or indifferent, and many are portraits of failed masculinity. These include Major Tetley, another of the legion of southerners with questionable pasts, who is obsessed with a son he regards as effeminate and whom he is determined to "make a man" to compensate for his own impotence.

The issue of race is introduced through the character of Sparks, a black minister whose younger brother had been a victim of lynching (as looms for the suspects) and who underscores the ineffectiveness of religion to regulate the community. In the introduction of a racial portrait, the film prefigures other 1940s war films that gradually include black characters and situations (Landy 2005b, 239). The film (shot in the studio and not on location) eschews any scenes that might contribute to the mitigation of the posse, devoting a large portion of the narrative to the degeneracy of the spokesmen for this hasty revenge perpetrated on helpless and innocent men. *The Ox-Bow Incident*, in its unsettling of prevailing conceptions of western justice, approaches a horror film. Its ultimate irony involves the arrival of the sheriff after the men are hanged, who reveals that the actual rustlers have been caught and indicts the posse as murderers. Thus, the final confrontation between the posse and the law is a travesty of civilized society and Carter a witness to this travesty.

The film is anticipatory of a faltering belief in the "American dream" as portrayed through the western, despite (or because of) wartime propaganda efforts to solidify the national community (Crain 1976, 247). It joins other films of the war era, especially film noir, that dramatize the uncertainty surrounding the nation, its past and its future. Gone is the hero who through action has redeemed the community: Fonda's starring role contradicts those that would later present him as a champion of justice. The action-image identified with the epic has entered into its decline. Hollywood, despite itself and its imposed moralistic concerns, has entered a different regime of the cinematic image that is closer to naturalism.

The Ox-Bow Incident heralds a challenge to a form of organic representation through a cinema that has become disillusioned about past and present, if not future. The film contests the world of the large form,

A Crisis of the Movement-Image and Counter-History   19

Figure 1.3. Vigilante "justice," *The Ox-Bow Incident*, Wellman, 1943.

presenting a diminished photography of landscape; perverse gendered, sexual, and familial portraits; and an irate and adamant community. It substitutes mob action and expediency for heroic commitment and exhaustion for energy and just action. The film's closure, set once again in the town bar, gives little indication of change: instead, in Carter's reading of a letter written by the condemned Martin before his death, silence reigns, and the only action, if it can be described as such, is Carter's willingness to deliver the angry letter to the man's wife. The final images of the film are of Carter and Croft slowly riding out of town into a desolate-looking landscape. Thus, the elimination of the retrograde forces of the past is accompanied not by a restoration of a community but by the memory of loss. Conceptions of the people as a benevolent community have been refuted through investigation of the betrayal of the law to enact justice. If, from Deleuze's perspective, cinema was in need of images to rethink the role of history that previously had held sway, the film's social realism reveals symptoms of the crisis of the movement-image. The film introduces the conventional conflict between moral antinomies but alters the constituents of the duel between the protagonist and the negative forces that he would be expected to overcome, thereby diminishing the force of the protagonist as well as of the community.

In its appeal to an alternative vision of society, *The Ox-Bow Incident* relies on memories of justice to imagine a rational alternative to the violence and destruction it portrays. Following the attributes of the movement-image, its social realism still remains largely entrenched in the nexus between affection and action characteristic of the traditional western, and thus constrained in confronting how spectators "hardly believe any longer that a global situation which can give rise to an action which is capable of modifying it" (Deleuze 1986, 206). According to Deleuze, "the soul of the cinema demands increasing thought, even if thought begins by undoing the system of actions, perceptions and affections on which the cinema had fed up to this point" (ibid.). Citing the work of Hitchcock, Deleuze introduces the concept of the "mental image," a form that entails symbols, links between natural and abstract relations that require interpreting. There are moments in *The Ox-Bow Incident* that invite the spectator to construe abstract relations—a third meaning involving Fonda's image as spectator, Rose's painting, and Martin's letter—that shift attention from a narrative resolution to raise questions about the starkness of the images as unsettling interpretation.

ACCOMMODATING TO THE POSTWAR WORLD

Memory, Myth, and History: Il mio nome è Nessuno

The western is not yet dead. It is, however, under erasure (see Kitses and Rickman 1998, 381–405). Unlike the large, monumental form of many westerns, *My Name Is Nobody* (*Il mio nome è Nessuno*, Valerii, 1973) is an elegiac, if not nostalgic, memorial to the passing of western, its myths, and its relations to history on film. The film's contribution to the "western genre" resides in its confronting "the myth with the negation of the myth" (Frayling 2000, 248) through parody. *My Name Is Nobody* captures the process of the Italian western's play on repetition and/as difference, just as the pre- and postwar Hollywood western has in various versions expressed connections and revisions to the literature, films, and legends of the West. The film is at a remove from conventional views of historicizing the West but not about counter-historicizing.

Directed by Tonino Valerii, *My Name Is Nobody* was made with the "supervision" of Sergio Leone, a major creative figure in the aesthetics and politics of the spaghetti western. Indeed, the film appears to be invested in solidifying the reputation of director Leone as the most internationally influential figure of the Italian western and the master of bridging the Italian and "the cherished myths of the Hollywood genre." The film self-reflexively reflects the character of spaghetti westerns largely produced between the 1960s and 1970s. The western is filtered through a burlesque of its characters and conventions. Borrowing from Foucault's description of Nietzsche's scorn of monumental history, the film offers a version "of history in the form of a concerted carnival" (Foucault 1977, 161). The film's burlesque treatment of western conventions, official history, and epic form is "a very appropriate arrivederci to the Italian western" (Frayling 2000, 255).

The film is a cornucopia of Leone-style images, scenes, and classical moments in his films, for example, *Once Upon a Time in the West* (*C'era una volta il West*, 1968) and *Duck, You Sucker* (*Giù la testa*, 1971), in addition to those of other Italian western directors such as Sergio Sollima and Enzo Barboni, and North American directors, especially Sam Peckinpah in *The Wild Bunch* (1969). *My Name Is Nobody* also pays tribute to Henry Fonda in the role of Jack Beauregard for both his Hollywood westerns and in *Once upon a Time in the West* for his work in Italian westerns (Kitses and Rickman 1998, 377), and to Terence Hill in the role of Nobody for the Trinity films such as *My Name Is Trinity* (*Mi chiamavono Trinità*, 1970) and *Trinity Is Still My Name* (*Continuavano a chiamarlo Trinità*, 1971).

The requisite journey of the western in this film moves in two directions, the first involving Jack Beauregard's slow movement eastward in anticipation of retirement to Europe, and the second, of a man with no name, Nobody, in his obsessive efforts to engineer Beauregard's confrontation with unfinished history in the form of the "wild bunch" of "150 pure bred sons of bitches" as obligatory ritual to procure Beauregard a place in the "history books." Nobody is a fan of the consummate gunfighter, Jack Beauregard, and Nobody's legend refers to Homer's *Odyssey* where Odysseus refers to himself as "No Man" to escape attack by Polyphemus's men. The film's reliance on the movement-image encompasses other dimensions of western scenarios: the revenge motif, greed for gold, the iron horse, the choreography of the gun flight, the male comic duo, and the homosocial elements of the genre.

The opening of the film also alludes to Leone's *Once upon a Time in the West*, presenting Beauregard confronted by three gunslingers (one disguised as a barber) who, having locked up a barber and his son, are intent on dispatching Beauregard. With aplomb, Beauregard sits in the barber chair (with a clock ticking loudly) and coolly places his gun in the "barber's" crotch. When the shave is finished, the erstwhile barber is dispatched, shot in lightening time, by Beauregard, as are his two cronies outside, and the barber and his son freed. After Beauregard's departure, the child asks, referring to the speed of the Beauregard's draw, "How did he do it, Pa?" And is told "nobody is faster on the draw than him." Thus, the legend of Beauregard the gunfighter assumes prominence in keeping with the film's parodic treatment of historicizing via the western, and Nobody plays the role of Beauregard's director/manager and his potential successor. The film's carnivalesque treatment stands out in Nobody's addiction to showmanship, prompting Beauregard to describe him as "shining like a door in a whore house" to which Nobody responds, "I like folks to see me."

The view of history as a "concerted carnival" referred to above in the reference to Foucault is enacted in Nobody's efforts to inscribe Beauregard in the history books through his management of the gunfighter's encounters with the 150 sons of bitches (*pace* Peckinpah's *The Wild Bunch*, 1968). Nobody's history making in the film becomes a matter of style, quotation, repetition, memory (Nobody's and the viewers), and vision: "I see it all clear as a crystal," says Nobody. Style becomes critical to the episodes that precede Nobody's articulated objective of getting Beauregard into the history books. Provoked by Nobody's shadowing, Beauregard's responds by shooting a hole through Nobody's Stetson, a gesture that Nobody returns. In the carnival scenes in the Street of Pleasure, Nobody shoots a threatening giant figure so as to reveal him as a dwarf on stilts.

Nobody stalks Beauregard, urging him to recall his many victories over adversaries who have unsuccessfully sought to compete for his status as premier gunslinger. He qualifies as trickster, a messenger, jokester, and intermediary between mortals and the gods. While associated with deceit, his tricks are usually in the interest of protecting and defending the helpless and marginalized against their exploiters. In a carnival tent, he undermines the game of throwing pies at the faces of blacks to one of throwing pies with much heavier weight at the face of the tent owner. In a saloon, Nobody humorously shows off his skill as a gunslinger, while drinking larger and larger glasses of both whiskey and beer before throwing a glass into the air behind him and shooting. The bystanders are awestruck by his precision. In the carnival's House of Horrors, he confounds his pursuers with multiple elusive mirror images of himself.

Nobody's plan for putting Beauregard into the history books involves Nobody's stealing the train carrying the gold to reach Beauregard and trick him into fighting the 150 men. Through trickery, Nobody has seen to it that the men's saddlebags carrying dynamite sparkle in the sun to enable the lone Beauregard to aim successfully at them. The film becomes operatic through image and sound in the wide-angle views of the landscape, the thundering hooves of the 150 men approaching on horseback to the music of Wagner and Morricone, and the sound of choral voices. In voiceover, Nobody reiterates the terms of this "historical" battle that involve a somebody like Beauregard who has to go out "with style."

Now the climactic moment in Beauregard's career as directed by Nobody explodes as the lone Beauregard shoots. Explosions are repeated a number of times, with Nobody keeping score, until the action is intercut by freeze frames, first in color, later in black and white, decorated to resemble pages from an old book. The scene ends with Nobody and Beauregard on the train departing after relegating the history to cultural memory through music, photography, and cinema.

On the train, Beauregard asks Nobody, "Well, now you got me in the history books, how do I quit?" Nobody answers, "You gotta die"; and, in public before spectators, the staged shoot out between Beauregard and Nobody takes place before a requisite mixed audience of women, children, whites and blacks, and a photographer on hand to commemorate the "duel." The "dead" Beauregard, now relegated to the history books

Figure 1.4. A message from the "dead," *My Name Is Nobody,* Valerii, 1973.

becomes a commentator on the cinematic events. Speaking from the ship, *The Sundowner,* he reads a letter intended for Nobody with reflections on his "death" and on the death of the western.

Drawing attention to differences between himself and Nobody, Beauregard reads: "I've always tried to steer away from trouble, but you seem to be looking for it." Since Nobody has now become a somebody, Beauregard reminds him that the only way for him to become a nobody again is to die. Moreover, Beauregard instructs him that the romantic world of the past, when "a pistol shot could resolve everything," no longer exists and "since violence has changed too . . . it's your kind of time, not mine." Thus, Beauregard can now articulate the meaning of a parable, posed earlier in the film by Nobody, of the bird and the coyote. In Nobody's parable, a coyote saves a bird stuck in cow manure. Unfortunately, the hungry coyote eats the bird. The moral of the tale, according to Beauregard who now meditates on its meaning is that "Folks that throw dirt on you aren't always trying to hurt you. And folks that pull you out of a jam aren't always trying to help you. But the main point is when you're up to your nose in shit keep your mouth closed," an allusion to a changed world in relation to aggression and violence at the basis of the film's elegiac perspective.

As a self-conscious and critical investigation into history making, the film reflects on a cinematic mode identified with the myth of the western as action-image, its appeal, longevity, and transformation. In terms described by Deleuze in his discussion of the crisis of the action-image, the film is self-reflexive of its altered character in terms of its awareness of limitations on epic forms of action. The crisis of the western as explored in the film can be related to "functionalism" that, in Deleuze's terms, is exemplary of Howard Hawks's westerns. He finds that the American cinema of Hawks surrenders itself "to a topological deformation of the large form" (Deleuze, 1986, 166), one that expresses itself through burlesque. In contrast to the epic and monumental form, the small form depends on a slight difference, where "violence becomes the principle impetus and gains from this as much in intensity as in unexpectedness" (ibid., 167). The film takes the route also evident in the Hawks's western; it "borrows the 'small form' directly, even on the big screen" (ibid., 166) where violence "becomes the principle impetus, and gains from as much intensity as unexpectedness" (ibid., 163).

My Name Is Nobody maps the various dimensions of the Italian western in parodic terms especially through its operatic character and its emphasis on of time. The film as a parody of the western is an encounter between mythic, historical, and clock time. The viewer is afforded the mirror referred to by Deleuze in his commentary in *Cinema 2* on the "crystals of time," which relate to recollection, memory, and modes of historicizing. Thus, the film in its focus on memory is on the passage of a form of history as myth making in which the cinema now reflects on its past and points toward its precarious future and, hence, to reconsiderations of history making as counter-history.

The Western in the Twenty-First Century:
Lost in Space through Meek's Cutoff

Meek's Cutoff (2010) differs from traditional storytelling and from a conventional emphasis on spectacle, melodrama, and the classic male duel inherent in the western film's predilection for the action-image. The film invites the viewer to contemplate a historical event from a position of indiscernibility that frustrates expectations of the time-honored journey westward. The film is a minimalist and philosophic exercise demonstrating great restraint in contrast to the stylistic exuberance characteristic of epic and revisionist westerns. *Meek's Cutoff* investigates questions of repetition and difference in its investment in narrating the North American past by thinking counter-historically.

Based on documented accounts of events, the narrative takes place in 1845, featuring a group of potential settlers traveling to the Oregon territory. Steven Meek (Bruce Greenwood) is the wagon-train guide. Three families, the most prominent being Emily (Michelle Williams) and Solomon Tetherow (Will Patton) have chosen to separate from the main wagon train to follow Meek's alternate route. For reasons not spelled out, Meek erroneously directs the pioneers not to the foothills of the Cascade Mountains but to a saline desert. The group's potential savior is a Native American (Rod Rondeaux) who strays into their encampment and is taken captive.

According to J. Hoberman, writing in *The Village Voice* (2005a), the western journey into the wilderness "recalls Jim Jarmusch's *Dead Man* and even Werner Herzog's *Aguirre: The Wrath of God* in its evocation of frontier surrealism and manifest-destiny madness." However, by contrast to these films cited by Hoberman, *Meek's Cutoff* eschews the monumental form and also akin to *My Name Is Nobody,* the film resists elegiac form in favor of an allegorical mode, posing questions of knowledge and authority as the basis for dramatizing this journey. While the narrative traces the emigrants' path out of the wilderness to a new home in Oregon, the wilderness challenges certainties about historical events and about figures credited with power. *Meek's Cutoff* embellishes the existing factual account of the journey (credited in the film's titles) to offer a self-reflexive and critical investigation of the nameless Native American and the woman Emily. Reichardt's film situates the Native American as an enigma in his physical appearance and in his inability (or refusal) to be verbally intelligible to the emigrants, while Emily alone forms an empathetic bond that reaps rewards for the group.

The film resists making Rod Rondeaux, a Crow, appear exotic or ugly. Rather, his gestures and the sounds he makes are as indecipherable as the chalk signs he leaves on rocks and his burst of songs, chants, or prayers. In Hoberman's terms, "he's the material projection of the unforgiving, unknowable wilderness in which they find themselves" (2005a). Unlike other revisionist westerns that work within an identity model to soften racial distinctions, this film resists familiar efforts to render exotic, interpret, and explain the Native American. Even Emily expresses her initial fears of Rondeaux's character by asking Solomon, "Is he ignorant or is he just plain evil?" Then she answers her own question with "It's impossible to know." Thus, the film introduces the issue of uncertainty in the confrontation that emerges between her and Meek.

In an early morning scene with domestic vignettes of the emigrants seated by their wagons, a boy reads a passage from the Old Testament relating to the Fall and man and woman driven from the Garden of Eden: he "has now become as one of us to know good and evil." Adam and Eve in the passage are reconfigured by the trio of Meek, Emily, and the Native American who are central actors in the film's investigation of knowledge. The passage underscores the film's portrayal of the physical and psychic hardships faced by the settlers in the hands of a guide who has misrepresented his knowledge of the wilderness, in Emily's terms, either from ignorance or "evil." In the western, the movement westward has been equated to the conquest of a "virgin" land, and, thus, as territory, morality, action, and, knowledge. *Meek's Cutoff* visualizes and questions this trope aesthetically, historically, and philosophically.

Emily is forthright in her view that they are "lost," and Meek corrects her by saying that we are merely "finding our way," to which she snaps back, "You don't have to patronize me." He interprets her behavior as flirting with him, and she responds that he does not seem to "know women":

> MEEK: Well, I know somethin' or other.
> EMILY: If you say so.
> MEEK: Well, I know women are different from men. I know that much. Well, I'll tell you the difference if you care to hear.
> EMILY: I don't doubt you will.
> MEEK: Women, women are created on the principle of chaos, the chaos of creation, disorder, bringing new things into the world. Men are created on the principle of destruction. It's like cleansing, ordering, and destruction.

As in this exchange, the film visualizes distinctions between men and women, between their labor, between the male and female group, the women's tasks being doing laundry, cooking, cleaning the dishes, tending the animals, and gathering firewood in contrast to the men's task of making decisions. The women's access to knowledge is limited to overhearing what the men say, and the women do not get to vote on the decision to persist onward, despite the group's common recognition of being lost. Access to knowledge is central to the counter-history dimension of the film that explores and challenges secure identity and agency. Emily's encounters with Meek, thus, draw on the physical and behavioral aspects of his persona. Not only is he slovenly and unkempt, but he is contemptuous of women, a man who espouses violence and whose attitudes toward the Other—whether Native American or Woman—beg Emily's question: is *he* ignorant or evil?

Emily does not hesitate to test their prisoner. She approaches him, offers him water, and points to his torn moccasin. He responds by removing it with her help. Another of the women, Glory White (Shirley Henderson) is aghast, but Emily explains that she wants him to owe her something, since she would like to know if he can guide them to water. Indeed, the episode suggests that Emily has the capacity (empathy?) to intuit the prisoner's gestures, and he, in turn, communicates with her.

A critical turning point occurs when Rondeaux bursts forth with a long speech that causes others in the group to stop and observe him, but Emily translates this outpouring to them as his saying and pointing to the possibility that water is beyond the hill. In order to progress, however, they must roll the wagons down a treacherous hill. After a brief discussion among the men who vote to advance, two wagons are guided downward, but the third topples and is demolished. In addition, a valuable keg of water spills. Millie Gately, the third woman in the group, becomes distraught and screams, "They're coming." Meek seizes this moment to claim that the Native American is stealing from a basket that has fallen off the broken wagon. Meek aims his gun at the man as reprisal for this "theft," but Emily picks up a rifle and aims at Meek. "What does it matter?" she asks.

Meek responds by invoking the cliché "[it is] the principle that matters." In a series of close-ups, the others, men and women, appear paralyzed at the sight of Emily's militant action. Emily does not back down, despite Meeks' scornful comment that "You don't know what you are dealing with," another evocation of the problematic of knowledge. He challenges

Figure 1.5. The wager, *Meek's Cutoff*, Reichardt, 2010.

her action, accusing her of posing a wager involving a choice between "water or blood." Indeed, he tells her condescendingly that, in defending the life of the Native American, she is playing a card game in which she is unaware of her cards.

Meek's earlier description of a difference between the female chaos of creation and male ordering and destruction is dramatized in this confrontation. Emily's response is to take the wager, though not in the deterministic terms suggested by Meek's language. The film treads on a philosophic terrain involving imperfect knowledge of the consequences of her choice. Meek challenges her by exposing the uncertain consequences of her action and by accusing her of placing others in a potentially dangerous situation, as if he had not himself done the same earlier.

In commenting on the "wager," identified with Pascal and Kierkegaard, Deleuze says that it is a model of a "bad game, with its manner of fragmenting chance ... under the constant glue of a God who is never put in question, [and] this game is indistinguishable from the practice of representation" (Deleuze 1994, 282–83). In the "divine game ... there is no pre-existent rule" (ibid., 283). Deleuze poses a conception of chance that involves different thinking about events. His notion of the wager, much as in *Meek's Cutoff*, the imperative of adventure, applied to Emily's dilemma (provoked by Meek) is an encounter with chance. Her decision constitutes an open-ended potential for rethinking the situation in which the emigrants find themselves.

In counter-historical terms, the rules of the game posed by Meek are based on a different and determinist sense of thinking and choice, while Emily invokes chance in a different sense of power as well as an affirmation of knowledge. *Meek's Cutoff*, thus, abandons the world of the historical western with its large and didactic form in relation to action and instead invents a style to introduce other terms into the equation, involving connections between mental images, time, earth as territory, and the prospect of a different relation to the knowledge of "good and evil."

When all seems lost, the emigrants discover a tree that also serves to locate objects as a matter for discovery of possible worlds through new forms for thinking. The earth is not indifferent. As Deleuze and Guattari indicate, "thinking takes place in the relationship between territory and the earth" (1994, 85). The emigrants run to the tree and assume that there must be water near at hand, though the viewer does not follow them to a new ground to confirm this belief but leaves them at the base of the tree. The film ends with a long take and the gradual disappearance from view of the Native American until only an image of the earth is visible. The long take and receding image are at a remove from realism, more like a dream or trance that belongs to counter-historical thinking in which fabulation as invention plays a critical role in rethinking the meaning of an event and in situating its actors, both the woman and the Native American, in a different relationship to thinking, representation, and identity.

The style of *Meek's Cutoff* emphasizes that earth is more than background: it becomes territory, playing a critical role as a form of geophilosophy in which the earth portrayed is more than the material render-

Figure 1.6. The tree of life, *Meek's Cutoff*, Reichardt, 2010.

ing of places and objects: it is a virtual coming together of the people (Deleuze and Guattari 1994, 109) in this unknown world. *Meek's Cutoff* is dependent on the earth in its depictions of the wilderness, desert, rocks, the cracked and hardened soil

As Deleuze and Guattari indicate, "thinking takes place in the relationship between territory and the earth" (1994, 85). Territory projects the Native American as a man of the future and Emily as a woman of the future, who, in their transformations, are becoming "other." Both figures call "for a future form, for a new earth and people that do not yet exist" (ibid., 108). Thus, the cinematic creation that animates *Meek's Cutoff* invites counter-historical thinking.

2

History Growling at the Door

Horror and Naturalism

> The originary world ... is thus a world of a very special kind of violence (in certain respects, it is the radical evil); but it has the merit of causing an originary image of time to rise, with the beginning, the end, and the slope, all the cruelty of Chronos.
>
> This is naturalism. It is not opposed to realism, but on the contrary accentuates its features by extending them in an idiosyncratic surrealism.
>
> —Deleuze (1986, 124)

THE POWER OF HORROR, NATURALISM, AND THE IMPULSE-IMAGE

If the action-image is largely characterized by interaction of perception, affect, and agency to generate belief in ethical action, it remains burdened by inherited forms of social and cinematic history that reveal them as inadequate to address political and aesthetic crises. In Deleuze's examination of the multifaceted responses to what he has termed a crisis, he identifies films that present altered landscapes and characters who are missing from themselves and other characters who are symptomatic of their bearing the burdens of the immediate past and the uncertainties of the present and future.

The crisis of the movement-image is one of belief in moral action, producing modes of expression that qualify, if not alter, the character of cinema in the direction of embedding a form of history that is rendered ambiguous through naturalism and its expression through the impulse-image. It thus becomes a form of cinematic counter-history that resists overt historicizing but is, nonetheless, not exempt from considerations of history. The films that I have selected to discuss in this chapter as exemplary of a crisis of history and cinematic form are identified with crime and the horrific: *Profondo rosso* (*Deep Red*; Argento, 1975), *La sindrome di Stendhal* (*The Stendhal Syndrome*; Argento, 1996), *Profundo carmesi* (*Deep Crimson*; Ripstein, 1996), and *Bakjwi* (*Thirst*; Park Chan-wook, 2009). Cinematic counter-history as embedded in these works undoes the emphasis on the community as an intermediary in conflict, the positive moral force of the hero as agent, and the reconstitution of a community. Instead, this form of historicizing relies on weak links among the people, a community with no moral anchoring, and on affects, involving rage, hysteria, and violent actions, that are inherent in conspiratorial and dispersive situations.

The films are located in "any-space-whatever" and, hence, are radically different to the regime of the action-image "actualised in states of things, in milieux which are geographically and historically determinable" (Deleuze 1986, 123). They are related, however, to the works of filmmakers such as Carl Theodor Dreyer, Robert Bresson, Michelangelo Antonioni, and Ôshima Nagisa in presenting forms of the affection-image realized not in action but rather through an expression that is aesthetic, spiritual, or religious. Deleuze examines this form of the expression in *Cinema 2* (1989a), where he develops conceptions of the time-image more fully in relation to the crystalline image that reveals different circuits of time. In this chapter, however, I focus on naturalism as expressive of a form of historicizing productive for thinking counter-historically in relation to forms that resist overt historicizing. Set in motion, nationally and internationally, in fiction and nonfiction films, this cinema is characterized by an elliptical form, weakness of linkages among events, a journey form, and attention to the detection of habitual formulas that have become clichés, thus cutting up historical narratives with an eye to reworking the prefabricated roles identified with the characters and situations of the prior popular cinema.

In commercial cinema, there was evidence of "a negative or parodic critical consciousness," but films would also give rise to the problem of how to create a cinema that enabled a "thinking image" (Deleuze 1986, 215), which Deleuze would particularly identify with the films of Alfred Hitchcock, in a remaking of popular forms and experimentation with their impact on viewers. In the revaluation of popular cinema, Hitchcock plays a key role in postwar alterations in critical thinking about the question of what cinema is. He became recognized as a filmmaker who introduced a mental image into his scripts to enlarge understanding of the components of this form of cinema, involving three axes: the director, the image-text, and the spectator. Featuring crime detection, this cinema emphasized the perpetrators of a crime committed, affect identified with its discovery, the viewer placed in a position of detective, and, hence, access to a doubling of the narrative and its modes of narration. Hitchcock did not destroy action-images, however; rather, through the mental image he transformed them into a "re-examination of their nature and status" as images (ibid., 204, 205).

These "thinking images" challenged historicism not only through crime detection films but also through a horror genre that worked against clichés of a cinema of gore to become "the genre of our time that registers most brutally the legacies of historical trauma" (Lowenstein 2005, 10). Instead of giving us social realism, these films constitute a transformation in historicizing that confronts these legacies through a form of narrative fiction and fact.

In the words of Jacques Rancière, "The notion of 'narrative' locks us into oppositions between the real and artifice where both the positivists and the deconstructionists are lost. It is not a matter of claiming that everything is fiction.... [T]he aesthetic age defined models for connecting the presentation of facts and forms of intelligibility that blurred the border between the logic of facts and the logic of fiction" (2004, 38). I extend this thinking on relations between fiction and fact to interrogate the supposed absence of historicity assigned to popular cinema, to explore the different, even shocking ways in which a violent and cruel history is epitomized in a cinema of naturalism, of impulse, and of entropy that signals a form of counter-historicizing in cinematic sites that might seem resistant to such an analysis.

In both literature and cinema, naturalism is a designation most often associated with forms of nineteenth-century realism identified with the Goncourt brothers, to a lesser degree with Honoré de Balzac, and certainly with Émile Zola. As exemplified by Zola, this naturalism is expressive of hyperrealism based on excessive descriptions of passion, degradation, and grotesque bodies. Naturalism is tied to the biological body in its privileging of horrific bodily transformations. Its treatment of historical time is identified with a form of evolution, albeit in a downward spiral (Deleuze 1986, 127). Following Deleuze, naturalism, though often referred to as realism, is rather the real of a primeval, originary world given to impulsive behavior, to violence and repetition (ibid., 126). Naturalism thrives in imaginary places and in a form of time that he describes as primitive or originary. It is a world of fetishes, partial objects, and characters who are parasitic and obsessive, attached to perverse modes of behavior (ibid., 128).

I avoid discussing Hitchcock at length as Deleuze's prime exemplar of a crisis in the action-image; instead, I consider various non-Hollywood and even non-European cinematic forms of the postwar body and landscape through forms of the horrific that are expressions of a crisis in historicizing. Following David Martin-Jones's work in *Deleuze and World Cinemas*, I regard Deleuze's work on cinema not only as increasingly germane to transnational film production but also as an enterprise that "takes us one step closer towards a freeing of Deleuze's *Cinema* books from accusations of Eurocentrism" (Martin-Jones 2011, 235).

In Deleuze's description of the movement-image, as manifest through a set of responses involving perception-, affection-, and action-images, he acknowledges a form of response that is "like the 'degenerate' affect, or the 'embryonic' action" (Deleuze 1986, 123). This is the "impulse-image" removed from realism but not from a real world in which the characters are like animals insofar as their actions are "prior to all differentiation between the human and the animal" (ibid., 124). Naturalist films have a wide reach of performance, including animation, avant-garde, horror, and fantasy, and span the international cinema of the twentieth to twenty-first centuries, including the films of Erich von Stroheim, Luis Buñuel, Marco Ferrari, Arturo Ripstein, and Park Chan-wook. Their films are exemplary in their use of the cinematic image to address historical crises in experimental and popular forms. The period after World War II that Deleuze correctly identifies as a crisis of the action-image was not confined to neorealism; it thrived too in the popular cinema of crime detection and the horrific in ways that evoke Hitchcock's "pushing the movement-image to its limit," along with "including the spectator in the film, and the film in the mental image" (Deleuze 1986, 204).

Hitchcock's films found further elaboration through the cinema of Dario Argento, whose cinematic and televisual productions span four decades, although the films that bear Argento's name are more controversial. His works have created a following of fans in Europe and internationally that has reached cult proportions, but appreciation of the experimental character of his films, and of their contribution to an understanding of contemporary politics and aesthetics, has been delayed. Direct and indirect censorship has still been the fate of many of Argento's films. The ongoing charges of "bad taste," "sensationalism," and "sexploitation," if not of pornography, have plagued their critical reception. They have been trapped also in the prison house of genre analysis or in an attempt to redeem them from "trash aesthetics," exercises that have often impeded a careful investigation of their experimental character.

My focus on horror cinema in the context of naturalism is to underscore its genealogical and aesthetic contributions to cinematic expression, particularly as a response to a crisis in historicizing. The legacy of the baroque in modern art and thinking have been acknowledged in the writings of Walter Benjamin, Deleuze, and Tim Murray (for example, his *Digital Baroque,* 2008), with an emphasis on different aesthetic and political moments in time, from painting to cinema to digital art. Central to the baroque in its various manifestations is its appeal to the senses; its employment of allegory, metaphor, and artifice; its attention to the body; violence; a folding of space and time; and the changing character of art. I situate Argento within a form of filmmaking that investigates the question "What was and what is cinema now?" in connection to spectatorship, temporality, and historicity. Argento's films are an opportunity to rethink critical concerns regarding the potential of popular media to engage the contemporary spectator in problems posed by transformations in media. These transformations are linked to altered social and historical realities involving more than a century of living in the "society of the spectacle" (Debord 1983) so as to investigate how an awareness of spectacle has inhered in various forms of filmmaking over the course of the twentieth century (and in the twenty-first) and how spectacle works.

I invoke writers and artists who, from early moments of cinema to the present, have adopted forms of historical expression that, while aware of the potential of indexical imaging, prefer a view of cinema that constitutes a different relation to the cinematic image and its engagement with history and memory. These works include surrealist films of the 1920s and 1930s, as well as writings by such filmmakers as Jean Vigo, Antonin Artaud, Germaine Dulac, and Luis Buñuel, involving the focus on the horrific, the contingent, and the violent, with attention to the character of cinema spectatorship. In 1930, Jean Vigo, commenting on spectators' upsetting reactions to the eye-slitting image in Buñuel and Salvador Dalí's *Un Chien andalou* (1929), stated that "our listlessness, which makes us accept all the horrors men have committed on the earth, is put to a severe test when we can't bear the sight of a woman's eye cut in two by a razor on the screen. Is it more dreadful than the sight of a cloud veiling a full moon?" (quoted in Abel 1988, 1: 61).

Vigo insisted on the necessary connection between visions of the horrific and the creation of a social cinema: "To aim at a social cinema is therefore simply to underwrite a cinema dealing with provocative subjects, subjects that cut into flesh" (quoted in ibid., 62). The viewing of earliest cinema from the last decade of the nineteenth century offered numerous instances of such subjects, and the writings and certain films of the avant-garde testify to the philosophical, aesthetic, and ontological potential of cinema. The films "make visible what was not in ordinary, everyday experience" (Doane 2002, 133), rendering the ordinary as extraordinary and vice versa. Viewing is conceived as confronting the discordant, the disorganizing, and the discontinuous. The loss of control is based on an uneasy encounter with the unexpectedness of viewing the mutilation of a part of the physical body.

In the Buñuel-Dalí film, when viewing the slicing of the eyeball, the element of shock arises from the spectator's direct frontal experience of the destruction of the physical organ of sight, which starkly throws the viewer into another affective response. The relation between the cutting of the eyeball and the cut of montage dramatically links vision to the vulnerability of vision, its potential destructiveness, and its metaphoric power to insert the spectator into another world of sensation and thought. This shot is, in Barthes's terms, a *punctum*, a point of disturbance wherein viewing becomes traumatic for the viewer. What is made manifest through the montage is another conception of viewing that steers away from a conventional engagement with meaning and is lured to a threatening elsewhere.

Artaud's "raw cinema" is "literally a stimulant and a narcotic" (Barber 2004, 26). It addresses the crisis of the movement-image through an appropriation of sensation. Similarly, Georges Franju's *Le Sang des bêtes* ([Blood of the Beasts], 1949) approximates Artaud's conception of cinema: the spectator is placed "at the very extremes of visual experience, physically exposed to a multiple crisscrossing of expulsive forces which necessitate a transformation of the conditions and nature of visual perception, and impel a resistance towards society and towards cinema itself" (ibid., 28). In familiar terms from a contemporary perspective, Artaud inveighs against representation as being inextricably linked to normative social and religious institutions and, therefore, as dangerous for life in annihilating alternative perceptions of the world. Artaud's ruminations on cinema are predicated on a necessary bond with spectators, engaging them in a "dangerous state of interaction" (ibid., 25) that threatens the integrity of conventional responses. In *The Logic of Sense*, Deleuze (1990, 82–93) devotes a lengthy section to Artaud, situating his fulminations on the human body, language, theater, and cinema within a context of excess in a radical reaction against conventional conceptions of space–time, where "meaning is predetermined not in ideal forms but in a process of emergence and surprise" (Doane 2002, 180). The surprise in Artaud, as his form of nonsense is presented by Deleuze, is related to graphic dimensions of the physical body that challenge conceptions of representation.

THE ARGENTO SYNDROME

A persistent function of Argento's films, whether in his earlier thrillers (*gialli*) such as *Deep Red* (1975) and *Suspiria* (1977) or in his experimental *Opera* (1987), *The Stendhal Syndrome* (1996), and *Il fantasma dell'opera* (*The Phantom of the Opera*, 1998), is their creation of profound dislocations in space and time by unsettling the viewer with a surreal and primal world. The characters often appear in the way that Deleuze characterizes the cinema of naturalism as indicative of manifestations of a crisis of the movement-image: as animals, human animals, made up of "heads without necks, eyes without faces, arms without shoulders, gestures without form ... a world of ... radical evil" (Deleuze 1986, 124) The camera and editing tricks and digital special effects undermine certainty about what is shown.

Hovering between states of bewilderment and a refusal to look yet the compulsion to see, the spectator moves between surface and depth, encounters works of art (opera and paintings) that lose their shape, probes boundaries between the real and the imaginary, and experiences uncertainty between the subjective and objective. Thus, the characters (and spectator) become prey to the terrors of a constantly altering visible world. The horrors and the cruelty portrayed are evident in the loss of familiar landmarks (often identified in terms of architecture). The viewers are frequently in the position of discovering that what they thought they had seen was inevitably misleading (as is Marcus's case in *Deep Red*). In *Deep Red*, *Opera*, and *The Stendhal Syndrome*, vision becomes literally more blurred and images harder to discern.

The Stendhal Syndrome involves a world where the quotidian is metamorphosed into nightmare, creating a tension between the visual and auditory milieus of the film, among its characters, and in the extradiegetic viewer via the film. Argento's adoption of the Stendhal syndrome is based on his memory of a childhood experience of becoming ill while viewing Greek architecture (Cooper 2012, 17). Years later, he came across the psychoanalytic writings of Graziella Magherini on powerful reactions to painting and architecture that she named the Stendhal syndrome. Stendhal (pseudonym of Marie-Henri Beyle), author of *Le Rouge et le noir* (*The Red and the Black,* 1830) and *La Chartreuse de Parme* (*The Charterhouse of Parma,* 1839), had recorded in his journal a disturbing response to art, one conducive to altered states of feeling, rapid shifts of affect, and blurred boundaries between life and death, ecstasy and abjection.

In 1817, after a visit to the Basilica of Santa Croce in Florence, Stendhal wrote: "My emotion was profound, aspiring to pity. The gloomy religiosity of this church, its timbered ceiling, the unending façade, all spoke intensely to my soul" (Stendhal, quoted in Gallant 2001, 136). He further described his disturbed physical and psychic response to the church as "initial confusion, followed by a sense of suffocation, nausea, fainting, high fever, depression" (ibid., 30). *The Stendhal Syndrome,* set in a contemporary landscape, takes this disturbed state further by drawing on an allegorical mode to investigate the effect of art, of vision (as both painting and cinema), on the central character of the film.

The film, more intensely than other of Argento's thrillers, undertakes a dual focus: it is a cinema of the action-image, a crime investigation, involving a serial rapist with a penchant for art and for violently attacking the bodies of beautiful young women (including a female police detective assigned to the case, played by Asia Argento, the director's daughter). It is also a form of cinema reminiscent of the time-image in its exploration of the disturbed and hallucinatory state of both the criminal and the victim as an investigation into the effects of visual art (painting and cinema) on viewers. The emphasis on "the violence of a sensation (and not of a representation), a static or potential violence, a violence of reaction and expression" (Deleuze 2003, xxix) is evident particularly in Detective Anna Manni's responses to Botticelli, Caravaggio, Brueghel, and Rembrandt paintings that cause her to swoon. Her vulnerability bonds her with killer Alfredo Grossi (Thomas Kretschmann) and arouses his desire, which produces his violent rapes of her. The two rape scenes of Anna and those of the other female victims are equally lurid and cruel. As if a portrayal of rape is not enough to compel the spectator to shield her eyes, the raw scenes of torture with the razor the rapist brandishes, the grotesque shooting of the faces of the victim at the moment of his climax, and the vaginal penetrations coupled to the copious amounts of spewing blood are tests of one's capacity to sustain looking at violence.

The scenes of violence are an act of cruelty on the viewer, such as the images of a broken fingernail thrust into an eyeball or a car hood repeatedly slammed over the head of a victim. These scenes would qualify the film as being what Argento described "as the most brutal movie I ever made." Argento asserted that he tried to "engender the same accumulation of weird sensations and unsettling emotions in the audience that Anna is feeling" (Jones 2004, 230). However, regarding these graphic depictions, which might produce laughter as often as screams, Mikel J. Koven argues that these set pieces of violence and mutilation "disrupt the continuity," so that "we are asked to think about the image on its own.... [The] artificiality brings to the fore the film's own constructedness, breaking the continuity of narrative cinema" (2006, 150) in the interests of allowing us to "think about the very ontology of the cinema and our pleasures of watching such images" (ibid., 157). In terms of Deleuze's examination of Francis Bacon, Argento seems to be plumbing sensation through cliché, absurdity, and grotesque acts of violence to liberate *"figures from figuration"* (Conley 2003, 132; italics his).

Another dimension of Argento's filmmaking relates to an affinity for the baroque. According to George Steiner, the baroque was an obsession with the pervasiveness of evil, the "blackness in the individual soul . . . the literal hell which haunts Baroque reflexes" (1977, 19). In Argento, the assault on art, with its corollary of an assault on cinematic representation, functions to radically derealize inherited images of the world by challenging the viewer through sensation. Argento's "theater of cruelty," reminiscent of Artaud, attacks commonplace voyeurism, as if challenging the spectator to participate in—not merely passively to view—the nature and consequences of torture and death. His experimentations with cinematic forms are akin, in Gianni Canova's view, to the "baroque effect to render death and terror visible" (Canova 2003, 108, 230; translation mine). The film collapses the gaze, much as Francis Bacon's paintings elicit the sensation of active witnessing, in which "the gazing figure bears witness or attends to the variation it elicits" (Conley 2003, 138).

According to Karl Schoonover, "The scenario of witnessing an endangered body triggers an opening out of the viewing subject's authority over the world viewed" (2012, 29). *The Stendhal Syndrome* further draws the viewer into a frame where images overflow, dilate, or explode into violence. This implosion produces an uneasiness concerning space and time, an essential element of the baroque, emanating from the perception of numerous folds of space, time, décor, and tableaux. Stendhal's hallucinatory experience of Santa Croce (and Anna's of the museum) can be compared to Deleuze's description of the experience of the baroque as "neither falling into nor emerging from illusion but rather *realizing* something in illusion itself" (Deleuze 1933b, 125). The baroque protagonists are "prey to the giddiness of minute perceptions": they are subject to swooning or "converting illusion into presence." Argento forces the spectator of the film to experience similar sensations, much like Anna's when she views the canvases at the museum, as well as in her own creations. Through images of violence perpetrated on her body and on other female victims, a radical decentering of the world transpires through cinema.

FIGURE 2.1. An excess of viewing, *The Stendhal Syndrome*, Argento, 1996.

In developing his conceptions of the baroque, Deleuze in *The Fold* invoked Walter Benjamin's writing on allegory as a

> decisive step forward in our understanding of the Baroque when he showed that allegory was not a failed symbol, or an abstract personification, but a power of figuration entirely different from that of the symbol: the latter combines the eternal and momentary, nearly at the center of the world, but allegory uncovers nature and history according to the order of time. It produces a history from nature and transforms history into nature in a world that no longer has its center. (Deleuze 1993b, 125)

Allegory is evident throughout *The Stendhal Syndrome:* in the choice of classical paintings, in Anna's own tormented vaginal paintings, in the image of the animated Devil with a huge erection as she lies pinioned in the cave after the rape, in the various transmutations of character that follow her enthrallment to the syndrome and her familial history—but most especially in the link between her various masculine and feminine costumes and her vulnerable body that undergoes the pains of abjection. However, the final image of her, overcome by the police after the murder of Marco and carried like a pietà through the street, embodies the allegory.

The quality of allegorizing pertinent to this Argento film is its connection to a game of riddles. The spectator is confronted by painful enigmas that are not solved through narrative logic but that emerge from the disturbed protagonists and are complicated by the fragmented dislocations throughout the film: from the museum and the paintings, to Anna's hotel room that dissolves into the street, and her fateful encounter with Alfredo culminating in the grotesque cave where she murders him. The persistence of eyes, seen collectively onscreen and individually in close-ups, is not merely another instance of self-referentiality: it is the *raison d'être* for the film's challenges to prevailing conceptions of the world purveyed through art and other contemporary media technologies. For Argento, "television is the literal nightmare of cinema" (Thoret 2002, 130), not only in its censoring practices but even more in its mundane view of the world, emblematic in the "murderous figure of the television talk show as well as in the censuring role of formulaic fixed patterns" (ibid., 129–30; translations mine) to which viewers are accustomed. The violence of his cinema addresses a world that has become exceedingly brutal, though his conception of brutality involves banality and repetition rather than acts of gore. Hence, Argento would insert gore into the country of sitcoms to arouse the viewers. Argento's counter-history is differentiated from historical narration in its concern with the role of vision in the society of spectacle.

The most recent attempts at theorizing time, history, and the death of cinema are connected to the emergence of new electronic and digital technologies that are assumed to operate differently from cinema, tending toward rationalization and standardization, and further obliterating history. Argento's reference to TV seems to echo this view, but a closer examination of his eclectic mode of production suggests otherwise. Rather than presenting himself as a filmmaker who remains committed to the traditional cinema, one who is waging a war against incursions by new technologies, Argento's experimentation with special effects by way of digital technology is situated in an interface between cinematic and digital modes. Commenting on surrealism as an earlier form of treating internal states and on his use of computer graphics, Argento has said,

> Surrealism used to be hard to put on film properly. Although I was reticent about it at first, computer graphics allow me to depict my extreme dreams and dark fantasies. Exploding heads, slicing up bodies—it's all easy to show today. It's hard to come to terms with the thought that you are only limited by your imagination when it comes to what you can achieve visually using today's technical tools. (Argento, quoted in Jones 2004, 230)

Digital technology enables Argento to probe the boundaries between the real and the phantasmatic in behalf of reconfiguring history and memory. His emphasis on an excess of vision is enhanced through the opportunities afforded by the union of cinema and digital media, furthering his commitment to a cinema of poetry that has marked his work. The poetic potential of digital effects in *The Stendhal Syndrome* is evident not only in the painterly composition of the scenes that portray Anna's disturbances but also in the dark and cruel poetry of her role first as victim, then as aggressor. His work with computer specialist Sergio Stivaletti does not strive for realism. His special effects invite the spectator to see into another dimension by foregrounding the potential of the image to reimagine the world through a particular emphasis on spectacle via the body and face and a sensorimotor response to movement.

Linda Williams has written, in relation to horror as a "body genre," that "the body of the spectator is caught up in an almost involuntary mimicry of the emotion or sensation of the body on the screen" (1995, 144), thus appearing to echo Argento's ostensible designs on his viewers. This view would seem to reinstate Argento as a purveyor of sensationalism rather than a cartographer of the senses. To lock Argento's films into a narrow point of body genres is to fail to distinguish their distinctive contribution to his investigative mode of cinema. His films do not merely mime emotion: they incite the viewer to react viscerally and also intellectually. The Argento syndrome is a propaedeutic to an investigation of the nature and effects of art. His gruesome images of torture, mutilation, and cruelty are not the terminus of his works any more than is Artaud's unrealized script for *The Butcher's Revolt*, Michael Powell's *Peeping Tom* (1960), Rainer Werner Fassbinder's *Querelle* (1982), Michael Haneke's *Funny Games* (1997). Argento's films share with these films an unrelenting investigation of the cinematic uses of the past and their persistence in memory through identification with newsworthy and cinematic forms of violence.

FACT AND FANTASY: *DEEP RED* AS COUNTER-HISTORY

Among the different forms of experimentation with cinematic style that Argento has undertaken in his appropriation of the thriller, the 1975 *Deep Red (Profondo rosso)* is a "quantum leap in all respects" (McDonagh 2010, 93). It demonstrates Argento's abiding exploration of violence in cinema as a complex exploration of the crisis of the movement-image, of perception and action. The film is an instance of a mode of counter-historicizing that both links as well as separates his films from other more vernacular forms (Koven 2006, 160). Films such as *Deep Red* invite the spectator to become aware of Argento's self-conscious, contemplative cinematic treatment of violence. His work does not adhere to theories of the historical avant-garde, in which art was not to be destroyed but transferred to the praxis of life, where it could be transformed to a different politics and aesthetics. His difference resides in their blurring of fact and fantasy, their challenge to conventional forms of realism, their hallucinatory quality, and in their particular strategies to incorporate the spectator into their world of impulsive behavior. In Argento, the real and illusory have lost their clarity, and art is as dangerous as life. His films are not manifestoes in the name of art redeeming life or of life redeeming art; they investigate the powers of internalized and externalized horror that inhere in late modernity and are particularly tied to the uses of media technology, including, in later films, computer-generated effects.

His films do not fall into utopian or dystopian forms common to critical writings on the technological sublime. They are, in a very cogent sense, attempts to investigate media, cinema, and television, animating and unsettling institutional and cinematic clichés. His uses of media are predicated on the importance of actively engaging his viewers in experiencing and contemplating the horrors displayed. Through riddles and deadly games, he fuses older cinematic forms with current digitalized ones (as in *The Stendahl Syndrome*), conventional genre forms and avant-garde styles, and nightmares of sexuality and violence and everyday banality. His baroque sensibility as identified by critics (as well as by himself) might be understood as existing in a virtual world, where thoughts of infinity give rise to reflections (on the body, on the senses, on organic and inorganic life, and on violence and power) evoked through his experiments with the changing properties of media that are part of the contemporary world of both popular nonfiction and fiction films, of television as well as cinema.

Films of horror and the supernatural are most often examined in terms of reiterated generic characteristics, social value or decadence, or of their direct connection to given events. In her study of Deleuze and cinema, Patricia Pisters (2003) focuses on the impulse-image in its relation to violence on the body to identify a form of filmmaking that invites thinking on and through the body. Mikel J. Koven (2006) also presents a complex and persuasive discussion of Argento's films that he links to a "cinema of poetry" in which the formal means of construction rupture the traditional form

> through the presentation of the character's subjectivity with the mechanical reproduction of the camera thereby fusing the character's subjectivity with the mechanical reproduction of the camera itself, we are invited, if not *required*, to question the very poetics that are presented to us. (Koven 2006, 145; italics his)

The role of the amateur detective is a significant way in which Argento deprofessionalizes the role of the police inspector and of crime investigation. In *Deep Red,* Superintendent Calcabrini (Eros Pagni) is a comic, inept police inspector; the burden of the investigation falls to a musician, Marcus (David Hemmings) and his journalist helper, Gianna (Daria Nicolodi), whose professions are removed from conventional presentations of the detective. Through these two characters, Argento alters the conventional concern with up-to-date enforcement technology and situates crime so as to enhance the dimensions of connectedness among violence, history, the aesthetics of violence, the role of cinematic vision, and designs on the spectator.

Argento's cinema is, in certain conceptual modes, reminiscent of Antonioni. Indeed, Antonioni's *Il deserto rosso* (*Red Desert,* 1964), Ripstein's *Deep Crimson,* and Argento's *Deep Red* share experimentation with color, sound, music, and a visionary landscape; the exploration of mental states; and a challenging of visual and verbal clichés. Significantly, both Antonioni and Argento probe the potential properties of cinema. *Deep Red* is self-reflexive in its manifold allusions to other filmmakers' work (for example, that of Hitchcock and Michael Powell), such as its use of David

FIGURE 2.2. Confusion between the visible and invisable, *Deep Red*, Argento, 1975.

Hemmings—a star associated with Antonioni's *Blow-Up* (1966), another exploration of a crime—and the naming of his musician-detective, Marcus, after Mark in Powell's *Peeping Tom*.

Argento's films not only acknowledge other filmmakers but also contain allusions to the other arts: popular, electronic, and classical music, including opera, painting, and architecture. His uses of landscape have been attributed to his fascination with Antonioni's filming of Roman landscapes (Newman 1988, 349–50). Also, Argento maintained the practice of using international stars much as Antonioni had done in his trilogy on modernity. Further, Argento utilizes paintings, mirrors, and windows to produce a disjunction between exterior and interior, nearness and proximity, subjectivity and objectivity in his exploration of the mechanisms of vision. The spectator is drawn to the character through familiar strategies of identification that are unpredictably disrupted, distancing the viewer alternately between reassurance and disorientation, the pleasures and threats of viewing violence. Distinctively, *Deep Red* calls attention to the senses—not only sight and hearing but also touch and proprioception (even telekinesis)—that are inherent to the scenes of violent murder but also to the strategies of crime detection.

The confusion about the visible and the invisible will persist in relation to the conflating of a painting with a mirror reflection that Marcus passes in the corridor on his way to the crime scene. But such confusion is also connected to other images: the shadow of the menorah on the wall of murdered telepathist Helga's apartment, the shadow of a Star of David that will be connected to the subsequent Jewish funeral attended by Marcus and Gianna.

These provocative images are emblematic of Argento's focus not only on sensation, as they relate to bodily states, but on the problematic of history and memory that haunts the characters, murderer and victims, detectives and amateurs, and the spectator. The enigmas posed by these visual signposts are reminiscent of Argento's rhizomatic form, namely, of an assemblage of images that open onto the multitude of possibilities attendant on violence: allusions to domestic childhood trauma incrementally repeated and augmented through images of partial objects, a haunting childhood melody, toys, and children's drawings. Through these visual and even aural images, Argento invokes the psychic world of the killer and that of his victims—but especially the historical resonances of the traumatic events identified with Fascism and cinema (especially in the casting of Clara Calamai, a prominent star of the Fascist era).

The killer's particular mode of stalking prey in *Deep Red* invites the vulnerable and perceptive spectator to experience threat through the unsteady and unsettling camera movements displayed in the scenes of pursuit, entrapment, and violence. These effects solicit cinematic and cultural recollections from the work of other filmmakers, from dreams, and from intuitions of impending violence. The film's treatment of violence in relation to Helga is not merely a replay of conventional stereotypes of menacing stalker and helpless victim, since Argento's treatment of aggression and physical violence is intermingled with epistemological concerns inherent to his reworking of the thriller. His films involve the pursuit of the perpetrators of crime, but they also complicate the desire to see the cruelty and violence, both in the rhythm of the editing and in the use of close-ups in these scenes, as if reproducing the sensations but also making them seem repetitive and familiar to the spectator.

Deep Red goes farther than reflexivity in that it embeds a number of historical allusions to problematic identities and behaviors identified with the

FIGURE 2.3. Helga's burial in a Jewish cemetery, *Deep Red*, Argento, 1975.

Jew, the child, and the maternal figure. The primary identity is that of the Jew, the killer's first victim. That Helga (Macha Méril) is a Jew suggests but does not stipulate specific connections; instead, it refers visually and enigmatically to her murder and to her funeral, suggesting undefined connections between her Jewishness and victimhood.

Although Helga's death in relation to the long-ago murders remains suspended and is never clarified by explicit reference to her Jewishness, it clearly is related to her prescience of a killer in her presence. The violence enacted on her is reserved for Argento's more exploratory investigation of the multilayered connections of each of the characters' penchant for violence. But this oblique evocation of the Holocaust does not diminish its power in relation to the traumatic effects of World War II, including those of Italian Fascism, on its victims. Other characters, however, are similarly problematic. For example, Carlo is presented as a likely killer, and the film complicates his role through his relation to his mother, his alcoholism, his homosexuality, and his penchant for violence. Each of the characters in the film, including Marcus, is a study in complexity, thanks to Argento's undermining reductive causal explanations. One of the characters, Dr. Giordani (Glauce Maura), is a psychoanalyst who, like the psychologist in *The Stendhal Syndrome*, is able to discern the murderer's identity; but Argento's silencing him through his murder also thwarts the possibility of a univalent psychological explanation to the killer's motives.

The film's strategies, then, involve not merely the discovery of the criminal's identity but a play with the spectator's desire to know in conjunction with ambivalent reactions to the clichéd perception of the "pleasures of watching such images" (Koven 2006, 157). The film's exploration of violence is not presented as a dilemma that demands explicit address. Instead, Argento's approach to the horrific is a self-conscious treatment of the connections among cinema, knowledge of the world, and art as medium for contemplating destruction of self and others. Marcus's role as detective involves his uneasy and intuitive sense of having seen something unusual, something to do with a painting, at the initial murder scene; his presence there both implicates him as a suspect and links him to the spectator, who enters the game of misrecognition. Marcus's fate is tied to Gianna, both bonded in a quest for the killer that alternately becomes comic, aggressive, and physically threatening. All of the characters, including the earlier police superintendent, are central to the problematic of misperception that haunts the film and renders it a baroque rather than gothic text. Particularly significant in a literary and cinematic form that relies on investigation and discovery of the truth is how Argento's film fractures and proliferates cause and effect to frustrate reductive explanation.

Each of the murders, as well as the threat to Marcus, contains elements of the domestic childhood trauma scene; these are gradually augmented by clues leading to fragments of the past alive in the present. In this way, the film enlarges its investigation of visual remnants that relate to the past, such as the fresco Marcus uncovers in the abandoned mansion. After the mansion burns in a fire set by the murderer, a picture is found that the caretaker's child claims to have reproduced from one in the archive at school. This is a potential clue that seems to point to Carlo. However, he is not the murderer, and his gruesome death as he is chased by the police is followed by the visual recall of the original murder scene of Carlo's father by his wife as their child Carlo watches, picks up the bloody knife, and stares at it.

The climax involves Marcus's return to the scene of Helga's death and recognition that the face that he had seen earlier was not a painting but a mirror and that he is now confronting not a portrait but the reflection of the murderer, Carlo's mother (Calamai). Fighting her off, he becomes the instrument for her death, as her head, chained to the elevator by a necklace caught in its mechanism, is severed from her body. The final shot is a reflection of Marcus's face gazing into a pool of blood. Hardly a moment of celebration and justification, this final moment dilutes satisfaction that the criminal has been exposed and punished at the hands of the just, thus reinforcing the difference between the action-image and the impulse-image. In the case of Argento's film, the naturalist element is evident in the film's insistence on repetition, on the obsessive animal-like character of the murderer, and on the downward trajectory into violence and death, as well as in the reiterative invocation of animality and fetishistic objects that come to be associated with the killer (see Deleuze 1986, 126–27).

In relation to counter-historicizing, the film's appropriation of memory images is another instance of a return to a scene of a crime and to its repetitive incarnations that run counter to expectations of resolution and clarification. The many visual allusions to the past in Argento's films are expressive of what Deleuze has described as conveying different "sheets of past" (1989a, 99) and central to the emergence of time to produce a different form of the image and of narration. The elements Argento has chosen to portray do not convey a linear sense of time but are characteristic of unusual, adventitious (rhizomatic) connections between the private and public world in which violence plays a major but not a specifically demarcated role. For example, the familial drama that sets the murders in motion has resonance in relation to connections among domestic violence, the law, and the public sphere. In addition, the forms of misrecognition attendant on identifying the multiple strands that contribute to the problem of truth seeking are emphasized through this form of investigative drama from the standpoint of the "amateur." Argento's portraits of the horrific are thus a form other than social realism for confronting the crisis of the action-image. Self-reflexive and self-conscious about the cinematic image and about its being embedded in a culture of vision, his films address the crisis of history as counter-history through a union of the naturalistic, the perverse, and the investigative.

NATURALISM, THE COLOR CRIMSON, AND PERVERSION

In a section in *Cinema 1: The Movement-Image,* Deleuze discusses naturalism, a form of literary and cinematic expression as an outgrowth of realism and identified with natural science. The influences of heredity and environment play a key role in eliciting instinctual responses to the external world, as is manifest in the writings of Émile Zola, Theodore Dreiser, and Jack London, among many others. In this deterministic world, behavior is governed by energy expressed through an "impulse-image." The impulse-image is caught between the affection-image and action-image and cannot be expressed through action or felt through affection. The cinematic world he describes is a world of artifice and violence closer to Artaud's cinema of cruelty and to expressions of the horrific. The world of naturalism is "not opposed to realism, but on the contrary accentuates its features by extending them in an idiosyncratic surrealism" (Deleuze 1986, 124).

The milieu of naturalism is one of extreme violence, deformation, degradation, and entropy, a world of fragments "*torn from* objects which have effectively been formed in this milieu," depending on symptoms that "are the presence of impulses in the derived world, and idols and fetishes" (Deleuze 1986, 124, 125; italics his). This world of perversions is made up of fragments or partial objects a where "the impulse is an act which tears away, ruptures, dislocates... a constant predator–prey relationship" (ibid., 128). Cunning is the dominant behavior in this world of violence, leading the predatory monsters to inhabit a degenerating milieu and remain there until they exhaust it and, therefore, move on to the next to repeat their death-dealing actions. Each passage becomes more violent and degraded, but the milieus are not totally deterministic: there is always the possibility of salvation through a form of repetition that is open through a direct image of time, but this is reserved for the viewer.

Naturalistic images transform actual milieus into primeval or "originary" landscapes, thus altering conceptions of history as linear and progressive and of the presence of figures of salvation who redeem time. The naturalistic world is a gloomy and destructive picture of history; its form of counter-history appears as a parody of melodrama and of manifest destiny. Arturo Ripstein's 1996 film *Deep Crimson* is exemplary of the qualities of the impulse-image and its effects (Deleuze 1986, 127–30). In the discussion that follows, I consider Ripstein's film from the vantage point of naturalism as a primordial cinematic world that relies not on a realization of heroic action in the interests of a community but on a prehistoric world that, through a downward trajectory, exhausts the organic and vital properties of a more recognizable one. Ripstein has indeed credited Buñuel for the intellectual and cinematographic role that Buñuel, for whom he had assistant-directed in Mexico, played in his career (Garcia 1998, 57), and the film bears the marks of Buñuelian satiric (and surreal) allegory in its focus on a milieu of increasing decadence.

Although *Deep Crimson* might seem a parody of *amour fou*, it is rather a grotesque exploration of perverse desire that unites sexuality and violence. The film is a fable that becomes a counter-history of Mexican culture and politics in the 1950s, related from a naturalist position to offer a bleak and destructive narrative of Mexican life. The film is populated by bizarre, cartoonish figures and their fetishistic attachment to partial objects expressive of their consuming impulses: the corpulent Coral (Regina Orozco), obsessed with cinema and with the figure of Charles Boyer, incarnated in the figure of Nicolás; the aging, self-centered Nicolás (Daniel Giménez Cacho), a con artist, who passes himself off as a Spanish gentleman and requires an expensive wig to appear as a masculine object of virility and desire; Juanita, a disturbed and alcoholic widow who responds to the advertisement, rages against a life trapped in an aging body but is granted a paradoxical release through rat poison administered to her by Coral; and Irene, a lonely widow who lives with religious fetishes as substitutes for her sexual desire and is brutally assaulted by Coral (with a statue of Christ) for daring to think she might have sex with and marry Nicolás.

The surreal images of the "marriage" between Irene and Nicolás in the cemetery, with Coral pacing like a caged animal, are prelude to her later killing of Irene with the widow's religious statue. The final victim of the couple is Rebecca, a younger woman, also a widow, seeking replacement for her dead husband to run her business. She is brutally murdered by Nicolás, and her small daughter is exsanguinated by Coral, albeit reluctantly.

Ripstein's film is a cinema of cruelty in its exploration of challenging the spectator to see and think differently about the marginal and dispos-

FIGURE 2.4. Coral contemplates a funeral, *Deep Crimson*, Ripstein, 1996.

sessed in Mexican society. It is not a neorealist film but a surrealistic one, its surreal treatment based on its violating popular forms of melodramatic attachment by exceeding its affective intensity through the horrific, not only in its images of blood and violence but in the manner in which the film invites the viewer to contemplate the world of its two outsider protagonists. The viewer is not spared encounters with an oppressive milieu and its connections to the bizarre and death-dealing impulses of Nicolás and Coral. Coral's claustrophobic and untidy dwelling is a clue to her disordered mind and only one of many clues to the film's focus on the banal and deadly aspects of the impulse-image. The film has been described as a "black comedy" (Ebert 1998). If indeed it is a comedy, it bears comparison to those elements of naturalism that border on the incongruous hyperrealism described by Deleuze as "idiosyncratic surrealism" (1986, 124).

If, in forms of realism (as in neorealism), the everyday is granted dignity, this film is the other side of realism, in which the familiar world is disfigured, made to carry the burden of social and psychic maladies in extreme and increasingly violent fashion. Coral Fabre, mother to two fatherless (and neglected) children and living in straitened economic circumstances, is a former embalmer now employed to administer inexpert and painful injections to an old man. Her unkempt appearance and behavior are reinforced by an eating fetish and obsessive attachment to Charles Boyer, whose picture hangs by her dressing table. She is determined to find a man in the image of Boyer, her desired lover, by responding to lonely hearts' advertisements.

When Nicolás Estrella comes to Coral's house after she replies to his personal ad for a companion, he presents himself as an incarnation of a Spanish gentleman. Expecting to find a young woman, based on a photo Coral had sent of herself prior to her weight gain, he instead confronts an obese woman whose desire is to possess him as the incarnation of her desire. She invites sex and he complies, but, during the night, he steals money from her purse and leaves. Determined to stay with him, and bringing her two children with her, she goes to his house with the intent of staying, though he is adamant that he cannot take them in. Undeterred by this rejection, she immediately abandons her children to a Catholic orphanage, returns alone to Nicolás, breaks into his house, reads his mail, confirms his practices of swindling women, and blackmails him into allowing her to remain and become his accomplice as his "sister." The two are fused by their imperfections: she is devouring in her desire, fiercely aggressive as a composite maternal figure, sister, and possessive child, while he is vain, grandiose in gesture, and increasingly dependent on Coral. The two consolidate their relationship and set out on the road to contact and swindle Nicolás's lonely and desperate applicants for companionship. Thus, *Deep Crimson* becomes a road film that, similar to many such pictures, ends in cataclysmic disaster for the two escapees from the real world.

The film focuses on the ways the couple becomes bonded with each other, on Coral's desperate and covetous desire for Nicolás, and on the desolate women seeking companionship—not unlike Coral herself. Her possessiveness of Nicolás intensifies her murderous hostility to the lonely women they seek to exploit. She will not share Nicolás, expressing the ultimate of devotion for her ideal lover and complete indifference to the lives of the women. Her murder of Juanita (Julieta Egurrola), their first client whom they arrange to meet in an out-of-the way bar, is an exquisitely cruel portrait of agony and jealousy: she hovers over Juanita, trying to separate her from Nicolás, until she goes to the basement of the bar and finds a container of rat poison with which to kill her. The act of dumping Juanita's body on a bench at the train station consolidates, even strengthens, the first grotesque phase of bonding with Nicolás through murder without financial gain. His dependency on her deepens. However, in the subsequent scene, again on the road, Nicolás, suffering from his persistent headaches, removes his hat and loses his wig in the wind, only to discover that it has been destroyed: "ruined like me.... I'm deformed."

Blaming her for his loss and desolate over its irreplaceability, he leaves her angrily her in a hotel and goes to a movie house where, coincidentally, a Boyer picture is playing. In his absence, Coral cuts her own hair and, utilizing her skills as an embalmer, creates an even "more natural" wig for him. Upon his return, kissing her before a mirror image of the two embracing and reconsolidating their oscillating masochistic union, the couple journey to their next contact, the widow Irene Gallardo (Marisa Paredes). When the couple arrives at her home, Irene is suspicious about the authenticity of Nicolás's Spanish accent and of the ethnic identity of both Coral and Nicolás; but Coral convinces her of Nicolás's pedigree as a hidalgo and, hence, of his Catholic piety and determination to convert the heathen populace. Initially, Nicolás and Irene indulge in hymn singing as Coral malevolently looks on.

A visiting neighbor, Señora Sara Silberman (Rosa Furman), identified by Irene as a Jew, injects a different perspective on the declared missionaries. Smoking a cigarillo, she articulates her skepticism of the pair and of their mission. When Coral describes their "missionary work," Sara says wryly, "I thought these lands were already Christian" as a consequence "of the last time the Spaniards came," when "they left a slew of dead Indians." Irene ushers this "professional anarchist and disbeliever" out of her house. The last we see of Sara is her peering at Irene's house from behind a curtain in her own. Thereafter, Irene and Nicolás's hymn singing is the evening's entertainment, again arousing Coral's fear and rage at being dispossessed. After Irene retires, she cajoles Nicolás into sex, but the following morning Coral appears at breakfast to learn that Nicolás and Irene will be married.

On the road again, with Irene as their third passenger, the group stops at a Christian graveyard where a surreal "marriage" takes place between

Nicolás and Irene. The ludicrous ceremony involves Irene in a white gown and veil, kneeling with Nicolás before her statue of Jesus on a tombstone as the two pray, with Coral looking on and pacing angrily. The climax of this encounter occurs when Irene insists during the night on sexual consummation with Nicolás, articulating, "Let your wine spill into my chalice." Coral enters the bedroom, hysterically claiming that he is "mine, only mine," touching Nicolás's private parts. Irene calls her a "savage." Coral, responsive to his pleadings to quiet Irene, picks up the statue and, blocking the view of the killing from Nicolás with her large body, finishes the job with a poker. Coral then props up the body, putting makeup on the face. The burial in a desolate field completes another gruesome, bloody episode (accompanied by tango music). This episode is not the denouement but rather an intensifying of the bizarre enactment of Coral's behavior as grotesque portrait of a maternal figure, conveyed in the changing relations of dependency between her and Nicolás, in which Coral increasingly assumes dominance. Claudia Schaefer interprets Coral's behavior as the grotesque underside of femininity and its relation to maternity played to the hilt: "Coral is absurdly and excessively society's epitome of the perfect woman who does everything for her spouse.... [T]here is no job she cannot handle" (2001, 97)—even murder, climaxing surreally in the final events of the road journey. Furthermore, by linking the Irene episode to religion, the film transgressively connects romantic love not only to the idealized cult of the Madonna but also to the residual history of Mexican colonialism by the Spaniards.

In the last fatal and most bloody episode, a young woman who has responded to Nicolás's lovelorn advertisement becomes their victim. Rebecca Sanpedro (Verónica Merchant), a widow left to manage an automobile business and care for a young daughter, Mercedes, is looking for a worker and mate. Skeptical about the brother-and-sister team who arrive at her homestead, she places Nicolás on probation, surveying him first to test his capabilities for business as a "strong man." She wants a Mediterranean man who is "old-fashioned and sympathetic," echoing Irene's desire for Nicolás as a man of pedigree. Quickly she learns that Nicolás is short on skills as a mechanic, while Coral, who tries to play with Mercedes, frightens the child with a suffocating form of affection. Angrily, Coral refers to Mercedes as a "snot-nosed little imp." In a long shot, Rebecca and Nicolás play tag as the child squeals with delight; the camera pans to Coral eating again, leering venomously at the domestic scene. Refusing Nicolás's plea to leave this house, Coral convinces him that the "slut" is rich and that their exploitation is justifiable since Rebecca is a "whore."

Coral's jealousy over his wooing of Rebecca erupts into a larger conflict with Nicolás when she now reminds him of her own children as having been nicer than Mercedes. Coral and Rebecca constitute two forms of maternal affection, Coral as a smothering caricature of motherhood and Rebecca as a conventional maternal figure. On Rebecca's command that Coral must go, Coral leaves with Nicolás's promise that she can return when the job is finished. As he and Rebecca have sex in a car, the camera revolves around the vehicle, then slowly pans to a travel suitcase of the temporarily banished Coral. Now the courtship between Rebecca and Nicolás proceeds as he undertakes to work for her. Unfortunately, while laboring, he is viewed by Rebecca without his wig. He angrily calls her a slut for laughing at him and toying with the now-bedraggled object fallen to the ground. Placing the unkempt wig back on his head, he rages about Rebecca's ignorance of honor and immerses her head in a large barrel of refuse, a prelude to the consequences of a crowning moment of his degradation that initiates the last phase of violent murder directed at the mother and her child.

On Coral's return (in the rain) to the house, she learns that Rebecca wants an abortion and violently berates Nicolás for breaking his earlier promise to her about chastity. He falls to the floor and abjectly begs her to punish him, to step on him "like a worm," and she complies. Furthermore, she tries to rip apart the toupee she made for him earlier by tearing it apart with her teeth. The bathroom becomes the site of the first bloody assault: the abortion administered by Coral is completed by Nicolás with a knife, killing Rebecca in the presence of her child. Now the more ghastly killing will take place as Coral tries to comfort Mercedes with a lollipop, refused by the child. The problem remains as to how to calm Mercedes, and, for a second time Nicolás, now assuming a commanding rather than dependent position, is instrumental: he informs Coral that the child too has to die, though Coral begs him to spare her.

In the bathroom, Coral undresses Mercedes, gently places her in the tub, and drowns her; then, disconsolate and claiming she is the mother, she tries to hold on to the dead child. Nicolás removes the body from her arms and digs a grave by a heap of dead tires and a truck frame that serves to cover the buried bodies. In a visually compelling scene, he comes to the bathroom with the bloody towel hanging over the tub and with the various instruments used in the killings arrayed on a chair next to Coral. She asks him, "Why did we do it?" He answers, "Things like this join two people forever.... We are united in blood." And she adds, "In blood and death." The film culminates in their brutal shooting by the police after they have been told to run: the final image, a close-up, is their bullet-riddled bodies in a bloody, stagnant pool of water, with their reflection, as the camera image slowly fades out on their bodies united in death.

Deep Crimson is not monumental history or a conventional melodrama but an antimelodrama presented as a counter-history of Mexican culture, offering clues to an ensemble of events for rethinking the past as well as present. The form of naturalism that it adopts connects to a historical world: the memory of colonialism via the Spanish conquistadores and its aftermath, the Catholic cult of the Madonna, and the minority status of the Jew. Through allegorizing, the narration evokes barbaric connections with an originary world. By means of its focus on impulse and sensation, rather than on sensorimotor perceptions and affection, the film creates a primordial sense of the rituals and psychic mechanisms (not easily accessible in disciplinary historical or sociologically inflected forms) that may not explain but do offer clues for the persistence of cultural forms that appear elusive, inexplicable, or mystifying. The treatment of violence places the spectator in a position "squarely in the middle of *la descomposición física y moral de la sociedad*" (Schaefer 2001, 88), plunged into the shadows, "rather than find[ing] the world which we inhabit more intelligible" (ibid., 100). The spectator is not spared the sight of their ultimate degradation but offered parallels to their brutal demise through the exhaustive treatment of this violent and exhausted milieu. This is naturalism in its most succinct form, in which perversion "is a constant predator–prey relationship" (Deleuze 1986, 128).

The film not only presents, in its portrait of Nicolás, a parody of the hidalgo as icon transposed onto the image of Boyer to allegorize his erotic masculinity but also probes the body of women in relation to sexuality, reproduction, maternity, and transgression. By undertaking a parodic, darkly humorous portrait of the reversal of spirit and flesh, the film in its religious irreverence and surreal extravagance is able to introduce, through the medium of mortified flesh and blood, a shocking view of transubstantiation. The clues involving Coral's maternity relate to her obsessive "maternal" focus on eating and feeding others. Her killings appear to literalize the Communion, "this is my body, this is my blood," fusing the actual with the virtual. Thus, *Deep Crimson* calls attention to the more diabolic and perverse versions of desire and behavior by exposing fraudulent devotional practices and missionary work as abjection, violence, and material exploitation. While the flimsy theater of the pseudo-missionaries is recognized by Señora Silberman as a swindle, Irene is too obsessed in her desire to possess Nicolás, her religious pretensions notwithstanding. Each of the episodes becomes more violent by emphasizing the mutilation of the physical body to reinforce the material rather than spiritual dimensions flaunted by Nicolás.

Employing the genre of horror, the film exposes the viewer to a morally and materially degenerate milieu that produces sensations of shock and repulsion at the vehemence of forms of violence both epistemological and physical. The film's evocation of religion, linking it to national identity and to social class, becomes an instrument that serves what Lowenstein regards as "a potential catalyst for the reawakening of experience to history" (2005, 16). In Ripstein's case of Mexican culture and cinema, however, this history is not conventional in its treatment of action, ethical judgment, and justice but exemplifies the impulse-image that can puncture conventional conceptions of morality, law, and social institutions. Its focus is on body politics, and its vision of becoming animal subjects the viewer to the stark knowledge of the flesh as meat (as in the last images of the film) to explode complacency about conventional values and liberal explanations of the human animal. Its theater of cruelty confronts the viewer with the holes created through naturalism to portray a "world of a very special kind of violence (in certain respects, it is the radical evil); but it has the merit of causing an originary image of time to rise, with the beginning, the end, and the slope, all the cruelty of Chronos" (Deleuze 1986, 124).

Unlike the movement-image in which time is subordinated, *Deep Crimson* offers an evident but different, primordial order of time that is a prime characteristic of naturalism, whose authors "diagnose civilisation" (Deleuze 1986, 125). The conspirators' journey through long stretches of desolate fields, an unproductive wasteland, and barren landscape becomes a correlative of their lives—even the place of their death, where they are ordered to run so as to legitimize their being shot like wild animals. Thus, the end of the film does not offer compensation to the viewer; instead, it provides a vision of cruelty as a counter-history to challenge reductive explanations of Mexican national history as conveyed through its legendary effects on the swindled and dispossessed. This form of history making comes close to conveying the effects of time, but in negative terms. In this negativity, the spectator is offered an entropic vision of life. However, in its excess of brutality and blood, *Deep Crimson*'s surrealism appears to produce less a frisson of excitement than an uneasy recognition of the film's naturalistic expression as diagnostic of a crisis of the image, providing a vision of counter-history to challenge the mythology of nation, religion, and desire.

VIOLENCE, SEXUALITY, NATURALISM, AND VAMPIRISM

Similar to *Deep Crimson* and to his own *Oldeuboi* (*Oldboy*, 2003), Park Chan-wook in his 2009 *Thirst* offers an example of monstrous depictions of desperate, obsessed, and violent bodies as characteristic of naturalism, though of a form that ultimately goes beyond fetishes and entropy. *Thirst* belongs to a hybrid form of filmmaking that has crossed between popular and traditional cinematic forms, crossed national boundaries exemplified in many other European and Asian transnational films, and crossed various generic boundaries, including horror, vampirism, Kung Fu, and even comedy. In the vein of many current South Korean filmmakers, Park too has dared to violate and undermine sexualized, gendered, ethnic, *and* racial tropes. Reviews and essays on Park's work are quick to point out his national and international auteur status, the astounding commercial success of his prior films, and affinities between his and Quentin Tarantino's films (Hu 2009; Ebert 2009), the continuity of the revenge narrative in his works to date. However, despite recent praise for *Thirst* as an enigmatic "vampire" film, there are instances of critics and reviewers who continue to regard the visual excesses of *Thirst* as problematic and allude to its style as not only sporting auteurism (Sharp 2009, 79) but making "a mockery of mor(t)ality" in its "comic book flippancy" (James 2009, 70).

Thirst is yet another instance of the contemporary uses of the horrific as a form of counter-history, with the vampire figure assuming a prominent aesthetic position. The Park film predictably does not overtly allude to a specific historical event, though it investigates complex conceptions about violence and sexuality that are transgressive through a lurid presentation of infected, diseased, disfigured, and maimed bodies in real time, as is consonant with naturalism. The film exemplifies an increasing transnational focus on a form of body politics "implanted directly in the flesh ... [in which] social forces permeate it right from the beginning" (Shaviro 1993, 133–34). The films of Park Chan-wook explore the politics of power by theatricalizing the agonies of monstrous bodies. In its investigation of subtle internal and external forms of control for maintaining docile bodies, the film links these bodies to threatening and decomposing physical and social forms, particularly those involving religion and altruism.

Thirst focuses on a Catholic priest, Sang-Sang-hyun (Song Kang-ho), whose burning desire is to mitigate the pains of the sick and dying. Several initial incidents prefigure his helplessness. The first involves a bedridden patient who describes his anticipation of the pleasures of savoring a sponge cake and how, after encountering two young starving girls, he relinquished his desired sweet. Desirous of serving the ailing man, Sang-Sang-hyun is responsive to the sick man's request to play a song. He runs to get his flute, only to discover that the ailing man has lapsed into unconsciousness and requires resuscitation, not music. The second image of the priest's helplessness is his encounter in the confessional booth with a woman who wants to commit suicide. He counsels her that suicide is "to die a martyr for Satan." Therefore, she is told to "Say 20 Hail Mary's, get lots of sun," and "take a cold shower." Furthermore she is advised to take antidepressants and "forget the bastard." Her response is that she "will deal with the bastard," and the priest can stick to his praying. The third and crucial incident involves Sang-hyun's encounter with his blind confessor, Priest Noh (Park In-hwan), in which Sang-Sang-hyun seeks permission to participate in an experiment involving a deadly virus, one that he claims will save the dying, despite his mentor's advice to stick to the confessional. Receiving absolution, he leaves to join the Emanuel Labs, where the experiments are taking place. The African doctor informs him about the deleterious effects of the virus: Sang-hyun will be inoculated, can expect blisters over his face and body, as well as internal bleeding, and finally will die, as there is no cure as yet.

The film does not take the route of conventional religious martyrdom promised in this episode; nor is it a conventional historical film, though readings of Asian films are rife with interpretations that focus on a film's historicity. In fact, similar to the naturalist films discussed above, *Thirst* is another instance of counter-history in which conceptions of chronology and interpretation are complicated by different registers of time that are nonlinear, asynchronous, and serial, invoking fantasy, dream, and recollection expressed largely through the body. More specifically, vampirism underscores the impulse toward the death instinct. Indeed, this is not a film relying on reflection theory, though time does play a critical role in falsifying narration to challenge prevailing forms of truth aligned to a belief in religion or science that are called into question. The film is not a predictable science fiction or horror film but a dramatic and philosophical investigation of fear, anxiety, and despair over an existence lived through a body subjugated through unthinking forms of belief. From the moment of Sang-hyun's "resurrection," the apparently realist *mise-en-scène* will shift into another cinematic register that will take the viewer into a world of sexual cruelty, passion, and violence—derived in part from Émile Zola's novel *Thérèse Raquin* (1867) as a guiding text—to develop a different and transgressive portrait of desire and despair (Niogret 2009, 25).

After Sang-hyun, covered as was predicted with eruptions and spewing blood, is pronounced dead while being given a blood transfusion, he inexplicably returns to life as a "bandaged saint." Crowds await his return and plead hysterically for a cure for their ailments. His resurrected appearance seems a parody of Christ's resurrection, with thanks to the blood transfusion administered in the hospital; but the parallels with a savior are comic given the eruptions on Sang-hyun's body and his addiction to the blood of a patient. Uncomfortable, he seeks to avoid such encounters. However, the critical moment in his "conversion" to vampirism begins when he meets Lady Ra (Kim Hae-suk) who pleads with him to save her son Kang-woo (Shin Ha-kyun) who, she claims, is dying of cancer. Thus begin the spiraling grotesque events portrayed in terms congenial to naturalism, with specific attention to mad love. The pivotal figure for Sang-Sang-hyun is the young woman Tae-ju (Kim Ok-bin) abandoned by her family, adopted by Lady Ra, and then married to the infantilized and sickly Kang-woo.

The Zola story was adapted first as a silent film by Jacques Feyder (1928) and later by Marcel Carné (1953) as a sound film. The appeal of the naturalist Zola novel resides in its intricate and downward trajectory involving Madame Raquin, a domineering mother and shop owner; her overprotected son, Camille; Thérèse, his wife; and eventually Thérèse's lover, Laurent. Park comments on the novel: "It has not an ounce of sentimentality. Its observations on the notion of love are so dispassionate that in certain parts, it almost makes you laugh" (quoted in Bell 2009, 43). Deleuze's comments on the Zola are relevant to Park's film. Park illuminates the workings of naturalism as they relate to the impulse-image, offering a radical, nonchronological sense of time as a threat to logical and rational accounting of behavior. According to Deleuze, naturalism in Zola entails a crack through which "the big appetites gravitate around the death instinct.... We could say initially that the instincts cover over death and cause it to retreat; but this is temporary, and even their noise is fed by death" (1990, 326).

In his reworking of the novel, Park loosely traces the disorganization that arises in a milieu that is more clearly related to the expression of originary or primordial impulses than to social or political amelioration. Park's film makes no pretense of realism in its treatment of body politics but offers a seriocomic portrait of connections among the different registers of death in life and life in death, thus playing with the vampire trope and its links to the torture of unrequited desire that not only awakens the impulses but goads them to increased acts of perverse pleasure and predation.

While certain critics (for example, Sharp 2009) are uneasy about the unevenness of the narration and gruesome visuals, from the moment of Sang-hyun's first drinking of the blood drawn from a hospital patient's IV drip to the consummation of his sexual coupling with Tae-ju, they are missing the more serious dimensions of the use of vampirism as counter-history. Through this bizarre, excessive treatment of the narration, the viewer is plunged into another time dimension described by Bliss Cua

Lim: spectral or ghostly time in which the return of the dead "refuses the linear progression of modern time consciousness, flouting the limits of mortality and historical time" (2009, 149). Sang-hyun's rebirth as a vampire entails his discovery of the power over life and death that he has acquired but also a recognition of the moral implications that arise from his growing sexual desire for Tae-ju, which exacerbates his struggle between altruism and personal survival. Tae-ju is more pragmatic and unconcerned about moral consequences. She is envious of Sang-hyun's great physical strength and his freedom to move in space and desires the same power for herself at the expense of others' lives. As her sexual obsessions grow, so does her penchant for violence, and so his.

As Sang-hyun observes the young woman's treatment by Lady Ra and her son, he identifies with her enslaved condition, thus placing himself in the position of Tae-ju's savior against Lady Ra and Kang-woo. Sang-hyun "frees" Tae-ju from her somnambulistic existence, but he is naïve about what an attachment to her entails in terms of his original, but now wavering, belief in his commitment not to cause harm to anyone. His ethical values are tested sorely not only by Tae-ju but also by Priest Noh, his mentor, when the blind priest begs Sang-hyun to aid him in becoming a vampire so as to be able to see, if only at night. Sang-hyun now declares that he is no longer a priest. Returning to Lady Ra's home, he informs her of his decision, and she invites him to stay in her house consonant with her maternal concerns for Kang-woo and the continuity of her domestic mahjong community. What is distinctive about the style is its fusion of the everyday with the primeval world of naturalism, thus calling attention to impulsiveness as inherent to the actual rather than reserved for the supernatural.

The living arrangements become desperate as Tae-ju continues to be tormented by her imprisonment in the house and in her marriage, and it is clear that Sang-hyun and she will kill Kang-woo on a fishing trip. Sang-hyun undertakes not only to kill Kang-woo but also to benefit from his victim's blood to rid himself of his resurgent blisters. The two men fall overboard into the water and struggle fiercely. Sang-hyun drinks the necessary blood as he wrestles with Kang-woo by acquiring it from a bleeding wound running out of Tae-ju's ear. Given the escalating number of victims, Sang-hyun visits Noh, confesses the crime, and agonizes over his fear of death, claiming if the blind priest gives him absolution, Sang-hyun will share his blood with him, thus granting him night vision. Unrepentant and unsympathetic, he then kills the priest and drinks his blood to clear his gruesome blisters and internal bleeding.

Sang-hyun's suffering has rendered him a cruel and literally bloodthirsty killer, despite his altruistic assertions about wanting to save innocent lives. The lapsed priest has inverted the Eucharist, in which the bread and wine are transubstantiated in the body of Christ; instead, to sustain himself, he kills and drinks the blood of men in a travesty of Holy Communion. The next stage of his degeneration is manifest in his brutal and ambivalent treatment of Tae-ju, who is now a vampire also thanks to his complicity in sharing his own blood with her. She has become as bloodthirsty and violent as he, determined to enjoy the forbidden pleasures, and their relationship has become cruel and competitive toward each other: she too has become monstrous.

Following the events in the Zola novel, Lady Ra, having suffered a stroke after Kang-woo's death, becomes incapable of speech but visually attentive to the bloody events that transpire as exposed by the mahjong players, who originally included Lady Ra; the retired police chief; Kang-woo, a friend; with Tae-ju, and a young woman, Evelyn, as observers. The game, identified by a player as having come from China, serves not only as a reminder of a world of gaming rules in the conventional world but also as a marker of the gradual shifting of power relations among the group that will culminate in an orgy of violence. First, however, the viewer is witness to scenes of madness enacted by Tae-ju, reminiscent of Thérèse in the Zola novel, in which Tae-ju desperately pleads for forgiveness despite her earlier vaunting, "I'm in charge now." Determined to end the recriminations and renounce his vampirism, Sang-hyun drives the car with the two women toward the sea, stops, and throws away the keys, so that he and Tae-ju can confront the daylight as they gradually decompose into ash, Lady Ra sitting immobile in the back seat and observing them. Lady Ra plays a critical role in the film as the bizarrely protective mother who, as in the Zola novel, confronts the two young people she had befriended after the death of her son, only to learn of their role in his murder. Hers is the last human presence in the novel; Lady Ra is also the last in the film, as Tae-ju and Sang-hyun, under the bright light of the day, slide to their deaths. Deleuze's description of the ending of the Zola novel is applicable to the ending of the Park film:

> If there is a transcendence, it is only that of a judge or of an inexorable witness who symbolizes the tragic destiny. This is why the role of the symbol or of a tragic god is held by Madame Raquin, the mute and paralyzed mother of the murder victim, present throughout the decomposition of the lovers. The drama, the adventure of the instincts, is reflected only in the logos represented by the muteness of the old woman and by her expressive fixity. (Deleuze 1990, 331)

Thus, it might be said that Sang-hyun and Tae-ju characterize the impulse-image identified largely with cinematic naturalism, whose creators are diagnosticians of civilization. They belong to the world of fetishes and symptoms in a world increasingly reduced to violence and cruelty. In the case of Park's film, the fetishes are strikingly marked in the repeated shots of Tae-ju's bare feet erotically caressed by the camera, then later bitten by Sang-hyun; but the film's innovative treatment of vampirism resides in its linking of science with religion as these relate to blood rituals. Sang-hyun's return to life is a consequence of the double failure of the experiment, which offers no cure but through the "foreign elements" introduced during the transfusion enables him to survive. Park's observation about Sang-hyun having become a "foreign object" (Bell 2009, 43) resonates through the mahjong game (imported from China); the introduction of the young woman, Evelyn, who in English asks Sang-hyun to pray for Tae-ju; and, above all, in Park's comment that vampire folklore is nonexistent in Korea and that the basis for this modern myth was imported from the West, as was Christianity.

Thus, the portraits of Sang-hyun and Tae-ju function as alien elements: namely, of forbidden sexual desire and violence. The grotesque comedy finally attributes this behavior not to the two protagonists but to forms of belief in medicine, religion, and the family, which are abundantly dramatized through Lady Ra's relationship with her son, Priest Noh, and the mutilated and dying victims of the experiment, as well as other exhausted and maimed bodies in the hospital. The everyday world, comprised of invalids, does not serve as a site of nostalgia so much as it embodies other

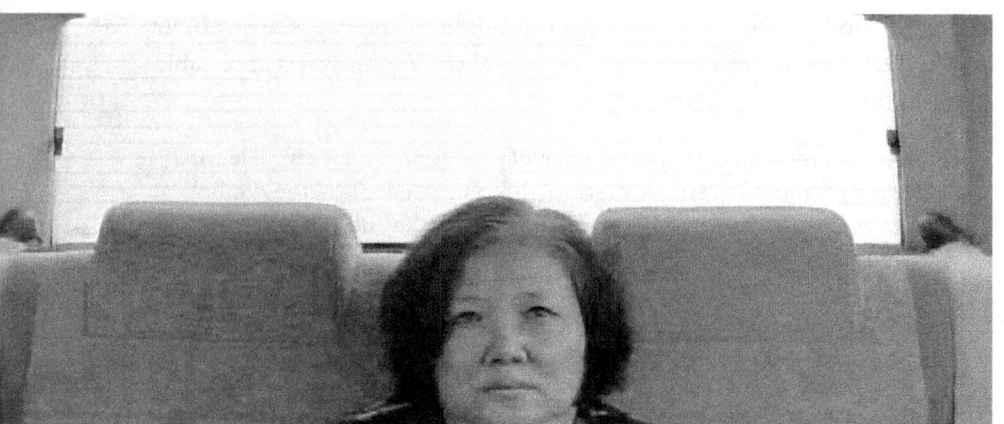

FIGURE 2.5. Lady Ra as spectator, *Thirst*, Park Chan-wook, 2009.

forms of obsession and contagion expressed through their diseased and damaged bodies. Similarly, the vampire body is also infected and is a source of contagion, though actively enthralled by the pleasures and pains of Otherness. Park in *Thirst* does not elevate and sentimentalize any more than he elevates the commonplace. Instead, he invites the viewer to contemplate the uses and abuses of the body in an instinctual world that offers portraits of degraded predator-prey relations in which the loser is life itself.

As noted, the film ends with the suicide of Sang-hyun and Tae-ju, while Lady Ra, like someone sitting in a drive-in theater, watches their demise. The final moments thus situate the spectator in the position of the paralyzed mother, inarticulate but imprisoned in the image, akin to the viewer. Here, in its ending, which closely adapts Zola's, *Thirst* seems to address the crisis of the cinema: it highlights the role of modern cinema as compelling the spectator to confront viscerally this deeply disturbing portrait of cruelty, but it also extracts from these inchoate images a potential for thinking differently, for interrogating conventional treatments of vampirism, if not of the cult of death that the film has explored. While adhering to a naturalist form, *Thirst* suggests finally that the former priest has not succumbed to diabolism but, in contrast to the conventional vampire, has experienced remorse; therefore, in violation of Tae-ju's desire to remain alive, he chooses to end their immortal existence and its turbulent actions according to his principles (Niogret 2009, 27).

Consistently, the film seems to be working toward a counter-history that emblematizes a large-scale reaction to sanctioned forms of historical analysis involving religious conceptions of the physical body, life and death, asceticism and excess, and morality. *Thirst* places emphasis on struggle, investigation, and a testing of existing forms of explanation for determination and indeterminacy. On the one hand, Sang-hyun has chosen to end his own and Tae-ju's mortal existence, but there is also the figure of Lady Ra to complicate the world being viewed. Her gazing at the doomed pair tantalizes the spectator to contemplate what is being *represented*. Having lost the power of movement, Lady Ra's image incites questions not only about what is being seen but who is seeing and what to think.

Throughout the film, crime and the horrific have played a critical role, evident in the bizarre murders throughout, the supernaturalism of Sang-hyun and Tae-ju, their deaths, and the film's uncertain ending with Lady Ra as the paralyzed last spectator. The film's unstable theater of innocence and guilt guides Park into counter-history. In its naturalistic treatment of character and landscape, its combination of different literary, cultural, and cinematic sources, and in its unsettling and manifold connections to conceptions of religion, the body, health and disease, and, by implication, cinematic form, *Thirst* unsettles the viewer with a form of tragicomedy that seems inherent in naturalism, a form that bespeaks a crisis in conventional historicizing.

3

Comedy, Theatricality, and Counter-History

> Comedy, not tragedy, admits the disorderly into the realm of art; the grotesque depends upon an irrational focus....
> Is it any wonder that along with our wars, our machines, and our neuroses we should find new meanings in comedy, or that comedy should represent our plight better than tragedy? For tragedy needs the "noble," and nowadays we seldom can assign any usable meaning to "nobility." The comic is now more relevant, or at least more accessible than the tragic.
>
> —Wylie Sypher, *Comedy* (1983, 201)

COMEDY HAS NOT merited the same attention accorded to epic, tragic, and dramatic forms as a medium for addressing history (Salmi 2011). Notable exceptions to this neglect are Marx, Nietzsche, Foucault, and Deleuze, who have insisted on the power of parody, masquerade, disguise, and carnival to unsettle versions of history by entertaining the power of nonsense and paradox to alter connections to the past by way of the present and future. Conceptions of history and the role of humor are central to clarifying my conception of counter-history that challenges conventional forms of historical narration through a reconsideration of the body (corporeality) to arrive at a rupture with the past. Comedy has the potential to engage with the body as "that which it plunges into or must plunge into, in order to reach the unthought, that is life" and, through humor, enables learning about "what a non-thinking body is capable of, its capacity, its postures" (Deleuze 1989a, 189). This position is consonant with aspects of Nietzsche's thought on history and Foucault's attempt to articulate the relationship between history and actuality that are closely tied to evolving conceptions about the care of the body often expressed through forms of comedy, theatricality, choreographed movement in forms of dance, phatic modes of communication expressed through language and music, human and other animal sounds, and physical gestures. The responses educed from comedy derive less from identification with the character and more from the incongruity of automatic responses to familiar situations removed from conventional expectations of accounting for behavior and action. Foucault's conception of "effective history" offers one form of counter-history, since his definition involves inverting traditional conceptions of the past to regard them not from superior heights but from a shortening of "vision to those things nearest to it—the body, the nervous system, nutrition, digestion, and energies.... [Effective history] unearths the periods of decadence and if it chances upon lofty epochs, it is with the suspicion—not vindictive but joyous—of finding a barbarous and shameful confusion" (Foucault 1977, 155).

Foucault distinguished three types of counter-historicizing that bear on a comic vision of addressing the past: (1) parody and farce to expose disguises and masquerades; (2) a dissolution of identity; and (3) a "sacrifice of the subject of knowledge" in the "rejection of traditional attitudes of reverence" (Foucault 1977, 160–62). In this respect, Foucault's view of counter-historical expression is closer to medicine and intuition than to the historical and the natural sciences, in that its "task is to become a curative science," in Carlo Ginzburg's distinctions between the natural sciences and medicine (ibid., 156). In many ways, this parts company from Deleuze in its historical and disciplinary diagnosis of institutional practices (madness, prisons, and disciplinary forms of sexual identity) that were previously considered unproblematic and unavoidable but that we might now perceive as symptomatic of punitive treatment and subject to a profound ethical rethinking.

For Deleuze, history offers a somewhat different sense of the real than that of Foucault through philosophy and aesthetics in order to redefine the actual as a state of becoming and of comedy as an art that resides in its ability to engage the viewer in a physical and mental realization that they are not yet thinking. Deleuze wrote, "the art of the aesthetic is humour, a physical art of signals and signs determining the partial solutions or cases of solution—in short, an implicated art of intensive quantities" (1994, 245) standing in contrast to molar, monumental, universalizing, and teleological forms for narrating history. Humor resides in an overturning of destructive personal and social fixities by offering a theater of cruelty to disconcert the viewer. The film comedies discussed in this chapter dramatize fixation, obsession, failure, underinvestment in self-consciousness and thought by situating the spectator in a position to confront the grotesque and incongruous forms of historical repetition and point toward difference.

In *Difference and Repetition,* Deleuze pursues Artaud's conception of a "thought without image" in which thought via sensation is "a new principle which does not allow itself to be represented" (1994, 147) but is nonetheless thought. Deleuze wrote,

> Artaud said that the problem (for him) was not to orientate his thought, or to perfect the expression of what he thought, or to acquire application and method or to perfect his poems, but simply to manage to think something. For him, this was the only conceivable "work"; it presupposes an impulse, a compulsion to think which passes through all sorts of bifurcations, spreading from the nerves and being communicated to the soul in order to arrive at thought. Henceforth, thought is also forced to think its central collapse, its fracture, its own natural "powerlessness." (Ibid., 147)

Deleuze pursues in his cinema books the powerlessness of thought, which he regards as necessary for acknowledging the intolerable and banal character of the world through the absurd, to "discover the identity of thought and life" (Deleuze 1989a, 170). This is a form of counter-history that invokes humor and sensation to undermine determinist and reductive beliefs in history through a multifaceted analysis of language and form so as to reveal the power of nonsense as a mode for challenging habituation. Deleuze rejects classical discourse as exemplified in the model of Socratic or tragic irony that assures the coextensiveness of being with the individual in the world of representation. Kantian or romantic irony speaks through the person, through the "I," as a personal extension of representation. By contrast, an "esoteric language" common to humor represents the subversion, from the ground up, of the ideal language and the dissolution of the one that holds the real language:

> Nonsense and sense have done away with their relation of dynamic opposition in order to enter into the co-presence of a state of static genesis—as the nonsense of the surface and the sense which hovers over it. The tragic and the ironic give way to a new value, that of humour. For if irony is the co-extensiveness of being with the individual, or of the I with representation, humour is the co-extensiveness of sense with nonsense. (Deleuze 1990, 140–41)

For example, in discussing cinematic expression in relation to the role of the small form that he identifies with burlesque, Deleuze indicates how juxtaposing gestures that appear akin to each other, as in Charlie Chaplin's films, can produce very different situations, creating a contradictory bond between laughter and tears, tragedy and comedy. The similarity in appearance between Chaplin and Hitler's moustaches in *The Great Dictator* (1940), contrasted to the distance between the situations of the Jewish barber and Hitler, can highlight "two opposable Societies, one of which makes the slight difference between men into the instrument of an infinite distance between situations (tyranny), and the other which would make the slight difference between men the variable of a great situation of community and communality (Democracy)" (Deleuze 1986, 171–72).

In this chapter, I focus on European and Asian films that illuminate versions of counter-history in their absurd, often surreal, treatments of historical characters and situations. In their forms, which span different moments in cinema history and film styles, they create chaotic and carnivalesque milieus through their invocation of gendered bodies in their parodies of the body politic. As my first example, I discuss *Carry On Up the Khyber* (1968), which employs parody, farce, burlesque, and at times allegory to unsettle, if not overturn, historical investments in the past. If, in the interests of comedy, the film adopts the theatrical trappings of imperial literature, documentaries, newsreels, and fiction films—including the use of a voice-of-God narrator to elevate the British "position in India," accompanied by the spectacle of public displays, ceremonial entertainments, and forms of ritualized duplicity in relation to diplomacy—it also includes clues to the incongruities of names, body parts, and actions that strip away the surface to reveal disorder, violence, and often farce.

The farce of empire invites audiences to encounter barbarism masked as civility. The film becomes a form of counter-history by virtue of the puncturing of monumental conceptions of the past, related to Foucault's conception of effective history and its "suspicion . . . of finding a barbarous and dreadful confusion" (1977, 155). Although *Carry On Up the Khyber* might seem to some a frivolous and vulgar, if not trivial, portrait of imperialism, with its emphasis on the body and on sexuality, the film introduces disorder and confusion into a system of beliefs and practices that have enormous consequences for a different assessment of its historical portrait of political force and power attached to the body—one of the signs of cinematic counter-history. It is not the literal body, the body with organs, that is the butt of humor but what this body expresses: "The body manifests the stigmata of past experience and also gives rise to desires, failings, and errors. These elements may join in a body where they achieve a sudden expression, but as often, their encounter is an engagement in which they efface each other, where the body becomes the pretext of their insurmountable conflict" (Foucault 1977, 148). It is this conflict that the joke makes visible and expressible and that becomes the basis of counter-history.

The Middle Ages also have been a subject for comedy as counter-history, exemplified in films set in an anachronistic medieval context: Mario Monicelli's *L'armata Brancaleone* (*For Love and Gold*, aka *Brancaleone's Army*, 1966) and *Brancaleone alle crociate* (*Brancaleone at the Crusades*, 1970), and the Pythons' carnivalesque *Monty Python and the Holy Grail* (1975). Monicelli's films are characteristic of *commedia all'italiana*, a fictional form that intermingles melodrama and comedy and that thrive on sentiment and laughter, proximity and remoteness, the ceremonial and the commonplace to entertain difference through the drama of comic repetition. Two other films of Monicelli's are given substantial treatment in this chapter: *I compagni* (*The Organizer*, 1963) is an illustration of the fusion of the comic and tragic set in the trade union struggles at the turn of the nineteenth century, and *La grande guerra* (*The Great War*, 1959), a counter-historical treatment of World War I. Both films eschew the conventional nostalgic sentiment associated with political struggle and portraits of the subaltern in their creation of counter-history.

Finally, I discuss the Taiwanese film *Ni Na bian ji dian* (*What Time Is It There?* 2001) as a comic variant on this hybrid mode of expression. By moving beyond Europe to Asia, the chapter entertains global cinematic expressions of the humorous as further expressions of counter-history through their close attention to the body, as well as to different spaces and times, as a mode for unsettling clichés concerning history. These films qualify as forms of counter-history in their disregard for conventional forms of realism and in their reflexive elements that foreground the power of vision as a mechanism of control, clueing the spectator to incongruities—names, body parts, and actions—inherent to history as comic theater.

HISTORY AND HUMOR

Marx's *Eighteenth Brumaire of Louis Napoleon* of 1852 (1990) is a drama in the service of counter-history to detail the rise to absolute power of a dictatorship. Marx's claim that the counter-revolutionary events in France in 1851 are farce, not tragedy, is a satiric strategy to characterize, caricature, invert, and puncture the abuses of power. More than a rhetorical flourish, the "farce" stages a theatrical scenario involving the various social classes, the monarch himself, and the uses of costume and stage setting for events to dramatize how "the tradition of all the dead generations weighs like a nightmare on the brain of the living," causing them to "anxiously conjure up the spirits of the past to their service and borrow from them names, battle cries and costumes in order to present the new scene of world history in this time-honoured disguise" (Marx 1990, 15).

Marx's view of history as farce is my opportunity to think how comedy can be regarded as a form of counter-historicizing, as more than mere occasion to produce laughter at human foibles, but also as an opportunity for critical reflections on the uses and abuses of the past and their effects on the future. Yet Marx's satiric treatment of the rise to power of Louis Bonaparte focuses on one of the key features of comedy: its reliance on theatricality, involving allusions to performance through the adoption of masks, impersonation, costumes, disguises, doubling, and mimicry. This validates Nietzsche's, Deleuze's, and Foucault's observations on the historical process as a theater of repetition that speaks "with a language which speaks before words, with gestures which develop before organised bodies, with masks before faces, with spectres and phantoms before characters" (Deleuze 1994, 10). The language relies on such terms as "disguise," "masquerade," "carnival," and "buffoonery," with Foucault (1977, 160–61), through Nietzsche, challenging belief in identity and authenticity.

Friedrich Nietzsche, in "On the Uses and Disadvantages of History for Life," undertook a dissection of Marx's "tradition of all the dead generations" as a dark and invisible burden. His 1874 essay foregrounds the necessity of "one's being just as able to forget at the right time as to remember at the right time; [of being in] possession of a powerful instinct for sensing when it is necessary to feel historically and when unhistorically" (Nietzsche 1991, 63), and is useful for thinking in counter-historical terms. His classification of the monumental, antiquarian, and critical forms of historicizing is critical for an understanding of how fiction and spectacle participate in negotiating between remembering and forgetting. His descriptions of excessive attachments to the past also suggest the presence of theatricality and of spectacle as germane to considerations of tradition as disadvantageous, even more, as destructive to life. His essay has played a key role in undermining official narratives of the past.

Comic theatricality as exemplified particularly through parody, farce, and satire entails not merely the acting of individual characters and of group performances to invert or overturn the histrionic situations in which they appear. Comic theatricality has relied on the trope of the world as a stage in the service of exposing how "everyone is engaged in acting out ... fantasies" in the interests of questioning and challenging the basis of common sense, "the very fabric of commonplace actuality" (Levin 1987, 120). Deleuze challenges commonsense formulations of language and behavior that are at stake in comic forms, as in *The Logic of Sense* (1990) and *Difference and Repetition* (1994). By emphasizing the role of recollection in relation to time and memory—the one habitual, functional, molar, and passive; the other attentive, molecular, chronologically fractured, and indiscernible in relation to the real and the imaginary—Deleuze (1989a, 44–68) opens the way to a cinematic consideration of how "characters/actors, and ultimately the film itself, pass from one bodily state to another, while performance constitutes its expression" (Del Rio 2008, 10). Performativity is at the basis of comedy that emphasizes human and animal bodies, their interactions, their changing dimensions, their sensory responses to the physical world, and their modes of expressing themselves. Performance takes place on all levels of life and history, enacting different levels of interaction, highlighting material properties of language that diagnose the present, and introducing the untimely and unthought history that runs counter to a pure past.

WHAT'S IN A HISTORICAL JOKE? *CARRY ON UP THE KHYBER*

The British "Carry On" films (from 1958 to 1992) are characteristic of their specializing in bawdy situations and "lower" physical functions associated with stereotypical characters situated in various social institutions (Jordan 1983, 316–17). One of the most popular films of this comedy series, Gerald Thomas's 1968 *Carry On Up the Khyber*, announces itself in a subtitle as addressing "The British Position in India." The film is a parody of British Empire novels and films such as Zoltan Korda's *The Drum* (1938) and *The Four Feathers* (1939), among numerous others, adopting their appropriation of the rituals, language, behavior, and landscape of imperialism and colonialism. The film is an instance of burlesque that relies on impropriety and vulgarity (involving the body) and on "joking turned theatrical" (Bentley 1965, 279, 282). Providing a farcical treatment of British imperialism, *Carry On Up the Khyber* extends beyond its mimicry of the familiar cinematic empire film to unmask representations of the Raj by subverting social and cultural practices that underpin British imperial power though an esoteric language in which sense and nonsense are coextensive.

The film is founded on a familiar riddle, namely, "What do the Scots wear, if anything, under their kilts?" (The reply: "Socks and shoes.") The film's narration is deceptively simple in its single-minded focus on a well-known jest that challenges the viewer about the means and ends of humor in relation to the film's historical setting. Set in 1895 in the Northwest Province of India under the "control" of Sir Sidney Ruff-Diamond (Sid James) with the military support of the "Third Foot and Mouth Regiment," also known as the "Devils in Skirts," the narrative is set in motion by the "discovery" that Private Jimmy Widdle (Charles Hawtrey), one of the recruits ordered to guard the Khyber Pass, is found by an Indian patrol to be wearing underpants. Reported by Sergeant-Major MacNutt to Major Shorthouse and conveyed to Governor Ruff-Diamond, this "infraction" sets in motion a rebellion led by Rhandi Lal, the Khasi of Kalabar, in league with Bungdit Din, the leader of the Burpa tribesmen.

The humor relies on the power of the myth of the "fearsome" bodies of the imperial "masters." Even the names of the characters suggest the sexual traits of the actors in this spectacle of imperialism. When we meet Lord and Lady Ruff-Diamond at the outset of the film, riding in a procession on an elephant, an elephantine fart undercuts the solemnity of the occasion, prefiguring their prominent lower parts becoming attached to phallic sexuality, racialism, and imperial power. The joke about lower parts of the male body pertaining to the kilt is dependent on spectacle, verbal language, and suggestive physical sounds to incorporate and render imperial spectacle as a travesty, involving the domestic relations between the governor and his wife, relations between the governor and the Khasi's wives, the sexual designs of Lady Ruff-Diamond on the reluctant Khasi, her fantasy of his randiness with his wives, and, finally, the terror of the Burpa warriors at the sight of the lifted kilts by the besieged members of the Scots regiment. The film's joke about the sexual power of the male organ covered by the kilt is contagious and expands to include Lady Ruff-Diamond's surreptitious viewing and photographing of the regiment revealing their lower parts to their superior officer, which she will use to seduce the Khasi. As a consequence of her machinations, the regiment is involved in various sexual antics. Keene, MacNutt, Widdle, and Brother Belcher, a missionary who preaches publicly against sins of the flesh, volunteer (or are volunteered) to recover one of Lady Ruff-Diamond's compromising photos from the Burpas. Accidentally gaining access to a harem, they disport themselves and then cross-dress in order to escape.

Princess Jelhi directly articulates the question that animates the kilt riddle. She asks her father, the regal Khasi, "What is there to fear from a warrior who wears nothing underneath his skirt?" and he responds, "Oh, my child, you have not made war! But think how frightening it would be to have such a man charging at you with his skirts in the air." The numerous allusions to what it is that "dangles" produces different responses from the governor and from Lady Ruff-Diamond, who is eager to betray her husband and experience sex with Rhandi Lal, and from Princess Jelhi, who is attracted to Captain Keene and, hence, willing to betray her father. Their betrayals are tied to conceptions of the sexed body—presented as a site of curiosity or pleasure in the case of women and of control in the case of the men—in which all the characters are implicated in desire for, and threat from, the fearsome men with flying skirts, whose private parts are never visible only alluded to. Decorum and censorship aside, the invisibility of this organ reinforces its imaginary character.

In the penultimate scene parodying ceremonial rituals of the empire film, a dinner is held inside the governor's palace including the governor, his wife, Brother Belcher, Princess Jelhi, and Captain Keene, all dressed formally. They are seated around a table set for the meal, with chandelier dangling overhead, and musicians enhancing the festive occasion. However, outside the Khasi and his men attack the British troops and bomb the compound. As disorder wages without, the group within is oblivious to the chaos. Learning that the British are at dinner, the Khasi describes this behavior "as typical exhibition of British . . . starched uniforms and stiff upper lip." While the musicians play a Viennese waltz, the group engages in small talk, windows are blown out, plaster falls from the ceiling onto the guests, and the chandelier crashes onto the dinner table. However, Lady Ruff-Diamond explains the falling plaster by saying, "the wind seems to be a little strong tonight," and Lord Ruff-Diamond validates the "terrible noise" by conceding, "It's not a first-class orchestra." The climax of the film involves the regiment fighting a fierce battle, until the governor orders a review of the troops that involves the display of the lifting of their kilts—followed by the hasty retreat of the Khasi and the Burpa warriors, horrified at what they, but not filmgoers, have seen.

Thus, this carnivalesque parody of British imperial power is based on the power of vision as social control through a contrast between "surface and beneath-the-surface" of events (Bentley 1965, 294). The issue of "surface" exposes the theatrical trappings of history as costume, treated by Marx in his conception of Louis Napoleon's rise to power. The historian Hugh Trevor Roper, in his comments on Scottish costume, the kilt in particular, argues that the wearing of the kilt does not originate in ancient practices but was an invention of the eighteenth and nineteenth centuries to bolster the martial prowess of the Scotsman. This culminated in

FIGURE 3.1. Is seeing believing? *Carry On Up the Khyber,* Gerald Thomas, 1968.

the British government's deployment of Highland regiments in India and America (Trevor-Roper 1985, 25) and, thus, has connections to imperialism. Initially, this costume was described derisively as "normally worn 'so very short that in a windy day, going up a hill, or stooping, the indecency of it is plainly discovered'" (ibid., 20). *Carry On Up the Khyber*'s playing with this "petticoat," earlier associated with effeminacy, serves to wreak havoc on the sexual potency and primitive virility mythically associated with its wearers and, hence, with the spectacle of British power. It thus becomes a counter-history through its naming and exposure of appearance and behavior identified with the kilt, the phallus, and the machinery of empire.

THE THEATER OF THE MIDDLE AGES: ANARCHIC AND SURREAL COMEDY IN MONTY PYTHON FILMS

Monty Python and the Holy Grail (Gilliam and Jones, 1975) is another parody, this time of Arthurian legend involving the Knights of the Round Table on a journey to find the Holy Grail. As is typical of early chivalric romances, the knights encounter threatening obstacles to the realization of their goal: monsters, the Black Plague, a witchcraft trial, magicians, battle scenes, and several dream visions. The Pythons' version of chivalric romance inverts expectations of heroic adventure and religious zeal and undermines historical clichés.

The film comprises episodes implicating each of the inept followers of King Arthur. As in *Monty Python's Flying Circus,* the group's BBC-TV series, the episodic comedy thrives on direct address, defamiliarization through an undermining of narrative expectations, discontinuities in time and space, reversal of physical and social characteristics, and the mixing of generic forms including comedy, romance, and adventure (Landy 2005a, 35–36). The film punctures heroic gestures by exaggerating commonplace gestures and languages, rendering them grotesque, and challenges pious conceptions of historical events, morality, and the literary and cinematic forms through which these conceptions are disseminated (including the Christian Bible).

The Pythons' perspective on comedy has commonly been labeled "anarchic," and "surreal" in adopting unsettling conceptions of the past to invert and undermine forms of storytelling. The quest for the Holy Grail becomes an encyclopedic recounting of the manifold strategies in place for regarding official history as truth and, as such, is deleterious to life and limb; but the film, through humor, enacts the seriousness of comedy as instrumental for puncturing history and/as legend. It is no accident that its conclusion involves the police search for the killer of "a famous historian" and the arrest of the knights as the culprits, thus bringing the past into the present, and history and art (in this case, film) into collusion.

Memorable dimensions of Python narration in the film involve numerous devices to call attention to itself as film and its relation to other literary and art forms. For example, showing pages of a book is a familiar cinematic device to call attention to fiction, but here they are cartoon images of an illuminated manuscript that caricatures each of the various knights and their encounters with strange characters and situations. There are also sudden and transgressive intrusions of a cartoon figure of God (with the visage of famed cricketer W. G. Grace). Through the uses of impersonation and animation, the viewer is treated to bizarre, even nonsensical visions that reduce the distance created between received sentimental and canonical views of historical events, corroborating Deleuze's view of the coextensiveness of sense and nonsense—here, with nonsense playing a crucial role in shedding light on the hypervalorization of sense. Nonsense is conventionally regarded as the absence of sense, as meaningless; but, in the world of the Pythons (as in Lewis Carroll), it becomes indicative of the nonsense that often passes for sense, "the sense that it produces in excess" (Deleuze 1990, 71).

In the Python film, epistemological violence is invoked through insults, name-calling, exaggeration, invective, and boasting. Physical violence abounds through the lopping off of limbs, hanging, burning, drowning, and bombing. The countering of history thrives on the ability to expose conventional and sanctimonious forms of historical interpretation examined by Deleuze and ridiculed by the Pythons in *Monty Python and the Holy Grail*. Mingling present and past, animation and live action, and the caricature of human figures, the film travesties realist conventions to question still-prevalent beliefs in religion. The movement between the mythic Middle Ages and contemporary events also entails other instances of animation injected into live-action scenes. At one point, mythic and idealized visions of Camelot are abruptly reduced to a variety show with a chorus line of the Knights of the Round Table doing a music-hall song-and-dance routine.

The film begins in the present with the insertion of a clip from another film, in black-and-white, titled *Dentist on the Job* (C. M. Pennington-Richards, 1961) interrupted to introduce *Monty Python and the Holy Grail*. Then titles are embellished with Terry Gilliam's distinctive animation figures including an image of clouds and an image of a disgruntled king and other grotesque figures, accompanied by stately music and Dutch subtitles, each time winding down and beginning with intertitles about all those who were sacked on the job of kingship. The title "England 932 AD" and an image of a rotting body stretched on a wheel set atop a pole appears, and King Arthur and his squire, Patsy, emerge from the haze, simulating galloping without horses. By knocking two coconuts together, Patsy supplies the sound of horses' hooves. Stopping in front of a castle, the two are greeted by a Frenchman who taunts them, claiming that they do not have horses but are merely using coconuts to simulate hoof beats. Arthur's demands to see the lord of the castle are ignored. Instead, a lengthy dialogue ensues,

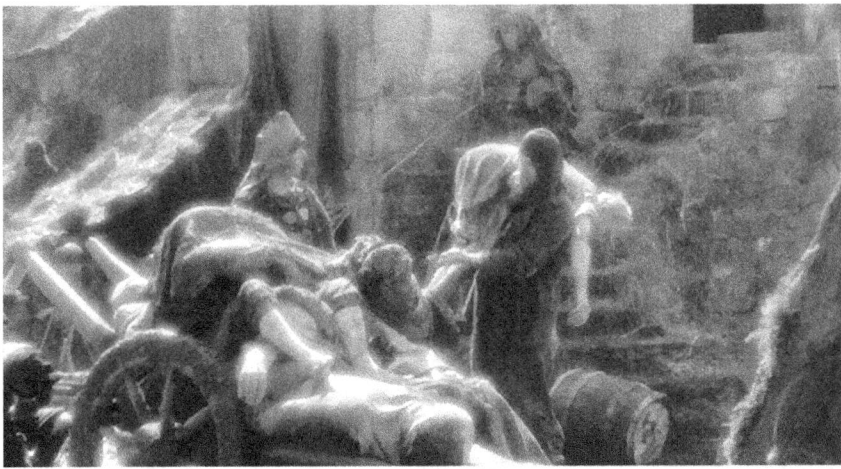

FIGURE 3.2. "I'm not dead," *Monty Python and the Holy Grail*, Gilliam and Jones, 1975.

replete with insults by the Frenchman about how Arthur was able to get coconuts in this temperate climate.

The film's self-consciously elliptical structure reveals its disregard for chronology and linearity, moving back and forth between the legendary past and contemporaneity. One abrupt transition is to a dirty village in which the Black Death is decimating the inhabitants. Several carts loaded with dead bodies pass through the village, while one man pushing a cart shouts, "Bring out your dead!"—possibly an allusion to Ken Russell's *The Devils* (1971). A man carries an old man out of his hut; the hostage yells, "I'm not dead" but is told that he will soon be. Resisting his captor, the old man is hit on the head sharply and thrown on the cart. Arthur and Patsy appear, and the cart driver comments, "Must be a king.... He hasn't got shit all over him."

Arthur's next encounter involves peasants' refusal to recognize the rightful "King of the Britons," and the king gets contemporary lessons in Marxism from the "autonomous collective" about dictatorship, exploitation, repression, and violence inherent to the system. When asked how he became king, Arthur explains in lofty terms that he was chosen by the Lady of the Lake: "Her arm clad in purest shimmering samite, held aloft

FIGURE 3.3. Momentarily saving an accused witch, *Monty Python and the Holy Grail*, Gilliam and Jones, 1975.

Excalibur from the bosom of the water, signifying by Divine Providence that I, Arthur, was to carry Excalibur." The humor of this sketch resides in the disjunction between the peasant's prosaic references to oppression and Arthur's lofty, epic language, exposed by the peasants as nonsensical: "Strange women lying in ponds, distributing swords, is no basis for a system of government." This is a humor of the surface that renders nonsensical the translation of the image of "strange women . . . distributing swords" by ridiculing Arthur's antiquarian language.

The Pythons' humor relies on deflating common sense, puncturing received truths, exaggerating sentiment, and caricaturing heroic pretensions that underpin conventional values and behavior. The devices employed by the film are a veritable encyclopedia of comedy—gags, slapstick, the grotesque, wordplay, and banter—employed to invoke a familiar world and render it strange by undermining traditional forms of history making. For example, in an episode that parodies conceptions of chivalric combat, Arthur encounters a Black Knight who will not allow the king to pass. After Arthur cuts off all of the knight's limbs, with copious blood spurting from each, in a bizarre example of litotes, the knight declares, "'Tis but a scratch" after losing his left arm and "Just a flesh wound" after losing his right. Sense and nonsense coincide to produce the inappropriateness of humility in the face of disaster.

An episode involving witchcraft provides a classic Python strategy for exposing irrationality posing as rational. While bloodthirsty peasants shout gleefully, "We've got a witch," Sir Bedevere, overseeing this auto-da-fé, assumes a rational position, asking the peasants, "How do you know she is a witch?" They respond, "She looks like one!" The "knight" also falls prey to appearances, telling the protesting victim, "But you are dressed as one." Sir Bedevere is no more rational than the accusers, offering advice on how "there are ways of telling whether she is a witch." His syllogistic premise is that witches burn; therefore, they must be made of wood; and, further, or alternatively, since wood floats, they can weigh her, and if she weighs the same as a duck, which floats, she is a witch. Her life is forfeit, since, in the face of the absurd premises put forward for establishing that a woman is a witch, there is no way to escape the reigning irrationality: the scales balance her with a duck, and the woman admits, "It's a fair cop." Sir Bedevere goes off with Arthur to become a Knight of the Round Table. This episode ridicules an excessive belief in the uses of contemporary science for social and political power.

In a parody of medieval dream visions, a cartoon reveals a figure of God, who chastises the knights for groveling. God asks Arthur what he is doing; he responds, "I'm averting my eyes, O Lord." "Well, don't," says the Lord. "It's like those miserable psalms. They're so depressing," the Lord complains. But finally the knights have a mission: "Arthur, King of the Britons ... it is your sacred task to seek this Grail." The cartoon ends with an image of clouds closing like a door. Arthur and his knights set out now on their journey to find the Grail. The theatrical treatment of both the Lord and Arthur (as well as of the Bible) is sustained in the cinematic interface between live-action filming and animation. Later in the film, in the episode of the "Holy Hand Grenade," a monk reads from the Book of Armaments, intoning, "'O Lord, bless this Thy Hand Grenade that with it Thou mayest blow Thine enemies to tiny bits, in Thy mercy.' And the Lord did grin, and the people did feast upon the lambs and sloths and carp and anchovies and orang-utans and breakfast cereals and fruit bats...."

Thus, not only is the purity of the Crusades debunked but also warfare in league with religion and biblical passages is ridiculed.

Among the other trials undertaken by the knights are their encounters with the French castle guard, who refuses to convey Arthur's request for a meeting with Sir Guy de Lombard about the Grail and who teases the king: "He's already got one, you see." Frustrated after a failed attempt to storm the castle, the knights at Bedevere's suggestion create a large wooden "rabbit" (with a red bow tied to it), in imitation of the Trojan horse; however the knights neglect to hide in it and thus fail to enter the castle. This episode is notable for the bawdiness of exchanged taunts, parodying combat rituals, and invoking the enmity between French and Briton. The Frenchman shouts, after Arthur has first threatened an assault on the castle: "You don't frighten us, English pig-dogs. Go and boil your bottom, sons of a silly person. I blow my nose on you so-called Arthur King, you and all your silly English knnnnniggets. . . . I fart in your general direction."

The knights leave without having gained any satisfaction, and the film returns to the present. We see a dignified older man, identified by a subtitle as "A Famous Historian," who, while commenting pompously on Arthur's difficulties, is abruptly hacked to death by a medieval knight barging into this contemporary setting. Not only is this episode another instance of the film's designs on historiography (and academic historians), but the death of the contemporary Historian, increasingly inserted into the episodes, becomes the *deus ex machina* to end the film, shifting genres to become a parody of crime detection films, involving the police as guardians of law and the performers as criminals. This self-conscious address of genres and temporality serves to conflate history making and filmmaking through the aggressive injection of humor.

Among other aspects of humor as litotes or understatement—in which the horror and cruelty are minimized through feigned ignorance, inappropriate response on the part of the perpetrator, and disjunction in the filming between image and sound—is the song of Sir Robin, a ditty that seems harmless in the instrumental style of madrigals, played by a troupe dressed in courtly costumes; but the lilting music is accompanied by gruesome lyrics with references to the knight's being "mashed into a pulp," having his "eyes gouged out," "limbs all hacked and mangled," and "penis split" (and so on) as an aggressive commentary on idealist expressions of medievalism. Galahad's adventure at Castle Anthrax also parodies medieval tales (for example, *The Decameron* and *Canterbury Tales* as adapted for film) about young men caught in a castle (or convent) with young women (or nuns) panting to partake of sex with a man who is "sworn to chastity." One of the women suggests that Galahad spank a woman for deceiving him by lighting a beacon that casts as image of the Grail, and the women all beg to be spanked, and "after the spanking, the oral sex." Brave Sir Lancelot saves Galahad from the women, but the episode succeeds in poking fun at the knight and at conceptions of abstinence.

The frequent allusions to bodily functions and to grotesque images of violence are, in the spirit of travesty, exemplary of the tendency to elevate material realities at the expense of individualized personal desire. In the case of the adventure of Sir Lancelot at Swamp Castle, the focus on violence arises from a familiar situation of a father's insistence that his son accede to an arranged marriage and, hence, be prepared to manage the estate. The son does not wish to marry and would rather be a singer, so the father keeps him imprisoned in his room until the young man assents. Speaking in the language of a self-made working-class Yorkshire man, the father says, "Listen, lad, I built this kingdom up from nothing. When I started here, all there was was swamp." The prince, with his bow and arrow, sends a note for help from his window. Lancelot finds the note and, thinking it is from a damsel in distress, arrives at the castle to save the beleaguered woman, indiscriminately hacking to pieces the guests assembled for the wedding. When confronted by the boy's father, Sir Lancelot says in the humor of understatement, "I'm awfully sorry," a frequent tool in the Python's lexicon of humor to minimize violence and death.

A familiar device in comedy is the blurring of the boundaries between humans and other animals by altering the stereotypes of certain animals: and, for the Pythons, the rabbit is a notable instance of this inversion, in which an animal identified with timidity assumes a trait of violent humans. As the quest for the Grail draws to a close, the assembled knights must confront a most horrible creature, a killer rabbit. Asked by Arthur to kill it, an underling scoffs at the possibility that a bunny could be dangerous: "One rabbit stew comin' right up." The knights do indeed discover its ferocity and thus realize that they need a powerful weapon to destroy the creature: the aforementioned Holy Hand Grenade. This episode is in keeping with the tendency of comedy to use animals through fables to focus on threatened human bodies. The images the Pythons have so often adopted in the forms of the sketches and in the animation rely on magical thinking, focusing on mutations in form. As in Ovid's *Metamorphosis* and in all kinds of fantasy and satire, animals are endowed with human attributes. The Python world is saturated with transformations from animal to human, from realist style to fantasy, from photography to animation, from sense to nonsense, and from cool delivery to hysterical and inappropriate rant.

Finally, the medieval journey abruptly shifts to the modern era as another quest takes over: the search for the killer of the Famous Historian. Just as the moment of victory over the inhabitants of the Castle Aaaarrrrrrggghhh is about to take place, the police enter with the professor's wife as she points at Arthur, "Yes, they're the ones, I'm sure," and after confusion, the police presumably arrest Arthur and his knights. The ending of the medieval fantasy in the present intrudes on the history of the past, reminding the viewer that this is a film, in fact, a contemporary film, bringing the many interfaces between past and present into focus by shifting the quest for the Holy Grail to a modern context: the police's arresting of the knights. The crime for which the Arthur and his knights will be charged is, pointedly, the killing of the Historian—not only physically but in their of making a travesty of serious historicizing by bringing the past into the present and dissecting forms of religious, sexual, and philosophical thought that bear on belief in the world as it is not.

In the conventional form of apologia, the Pythons disavow their satire on cinematic historicizing. The ending introduces ambiguity between madness and sanity, fiction and truth, sense and nonsense. The film's satiric comedy serves counter-historical thinking; it works against forms of portraying history as amenable to rational explanation, not to demolish but to challenge the straitjacket of historicism in which the present "is framed by the past and future" (Foucault 1977, 176). Their carnivalesque and nonchronological treatment of time emphasizes coexistence of "sheets of past," different regions that confer a new value on narration that distributes "different presents to different characters" (Deleuze 1989a, 101). In this sense, the Python's journey in cinematic form exposes nonsense that passes as sense to create a counter-history as "philosophy not as thought, but as theater: a theater of mime with multiple, fugitive and instantaneous scenes in which blind gestures signal to each other" (Foucault 1977, 196).

COMMEDIA ALL'ITALIANA AND COUNTER-HISTORY

Italian film comedy has been a major form of filmmaking in Italy indebted to earlier comedies (Roman, goliardic, Neapolitan theater, and especially the *commedia dell'arte*). These types of comedy are known for their use of social types, improvisation, clowning or masks, slapstick, and body mechanics that translated onto the silent and sound cinemas. Light romantic comedy (pejoratively identified as *telefoni bianchi* or "white telephone" films) flourished under Fascism in the 1930s and captured the imaginary sense of Fascist modernity in conformity with the regime. These films identified with such directors as Mario Camerini and Alessandro Blasetti and appealed to audiences through their uses of genres, visual and sound images, star personas, and a semblance of a fusion of everyday places and people with the fanciful. However, following the Nazi-Fascist alliance, racist laws, and the coming of World War II, a few indirect critical portraits of Fascist culture through comedy escaped the censors: *Il cappello a tre punte* (*Three-Cornered Hat*; Camerini, 1935), a satire on a lecherous and unscrupulous governor; *Sorelle Materassi* (*Materassi Sisters*; Fernando Maria Poggioli, 1944), a surreal, satiric film that focuses on a reprobate young man who cruelly exploits two elderly women; and *Quattro passi fra le nuvole* (*Four Steps in the Clouds*; Blasetti, 1942), featuring a traveling salesman who lives a ritualized city life and is enlisted to aid a young rural woman who, to the potential consternation of her family, is pregnant out of wedlock.

The post–World War II era witnessed literary and film forms identified as Italian neorealism for the uses of ordinary people, location shots in the city and countryside, and a critical treatment of conventional social, economic, and familial values. They focused on impoverished and oppressed characters struggling to survive in a contemporary devastated landscape. The films were melodramatic, though they occasionally included humorous characters and episodes (for example, Roberto Rossellini's *Roma, città aperta* [*Rome, Open City*, 1945]). In the quest for a genealogy of neorealism, these films have been cited as precursors, along with literary and cinematic works identified with nineteenth-century forms of realism, *verismo*, and naturalism. Neorealism as a phenomenon of the postwar era (Bazin 2005, I:29, II:19; Brunetta 2001a, 304–72; Deleuze 1986, ix) has been historically tied to effects of Fascism, war, and uncertainty in relation to the fate of the nation and of national cinema, whether Italian, European, or Asian. As described by Bazin, neorealism is "more an ontological position than an aesthetic one. . . . The word neorealist was thrown like a fishing net over the postwar Italian cinema and each director on his own is doing his best to break the toils in which, is it claimed, he has been caught" (Bazin 2005, II:66). Despite its ambiguous historical origins and its conflicting terms of definition, Bazin asserts, there are reasons to stick with the term for purposes of identifying the important dimension of its allusiveness in aesthetic and philosophic terms. It is not a faithful reproduction of reality; it is not a genre, nor is it merely a reliance on actual locations and nonprofessional actor. Neorealism is a poetic form of cinema that has remained protean and contentious, though it continues to be a yardstick against which much of Italian and global film production is still measured.

Recent studies of Italian cinema, such as Karl Schoonover's *Brutal Vision* (2012), have proffered analyses of neorealism that are germane to a different and more complex understanding of Italian postwar cinema. These studies bear fruit in relation to considerations of *commedia all'italiana*. Tied to conceptions of the everyday, the marginal, the suffering body, and poverty, neorealism provides a cinematic language that is self-conscious about seeing *as* believing, about the effects of the image. The immediate postwar neorealism, exemplified in such films as *Rome, Open City*; *Ladri di biciclette* (*Bicycle Thieves*; Vittorio De Sica, 1948) and *Paisà* (*Paisan*; Rossellini, 1946), was a challenge to conventional forms of realism that foregrounded heroism, action, affect, and future resolution. Neorealism eschewed this familiar model and had an affective design on its viewers. According to Schoonover, it enacted a "politics of pity," placing the viewer in "an extranational space of charity" (2012, 150). On the one hand, the films emphasize the suffering body as a preventive strategy against the repetition of violence, while, at the same time, "this aim is pursued cinematically through the virtual repetition of these atrocities" (ibid., xvi).

After 1948, with the triumph of the Christian Democrat Party and later with the "economic miracle," the Italian filmgoer was entertained with the return of genre films, including melodramas, peplum epics, westerns, documentaries, animation films, and a number of comedies that avoided direct engagement with past history. Producers' eyes were on the international market and on profit. Initially, Italian comedy was profitable exemplified by adaptations from the Don Camillo novels of Giovanni Guareschi, and such films by Luigi Comencini as *Pane, amore, e fantasia* (*Bread, Love and Dreams*, 1953) and *Pane, amore e gelosia* (*Frisky*, aka *Bread, Love and Jealousy*, 1954). These largely focused on rural life, reconciling tradition with modernity and geared to reducing complexity, by offering affective reassurance about a changing and uncertain social world, starring such actors as Gina Lollobrigida, Sophia Loren, and Vittorio De Sica.

In another version of the comedic, though allied to satiric comedy and fantasy, *Miracolo à Milano* (*Miracle in Milan*; De Sica, 1951) is akin to a neorealist fairy tale, a fable that visualizes the poverty and exploitation of the lower classes, the unemployed, and the elderly, conveying an ironic message of endurance, faith, and solidarity. While critical, if not pessimistic, of social institutions and the rich and pessimistic about their ability to contribute to social transformation, De Sica uses satire and humor to shatter the clichés and stereotypes associated with the poor so as to incarnate the love lavished on them through the magic of cinema, thus placing the film closer to the *commedia all'italiana* that became prominent in the 1960s.

Since *commedia all'italiana* is a complex form of cinematic comedy that employs a range of styles, characters, situations, and stars to create a form suitable to changing events in Italian cultural and social life, its contributions can be seen in a variety of cinematic forms, from those of auteur cinema to the popular forms identified with peplum epics, Italian (or "spaghetti") westerns, parodies of dominant film forms, and star vehicles. Definitions of *commedia all'italiana*, akin to definitions of neorealism, are notoriously elusive. *Commedia all'italiana* blurs boundaries—high and popular forms, masculinity and femininity, the real and the imaginary, represented by the films of Mario Monicelli, Federico Fellini, Dino Risi, and Lina Wertmüller—through recreating earlier eras in Italian social and political life to rethink the past and its impact on present forms of culture and politics. Totò (Antonio De Curtis), whose career in theater and film spanned the early years of cinema to the late 1960s, maintained a prominent position in the reemerging culture of comedy. His comic persona appealed to Italian audiences of changing generations for its ability through gesture, theatricality, and verbal language to parody and unmask the ineptitude and theatricality of the Italian male (Reich 2004, 36) and Italian social institutions.

I undertake here a mapping of elements and particular texts that offer insights into forms of postwar comedy that transgress the borders of conventional genre analysis. Recent writings on Italian cinema have been critical of the tendency of film critics to single out canonical texts produced by such filmmakers as Rossellini, Fellini, Antonioni, Bertolucci, and Pasolini to the neglect of popular genre films, with the exception of those texts that, like the Italian western, have achieved international acclaim (see Brunetta 2001b, 365–425, Günsberg 2005, 97–215, and Koven 2006). In what follows, I discuss a range of films that elude strict generic classification in their irreverent treatment of social institutions, social types, language, and bodily expression.

The popularity of *I soliti ignoti* (*Big Deal on Madonna Street*; Monicelli, 1958) heralded a form of comedy identified as *giallo-rosa*, a caper film, that focuses on the exploits of a group of incompetents to carry off a big heist. The 1950s witnessed several critical popular versions of this subgenre, namely *The Ladykillers* (Alexander Mackendrick, 1955), *Du rififi chez les hommes* (*Rififi;* Jules Dassin, 1955), and *Bob le flambeur* (Jean-Pierre Melville, 1956). Monicelli's film combines these international crime detection farces with an encyclopedic treatment of Italian social life at the margins to satirize courtship and marriage, unemployment, outmoded familial rituals associated with Sicilian life, and a problematical portrait of Italian masculinity that becomes identified with postwar cinema.

The commercial and critical success of Monicelli's film also derives from its selection of actors, figures largely identified with popular cinema and some with comedy in particular (Totò; Marcello Mastroianni; dramatic actor Vittorio Gassman transformed into a comic figure; and a new face destined to become a star, Claudia Cardinale), which enhanced not only the star appeal of the *commedia* but also the expectation of a film form that accentuated the role of dialect, slang, and seriocomic treatment of theft (including a humorous engagement with the "stealing" of cinematic forms). The films of Federico Fellini are often separated from the popular cinema and identified as auteur cinema; however, in addressing the caper film, Fellini's *Il bidone* (1955) belongs as well to this hybrid cinema that is self-conscious about its status as film. Using an American actor, Broderick Crawford, Fellini adopted the form of the caper film but then converted the film into a Christian parable of the good thief (Bondanella 2001, 25) in which the comic grotesque become undecidable in meaning. In Fellini's film, as in his *La strada* (1954), the body is visualized as an object of violence converted into an uncertain allegory of conversion and redemption.

Commedia all'italiana undertakes a dismantling of social institutions through caricature, ridicule, and parody, with an emphasis on gendered bodies, to create a grotesque form of humor that incorporates tradition, rituals, laws, customs, and codes that have imprisoned Italians. A key character is the roving male, a caricature of the Latin Lover, exemplified in such films as *Divorzio all'italiana* (*Divorce Italian Style*, 1961) and *Sedotta e abbandonata* (*Seduced and Abandoned*, 1964), both by Pietro Germi; and *Il bell'Antonio* (*Bell'Antonio*; Mauro Bolognini, with a screenplay by Pier Paolo Pasolini, 1960). *Divorce Italian Style* ridicules "the performative codes of Sicilian masculinity, in particular the *bella figura*, the *gallo*, and public manifestation of the honor code" (Reich 2004, 66). *Seduced and Abandoned* reaches deep into ritualistic *cum* legalistic social structures that reinforce the tenacity and violence underpinning the maintenance of traditions. The film is both a discourse regarding "the legal system and all its gender absurdity" and "a portrayal of an archaic mentality and its dire consequences on everyday people" (Lanzoni 2008, 115). Another comedy set in Sicily and focusing on the bizarre expectations of male and female comportment is *Bell'Antonio*, a dark comedy that portrays Antonio (Mastroianni), as the title suggests, as a beautiful figure (a *bella figura*: the ideal spouse, well situated, handsome in appearance, respectful to women—and sexually impotent). The grotesque humor exposes how Antonio's worship of the figure of the Virgin poses an obstacle to his amour proper as a man and, as such, his sexual consummation. Yet carnal creatures such as Santuzza (Patrizia Bini), to whom he will be yoked and with whom he can perform sexually, can establish that Antonio is finally "a man" (Reich 2004, 61–65).

MONICELLI, *MAESTRO DI COMMEDIA ALL'ITALIANA*

Mario Monicelli, whose filmmaking spanned from the Fascist era to his death in 2010, was considered a quintessential practitioner of *commedia all'italiana*. His 1968 *The Girl with a Pistol* (*La ragazza con la pistola*) initially set in Sicily, focuses on the violation of the honor code and dooms Assunta Patanè (Monica Vitti) to avenge her own and her family's honor by murdering the *gallo* (womanizer; literally, rooster) who debauched her. She sets out on a journey to the United Kingdom to find him and, on her travels, begins to inhabit a modern world in the Swinging Sixties of the UK that serves as a critique of the archaic values that she has left behind. The film is also an instance of how Monicelli uses actors in roles different to their well-known film personas, in Vitti's case in contrast to the enigmatic roles she had played in Michelangelo Antonioni's aesthetic and philosophic trilogy on modernity (1960–62), which had established her internationally.

Other familiar actors in Monicelli's comedies were Anna Magnani, Aldo Fabrizi, and the formidable Totò, all from Italian theater and screen. New faces also appeared on screen: Alberto Sordi, Ugo Tognazzi, and Marcello Mastroianni. These new star bodies became prominent in generating a different historical sense of the cinematic body (actually and virtually) as contributing to thinking counter-historically in terms of bodies, time, and space. Monicelli's selection of actors for his comedies was based on deglamorizing them and placing then in roles in which they are outcasts, marginal, and inept figures. Their ineptness exposes corruption often based on misrecognition: of themselves, their overvalued abilities, their underestimated friends and foes, and of the limits on their agency and capacity for action.

Not only do his characters serve to undermine clichés and stereotypes about behavior through appearance and gesture, but also the actors playing them undermine their own familiar star personae. Exceptional in their appearance and behavior, his actors are creatures of fixation, grandiosity, often indifferent to the counsel of others, and distinguished by their opportunism in the art of getting by. Monicelli exploited them and their social milieu to critical advantage. Their characters located in a specific historical milieu are revealing of counter-historicizing, in such films as

The Great War, The Organizer, Brancaleone's Army, and *Brancaleone at the Crusades.* Working in the generic mode of *commedia all'italiana,* Monicelli creates antiheroes who are "inept, self-centered, shallow, yet often lovable." He places them in absurd situations that often end in failure, portraying a "darker, more ironic, and cynical vision of Italian life" (Bondanella 2007, 145). The characters are no longer "truthful"; they are forgers, thieves, imposters, and confidence men; and "truth" becomes a matter not of judging their goodness or badness but of the power of storytelling to think differently. Monicelli employed dark humor, farce, and satire to unmask conventional beliefs through picaresque characters whose social performances, and the situations in which they function, serve to redefine comedy as well as reigning conceptions of Italian history.

The comedies were not a radical rupture from neorealism, but, in concert with other filmmakers' works of the 1960s (for example, Fellini) and 1970s (for example, Wertmüller) were instrumental in revising inherited fictions of Italy's cultural and political past. They exposed deleterious myths, injustices, and destructive social practices and were sensitive to the need to experiment with the potential for seeing, thinking, and reacting differently to the world presented on screen. The films utilize parody and farce as a pretext to explore affinities and discontinuities between the past and contemporary cultural and political life. Their narratives focus on the opportunism and ineptness of their picaresque male protagonists, who are not villains but marginal figures seeking to overcome the constraints of economic hardship and social constraints (Reich 2004, 16) in situations that reveal their failure to prevail over the severe cultural and social situations in which they inevitably find themselves.

Monicelli's Middle Ages: The Brancaleone Films

Monicelli's two comedy features set in the Middle Ages, *Brancaleone's Army* (earlier called *For Love and Gold*) and *Brancaleone at the Crusades,* starred the versatile Vittorio Gassman, a dramatic actor whose inept pugilist Peppe in *Big Deal on Madonna Street* had established him also as comedic—a designation his boastful Brancaleone (literally, lion's claw) would enhance.

Both are further instances of Monicelli's designs on the past, involving language, popular and canonical literature, intertextuality, and painting.

With his cowriters Agenore Incrocci and Furio Scarpelli, Monicelli was able to plan and execute these films, which earn the appellation of "mock epic." The comedies reveal a cinematic historian at work, drawing on numerous sources for his medieval imagination: Dante, Cervantes, folklore, and comic books. The films' counter-historical aspirations rely on strategies that have animated "the medieval imagination," involving myth, folklore, time, and memory, to introduce connections between that past and modernity. The *Brancaleone* films utilize satire, caricature, and farce to explore these affinities through pastiche, animation, and metacinema. Adhering to the quest narrative, the film journey form permits an encyclopedic and seemingly improvisational episodic treatment of characters and situations. Such parodies of quest narratives might lead one to assume that these films paint a negative picture of medievalism in contrast to enlightened modernity. However, the films do not set up a stark contrast between a retrograde Middle Ages and an enlightened present; rather, they not only indicate where medievalism offers insights on and parallels with modernity but also use that past to unsettle complacent views of both past and present.

Brancaleone's Army invokes the present as a site of repetition in which there are no "economic miracles" (or perhaps no miracles at all, except in cinema). A parody of the quest motif of chivalric lore by presenting a protagonist who inverts physical and heroic patterns of chivalry, the film becomes a seriocomic vision of knight errantry, with Brancaleone and his followers the figurative descendants of Don Quixote and squire Sancho Panza. Set during one of the Crusades, the film follows Brancaleone through a landscape fraught with obstacles. The stages of the journey situate him (and the spectator) in an encyclopedic confrontation with a medieval world: class, gendered and religious differences, disease, war, and economic practices that, in the spirit of parody, are indebted as much to medieval chronicles as to modern life.

The film begins with a marauding band of Hungarians attacking an Italian village. The brutal rape, pillage, and sacking are prologue to the film's gritty images of a medieval world that focuses on the underside of the chivalric ethos, demolishing the tendency to glamorize heroism and warfare, whether historical or contemporary. Hardly unique, and with a bow to medieval fabliaux, the images call attention to the physical hardships and the mercenary objectives of inhabitants of this world. The film is set in motion by the assumed brutal killing of a knight, Arnolfo Mano-di-ferro (literally, iron hand), by two Italian survivors of the attack, Mangold and Taccone, who will soon become members of Brancaleone's ragtag and opportunistic "army." They plunder Mano-di-ferro's belongings and sell them to a Jewish merchant, Abacuc, who, able to read, discovers among these pilfered goods a parchment that cedes Man-di-ferro's fiefdom of Aurocastro in Puglia to the "noble" bearer of the document. Abacuc, Mangold, and Taccone determine to find a knight who can lead them to this wealth. They chance on Brancaleone, an impoverished knight, who at first refuses the offer of future wealth, claiming that he will gain his fortune by winning the hand of a wealthy woman in a tournament.

With his wild hair, tattered garments, rusty armor, and his recalcitrant yellow nag, Aquilante, he is the antithesis of the ideal knight-errant. Arrogant, incompetent, and vain, he recalls the boastful Capitano of the *commedia dell'arte*. His ineptness in combat begins with his losing his tournament by being thrown from his horse, which refuses to obey his commands. Thus, he has no choice but to join the rogues and undertake a journey to claim Aurocastro. In a mock-epic scene, he proclaims himself the men's "Duce" and commands them to swear fealty. On the road to the refrains of a lyric, "Branca, Branca, Branca, leone, leone, leone," Brancaleone encounters a knight, Teofilatto dei Leonzi (Gian Maria Volonté), who refuses to let him pass. As expected of knights, the men duel; but despite three attempts, neither is able to overcome the other. Three times they declare truce and then return to combat. Each time missing their opponent, the men cut down trees with their axes and completely mow a wheat field with their swords, thus at least transforming their ridiculous dueling into practical consequences. Teofilatto, now their prisoner, offers them a reward from his father if they take him home, but the men vote to continue their mission, and Teofilatto chooses to remain with them.

The men's next encounter looks more promising for the fortune hunters. Coming upon a seemingly deserted castle and finding food, the men sack the place and, inspecting the premises further, Brancaleone finds a beautiful woman, who offers him sexual delights. The promise of pleasant entertainment is truncated when he discovers that her husband and the other inhabitants of the castle had died from the plague. Fleeing the place

FIGURE 3.4. Death of the Jew, *Brancaleone's Army*, Monicelli, 1966.

in fear, the men are on the road again, this time confronting Christian crusaders on their way to the Terra Santa (the Holy Land). Anti-Semitism is foregrounded through the monk Zenone, their fanatical leader (Enrico Maria Salerno), who inveighs against the presence of an impure Jew, Abacuc, insisting that he be "purified" by tossing him into a waterfall, which almost kills him. In a scene that tests the other men's faiths, they are ordered by Zenone to cross a dangerous footbridge. Brancaleone and his men succeed in crossing, but then it collapses, causing some of Zenone's men to plunge to their deaths. Unperturbed, Zenone ascribes this misfortune to God's will, though the catastrophe is due to less to God's will and more to Zenone's miscalculation and arrogance.

Thus far, the film has parodied tyrannical leadership, superstition, and the fanaticism of crusades by stressing the incompetence and opportunism of all the characters. Later, chivalric honor and courtly love are parodied when Brancaleone saves a young woman, Matelda (Catherine Spaak), from the violence of warriors seeking to restore her to a fiancé. However, Brancaleone swears to her dying tutor that he will respect her chastity and return her unsullied to her fiancé, Duke Guccione. Unfortunately, she does not share his commitment to this oath and instead has sex with Teofilatto. Upon her return to her promised spouse, the duke discovers that she has been sexually "abused," and Brancaleone is wrongly imprisoned for this offense. Saved by his men, he tries to find Matelda in a nunnery, but she now abjures sexuality and declares that her new spouse is Christ. Brancaleone and the men find themselves on the road again without any success to their trials. However, the episodes foreground not only Brancaleone's inadequate assessment of the "mission" to which he has been elected but also comic theater of history that involves misrecognition, illusion, chance, and difference.

The film returns to its focus on the Jew, to reinforce his low religious and social status in this Christian world. Abacuc becomes gravely ill, and Brancaleone reassures him that he will go to a better life than on earth, whether it is a Christian paradise or not. When he dies, it is Brancaleone who buries him. As in many episodes in the film, this scene underscores the background of religious superstition and discrimination against Jews—a subject rarely treated in Italian films despite the consequences of Fascism, the persecution of Jews under racial laws, and their roundup and shipment to concentration camps. Yet here, among the instances that Monicelli includes in his portrayal of the marginalized and oppressed, the Jew plays a critical role.

The journey is about to end successfully as the men arrive at Aurocastro to claim their booty. Unfortunately, the original document was deficient: a critical part had been torn from it, one that Brancaleone now learns stipulated fighting the Saracens. Almost burned at the stake by the Christians (since it turns out that Arnolfo Mano-di-ferro did *not* die but has returned to reclaim his patrimony), Brancaleone and his men are saved by Zenone and his crusaders. Astride his horse, Aquilante, who has reluctantly parted from a willing mare, Brancaleone joins the singing crusaders, leaving the film open-ended in resolving the men's quest for wealth and glory. The style of the narrative has resisted any opportunity to offer either material or spiritual resolution to the hardships encountered on this allegorical journey. Brancaleone and his followers have not succeeded in any of their worldly enterprises, though they have managed to escape from imprisonment and/or death and provided a view of a medieval landscape filtered through cultural imagination. The world of the Middle Ages has been portrayed from a bottom-up view of historical events, pitting the threadbare rogues against more powerful forces. This history from below has shifted the onus from upper-class characters to a nomadic and vulnerable band whose quest is not for glory but for material gain. In the vein of Foucault's genealogical method, the film "tracks down the min[u]scule, repetitive acts of cowardliness and all those features of folly, vanity, and complacency that endlessly nourish the philosophical mushroom" (Foucault 1977, 181).

This form of the comic constructs a counter-history, a transformation of history into another form of time, a form of "concerted carnival" (Foucault 1977, 160–61, quote at 161). This carnival is a travesty of both mythic and historical figures and events. Through its use of parody, intertextuality, caricature, and animated and colorful titles, the film dismantles the narrative of chivalry and its idealist dimensions as enshrined in cultural memory, focusing on the vulnerable physical body and on failure rather than success. The picaresque Brancaleone and his rogues become examples of "knight-errantry minus the delusions" (Nelson 1990, 93) in the film's demythologization of romance, leadership, warfare, and heroic identity. In its visualization of an unsuccessful quest, it portrays a world turned upside down, undermining religious and commonsense consolation of reward offered for earthly suffering, and posing failure as its pedagogical design on the spectator central to counter-historicizing.

Brancaleone at the Crusades delves even more deeply into the medieval landscape, focusing on witchcraft, leprosy, dwarfism, papal legitimacy, war, and religious faith. The film opens with animated cartoons drawn in childlike fashion under the credits, to introduce the disheveled Brancaleone and chanting Christian crusaders under the leadership of the "prophet" Zenone as the followers set out on their journey to the Holy Land, giving thanks to the Lord and praising Pope Gregory. Unfortunately, the crusaders land in the wrong place and are massacred by supporters of Pope Clement, and Brancaleone, who had hidden under a boat, is left alone to undertake the crusade. Viewing the bodies of his comrades buried head first in the sand with legs protruding, Brancaleone laments his survival; but, as in Ingmar Bergman's *Det sjunde inseglet* (*The Seventh Seal*, 1957), another counter-historical film set in the Middle Ages, Brancaleone too confronts the gruesome figure of Death that introduces themes relating to time, mortality, and chance.

Bargaining with Death (in appearance evoking Bergman's figure) about the length of his life, Brancaleone chooses a short and glorious life, and Death vows to return for him at the end of seven months. Thus, Brancaleone's first adventure on his journey to the Holy Land is the rescue of a baby, the son of Boemondo (Adolfo Celi), king of Sicily, who has been abducted by a knight, Thorz (Paolo Villaggio), in the service of the German king, an enemy. Thorz proposes that he and Brancaleone fight blindfolded, though he does not blindfold himself. However, thanks to the assistance of sympathetic observers, Brancaleone gains advantage and allows Thorz and the bystanders to join him on the journey to the Holy Land, causing the others to regard him as mad rather than pious for this folly. He also takes the baby along. This film, in comparison to *Brancaleone's Army*, focuses less on worldly enterprises, profit, power, and war and more largely on biopolitics, physical and mental diseases, deformity, madness, torture, and the potential for thinking in terms of biopower—that is, the enthrallment of the vulnerable body (*homo sacer*) to the reigning power.

As is characteristic of *commedia all'italiana,* the focus of this film is on outcasts, on the deformed, diseased, sinners, and witches who become Brancaleone's new followers. After adopting the baby, the group encounters a woman about to be burned at the stake for witchcraft. As in *Monty Python and the Holy Grail* (1975), this episode involves the bizarre "proofs" of witchcraft. Whereas, in the Python film, the confessed witch is left behind to suffer her punishment, Brancaleone rescues Tiburzia (Stefania Sandrelli, of both *Divorce, Italian Style* and *Seduced and Abandoned*). The motif of witchcraft becomes increasingly central to later events in the film in its exploration of connections between myth and history as they relate to femininity.

A dwarf who had claimed that Tiburzia was responsible for his diminutive appearance joins her and the group and maintains an antagonistic attitude toward her. Still another deformed character of the Middle Ages, the leper, also becomes a follower of Brancaleone. At first, the terrified crusaders order him to leave; but, through Brancaleone's intervention, they allow the "creature of God" to remain but stay at a respectable dis-

FIGURE 3.5. The damned, *Brancaleone at the Crusades*, Monicelli, 1970.

tance. The awfulness of deformed bodies is developed in the crusaders' next encounter with a grotesque Dantesque scene of human bodies hanging from the branches of a tree. Tiburzia then serves as a translator to communicate with the suffering sinners, who describe themselves variously as punished for adultery, eating meat on a holy day, being a Jew, and holding radical religious and political views. The film thus satirizes medieval Catholic orthodoxy to resonate with contemporary treatments of difference not unrelated to Catholicism and its cultural and political constraints.

Brancaleone now encounters and fights with Turone, the brother of King Boemondo, who has come for the baby, but the group saves both the baby and Brancaleone, who has been left to hang upside down from a high ledge. Now the issue of papal legitimacy comes to the fore when Brancaleone confronts a holy man, the stylite Colombino, who will determine the "real" pope from the antipope, in which Brancaleone will play a supportive role. As the followers of each pope face each other, Colombino tells Brancaleone to walk on hot coals and to bring a dove to the rightful pope. Brancaleone succeeds and gives the dove to Pope Gregory but burns the soles of his feet. As he is assuaging his pain in water, he discovers that the "leper" is a princess, Berta d'Avignone, seeking to regain her kingdom after the death of her husband. She had adopted the garb of a leper to protect herself from unchivalric assaults by men. Returning to the other crusaders, Brancaleone and Berta join them in a carnivalesque moment where all sing and dance, except for Tiburzia, jealous of Brancaleone's attentions to the princess.

The moment of gaiety is short lived. Turone and his men mortally wound the dwarf in a vicious attack on Brancaleone and his men. Before the dwarf dies, he asks (echoing Abacuc's last moments on earth) if he as a stunted creature will go to paradise. Brancaleone tells him that he will go to a special paradise for dwarfs, where all men are dwarfs. The dwarf's dissatisfaction with his body serves to highlight the medieval treatment of "monstrosity" (Bildhauer and Mills 2003), whether of wild, aberrant, and antisocial beings, giants, dwarfs, the physically or mentally ill—tying it to Christian beliefs in sin and redemption internalized by the victims of social ostracism. Repeatedly, the comedy complicates conceptions of normality by invoking religion as a primary fomenter of conflict.

The long-awaited arrival in Jerusalem brings further complications. King Boemondo is at first delighted with the return of his son, until he finds that the birthmark that he and his son share on their posterior parts is not to be seen; thus, he rejects the child, condemning the boy to death. Tiburzia comes to the rescue, confessing that she is a witch and had caused the birthmark to disappear. She is put to the test by being asked to render herself invisible, and she does so. Though her presence is evident through her voice, she is sent away, barred from witnessing the conflict between the Christians and Saracens. In a scene that draws on spectacle as a theatrical display of the contending legions in their ritual regalia, the leader of the Saracens proposes that, instead of a pitched battle, the Saracens and Christians conduct a tournament. However, the participants must be of aristocratic lineage. Brancaleone's lineage is challenged, and he is denied participation. Alone and rejected, Brancaleone laments his fate, accusing himself of being a false knight and spitting on his reflection in a pool of water. Tiburzia appears and urges him to flee, but, having learned that all four of Boemondo's knights have been defeated, he rides off determined to confront the king. He informs Boemondo that he can be knighted if the king so wishes; thus, Brancaleone is made a baron. He now defeats the Saracens and is about the finish off his last opponent when

Tiburzia, having observed the tournament from afar, causes a coconut to fall on his head and knocks him unconscious, thus spitefully depriving him of the glory of his victory.

In a desert, Brancaleone attempts to avenge himself on Tiburzia, who keeps altering her appearance from visible to invisible. He accuses her of being jealous but is interrupted in his vengeance when he hears the voice of Death, who has now returned. The new knight's seven months have elapsed. Brancaleone has had his brief glory, and his time has expired. He refuses to succumb but undertakes combat with Death; but, just as Death is about to end Brancaleone's life, Tiburzia intervenes and is mortally wounded, mysteriously causing Death to vanish. Asked why she did this, Tiburzia tells Brancaleone that it was for love of him, and he, moved, renames her "Felicilla" (happy one), rather than "Pazzarella" (crazy one), as she expires and is now transformed into a bird. Either name captures the role she is assigned in the film, or more properly the character of comedy that relies on magic, fantasy, and dream to present itself as counter-history. Henri Bergson, in discussing the comic, emphasizes the centrality of "repetition inversion and reciprocal interference" (1983, 201), as well as distinctions and distortions between large and the small, and connections between the actual and the virtual (ibid., 200–201).

Monicelli's comedy self-consciously appropriates verbal and visual language from various sources: Cervantes, Dante, folk tales, romances, theology, church history, chronicles of the period, current history, and other films; and these eclectic borrowings have their counterpart in the visual images involving cartoons, paintings, drawings, and a panoply of bodies, large, small, deformed, living, or dead. The verbal language is also eclectic, indicative of a mixture of various regional dialects, archaisms, Latinate constructions, and foreign phrases (Brunetta 2001a, 97). The second Brancaleone film, with the introduction of King Boemondo, also introduces poetry into the dialogue: the characters begin to speak in rhymed couplets, thus further fracturing the unity and credibility of a historical viewpoint, paralleling how the comedy strives to differentiate its personae, confounding the high and the low, sense and nonsense, and expectations of a familiar treatment of the past.

Counter-history is a narrative of "the vanquished, the abject, and the downcast of history" (White 1994, ix). In this context, literature (and cinema) is not to be dismissed as mere illusion, fancy, or untruth but instead is related to the problematic of finding a way to portray actors in situations in which they are powerless and constantly involved in a struggle to survive yet capitalizing on their lack of self-awareness, habituation, and obliviousness. However, since comedy is a social form, it entails spectators (Bergson 1983), both those internal to the events and external viewers as well, to appreciate the painful, absurd, yet also potentially corrective dimensions of the behavior and situations witnessed.

The emphasis on Tiburzia's physical metamorphosis (from human to bird and from visible to invisible) and the verbal and visual language used by her earlier as mediator between the language of the dead sinners and the living function self-reflexively to call attention to the potential of cinematic comedy to reveal "meanings that speech failed to express" (Rancière 1994, 46). Monicelli's *commedia all'italiana* validates Deleuze's conception of a cinema of belief through memory, recollection, and, above all, humor: "We need an ethic or a belief, which makes fools laugh; it is not a need to believe in something else, but a need to believe in this world of which fools are a part" (Deleuze 1989a, 173). Comedy as counter-history is not negative, but it is ethical, cruel, and perhaps partisan.

History as Comic Theater of Common Sense: The Organizer

Monicelli's 1963 dark comedy *The Organizer* is a historical film focusing is on the harsh, inhumane conditions of work in a Turin textile factory in the 1890s and the workers' struggles for socialism to improve those conditions. (Its Italian title, *I compagni*, actually means "The Comrades.") In the tragicomic vein of social realism, the film refuses either to glorify or to demean the all-too-human strikers, whom the film shows as "quicker to fight among themselves than to protect the interests of their class" (Bondanella 2007, 148). Gian Piero Brunetta regards the film as a great emotional and ideological treatment of nineteenth-century workers' protests (2001b, 186); however, these protests and their aftermath also evoke the labor conflicts in Italy identified as *operaismo* (a workerist communist movement) in the 1960s to the mid-1970s, associated with radical Left intellectuals, that were also to end in violence. Both centuries are evoked in this *commedia all'italiana* to suggest the complexity attendant on the failure of the strike, in which consensus is impossible.

The film, not a conventional comedy, focuses on the decision of the workers in a factory to strike after a man is seriously wounded at his machine. A montage, Eisenstein style, portrays the alienating milieu of the factory. The extended panning shots of the massive machinery, the focus on a wall clock, and images of workers toiling at their posts, subject to the rigors of a fourteen-hour workday, offer a mechanistic view of the working-class world in contrast to the familiar world of the economic boom of the 1960s and 1970s. The machinic portrait of the factory and the machinic behavior of the bosses connect to the film's problematic portrayal of the workers' attempt to overcome their oppressive social world. Again, landscape plays a preeminent role, and Monicelli has expressed a preference for location shooting, so as to create a realist effect through the behavior of the characters in interaction with their surroundings, the working-class milieu of late-nineteenth century Turin: the factory, the streets, the workers' lodgings, the railroad yard where they scramble to collect dropped pieces of coal.

Music is essential to the film's tragicomic technique, occupying a position of equality with the visual images in this black-and-white film (as well as in the Brancaleone films and *The Great War*). The music is a source of pathos in its capacity to evoke the historical events portrayed, using song reinforced by visual images from earlier paintings and photographs. The strains of a socialist workers' anthem recur throughout the film and serve a dual function: its militant lyrics and melody are identified with the history of Italian socialism, thus expressing the aspirations of the workers; but the song is also finally a reminder of the untimeliness of their efforts. In relation to the characters, the songs also stress group collectivity, as in the penultimate scene where the workers march to it, unfortunately to be dispersed by the guns of the army in collusion with the factory owners.

The characters speak in dialects; their personas are identified with different regions in their uses of language, gesture, and personality types. This form of realism produces a neorealist sense of an everyday world through its treatment of character and situation; it singles out representative members of the community and presents them not as mere caricatures or stereotypes but as physical and mental types, including different generational and regional figures from northern and southern Italy. Among the notable figures who play significant roles in the community are the rotund, explosive, and vacillating Pautasso, the suggestible Martinetti (Bernard Blier), the irascible and finally enlightened Raoul, the defiant and generous Niobe (Annie Girardot, whom we shall meet again in chapter 5). In their portrayals, *The Organizer* creates a portrait of their limitations but also of their responses to dire necessity. What renders the film exemplary of the *commedia all'italiana* is its focus on the drama of these individuals in conflict with a social world and material environment that exceed their capacity to comprehend or control. Thus, the (dark) comedy arises from failure: on the part of the workers and also on the part of the idealistic and middle-class Professor Sinigaglia (Marcello Mastroianni), whose mission is to create a milieu of social cohesion. The film ends in negativity, with neither romance nor constructive action to ameliorate the lack of social cohesiveness.

In physical appearance and demeanor, the portrayal of Sinigaglia reinforces the film's relentless address of the difficulty of collective action. His comedic treatment relies on his appearance and his halting but at times eloquent speech. Dressed in a moth-eaten suit covered by a cape, he is dirty, disheveled, and awkward in movement. Sought by the police in Genoa for his involvement in a strike there and in need of refuge, he arrives by train at a critical moment during the Turin workers' deliberations about whether to strike. Committed to their cause, Sinigaglia arrives in time to participate in their impending strike. He too is implicated in its failure.

Reminiscent of Charlie Chaplin's tramp and of Michel Simon's title role in Jean Renoir's *Boudu sauvé des eaux* (*Boudu Saved from Drowning*, 1932), Mastroianni's Sinigaglia joins the rank of comic characters that have adopted the pathetic but moving persona of the vagrant. Unfortunately, the state-backed power of the bosses contradicts Sinigaglia's exhortations to the workers to prevail militantly against their employers to achieve justice. Neither he nor the workers are villains of the strike's failure. Rather, there are intertwined obstacles confronting the community: the greed and manipulation of the employers and the dire material hardships and lack of education of the workers that make their survival tenuous.

Despite the majority of workers finally having met and voted to return to work, after internal controversy about this decision, they allow themselves to be persuaded by Sinigaglia's rousing rhetoric to demonstrate and take over what is theirs—the factory. They march to the factory singing, but the army enlisted by the employers to break the strike is ordered to shoot the demonstrators if they cross the line of the militia arrayed against them. In the melee that ensues, the soldiers kill one of the young men. The strikers disperse, but Bianca, the dead man's sister, goes to the scene, falls over the body, and berates and batters Sinigaglia. A pathetic and degraded figure, Sinigaglia searches for his glasses, which have been knocked to the ground (not the first time they have fallen off, demonstrating his limited vision). The last we see of him, he is being led away by two policemen, hardly the incarnation of the Latin Lover with which Mastroianni has been identified but closer to his comically inept character in *Big Deal on Madonna Street*.

This tragicomedy is a dour exploration of the workers' conflicts, both among themselves and with their leaders. Monicelli's gallery of antiheroes—"inept, self-centered, shallow, yet often lovable" (Bondanella 2007, 145)—find themselves in situations that end in failure. However, the film refuses to glorify, demean, or melodramatize the strikers. Their desperate situation, the images of their hardship and brutal treatment at the hands of the bosses, scenes of industrial accidents, and incidents of betrayal and death all appear to be in the vein of neorealism with the location shooting, focus on the everyday, natural lighting, contemporaneity, and so on; and yet the film has critical designs on rethinking history making on film. In creating a scenario of historical failure, by reconstructing nineteenth-century history, the film recalls the crisis of the action-image in producing indeterminacy through invoking a potential through situation and characters to pervert habituated forms of behavior (clichés) that previously held sway (Deleuze 1986, 206).

The strikers' inability to respond effectively to their present situation is the crux of this dark comedy in its challenging of a conventional social-realist scenario; the film engages the spectator in thinking in terms of time, enabling counter-historical thinking through the interaction of a tragic past, a comic present, and an unknown future. The strikers' failure to realize their action is a provocation to consider powerlessness as an entry to reconceiving familiar representations of a bridge between knowledge and action and of tragic repetition and failure as an entry to an awareness of time and historical process. Through the portraits of the strikers, including Mastroianni's Sinigaglia, this episode offers a version of "effective history" in which the cinematic world is not "a simple configuration where events are reduced to accentuate their essential traits, their final meaning, or their initial and final value" (Foucault 1977, 155). On the contrary, this counter-history is a profusion of entangled events that are reliant on the mercilessness of time, mistakes, error, and contingency.

The Organizer involves a productive confusion between the comedic and the tragic, drawing on emotion, visual and aural discontinuities, *mise-en-scène,* and intertextuality to portray events that pertain not only to the late nineteenth-century world but also to political, economic, and aesthetic crises in the world of the 1960s. The uses of both montage and *mise-en-scène* to juxtapose industrial machines and human machinic behavior and to dramatize the focus on the impossible conflict between cohesiveness and individual necessity and desire are an attempt to subvert traditional and reductive political treatments of history through cinema. This cinematic counter-history lesson aspires to be open-ended in its rejection of heroes, passive victims, and the attribution of a final meaning and resolution to the events. The film is not a cynical and negative portrait of a strike. It proffers a parable for the viewer that resides in its philosophic investigation of time and change, one that involves a focus on engaging the viewer through a visual and sensory register of both content and style in a tragi-comic form that challenges clichés; resists didactic, formal pedagogy; and is geared to becoming investigative even more than explanatory.

The film seems wary of a form of historicizing that relies on action to resolve the conflict between incompatible positions; rather, it invites the spectator to contemplate the ethical issues raised by the portrait of confusion, disorder, and death. The contrast between the strikers' situation and the forces arrayed against them invites reflections on forms of representation that rely on repetition to interpret and find solutions. Monicelli's film generates an affective response to the characters' plight through the images of their hardship, brutal treatment, and death; but the comedy of failure involves critical reflections on causality, agency, and temporality that pertain not only to the past but also, more imperatively, to thinking about the present and future as characteristic of counter-history.

Monicelli's tragicomic vision of irreconcilable difference is characteristic of 1960s Italian cinema, its treatment of both subject and spectator in its refashioning of film style. By shifting emphasis from the agency of the characters onto their circumstances, the film as tragicomedy dramatizes a break between a massive situation and the limited capacities of the protagonists—not to diminish either but to invoke crisis and uncertainty about explaining events. The film's narration places truth into crisis, introducing uncertainty in relation to action, but it also opens onto the potential of thinking differently about agency and events. This form of counter-historicizing places the viewer in a more active relation to the narration, in which the terms of historicity are diverted from clichéd representations about the body politic and the politics of the body in a way that introduces different perceptions of violence, knowledge, and power.

History, "The Art of Getting By": The Great War

Monicelli's 1959 film version of World War I in *The Great War* portrays with grim humor the sacrifice of a generation of young men in a war to end all wars. His transgressive treatment of war is another tragicomic counter-history. The film evokes *Paths of Glory* (Stanley Kubrick, 1957) with its satiric portrait of the "just" war; in fact, Monicelli's comic portrait, in its bold dissection of war, suggests that he had the Kubrick film in mind as he worked on *La grande guerra*. Like Kubrick's, his film elicits connections to Foucault's discussion of "the historical sense" in which monumental, antiquarian critical history are transformed into parody or masquerade (Foucault 1977, 160).

By returning to the past through World War I, Monicelli's film investigates the common sense of opportunism—the destructiveness of the art of getting by, of survival at any cost—as pivotal to unmasking pretensions about war and patriotism. The film presents its tragicomic narrative through two unwilling, scheming, and unpatriotic soldiers who are drafted to serve in World War I. The two draftees, Giovanni Busacca (Vittorio Gassman), a Roman, and the other, Oreste Jacovacci (Alberto Sordi), a Milanese, are followed through the rigors and bungling episodes of military training, errors in recognizing distinctions between their own troops and the enemy, and fateful confrontations with the enemy in brutal battle scenes. Unlike the Kubrick film, these two men are at the center of the action, carrying the burden of the *commedia* through their competition with each other in the vein of banter and burlesque.

The comedy offers a version of history that inverts the patriotic myths associated with war and undermines reigning conceptions of human agency: even the ultimate heroic "choice" to withhold information from the enemy is fraught with failure for the two men and for the understanding of the spectator to whom this counter-history is addressed. The film not only undoes clichés identified with monumental history, such as heroic sacrifice for the common good of the nation, but also takes every opportunity to introduce an alternative mode of history making. It is not heroism that triumphs. The two men and the spectator are faced with a different and too-late revelation of history. This "'too-late,'" as Gilles Deleuze reminds us, "is not an accident that takes place in time but a dimension of time itself" (Deleuze 1989a, 96).

Their deaths are not an invitation to think in terms of a final moment of heroism that would reinscribe the values that the film's union of the comic and tragic seeks to unmask. In the penultimate episode of *The Great War*, Busacca and Jacovacci have complied with their orders to deliver a message to beleaguered Italian troops. The two have then taken refuge from torrential rain in the stable of a farmhouse before returning to the front, and they don Austrian uniforms they find there; but, during the night, the Austrian enemy has occupied the surrounding territory, and the two men are surprised to find themselves in enemy territory as their prisoners. When Jacovacci accidentally lets slip about a bridge being built by the Italians, the officers insist on knowing the location. Initially, Busacca and Jacovacci agree to comply with this demand, habituated as they are to the rewards of opportunism, in which their cleverness, in the final analysis, has saved them. However, after witnessing the officers' contempt for their identity, comparing them to Venetian cooks of liver and onions, Busacca, enraged, refuses to be an informer and is shot; Jacovacci will share the same fate.

This is the decisive moment in the film's unmasking of traditional forms of history making. Thanks to Gassman and Sordi's acting styles as animated, theatrical display, though ultimately hopeless, this episode exemplifies Monicelli's tragicomic treatment. The scene has potential for low comedy through the familiar presence of a comic duo whose interactions involve the element of surprise: they find themselves in the wrong place, in enemy uniforms, inadvertently revealing secret information, and they contemplate a strategy based on the success of their past opportunistic behavior. The scene exploits their character traits by emphasizing their ordinary physical appearance. It distinguishes between Busacca, his defiant posture, his theatrical wink to Jacovacci and swagger as he is led to his death, and Jacovacci, left a shivering spectator to the shooting. Framed by the open shutters, his view of Busacca's death through them, serves as surrogate for the cinematic frame, a reminder to the spectator of the shooting as cinematic historical reconstruction. The final words of the film are Jacovacci's before he is dragged protesting to meet a similar and senseless demise. The theatricality and complexity of this moment raise questions for the viewer of how to react to what they have witnessed.

Clearly, the two men are confronting a limit situation that breaks from past repetition, and Brunetta describes this moment as "revealing their true identity [by] suddenly breaking from their old ways," revealing "their sense of altruism, their respect for others and the law, their solidarity, their honesty, and their willingness to sacrifice" (2001a, 165; translation mine). In this formulation, we have a portrait of conversion, sacrifice, and redemption. But is it any of these? Or does the film become a diagnosis of thinking historically that produces a shift from the individual actions of the men onto their situation (as exemplified by the film's ending after their deaths on the battlefield). Bereft of their habitual strategies of evasion, death is inevitable, and through them, the spectator is faced with a different revelation about historical agency. Their deaths, though moving, are not a repetition of the transcendent moment of a tragic hero, but an exploration, characteristic of *commedia all'italiana*, both of the failure of the art of getting by and, even more profoundly, of the impossible situation, the double bind in which they are placed.

This episode invokes the significance of historical repetition and its theatricality—as Gilles Deleuze, following Marx and Nietzsche, has written, "Historical actors or agents can create only on condition that they identify themselves with figures from the past. In this sense, history is theatre" (1994, 91). In this film's form of theatricality, however, the viewer is diverted from time-honored heroics: although the men's situation recreates the familiar prisoner's dilemma, it deprives the spectator of transcendental reassurances derived from repetition (and consolation) of past tragic forms. *The Great War* brings fiction and documentation, material events and virtual memory, affective involvement and distancing all into play, creating a counter-history that raises questions about received forms of causal explanation, reductive considerations of behavior, and alternative, if incomplete, possibilities of thinking differently about the past.

CLOCK TIME, CINEMATIC TIME, AND COUNTER-HISTORY: *WHAT TIME IS IT THERE?*

Tsai Ming-liang's 2001 *What Time Is It There?* is a further enactment of counter-history by invoking conceptions of time irreducible to equivalence or linearity of past, present, and future, traditional allegory, or representation. The film prompts thinking on globalization to investigate time as expressed in constraining or potentially emancipatory forms. It commingles past, present, and future to redraw boundaries between the real and the imaginary.

Through the frequent long-take filming of characters and landscape—protagonist Hsiao-kang especially but also his mother—the film self-consciously reinforces the tyranny of the clock, symptomatic of what Deleuze describes in *The Logic of Sense* as linear Chronos that "orients the arrow of time from past to future, *according to this determination; it assigns to the* present a directing role in this orientation . . . in which all of the preceding characteristics are brought together" (1990, 76; italics mine). By contrast, "Aion is the locus of incorporeal events, and of attributes which are distinct from qualities. . . . [P]opulated by effects which haunt it without ever filling it up . . . [it is] time: *pure empty form of time.* . . . It is the present . . . of the counter-actualization" (ibid., 165, 168; italics his). The father's ghostlike appearance at the end reveals an investment in the past, but through the potential of the cinematic image to bring the past into the present, through a virtual treatment of space and time. Thus, the pathos of Hsiao-kang's clock changing has resonance in relation to a different conception of history: as becoming. Time as becoming injects difference into repetition in an active—that is, an attentive rather than passive—form: through cinema and its potential to think differently about the real. The film plays humorously not only with clock time but also cinematic time by juxtaposing the visual faces of the clock to the tired faces and bodies of the filmed protagonists imprisoned in time.

What Time Is It There? recalls Henri Bergson's thoughts on comedy and the body: how the body becomes comedic in its rigidity and automatism. The Bergsonian emphasis on "*inelasticity* of character, of mind and even of body" (Bergson in Sypher 1956, 73; italics his) constitutes one part of the tragicomic dimensions of Tsai Ming-liang's film. These attributes are evident in Tsai's films and serve a dual function: they focus on the clock face of habit and repetition but also explore another face of time—duration. Like his 1998 *The Hole* (discussed in chapter 4), *What Time Is It There?* involves bodies trapped in clock time; but it also injects the role of film within film by inserting clips from François Truffaut's *Les Quatres cents coup* (*The 400 Blows*, 1959) and referring to Alain Resnais's *Hiroshima Mon Amour* (1959) and, thus, a conception of cinematic time. However, the film appears less concerned to produce humor, in the sense of slapstick or gags, than to explore philosophic, historical, and aesthetic questions in its focus on memory, time, habit, and repetition through characterization and the uses of the body and the city landscape. Further, as in *The Hole*'s counter-history, the film's emphasis on time seems to experiment with forms for escaping from history that are connected to the comic and its bodily expressions.

The film begins with an image of an unidentified exhausted man standing at a sink with the sound of running water. This single-take sequence follows the man's movements from a small kitchen to a table. Placing a plate of food beside him, he rejects the food, smokes a cigarette, rises, calls out the name Hsiao-kang, sits again, continues to smoke, and finally rises and goes to the rear of the kitchen, opens a door, moves a plant aside, and gazes vacantly into space. This opening offers clues to the film's style in its use of long takes, offering a sense of the everydayness of place and "idle periods" with a dreamlike evocation of slowness, boredom, and of bodily exhaustion. This opening scene captures cinema's ability to expose the attitudes and gestures of the body, specifically in terms discussed by Deleuze on the effect of Antonioni's films: "To think is to learn what a non-thinking body is capable of, its capacity, its postures. It is through the body (and no longer through the intermediary of the body) that cinema forms its alliance with spirit, with thought"—and, ultimately, with "the 'unthought' life" (1989a, 189).

An abrupt cut from the image of the kitchen to a young man, Hsiao-kang (Lee Kang-sheng), in a taxi on the way to a mausoleum reveals him holding a covered funeral urn. He is the person called for by the man in the opening sequence and turns out to be the son, carrying the father's remains. From the window can briefly be seen images of the traffic and high-rise buildings of Taipei as the young man passes into a tunnel and addresses the urn. The third cut is a middle distance shot of Hsiao-kang at the mausoleum with two women, his mother and a priest's assistant, and a male priest/conjuror who inserts the urn into a requisite compartment for the remains of the dead and performs the prescribed prayers, while the others chant.

On Hsiao-kang's return home from work the next day, another ritual of mourning performed by the conjuror and witnessed by Hsiao, his mother, and two other women ensues. A table is covered with food and flowers and a fish tank containing a large fish visible at the extreme left of the frame, an image that will recur significantly several times thereafter. The food is blessed by the conjuror, and he directs the mourners to bow before the table of food as he chants. The ritual continues with the mother pouring a bowl of water for the priest to bless, as Hsiao removes remnants from the table and burns them. In another subsequent scene, the priest dedicates the bowl of water to the dead, telling her that "this is yin-yang water" on which he is casting a spell, and it is to be placed on an altar in the room in case the dead returns. The sign of his return will be the diminution of water in the bowl. Encouraged by him, the mother increasingly begins to blur the boundaries between the physical and virtual by beginning to act as if the dead man will literally return in his body.

Images of flowing liquid will play a critical role in this film, as they do in *The Hole*. At night, in the almost completely dark apartment, Hsiao-kang's shadow emerges as he slowly approaches and gazes at the large fish tank that is to become identified with the father. The dialogue is minimal, and there is no musical accompaniment—only the sound of the water flowing in the tank to enact the slow passage of time as an experience of loss and mourning. Hsiao walks furtively into the room, looks about, and hastily exits. In contrast to the conjuror's designation of the water as symbolizing rebirth, the following scene offers a physical image of fluidity in the image of Hsiao urinating in his bedroom. Conceding to his mother's concern about circumventing the return of the dead man, Hsiao-kang, in his room, lying in bed, abruptly throws the covers aside, rises, and looks for a container. He finds a plastic bag and, with his back to the camera, slowly urinates into the bag (for over a minute) and then quickly runs back to the bed. His mother, in the kitchen, slowly, checks the condition of the altar for signs of life, thus increasing the intensity and fixity of her mourning.

Again in an abrupt transition, Hsiao is at work selling watches on the street, when a young woman Shiang-chyi (Chen Shiang-chyi) approaches and wants to buy a dual-time watch for going abroad. She insists on wanting his watch and no other, though he informs her that, since he is mourning, it would be improper to part with it. However, a tenuous bond is forged. He promises to find her another similar timepiece and gives her his phone number. Shiang-chyi is now filmed inside a bakery as she emerges with a box of sweets. She telephones him, and, though he is still reluctant, informing her that his watch would "give her bad luck," she responds that, as she is a Christian, this does not trouble her. Having successfully bargained, she hangs up the receiver, returns to Hsiao's stand, pays for his watch, sets the time, and places it on her wrist. When asked by him where she is going, she says "Paris," and he responds, "France." Before she leaves, she gives him the packet of sweets. Though this is the last time they will be together, her persona, identified with her destination, lingers in Hsiao's memory—as he does in hers—through the trope of the watch.

The world of clock time is reinforced by images of the shop, crowded with timepieces of every conceivable size and shape, where Hsiao-kang acquires his watches to sell on the street. He returns to the street with his display case filled with assorted watches. Looking bored, he bangs one angrily on a railing to garner the attention of pedestrians emerging from an underground passage and walking on the street.

If Hsiao-kang's mother is fixated on turning the clock back, he is identified with images of changing time, exemplified by his owning a watch that indicates local and European time. However, he tries to comply with his mother's demands, though the sorcerer's rituals are not congenial to him. For example, when he returns home from work for a meal, he picks up a cockroach on the kitchen floor. She berates him, reminding him that

FIGURE 3.6. *What Time Is It There?* Tsai, 2001.

no living creature must be killed for forty-nine days after the death of a person, since it would hinder his or her resurrection. Indifferent to her, Hsiao drops the cockroach into a fish tank displayed prominently in the next room. Chastened, Hsiao-kang sits alone and eats. If the mother becomes obsessed with the actual resurrection of her dead husband, Hsiao-kang's own mourning and attendant loneliness will settle on his memory of Shiang-chyi, whom he identifies with Paris, French cinema, and more particularly with the films of Truffaut. In his room, Hsiao-kang sets his clock to Paris time, while his mother, alone in the kitchen, prepares food, examines the water on the shelf where the priest has placed it, and walks to the porch to water the father's dying plant. Hsiao-kang becomes preoccupied with altering the time on all the clocks throughout the house to Paris time. Becoming increasingly nomadic, he goes to a video store and asks to rent a French film (Tsai has expressed his predilection for films of the French New Wave); thus, the film further implicates film time, aligning it to a history of cinema and more specifically to questions of spectatorship. Rejecting popular Taipei and Hong Kong videos as well as Resnais's *Hiroshima Mon Amour*, he selects Truffaut's *The 400 Blows*. At night in bed, he views Antoine Doinel, played by a young Jean-Pierre Léaud, standing on a spinning fairground ride that resembles a zoetrope (Bloom 2005, 319)—an image aligned to the moving Ferris wheel in the final moments of the film, suggesting cyclical rather than linear time.

Another episode from the video of the Truffaut film is an extended scene of the young Doinel on the street stealing a bottle of milk, gulping it down, and discarding the bottle. (Later in the Tsai film, an adult Léaud will appear as himself.) Tsai's allusion to the child is reminiscent of Deleuze's comment on the role of the child in postwar cinema, where "the character has become a kind of viewer... affected by a certain motor helplessness... that makes him all the more capable of seeing and hearing" (Deleuze 1989a, 3). It is not only the child, afflicted in this manner, who "records rather than reacts." Others too are "prey to a vision, pursued by it or pursuing it" (ibid.).

Hsiao-kang's synchronization of the clocks is paralleled by scenes that are counterparts to the actions of the three characters enthralled to clock time, foregrounding the characters' loneliness and vain expectations of physical contact and solace. The long-take camera work accentuates the burden of time as a perpetual waiting for something to happen. The film takes another absurd route when Hsiao-kang is summoned from bed by his mother. Unaware of his changing of the clocks, she calls him to the kitchen to examine how the altered time on the clocks portends the return of his father. Further, she will cover all the windows to block entering light and thus keep out signs of time change to accord with the time on the clocks.

Shiang-chyi's visit to Paris produces boredom, uncertainty, and disenchantment. Her encounters with the city are a parallel expression of the intolerability of self and the weight of time, from which Hsiao-kang suffers, as does his mother. In her hotel room, she sits on the bed, munches candy, puts on her dual-time watch, gazes at it, and goes to a bathroom, where she scrutinizes her face. Later, she is seen in a café sitting alone at a table, looking off into space. The viewer is aware of the rear of a man's head in the foreground, but it is not clear if he is trying to make contact with her or she with him. Similarly ambiguous is a view of Hsiao-kang in his car listening to traffic report about a dog on the highway to be avoided and about other hazards, ending with a truncated report about what happened to the dog.

Shiang-chyi's lonely touristic saga unfolds further in a restaurant, where she struggles to read the menu. Observing her confusion, a Frenchman seated behind her tries to explain the contents, but she rejects his advice and insists on having an English menu. In a parallel scene, Hsiao-kang sits at a counter by a nearby waterwheel; he rises and angrily throws his watch into the water. His loneliness is further rhymed by Shiang-chyi in Paris. Entering the subway, she is stopped by inspectors; awkwardly she spills the contents of her purse as she seeks her ticket. She stands and waits by the subway tracks, she on one side, a young man on the other. A train comes; the man gets on, looks at her on the platform; but she remains rooted, waiting for another train.

In Taipei, Hsiao-kang sits in a restaurant alone, surrounded by bowls of food, and then repairs to a shop with clocks, which he sets to Paris time. Observed by a young man, Hsiao-kang wanders along a corridor, overturns a waste container so that he can stand on it, takes down a clock on the wall, hides it, and enters a movie theater. The theater is not full, and there is no indication of a film playing, but the young man seen earlier in the clock store comes to sit beside him. Hsiao-kang moves away, leaving the clock on the floor. The young man picks it up and exits. Hsiao-kang follows him into the toilet to find the young man, pants down, holding the clock over his lower parts in a homosexual invitation that Hsiao-kang angrily rejects.

In still another moment of waiting, his mother rises from her bed at midnight, goes to the kitchen, and cooks a meal. She enjoins Hsiao-kang to eat with her, serves him, and sets another place before an empty chair at which she places bits of food in a bowl, presumably for the return of the dead. The moment is interrupted by an image of Shiang-chyi soaking her feet in a tub in her Paris hotel room, eating candy and listening to sounds emanating from an upper floor that bring her out into the corridor and up the stairs to listen at the closed door above her room.

The spectator processes these images differently from conventional historicizing about modernity or postmodernity. Its portrayal of the banal and commonplace, its tired bodies of death and loss, solicit the spectator to think differently about time and history as they connect to the senses. Time determines the quality of the image to foreground how the characters are "suffering less from the absence of another than from

FIGURE 3.7. Another missed encounter, *What Time Is It There?* Tsai, 2001.

their absence from themselves," replacing "'traditional drama with a kind of *optical drama* lived by the character'" (Deleuze 1989a, 9, in part quoting Claude Ollier). This statement applies to the mother in her darkened chambers, to the nomadic Hsiao-kang, and to Shiang-chyi in Paris. The film incrementally introduces synchronous situations, involving loneliness, obsessional behavior, and the quest for intimacy through sex. In each of the segments involving the three characters, boredom, uncertainty, and preoccupation with loneliness are rhymed: the mother masturbating while gazing at a photograph of her husband; Shiang-chyi in a lesbian encounter with another tourist; and Hsiao-kang's sex with a prostitute in his car. These scenes, writes David Barton, are less instances of a "sexual fling than absorbed despair and desperate loneliness masking as rather aborted lust" (2008, 288). By contrast to this melodramatic description of the characters, Aysegul Koc holds that the film "is unaccustomedly true to ordinary life details ... taking a position against contemporary fast-paced, plot-driven commercial cinema," revealing instead "a cinema of patience, reflection, a subtle sense of humor and a cynical hope for life" (2003, 57).

Shiang-chyi's encounter with Jean-Pierre Léaud, in the Montmartre cemetery, is a further link between Tsai's and Truffaut's films, as well as a diegetic link between Shiang-chyi and Hsiao-kang as another moment of missed opportunity. Preoccupied as she is with hunting in her purse for a telephone number (no doubt Hsiao-kang's), she fails to register where she is or to acknowledge the advances that Jean-Pierre has made toward her. She shares with Hsiao-kang a relation to the world expressed in her ineptness in encounters that seem threatening in their strangeness and produce a mechanical, banal, or hallucinatory response on her part. However, through the equivalent of pillow shots and long-take episodes in the vein of Yasujirō Ozu's films, Tsai produces spaces of contemplation for the spectator, if not for the characters.

In the case of Shiang-chyi, in the Tuileries asleep aligning with the final image of Hsiao-kang's mother asleep after masturbating before her husband's photograph), she is filmed as oblivious both to the children playing with her luggage floating in the water and to its retrieval by the ghost of Hsiao-kang's father, who appears and then diminishes in long shot, moving toward a Ferris wheel in the distance that begins slowly to rotate. At the end of the film, all three dominant characters are asleep, the ghost disappears, and the wheel turns, another reminder of time and of counter-history. The film's investment in history has been noted. For instance, Guo-Juin Hong has written of this film that Taipei offers a view of the postcolonial city portrayed as "an image of coalescence, if not of willing complicity... of twenty-first century Taipei" where "a listless individual manipulates the time of a clock atop a stock exchange office building... to synchronize a foreign time with that of the local space" (2011, 184).

For David Barton, however, the film's historicizing is connected to colonialism and postcolonialism in its "baroque melancholy in his [Tsai's] mourning for dead fathers" (2008, 281). In the vein of Benjaminian allegorizing, it is built on the material and immaterial "ruins" of the past. A scene showing the removal of a name on a statue dedicated to of Chiang Kai-shek, the father of Taipei, exemplifies the death of a nation. Similarly, the father's death plays a central role in this film as a work "under the spell of the father" (ibid., 283), a cinematic father, Taipei's father, and Tsai's own father. The film's counter-history resides in the invitation to the viewer to consider what Hanjo Berressem has described in relation to Deleuze's investment in [counter-]history as involving "the laws of forms and formations, of metaphysical relation, psychic affection and contemplation. Its time is that of immaterial, empty durations that encompass past and future but that always 'miss' the present, and its history is an aionic history of pure effects" to become humorous (2012, 206). The counter-historical as enacted by Tsai's film invites the spectator to recognize the ineptness of the characters' relations to each other, to nature, time, death, and to what they have missed. On this open note of waiting, the film ends.

4

Minoritarian Cinematic Forms as Counter-History

There is a universal figure of minoritarian consciousness as the becoming of everybody, and that becoming is creation. One does not attain it by acquiring the majority. The figure to which we are referring is continuous variation, as an amplitude that continually oversteps the representative threshold of the majoritarian standard, by excess or default. In erecting the figure of a universal minoritarian consciousness, one addresses powers (*puissances*) of becoming that belong to a different realm from that of Power (*Pouvoir*) and Domination.

—Deleuze and Guattari, *A Thousand Plateaus* (1987, 106)

THIS CHAPTER EXPLORES counter-historicizing through the ways in which "a deterritorialising minority uses the language of the dominant, major voice but makes it speak in a minor way" (Martin-Jones 2008, 36). Minority expression addresses "a people who do not yet exist ... a cinema of the body ... a potentiality defined by relations and forces, or the power to affect and be affected" (Rodowick 1997, 154). These relations and forces are aligned to an emphasis on time that puts all into crisis, involving connections between past and present, objective and subjective perception, physical and mental sensations, and indeterminacy between the real and the imaginary. Time is present in both the movement- and time-image, indirect in the former and direct in the latter.

Different circuits of, and splits in, time (as forking) are manifest through flashback, memory, recollection, and dream images, but Deleuze asserts that it is "the disturbances of memory and failures of recognition" that provides "the proper equivalent of the optical-sound image" (Deleuze 1989a, 55). In discussing a cinema of the body and its relations to thought, Deleuze introduces his view of "modern political cinema" as it "applied to the West" (ibid., 216–17) through forms of minoritarian filmmaking. His examples are largely drawn from black American cinema and films from Turkey, South America, Quebec, and Africa. In their book *Kafka* (1986), he and Guattari elaborate their conception of a mode of fabulation that narrates relations between author and subject through intercessors, real and not fictional characters, engaged in a process of making legends and stories that produce "collective utterances" (Deleuze 1989a, 222).

In its modes of addressing history, language, and styles, minority expression "does not entail a third world because it develops a concept based on singular traits that may just as well be located in any world—in our world.... The conditions of the minor do not refer to any infinitely particularized attribute nor to any transcendental condition... *not the third world but the third person*," the impersonal figuration of "a people to come" (Flaxman 2012, 229–30; italics his). Thus, minority expression entails a reconfiguring of national, ethnic, racial, and sexual identity (Martin-Jones 2008, 36) to render narration as absurd, estranged, and queer, deviating from existing forms to invent the possibility of *becoming* by creating a narration to express the forces of domination and exclusion misrecognized in, or occluded by, a dominant major voice. Martin-Jones (2008) argues for a broader spectrum of connections between movement-images and time-images exemplary of different historical and global contexts and different considerations of genre and spectacle, evident in instances from silent cinema, silent and sound narrative forms from other nations, and from pre- and post–World War II cinema. My discussion of comic, horrific, and, in this chapter, minoritarian films identifies these forms as global, as popular and generic, and as counter-historical in their irreverent treatment of monumental forms of memorializing.

In another work, *Difference and Repetition* (1994), Deleuze contends with prevailing philosophies of history to question investments in the past, memory, and repetition exemplified in reigning forms of historicizing:

> Historians sometimes look for empirical correspondences between the present and the past, but ... this network of historical correspondences involves repetition only by analogy or similitude. In truth, the past is in itself repetition, as in the present, but they are repetition in two different modes that repeat each other. Repetition is never a historical fact, but rather the historical condition under which something new is effectively produced. (1994, 90)

While Deleuze confronts images of history, his focus on the cinematic image via the time-image is revealed in crisis through a journey form (the trip ballad), faltering sensorimotor responses, concerted and multiple organization of clichés, and a conspiratorial plot. Also, he explores whether it is possible to extract from this situation the possibility of thinking differently about the relation of cinema and thought through expressions of bodily sensations and their connections to becoming. Deleuze's writings on minority forms are an engagement with concepts that account for the power (or "impower" [*impouvoir*]; 1989a, 166) of the cinematic image to give rise to different modes of perception, sensation, and thinking that run counter to more explicit forms of history making. Minoritarian expression is political: "its cramped space forces each individual intrigue to connect immediately to politics" (Deleuze and Guattari 1986, 17). Out of this intrigue, a collective enunciation emerges but "only as diabolical powers to come or revolutionary forces to be constructed" (ibid., 18). In minoritarian expression, to borrow Walter Benjamin's words, "the adherents of historicism actually empathize ... with the victor" and thus affirm existing social and political conditions of mastery (1969, 256), and individual conflicts become political and collective in enunciation. This literature sets out to summon a missing people through a pedagogy that involves failure and minorizing the language through stuttering or stumbling (Deleuze 1989a, 109).

Counter-history, as I derive it from Deleuze's thinking on becoming, is "its acting counter to the past and therefore on the present, for the benefit, let us hope, of a future" (Deleuze and Guattari 1994, 112). Deleuze's concern with history may be omnipresent, but it is starkly different to prevailing conceptions of history making, in particular not only as constituting an escape from it but as offering alternatives to a univalent and determinist assessment of events. Although one can make a case for Deleuze as having a philosophy of history that contains empirical claims—an ordering of events, a theory of causality, and a sketch of the "main stages of actual human history" (Lampert 2006, 1)—Deleuze's conceptions of history undertake a more complex political and philosophical direction. This direction relies on the notion of "incompossibility" (Deleuze 1994, 48) expressed in *Difference and Repetition,* where Deleuze introduces Gottfried Wilhelm Leibniz's conception of possible worlds (ibid., 47–48, 197) and Jorge Luis Borges's treatment of time as a game of chance that involves the possibility of "'various futures'" (ibid., 116). Steven Shaviro underscores the affinity between Deleuze's thinking and that of Alfred North Whitehead on complexity, "one that does not exclude dissonances, apparent contradictions, and incompossibilities" (1992, 25–26).

Deleuze projects the viewer into a time in which the corporeal and the virtual intersect in relation to his conception of becoming, not as a replication of existing forms of historicizing but as a philosophic intervention in rethinking conceptions of agency and causality through the intervention of time. For Deleuze, "becoming is the principle of time as force, and time is the expressive form of change: the fact that the universe never stops moving, changing, and evolving" (Rodowick 2010b, 100). The force of becoming depends on a nonlinear conception of time in which contingency operates to conceive of history through creativity as invention to produce the new, to release the entrapment of the event in forms of thought that resist change. In *What Is Philosophy?,* becoming is not History (there identified with a capital "H"), but an escape from it rendering it as philosophy:

> Becoming is the concept itself. It is born in History, and falls back into it, but is not of it. In itself it has neither beginning nor end but only a milieu. It is thus more geographical than historical. Such are revolutions and societies of friends, societies of resistance, because to create is to resist: pure becomings, pure events on a plane of immanence. What History grasps of the event is its effectuation in states of affairs or in lived experience, but the event in its becoming, in its specific consistency, in its self-positing as concept, escapes History. . . . History is not experimentation, it is only the set of almost negative conditions that make possible the experimentation of something that escapes history. Without history experimentation

would remain indeterminate and unconditioned, but experimentation is not historical. It is philosophical. (Deleuze and Guattari 1994, 110–11)

Deleuze's philosophical thinking as experimentation in the creation of new concepts depends on "a particular kind of belief" that only "replaces knowledge when it is belief in this world" (Deleuze 1995, 136). Thus, becoming resides belief in the body, by "giving discourse to the body, and for this purpose, reaching the body before discourses, before words, before things are named: the 'first name,' and even before the first name" (Deleuze 1989a, 172–73). His conception of this cinema of the body as "the germ of life" (ibid., 173) is aligned to Foucault's genealogical conceptions of "effective history" via Nietzsche through the parodic, the farcical, and masquerade that challenge traditional forms of knowledge as they affect historicizing (Foucault 1977, 157,160). In his articulation of minority literature and filmmaking, particularly exemplified by the writings of Franz Kafka, Deleuze too challenges conceptions of origins, identity structures, and essentialist conceptions of the body. This form of narration relies on inventing stories through a "collective assemblage of enunciation [that] can be defined as nothing less than the deterritorialization of the subject" (Flaxman 2012, 215). Deleuze's focus on minority forms falls within the regime of the time-image that characterized the search for a "new thinking image" (Deleuze 1986, 215) by introducing weak connections, hallucination, trance, nonchronology, and deterritorializing forms of language, all of these identified in various modes with cinematic New Waves, the films and the writings of Pier Paolo Pasolini, and particularly with minor cinema. Moreover, "the direct-image of time is an ever renewable possibility recurring throughout the history of cinema" (Rodowick 2010b, 108). If the movement-image applied to belief in a world transformed, the time-image applied to a world in which belief is renewed by confronting images of thought based on the world as it is.

The films discussed in this chapter are drawn from art films and from popular European, Hispano-Latin American, Asian, and African forms to elaborate on the political and aesthetic character of minority discourses that contaminate familiar styles, genres, and national cinemas, as well as cinematic language. In the first main section, I discuss the biopic, a staple of film and television, to reimagine the telling of actual stories that resist hagiography, are irreverent to the past, develop a counter-historical language through spectacle, fictionalize real subjects, and produce a pedagogy "to read the visual" (Deleuze 1989a, 247), as in the case of *La prise de pouvoir par Louis XIV* (*The Rise of Louis XIV*; Roberto Rossellini, 1966 [TV]) and *An Angel at My Table* (Jane Campion, 1990). Many of these films selected do not deal explicitly with the historical past. Rather, these films are selected because they offer an *access* to the past that is investigative and inventive in narration, often overturning conventional modes such as biopics, musicals, and historical films. In each of the biopics, the viewer is compelled to confront a form of historicizing that marks the passage from an older world to the emergence of a newer aesthetic and political world, in which the protagonist emblematizes this struggle into emergence.

In the second main section, I examine three films that, through their emphasis on music and dance, explore the deterritorialization of the subject in the foregrounding of the tango as an aesthetic and political form. *El exilio de Gardel: Tangos* (*Tangos: The Exile of Gardel*; Fernando Solanas, 1985), *Tango* (Carlos Saura, 1998), and *The Tango Lesson* (Sally Potter, 1997) involve portraits of political and self-imposed exile to enact the potential of becoming. The final main section first reexamines two African films, *Camp de Thiaroye* (*The Camp at Thiaroye*; Ousmane Sembène, 1988) and *Hyènes* (*Hyenas*; Djibril Diop Mambéty, 1992) as counter-historical cinematic treatments that enact the elimination of the people and how the terms of that loss invoke the possibility of a people to come. In Tsai Ming-liang's *Dong* (*The Hole*, 1998), which explores the dystopic and the utopian by anastomosing the disaster film to the musical, the viewer is treated to another form of minoritarian expression that involves the everyday, the private, and the public, and where threatened bodies engage with potential through popular forms to imagine different worlds.

THE BIOPIC AS COUNTER-HISTORY

From the earliest years of cinema to the present, the biopic has been a dominant form. The intense interest in creating visual biographies has also migrated to television and even to the Internet, but its status as history remains elusive. Robert A. Rosenstone's definition of the biopic as history on film is "that either individuals are at the centre of the historical process—or are worth studying as exemplars of lives, actions, and individual systems we either admire or dislike" (2006, 90). The biopic joins historical films in their investigative and critical stance toward the figures they examine and the questions they raise about authority, power, and forms of control, as well as implied or overt conceptions of subaltern life. This genre has received much less critical attention than others and was described by one film scholar as "the butt of jokes rather more often than it has been the focus of serious analysis" (Neale 2000, 54).

The difficulty of developing a "serious analysis" of the biopic resides not only in its hybrid character, its diverse emplacement within other genres (musicals, melodramas, westerns, and crime films, to name a few), but in its complicity with the cult of fame and personality that privileges the individual as the motor of history, focusing especially on the lives of monarchs, political leaders, artists, popular entertainers, and even criminals. The biopic can assume a number of forms: religious portraits of martyrdom (hagiographies), romantic narratives of famous doomed lovers, celebrations of physical and/or psychic triumph over adversity, dramatic recounting of the accomplishments of famous scientists, mythic treatments of national heroes, and various renditions of the rise and fall of entertainers, including theater and movie actors. The tendency to favor biographical narratives is not restricted to Hollywood: it has a long history within transnational cultures.

Often tied to foundational narratives of nation and empire, the biopic as it evolved from early cinema to the era of sound was represented in numerous remakes of the lives of such national heroes as royalty, statesmen, military heroes, poets, painters, and scientists. Early Italian silent films featured such historical figures as Hannibal, Scipio Africanus, and Catiline, involving imperialism, masculine leadership, and nationalism, thus linking ancient Rome to the Risorgimento, and later to Fascism. The French cinema of the silent era produced biopics of an experimental character, the most notable being Abel Gance's *Napoléon* (1927) and *La Passion de Jeanne d'Arc* (*The Passion of Joan of Arc*; Carl Dreyer, 1928). The Gance film, while it dramatized the life of Napoléon from his time at school to his rise to power, marriage to Josephine, and victories in the Italian campaign, is characteristic of the biopic as a monumental form of historicizing. Gance was never to finish the epic to his satisfaction, but the director's struggles are testimony to the experimental character of the film. In its treatment of his protagonist, a union of epic and melodrama, cinematic theatricality creates a romantic spectacle of the great man who is enigmatic. The excesses of its epic style have occasioned controversy as to whether the film is a celebration of or critique of Napoléon as fascist dictator (King 1984, 140). The film has rightly been regarded as an exploration of the potential of the movement-image to generate strong affective responses through spectacle evoked through tableaux, rhythmic editing, postured acting, superimposition, and double and triple screens to create a moving epic cinema of the sublime.

Similarly, the German cinema produced biopics of Frederick the Great, Ohm Krüger, Friedrich Schiller, and Otto von Bismarck, often starring Emil Jannings in films emphasizing German power and accomplishments. The cinematic attractions of colonialism and empire were evident in British biopics focusing on the lives of Queen Victoria, Benjamin Disraeli, William Pitt the Younger, and Florence Nightingale. Actors who played these eminent figures basked in the reverence accorded them. The popular biopic is elusive, hard to define, and harder to situate within a single genre form, since its style often depends on the profession of its subject (for example, musician, political leader, actor, scientist). Moreover, it concentrates on actual people, living or dead, associates with the identifiable historical, and has a tendency to unite fact and fiction.

A number of prestigious nineteenth-century historians were instrumental in advancing forms of monumental history dependent on the figure of the "great man" as a motive force of historical process. Thomas Carlyle emphasized the distinctiveness of such men from the common run of humanity (White 1973, 148). He held that the actions of these exceptional individuals (for example, Frederick the Great) were instrumental in imposing order over chaos. The Enlightenment was more skeptical about the achievements of individuals. Johann Gottfried Herder espoused a view of historical progress characteristic of an organicist conception of life in which individuals and groups were united by nature *and* spirit and, hence, could overcome their natural tendencies. Such a struggle could harmonize natural and spiritual tendencies in the direction of purposive action and "movement toward a goal" (ibid., 72). Relevant to thinking about the process of biography is its dramaturgical character, where history is viewed as a theater in which antagonistic forces engage in moral combat to arrive at or move toward moral and political enlightenment. A narrative of progress was bolstered through rhetoric and affect. The biopic has offered numerous portrayals of exceptional individuals implicated in a drama of agency, social, and historical progress.

Deleuze's writings on cinema are an engagement with philosophical concepts to account for the power of the visual image in animating belief and confidence in historical agency, as well as symptoms of its decline. His is not an empirical study of history proper but an analysis of cinema's expressive uses of the body, of faces, and of spaces that engender affects organized around action and, hence, directed toward transformation of a community—or, conversely, its dissolution. Deleuze describes it thus: "monumental history considers effects in themselves, and . . . the only causes it understands are simple duels opposing individuals" (1986, 150). As I discussed in chapter 1, Deleuze explores how this form of monumental history inspired the American cinema of the pre–World War II years:

> The ancient or recent past must submit to trial, go to court, in order to disclose what it is that produces decadence and what it is that produces new life; what the ferments of decadence and the germs of new life are, the orgy and the sign of the cross, the omnipotence of the rich and the misery of the poor. A strong ethical judgment must condemn the injustice of "things," bring compassion, herald the new civilisation on the march. (1986a, 151)

Deleuze identifies this epic mode of cinematic historicizing with a crisis in belief related to the unsteadiness, if not waning, of the movement-image that he regards as being connected to,

> in no particular order, the war and its consequences, the unsteadiness of the "American Dream" in all its aspects, the new consciousness of minorities, the rise and inflation of images both in the external world and in people's minds, the influence on the cinema of the new modes of narrative with which literature had experimented, the crisis of Hollywood and its old genres. (ibid., 206)

The movement-image involves situations that were once globalizing, based on universal assumptions about monumental and antiquarian history, but the cinema of the time-image can be understood better as relying on crystals of different layers of broken time. This crystalline narration is evident in the cinema through the presence of water, mirrors, and seeds as caught up in formation and growth, or (as in sound) the musical ritornello or gallop to convey passing time. This narration "presents differences in the present that are *inexplicable* and alternative versions of the past whose truth or falsity are *undecidable*" (Rodowick 1997, 86; italics his). Not only does Deleuze question prevailing orthodoxies about chronology, but he also probes different cinematic expression to investigate the possibility of the emergence of a new mental, thinking image (Deleuze 1986, 215). The mental image is more fully realized through the French and later German New Waves that enabled "an analytic of the image, implying a new conception of cutting, a whole 'pedagogy' which will operate in different ways" (Deleuze 1989a, 22). This pedagogy is instrumental in establishing differential relations to time that dislodge reductive and univalent forms of habitual recognition derived from historicism to open onto an understanding of the creative dimension of counter-history.

The time-image in its smallest circuits brings past and present into coexistence, the present being actual, the past virtual. This creates a (historical) process with (a) many entrances, (b) repetition in different forms, and (c) characters and viewers situated in a position of uncertainty, if not of skepticism, all of which contribute to an understanding of Deleuze's distinctions between the cinema of action and that of time. In his description of the action-image, Deleuze describes a cinema in which becoming is real but not actual, ideal without being abstract. The world of the time-image, inhabited as it is by seers, somnambulists, counterfeiters, and imposters, is symptomatic of changing relations in the world as expressed through modern cinema, whose greatness lies in exploring new links to the image through the process of becoming. If the crisis of the action-image refers largely to a world in which a belief in the unity of "man and the world" is severed (Deleuze 1989a, 169), various expressions of the time-image reposition film characters and the viewer in relation to "an imaginary gaze" that refers "to the lost gaze of the being who is absent from the world as much as from himself" (ibid., 9). Deleuze's description of the imaginary gaze applies to certain historical/biographical films produced in Europe in the 1960s and 1970s and to other non-European films from the 1990s to the present.

COUNTER-HISTORY AS SPECTACLE AND PEDAGOGY: *THE RISE OF LOUIS XIV*

Pre–World War II biography had an affinity for historical representation expressed through the action-image, in which historical actors and agents can act only on the condition that they identify themselves with recognizable figures from the past. Biopics such as *Queen Christina* (Rouben Mamoulian, 1933) and *The Scarlet Empress* (Josef von Sternberg, 1934) offer the spectacular face of theatricality, closer to the rhetorical conventions of the stage, through tableaux, and stylized acting. In such films as Rossellini's *The Rise of Louis XIV* and Todd Haynes's *I'm Not There* (2007) it is used as a means of fracturing the identity of the biographical subject through shifting and unreliable perspectives. Theatricality deprives the spectator of transcendental reassurances derived from repetition of past tragic forms. One way, as Deleuze describes it, is by presenting a portrait of powerlessness as prologue to rethinking relations between the world and life through "grasping of the intolerable even in the everyday and insignificant" (1989a, 170). What the viewer confronts in this theater is a focus on images of time "wherein each passing present yields to the unforeseeable, the unpredictable, and the emergence of the new" (Rodowick 1997, xviii), which exemplifies counter-history.

Historical theater becomes counter-history when, like Foucault's "effective history," it "shortens its vision to those things nearest to it" (Foucault 1977, 155). Reminiscent of Carlo Ginzburg's writings on historical method, Foucault's historical sense is closer to medicine in that, as noted in chapter 3, its "task is to become a curative science" (1977, 156). This entails focusing on symptoms and clues based on the senses, intuition, or conjectural knowledge to render a critical perspective on forms of historicizing that apply to the biopic in its incarnation as counter-history. Robert Rossellini's eccentric biopic *The Rise of Louis XIV* is an exemplum of counter-history, an inquiry into "the inner longing for a role and mask, for an *appearance* (*Schein*); an excess of capacities for all kinds of adaptation ... that art of perpetually playing at self-concealment" identified with historical figures (Nietzsche 2001, 225–26).

Set in the seventeenth century in the court of the ascendant Sun King, *The Rise of Louis XIV* becomes a pedagogy. In returning to that earlier time, the film challenges deep-seated assumptions about the past and the present by adopting irreverent dark humor, parody, and even satire. The film as biopic involves Louis's relationship to his mentor Cardinal Mazarin and his resistance to his mother's rule. As the film develops, it shifts to its theatrical staging of two tableaux in Louis's rise to power. The first is the illness and death of the cardinal; the second, the spectacular performance that Louis stages for the court, entailing the preparation and then serving of a sumptuous banquet for himself alone before his courtiers as spectators. The conventional emphasis on the individual is destabilized through a camera language and editing in which the visual and verbal "becomes legible for itself" by tearing away the old style to give rise to a "new space ... in tectonic opposition to the old" (Deleuze 1989a, 247–48), as visible in the palace of Versailles.

Through a self-conscious narration, a deliberate foreshortening of perspective, and a focus on embodiment, Rossellini's biopic addresses "the imponderables of history" (Bingham 2010, 9) rather than its certainties to rescue its real-life subject from static forms of monumentality. However, the film demonstrates that the biopic belongs to a cinematic world that has lost faith in illusions of redemption, though perhaps not in the capacity of the spectator to discern and contemplate difference through a form of theatricality that draws on parody, humor, or irony to place social actors and events in situations that undermine habitual expectations, thereby revealing its designs as counter-history. Louis's rise to power connects to "cinematic uses of the past" (Landy 1996) and prefigures a modernity where "fashion and film industries in close alliance" have formulated "fantasies of the 20th century" (Kunzle 1982, 282–83) through elite and popular culture. Commodity fetishism provides an indispensable source for thinking about the past and present, in relation to changing conceptions of the body as a display that captures "inescapable ambivalences and affective intensities" (Shaviro 1993, vii).

Deleuze conceives of the cinematic body as "necessarily social and political ... bio-vital, metaphysical and aesthetic" (1989a, 194). The body becomes central to a cinema in which "'characters are constituted gesture by gesture and word by word' ... less to tell a story than to develop and transform bodily attitudes" (ibid., 193). Walter Benjamin's writings on historical processes are also concerned with reconfiguring the body in relation to material culture in Ur-modernity. His emphasis in *The Arcades Project* (2002) on objects—fashion, street life, landscapes, and architecture—critically explores the existence of the past in relation to emerging social power, and to its expression in cinema. Dana Polan notes that Deleuze strives "to go beyond the surface fixities of a culture and find those forces, those energies, those fluxes, those sensations that specific socio-historical inscriptions have blocked and reified into . . . stultifying patterns of representation" (1994, 231). In short, Deleuze is invoking a form of theatricalization as a counter-history in which attitudes toward Louis's acquisition of state power and its connections to "surface fixities of the culture" are called into question through a form of inquest rather than a commentary or analysis. Rossellini's form of investigating the past "calls up the comic and the dramatic, the extraordinary and the everyday: new types of speech-act and new structurations of space" (Deleuze 1989a, 248).

Rossellini turned to television as an opportune medium to explore his views on historical narratives and their relation to the spectator. *The Rise of Louis XIV* focuses on the court of the Sun King as an allegory on the relations among commerce, visibility, and absolute power through the machinations of a historical persona likened to a "consummate swindler" (Bondanella 2007, 166). His television film biopic entails a visualization of ceremony, ritual, and *mise-en-scène* as spectacle. Rossellini aimed "to show the customs, prejudices, fears, aspirations, ideas, and agonies of an epoch" (Forgacs et al. 2000, 162). Clearly, he had in mind a different form of historical film that follows "the thread of the transformations in thought" in relation to modernity (ibid., 127), a form of history through audiovisual media that was educational (ibid., 129). In his writings and in his creation of historical films for television, Rossellini asserted that cinema was on the wane (Frappat 2008, 76–79) and that television was a more opportune medium to explore his views on historical narratives for their cultural influence on a "mass audience of nonintellectuals" (Brunette 1987, 260). *The Rise of Louis XIV* being a television film, writes Adriano Aprà, was central to Rossellini's project of "addressing an audience whose gaze was not yet polluted by the 'aestheticisms' of cinema" (2000, 135).

One of the major ways Rossellini sought to convey his sense of history was to prevent the actors from "'acting,' from immersing themselves in a role, appearing natural and lifelike. . . . [T]hey talk like a book, they are not individualised voices but mouthpieces" and must view a performance that is plainly artificial, staged, "'false,'" thus making it "impossible for spectators to merge with the film" (Aprà 2000, 135–36). The film's counter-history is a tantalizing, even cruel exercise in the spectacle of power and the power of spectacle, frustrating the viewer's submission to the image. Rossellini's choice in dramatizing the significance of display and fashion appears eccentric considering the prevailing documents and official histories that address the role of the Sun King, until a close examination reveals how the film becomes a "pedagogy" that focuses on clothing and architecture. Proleptic of connections between Louis and modernity, Louis's machinations are critical to thinking about time as inherent in the exchange value and power of the commodity, as a strategy for controlling his subjects. In the scenes with Louis's finance minister, Colbert (Raymond Jourdan), the viewer begins an education in the power of the visual image to communicate the operations of social power.

As recounted by Rossellini, the film is based on the work of historian Philippe Erlanger. Rossellini claims that he and his writer, Jean Gruault, did not know anything more about the Sun King, "except that . . . he had invented a trick to get the nobles to forget their claims and leave him in peace; he led them to the point where their sole preoccupation was to have ribbons and lace sewn on their clothes and feathers stuck on their hats—in other words, he invented *fashion*, domestication, domination through fashion" (Gallagher 1998, 571–72, quote at 572). Rossellini abandoned a prescripted text for a form of realism that was improvisational, "tricks" as he described it, relying on the actor's physical appearance, awkward behavioral tics, and gestures to dramatize how "men are ruled by appearance, not by the true nature of things" (quoted from film). Rossellini chose for the role of Louis one Jean-Louis Patte, not a professional film actor but an office clerk who had been involved in theater. Patte was a short man, unimposing, and awkward in his appearance and speech, closer to a caricature of Louis's portraits as the Sun King.

Louis's selection of Colbert as his finance minister aligns the monarch and his minister with the pragmatic monetary values of the merchant class. Money, fashion, and the fetishism of the commodity become instruments utilized by Louis in his taking of power and significant in the birth of modernity. The writer Alberto Moravia identifies the strategies of this film as dramatizing a "certain conception of history" showing how "ceremony and ritual ... make the irreal real ... [and] the advent of life as ceremony" (Gallagher 1998, 579). Fashion under Louis's tutelage is inseparable from theater, the arts, clothing, and the architecture of Versailles. The film is an allegory that presents fragments of a passing world and its residual connections to the modern present to explore "the changed relationship between subject and object that results from the 'new' character of commodity production" (Buck-Morss 1997, 97). The film's visualization of the transition from feudalism to modern statecraft in Rossellini's film is in the vein of Walter Benjamin's (2002) cataloging and description of the arcades of Paris. Benjamin's accounting of the Paris arcades takes on resonance through the role of objects as commodities inherent to an emerging world, "captured in the transitory, material images of history itself" (Buck-Morss 1997, 20), applicable to Rossellini's film.

Through early episodes in Louis's taking of power, the viewer is treated to tableaux of a world seemingly impermeable to change and associated with a medieval landscape. Cardinal Mazarin's death, which opens the film, focuses on the archaic social and medical practices portrayed in the bloodletting and smelling of urine by physicians and in the ritual of worldly confession. Mazarin's death makes way for a modern rendition of statecraft embodied in the figures of Colbert and Louis, the latter emerging as the absolutist Sun King, which will have deleterious effects for the lower classes. This new order is based on commerce and intrigue, and on the cinematic uses of spectacle portrayed in Louis's designing the elaborate dress that is to become requisite, as well as the building of Versailles as an awesome instrument of economic and political display. In the initial stages of his rise to power, Louis eliminates plots to his accession involving the machinations of different political factions associated with the Fronde (two groups in opposition to Parlement and another faction of nobles intent on limiting the power of the king). Louis's first decisive act is opposing his mother by imprisoning Nicolas Fouquet, who was initially responsible for the economic administration of the realm, and selecting Jean-Batiste Colbert for his finance minister.

The banquet scene that Gallagher has described as a "baroque funeral mass" (1998, 577) is preceded by a tour of the gardens, where the monarch is trailed by his courtiers. Inside, in a hectic and crowded scene, the

FIGURE 4.1. Louis and his court, *The Rise to Power of Louis XIV*, 1966.

kitchen staff works on an exquisite meal comprising numerous courses, supervised methodically by a pompous master of the kitchen, and overseen by the Musketeers, as if this were preparation for a state banquet. All this labor is expended on a single person and on prodigiousness and prodigality realized in the next shot: Louis alone on the dais, served by his brother and influential members of his court. The scene functions to convey the labor expended on spectacle and its realization in the form of commodities in the service of appearance, implying exchange—not use-value. Louis's courtiers are the captive audience to this visual display intrinsic to the theater of power. Also inherent in the film's design is the insinuation of this moment in the past into the modern, not yet postmodern, present of media.

The film ends with Louis, alone in his chamber, removing his accoutrements as he philosophizes on the role of appearances. He reflects on "how neither death nor the sun can be looked at directly," underscoring the force of the film as parable of modern power and its political implications for the future. The film can be described as an essay on culture as politics made evident through its focus on "the everyday manufacture of objects, small or large works, crafts or industry" (Deleuze 1989a, 247). The spectator is offered "lessons in things" and "lessons in words" to portray the transformation from one historical moment into another through a portrayal of "a struggle marking the itinerary of a world which emerges from one historical moment to enter into another" (ibid., 248). While James Roy MacBean regards the film as conveying a feudal, not modern, view of history (1975, 214), I disagree with the notion that the film is confined to a retrospective position. I regard the film's engagement with history and manufacture as initiating reflections on the role of governance as spectacle and theater that looks ahead in time to the rise of capitalism, spectacle, and consumerism.

The film proffers the spectacle of power, which serves multiple functions to points forward in time: (1) to map a genealogy of spectacle; (2) to offer an alternative way of rethinking historicizing from an ostensible top-down perspective; and (3) to offer a cinematic language through an excessive visual form by "introduc[ing] lines of fracture and disincorporation into imaginary collective bodies" (Rancière 2004, 39). Finally, Rossellini's choice to adopt a televisual mode produced an enigmatic but provocative interrogation of historical representation, introducing revisions to conventional historicizing that contribute to creating a counter-history, particularly through its deformation of the biopic.

The Rise of Louis XIV invites the viewer to identify it as a multifaceted and investigative form of counter-history, not merely about conceptions of the seventeenth-century world but especially about the film's style, in which the union of fact and invention, spectacle and theatricality (not melodrama) suggests an interrogation of historical accounting as a pedagogy for the spectator. The style of the film relies on the gestural rather than on the transparency of the verbal, on dissonance rather than resemblance, and on difference rather than repetition. Rossellini's treatment of the Sun King places the spectator in a position, along with the filmmaker, of trying to engage with the events rather than passively receive them solely through the figure of Louis, and it fosters ambiguity regarding the spectacle.

Though this unusual biopic focuses largely on Louis's "taking of power" in his authoritarian relations to his nobles and family, there is also evidence of a subaltern component that plays an inarticulate but nonetheless critical role in the film This involves the peasants seen briefly at the beginning, the silent tailors who realize Louis's design of sartorial excess, and the many silent cooks who concoct the food for Louis's spectacular banquet. In the final episode, as his subjugated courtiers observe him at his high table, the minoritarian dimension becomes palpable: the people are missing, and the future looms in the spectacle of their disappearance, despite the revolution to come. The film ends with Louis alone, removing his finery, reflecting on appearance and power.

AN ANGEL AT MY TABLE: TELLING WOMEN'S LIVES

In the genealogy of the biopic, there are many narratives of female subjects (Custen 1992), but what has altered, if slowly, are the affective and aesthetic forms for portraying the female subject through a minoritarian language and style. Adapted from New Zealand writer Janet Frame's autobiographical writings, Jane Campion's film translates autobiography into biography to forge bonds between herself, the biopic's subject, Janet Frame, and the viewer. *An Angel at My Table* was originally made as a television miniseries, suggesting that Campion conceived of a more intimate form of viewing the events derived from Frame's autobiography. In addition, she was not without reservations about transferring the work to the big screen (Taubin 2005a), but the television production was successful enough with audiences to merit its subsequent release as a film.

The New Zealand milieu plays a critical role in the film in ways connected to other New Zealand–centered films, such as *Heavenly Creatures* (Peter Jackson, 1994) and *Once Were Warriors* (Lee Tamahori, 1994), that orchestrate issues relating to family, colonialism, and nation. Campion's film further complicates the largely social and ethnic orientation of Lee Tamahori's film, as well as the social-class orientation of Jackson's film. *Angel* as biopic presents different facets of Janet Frame's life—the geographic, familial, and institutional (school, college, and mental hospital)—to illuminate Frame's various engagements with New Zealand culture and their effects on her conception of herself and of her minority relationship to the also minority culture of New Zealand literature, of which people spoke "as if it were a shameful disease" (Frame 1991, 192). Here it seems her

New Zealand writerhood constitutes her as belonging to a minority, while her womanhood as an actual majority relegates her to a political minority.

Angel delves deeply into the public and private landscape of what Deleuze and Guattari call "becoming-woman" (1987, 117) through the act of writing. Frame describes herself virtually as "having been an orphan who discovers that her parents are alive and living in the most desirable home—pages of prose and poetry" (1991, 193). Autobiography merges with biopic. Frame (and Campion in her inclusion of episodes from her own childhood [Bingham 2010, 318]), articulates the struggle for "becoming more than his or her nominal self. . . . [Through writing] the romance of the individual life is exceeded, deterritorialized, and escaped" (Polan 1986b, xxiii). The film portrays Janet Frame's struggle toward "becoming-woman" as a struggle that is "basically a question of the body: the body that is stolen in order to give it a fixed organization" (Pisters 2003, 111).

Frame's story enunciates the minority position of women within the majority culture through a deterritorialization of language, a politicization of the private, and focuses on her individual story as a collective utterance in relation to her being "outside . . . her fragile community" (Deleuze and Guattari 1986, 16–17, quote at 17). Her expression of her sense of difference though the figure of the orphan "forms a block of deterritorialization that shifts with time, the straight line of time, coming to reanimate the adult as one animates a puppet and giving the adult living connections" (ibid., 79). The biopic's underscoring of the figure of the orphan as inherent in the narrative of childhood invokes a sense of homelessness in the world of the working-class family in New Zealand culture. The film enacts Janet's Frame's becoming-woman through a discovery of other worlds of expression. Reading and writing characterize her growth from childhood to adulthood despite (or perhaps because) of her being diagnosed as schizophrenic. Her struggle to find a voice or voices focuses on the creative word as it invokes its power of transforming conceptions of a self in a mundane world. *Angel* dramatizes a class-bound, provincial, colonized culture in which uniqueness is threatened and language offers the young woman a way to get out of the black hole of sameness in the face of the obstacles she confronts.

Campion's narrative of Janet Frame's life begins with her childhood in an economically and socially difficult world made visually evident

FIGURE 4.2. Janet as adult, *An Angel at My Table*, Campion, 1990.

through the cramped quarters in which she lived under the constraints of working-class existence. Alexia Keogh plays young Janet as a plump, somewhat ungainly child, crowned with a flaming nimbus of untamable red hair; Karen Fergusson plays the author as a young woman, and Kerry Fox as an adult.

Through each actor, hair becomes an emblem of Frame's consistent difference from others that carries over into adulthood—and at one point becomes a source of humor, when she is urged to have it tended to. (Later, she complies, only to produce an even more bizarre image of herself as she views herself in the mirror.)

Though the young girl is not a victim of physical abuse by her parents and she has a sense of solidarity with her sisters, her experiences at school provide a vision of an awkward child conspicuously reduced to humiliation by her teacher, who shames her before the class for having taken money from her father's jacket pocket to buy chewing gum for her schoolmates. This episode initiates a number of conflicts for Janet between what is assumed as proper and improper. The episodes at school portray her eccentricities and also tie them to her growing perceptions of separateness from other students. Part One is an interior journey that also hinges on chance encounters that involve a brief friendship with another outcast child, Poppy, which introduces her to sexuality and also to the discovery of fiction through Poppy. However, her father plays a role in separating Janet from Poppy, as punishment for articulating her newfound knowledge about sexual bodies. This episode is narrated less from a bitter judgment of the father and more as a critical stage in Janet's learning about how to channel her responses into the language of fiction, thanks to Poppy's gifting of *Grimm's Fairy Tales*, which leads to Janet's reading further literary works, such as Tennyson's *Idylls of the King* and Matthew Arnold's "The Scholar Gipsy." If her difference functions to isolate her, so does her desire for making herself what she terms "a third person—as children are" (Frame 1991, 65). Janet's childhood entails the threat of the loss of a sense of the real, to which she responds by withdrawal into herself and particularly from her connections to *those* persons she meets as she evolves into a young adult.

The film situates the young Janet in an earlier New Zealand provincial world in which creativity is deemed unprofitable, disruptive, and threatening. However, Frame's autobiography and Campion's biopic are not expressive of harsh or vindictive judgment of this world in which she grew up for its cultural, social, and economic constraints. Despite her attempts at sociability and acceptance, she is often filmed as alone in the natural landscape and in her encounters with teachers and schoolmates. One instance of her apartness is conveyed in a middle close-up shot of her when her brother, Bruddie, is set upon by his schoolmates, while Janet remains at a distance observing his humiliation and failing to extend sympathy to him after the boys depart, leaving him alone to recover. The event is revealing of a vision of minority status, her own and Bruddie's, as outsiders, which she will continue to confront through subsequent events that underscore her encounters with suffering, loss, and death. The first part ends with Janet leaving home for a teacher's training college.

Part Two is introduced by a train journey, rhyming with an earlier train journey with her family to move into their new home. A major image of the film is mobility, from the train ride at the beginning to the family's new home; to Frame's journey to teacher's college; then to Seacliff, the mental institution as a middle region, a center of indifference; and, finally, to Frank Sargeson's trailer, where she finds the freedom to write again after her hospitalization. In the second part, Frame's isolation from others becomes more pronounced, revealing her discomforts with her body, her fearfulness in the presence of others, her growing resistance to becoming a teacher, and her hesitancy about herself as a poet. Starkly pronounced is the emphasis on her ongoing scrutiny of her own mirror image, as well as her discomfort at the observations of others: teachers and schoolmates who reinforce her growing sense of self-division. However, her writing, encouraged by the ambiguous Mr. Forrest, appears compensatory and enables Frame to take risks with her language.

 Frame's decision not to teach is presented wordlessly during a class visitation by an examiner. She stares at the blackboard with the camera intercutting between her, the whispering pupils, and the examiner at the rear of the room. Captured in close-up, she clutches a piece of chalk between her fingers, stands silently, and then merely expresses her cryptic request to be "excused." A decisive moment of betrayal occurs after this episode when Mr. Forrest confronts Janet and tells her, "you have a real talent for writing." Coupled to his praise is a reference to her mental condition couched in terms of concern and condescension: "Lots of artists have suffered from schizophrenia." The close-up in her response to him is indeterminate: Is she seduced by his affirmative assertion about her talent, indicative of an amorphous comprehending of his condescension, or an expression of an overwhelming sense of shock in relation to her ongoing sense of difference? The years of electroshock and confinement at the hospital are revealing of the political and cultural apparatuses in place to contain symptoms that threaten difference. Frame's incarceration in a mental institution for schizophrenia is symptomatic of her foreignness within the culture, made manifest in the alien character of her writing, interpreted by others as expressing bizarre behavior.

 Many of the hospital sequences are visualized through Frame's eyes and present her behavior as quite unlike that of the clinical diagnosis of schizophrenia: it is not paranoiac, hallucinatory, schizophrenia, and dysfunctional. She is not portrayed as either angry or abject: if she is dissociated, this is expressed by her writing, even to the degree of writing on walls if no writing materials are available. Rather, the caretakers are in understated images portrayed as mechanical in their service in the interests of the institution. Her receiving an award for her book, which saves her from a lobotomy, is also treated briefly and in understated fashion. This episode in her life is incorporated with, and instructional about, the stages of her becoming. In discussing the later verification of the faulty diagnosis of schizophrenia that Frame describes in the autobiography, she writes, "I was never withdrawn from the 'real' world, however, although I was convincingly able to 'use' this symptom when the occasion required" (1991, 202). Thus, she articulates yet another dimension of minority expression that dramatizes that writing, for her, is also to become something other than a writer.

Finally, thanks to positive reception for her writings, her journeys take her beyond New Zealand to England, Paris, and Spain, and then a return home. These later journeys expand and deepen her narratives as movements toward "becoming-other" (Deleuze and Guattari 1987, 262). The film portrays Frame's character as both vulnerable and resilient through direct or implied reminders of her story as narrated from a contemporary position of her reflections on the past in the present. Consistently, she is a portrayal of a refusal to succumb to a melodramatic portrait of victimhood and pathos. The transformation from an autobiography to a biopic complicates the narrative's discourses and chronology, by injecting multiple responses to the narration in connecting past and present through voice-over, thus frustrating a strict linear narration. Further, the film understates the conventional familial and romantic conflicts inherent to the conventional biopic that tend to resolve themselves in romance.

The biopic of Janet Frame's life ties her to a minority culture as woman and writer and conveys the multifaceted components of this position: gender, sexuality, social class, and forms of language. Her return to New Zealand does not terminate in a resolution of identity and of reconciliation. The ending of the film maintains her orphan position as one of acceptance that entails her potential to write not "as a solution to the interiorized problems of an individual psychology" but rather for the "possibility of becoming more than his or her nominal self, of trading the insistent solidity of the family tree for the whole field of desire and history" (Polan 1986b, xxiii). This is where the orphan, a minoritarian figure, becomes the motor of a counter-history in which the childlike or mad person is the instrument for thinking issues relating to femininity, nation, and colonialism, an issue referred to earlier in relation to the Tamahori and Jackson films.

MINORITARIAN PEDAGOGY: THE DANCING BODY, THEATRICALITY, AND BIOPOLITICS: *TANGOS: THE EXILE OF GARDEL*

Deleuze refers to the body as that which "forces us to think, and forces us to think what is concealed from life and thought" (1989a, 189). Music and dance enact a migration from one world to another in which the performers enter into the world of another. If one mode of expressing the body is through the daily attitude of the body as a revealer of time as deadline, another mode is the cinema-body-thought link in which, through theatricalization, the everyday body passes through a ceremony (ibid., 190). In this section, through the tango, I explore the dancing body as a form of minoritarian expression and, hence, as counter history.

Initially, a politics of domination is associated with the Spanish conquest in the sixteenth century that brought with it wars of extermination against indigenous populations and hierarchical political control of economic and social life. Independence in the early nineteenth century from the Spanish (briefly British) colonizers perpetuated neocolonialism through an elite white domination acting in the name of progress for its own economic and cultural interests (Savigliano 1995, 21–25). In the late nineteenth century, Argentina embarked on a plan to increase the workforce through subsidizing the immigration of European farmers and artisan classes. The immigrants (mainly Spanish and Italian) in the mid-nineteenth century were lumped with earlier *criollos* (of colonial Spanish and also of Amerindian parentage) to become objects of "purification," "whitening," and campaigns of "national pride" (ibid., 24–28). Both the immigrants and *criollos* came to be identified with the tango that was associated with their cultural and economic dislocation "rooted in long-standing conflicts over race, class, and gender supremacy" (ibid., 32). The tango was originally identified with bordellos and other clandestine meeting places for singing and dancing, and the figures that dominated this underclass world were prostitutes, pimps, criminals, the lady's man, and a language (Lunfardo) tied to mixed ethnic forms, slang, and argot.

Initially, the poetry of the tango was oral, later written, and changed further with its popularization with polite society. It moved to dance halls, cafes, and the theater. Certain names stood out as preeminent: Celedonio

Esteban Flores, "a poet of the people" who expressed the frustrations of the working class, Enrique Santos Discépolo and his brother Armando who were associated with the "grotesco criollo" (a tragicomic form) that was "a cruel art of making fun of others via self-aggrandizement at the come[d]ic expense of others" (Castro 1991, 76–77). The tango enacted a duel that involved antagonism between the creole and the immigrant in which the knife played a critical role in a "battle for cultural survival and a clear demonstration of class conflict" (ibid., 123). The masculine figures included the flashily dressed swell, decked out with a homburg, high heels, fancy vest, and balloon pants (ibid., 117).

By the 1920s and 1930s, the music was disseminated through radio, the phonograph, and cinema. Among the number of culturally prominent tango singers and musicians, Carlos Gardel 1890–1935) stands out as the epitome of creole cultural values. Fernando E. Solanas in *Tangos: The Exile of Gardel* singles him out as exemplary of Argentinian national form and also of the condition of exile. Born in Toulouse, France, but emigrating to Buenos Aires with his mother, he began first as a street singer and performer in neighborhood bars as a tango-cancion singer where his popularity spread to catapult him to national stardom through radio, gramophones, and movies. His successful performances captured the basic conditions of the male tango singer: machismo, self-confidence, financial and social success, "lady's man," albeit with a sense of vulnerability in relation to women, particularly in his attachment to and praise for the mother in his songs.

The situation of tango for women was different from that of the male singers and dancers. The position of woman in this world was largely one of subjection, and the sentiments they expressed through gestures and music communicated deep conflicts in relation to sexual power. Popular lyrics and music were created by prominent women tango performers, particularly Rosita Quiroga, Azucena Maizani, Rosi Rodriguez, Ada Falcón, and Libertad Lamarque and conveyed in their tangos portrayed "women as prostitutes, deceivers, and betrayers" (Castro, 230), as victims. While women were " object[s] of dispute between men as well as ... mediating figure[s] in the resolution of conflict, they were not always passive victims. These *milonguitas* could adopt "a whole array of manipulative stratagems, deceptive behaviors, and strategies for subversion" (Savigliano 1995, 57):

their popularity, among women, in particular, resides in the blatant exposure of insurgencies on the part of victimized heroines (ibid., 71)

Between the 1920s and 1930s modest changes in the Argentinian economy were to have an impact on women's physical appearance and behavior. A gender-neutral figure became apparent not only in sporting bangs, bobbed hair, and smoking but also in the increased position of women as not only subjects of the tango but as tango interpreters (for example, Rosita Quiroga's association with Gardel [Castro 1991, 180]). While women who worked in this dance world were considered déclassé, some dressed in male attire, changed their names, and sang lyrics that were identified with "a manly voice quality" (ibid., 190).

The tango itself was a migrant form moving from the ports of Buenos Aires to the bordellos and bars to legitimate theater and cinema, and on to Paris and London in the early 1900s as well as to the port of Marseille. According to Savigliano, in Paris the tango "reshaped its style, and [was] promoted to the rest of the world as an exotic symbol of heterosexual courtship" (1995, 122). Fashions were created to suit the bodies and footwear of women, and the tango further migrated to popular music halls and revues and became intrinsic to dance schools with a focus on ballroom dancing. The cinema with its penchant for the commodified exotic and spectacular promoted Rudolph Valentino, but in a Frenchified not Argentinian fashion. The Perón years of 1943–55 are another mutation in the transformation of the tango as described by Donald Castro: "Juan and Evita Perón ... were tango.... The rags to riches story of Perón's success from a poor boy in the provinces to president is Gardelian in its scope" (1991, 234). In the last decades of the twentieth century, the tango underwent a political mutation as exemplified in Fernando Solanas's *Tangos: The Exile of Gardel* (1985) aligning it with minority expression.

Tangos is an experimental political film involving Argentina's Dirty War in the post-Peronist period, when a brutal reaction by the military against the Left witnessed the torture, murder, and disappearance of thousands of trade unionists and leftist intellectuals. The years 1976–83 brought on brutal repression by the regime in revoking the freedom of the press and speech, the "disappearance" of at least nine thousand persons, and the exile of Left intellectuals and artists. The film centers on Argentinian exiles during the repressive and brutal reign of the military during this period but takes a different direction from documentary or commercial cinema to extend the sense of exile "multiplied in its meaning... to speak of the exile of those within their countries and outside their countries" (Fusco 1987–88, 59). Self-consciously, *Tangos* functions as a political spectacle, a performance for producing a counter-history of deterritorialized and struggling bodies through the vicissitudes of exile.

From the perspective of displacement and homelessness, the film unsettles conceptions of gender, sexuality, and national identity and appropriates conceptions of the tango as a mobile expression capable for confronting the past that relies on the singing and dancing body. This transnational film is characterized by a dual focus on the affective and performative body in which performance becomes a means of reflection on personal and political loss and on the potential of thinking about a different future. Eschewing the formal and requirements of the revolutionary film, Solanas and his collaborators saw the film "as a prologue, as a detonator for a moment of reflection in the theatre" (Fusco 1987–88, 57). Solanas regarded the film as "an experience of liberty for the spectator" based on emotion in "an attempt to recover history and memory" through the "*tanguedia*—tango with comedy and drama" (ibid., 59).

The tango film's multifaceted treatment of popular music and dance is an example of the dynamic, mutable, destabilizing, and multiple determined appropriations of cinematic forms, involving competing institutional forces (producers, exhibitors, and users) and alternative discursive positions for illuminating the politics of the body through the intimate sexualized movements between a man and a woman (Savigliano 1995, 32). In the case of *Tangos,* other forms of body politic are enacted: one involves men and women's bodies subjected to indiscriminate violence in which the desexualized victims are reduced to bare life (Agamben 1998) and destroyed in the period of the 1970s. Another involves the *tanguedia* as an exploration of survival and the potential of freedom through an expanded conception of exile as deterritorialization not merely "of those within their countries and outside their countries, [but] of exile within their bodies, and of [self-] exile in creation" (Fusco 1987–88, 59).

In its focus on invention, Solanas appropriates history and memory through the ghostly figures of José de San Martino (Michel Etcheverry), a liberator of southern South America; Carlos Gardel (Gregorio Manzur), an icon of mass culture and of political Peronism (Newman 1993, 72); and Enrique S. Discépolo (Claude Melki), another iconic tango performer. Focusing on a group of exiles primarily from Argentina and from France, the film depicts a collective effort on their part to stage their struggles to survive. The film appropriates a number of theatrical, musical, balletic, literary, and cinematic allusions in a style that can be considered as a minority form of expression in its uses of cinematic language that connect the exiles to a personal and political immediacy.

Tangos: The Exile of Gardel is a blending of song and recitative, dance scenes on the street and rehearsals in a theater. The city of Paris is the stage for the exiles' struggles for personal, creative, and economic survival. Not only is the tango a transatlantic artistic form that has travelled between Argentina and Europe from the nineteenth century, but, in the film, it also the image of Paris as a place of refuge from ongoing political crises in Latin America. The Parisian streets, the train and metro stations, parks, and domestic domiciles become a theater to perform different, at times comedic and carnivalesque, individual and group responses to express their alienation and disaffection such as the exiled musicians' adoption of a dog's costume to traverse the city as a form of gaining attention. The subway station and telephone booth provide another locale for diverse characters as they are shown in the inevitable mobile lives they and their visitors are forced to lead. The telephone scenes in the subway station highlight acute conflicts among the exiles where this underground serves as a bridge between life in Paris and torture and repression in Argentina. The use of location and documentary footage of a street demonstration is a collective expression on the part of the larger exilic community to make public the dire situation of the disappearance, torture, and repression of the people in Argentina.

Through the *tanguedia,* the film assembles a cast of exiles: Gerardo, an elderly philosopher/historian; tango dancers such as Mariana and her daughter Maria; Juan Dos, a tango composer and Mariana's lover; Pierre, a self-styled French exile in his own homeland; Florence, a Frenchwoman seeking to aid the *tangueros;* and Misería who aids the group in illegally arranging telephone calls from Paris to Buenos Aires. Through them, the film explores the distinctive ways in which they confront their personal situation, putting time into the body to introduce affect and thinking via the characters and their milieu as, in Solanas's words, "a game which at moments is sad and serious, at other moments, grotesque, and, at others, enjoyable" (Fusco 1987–88, 58).

The sad moments include the departure of Alicia with her children for Barcelona for work that further undermines the collective ties of the group. Also, Mariana's overwhelming melancholy about her inability to acclimatize to life in Paris results in conflicts with and separation from her daughter María. Gerardo's anticipation of the burning of his books is serious, as is the loss of $6,000 to aid the exiles brought by Ana from Buenos Aires that is by accident flushed down a toilet. The disappointment of the group on hearing that their *tanguedia* is "too local" and "too Argentinian" highlights the difficulty of making their plight intelligible to a French audience. Quasi-comic elements involve the Uruguayan Misería's instrumental role in successfully fiddling with a public coin telephone to enable phone contact to Buenos Aires, and, unbeknownst to him, perform his machinations under the surveying eyes of the police, and Mariana's accidental discovery on opening a door in her apartment that her daughter is in bed with a young man and not in school.

Among the grotesque elements is the interspersing of mannequins and tango dancers as partners as well as with the images of angels that float over the ballroom, thus emphasizing a major motif of the film, involving actuality and artifice, history and invention.

The street dances by the young people and the creation of the *tanguedia* are an expression of freedom through song and dance in a mélange of playful and expressive bodies. Similarly, the fantasy appearance of the image of Carlos Gardel evokes an attentive memory that might enable a means of rethinking their past and future. In relation to the deterritorializing dimensions of exile, Deleuze asks in *What Is Philosophy?*

> Are there not territories and deterritorializations that are physical and mental but also spiritual—not only relative but also absolute in a sense yet to be determined. What is the Homeland or Fatherland invoked by the thinker, by the philosopher, or artist? Philosophy is inseparable from a Homeland to which the *a priori*, the innate, or the memory equally attests. But why is this fatherland unknown, lost, or forgotten, turning the thinker into an Exile? What will restore an equivalent of territory, valid as a home? (Deleuze and Guattari 1994, 68–69)

FIGURE 4.3. Mixed *tanguedia* style, *Tangos: The Exile of Gardel*, Solanas, 1985.

The film through tango in a cinematic form seeks to locate answers to these questions. Throughout the film, the group of *tanguedia* dancers is unable to confront how to create an ending for their performance: "We need an ending." The most philosophical and aesthetic dimension of the film involves the issue of closure not merely of the film itself but of a philosophical and political stance toward the future of the exiles. *The Exile of Gardel* struggles with uncertainty, with time as a game of chance that involves the possibility of various futures.

Frank Kermode's sense of an ending recalls Deleuze's reference to time as "change [existing] between remote and imaginary origins and ends that our interests are fixed ... in a freedom which is the freedom of a discordant reality. Such a vision of chaos or absurdity may be more than we can easily bear" (2000, 179). Kermode's comments apply to thinking counter-historically. The cinematic game of *tanguedia* as the coda of the film invokes the possibility of freedom inherent to thinking of history not linearly as Chronos but as Aion, as both past and future in which the event functions in two directions: in terms of both what has happened and what is to happen, "a proximate past and an imminent future" (Deleuze 1990, 63–64). In the idiom of minoritarian expression, the film brings together the deterritorialization of language though exile, the merging of the public and the private, and the potential of a collective enunciation. If the people have disappeared through their persecution, the film seeks to invent a future through invoking the image of General José San Martin along with that of the tango as a memory of that history and contemporary art but as a prefiguration of the people to come inherent in counter-historicizing.

THE POLITICS OF EXILE AS COUNTER-HISTORY: *TANGO*

Both Solanas's *Tangos: The Exile of Gardel* and Carlos Saura's film *Tango* (1998) in their styles explore the politics and aesthetics of the tango through cinematic forms that explore political exile. Both invoke the history of the tango through the figure of Carlos Gardel and other prominent earlier tango performers, and both present a multilayered history as an intersection between past and present. Also, similar to Solanas's film, Saura conceives of the tango as "lending itself to making a story about emotions, which is part of the tango itself" (Willem 2003, 151). In the Solanas film, the affect is generated through the experience of exile during the Argentinian dictatorship. In the Saura film, that dictatorship is evoked not only through the Argentinian experience but also through the memory of the Spanish Civil War. Another major difference between Saura's uses of the tango and Solanas's of the *tanguedia* resides in the reworking of genre. In the *tanguedia,* the emphasis is on tragicomedy, whereas melodrama prevails in the Saura film. Both filmmakers are self-conscious in their uses of the medium: the Solanas film adheres to the narrative strategies of an imperfect, experimental cinema; the Saura film is attached to narrative, romance, and spectacle. Visually, if the Solanas film relies on lightly saturated colors, the Saura film is shot in highly saturated, vivid color.

The Saura film begins with a brilliant red sunset shot of Buenos Aires and then cuts indoors to a shot of a man in bed. Mario Suárez (Miguel Ángel Solá) rises, goes to his typewriter to examine a movie script and then to his bed. Images of a movie camera can be seen as dancers, Cecilia Narova and Carlos Rivarola, perform a contemporary tango (composed by Lalo Schifrin for the film). Mario, seen in silhouette in his bedroom, appears in a rear shot directing the dancers. He is shot in close-up, with his hands holding a knife, and he stabs a woman—his estranged wife Laura (Cecilia Narova). This scene is revealed as a fantasy when the subsequent scene shows her alive in their apartment. Mario rises from the bed and, after pleading for reconciliation, becomes violent toward her. Rhyming the previous scene of violence between the couple, it becomes unclear whether this scene too is not a further extension of his fantasy. In addition, both scenes prefigure the film's exploration of eroticism and violence between males and females through one form of tango as a drama of sexual desire and conflict.

These two scenes set the stage for an investigation of the tango through forms of cinema operating at the limits between real and imaginary, private and political/historical (Barroso and Javier 2001, 115). Thus, the film involves the actual appearances of the film's director Carlos Saura and his fictional counterpart Mario, professional dancers and actors, older tango dancers (for example, Carlos Nebbia played by Juan Carlos Copes), professional dancer Narova as Laura, and new performer Mia Maestro as Elena, the history of tango and its further iterations in the present. The dances of the tango are mirrored through Mario's relationship to his estranged wife but also through the introduction of a new young female dancer. At the request of Angelo Larroca (Juan Luis Gallardo), a powerful and dangerous figure and an investor in Mario's theater production, Mario is asked to try out Larroca's protégée Elena for his troupe. Attracted by her beauty and her graceful tango movements, Mario agrees to test her.

The film features tangos through tryouts for dancers, rehearsals, and also performances, focusing on the nuances of their bodily movements, their affective interactions, and the type of tango they are performing. The camera also foregrounds the musicians: the pianist, cellist, violinist, accordionist, and guitarist. Documentary footage is introduced of earlier tango dancers and musicians, along with a film clip of Carlos Gardel. Laura (Narova) performs a percussion tango with Nebbia (Copes) emphasizing the torsos of the two dancers, their foot movements in close-up, and dramatic lighting and color (alternating red and purple) to express the sensuous and suppleness of the performers. The tangos are examples of mixed forms—tango, ballet, and even jazz—to underscore the dance's potential to address politics and aesthetics in the contemporary terms that the film invokes.

Scenes of Mario's increasing erotic interest in Elena, who has become a principal in the troupe, are intercut with tango scenes that will later become increasingly political and historical: several enact the brutality of sexual politics, another the torture identified with the Argentinian regime, ending with an immigration tango that links Europe to Latin America. The dances are performed in duos, trios, and ensembles. The romance elements converge with the politics. For example, a critical dance scene takes place in a dressing room and focuses exclusively on women with other women dancers. The scene involves a wind machine operated by Mario who vicariously views the women in a simulated dressing room. The camera pans rows of billowing tango costumes and women clothed in '20s costume at the makeup table or dancing together unaware of being observed. Laura invites Elena to dance with her as the other dancers look on. The focus on the women's bodies captures their fluid but disciplined movement, and their intense absorption in each other, bordering on hostility and desire, differs from their dancing the tango with male partners. Elena is dressed in white gossamer dress with a pearl cloche to cover her hair, Laura in a dress in sequined gold top and black gauzy skirt, her hair piled atop a headdress. Mario's gaze in close-up is intercut with varying shots of their bodies, caressing hands, and foot movements that culminate in a lesbian embrace and kiss. Thus, the viewer is given a different view of tango by calling attention to Mario's fantasy of homoerotic desire among women that will connect to the violence of heterosexual desire that was visible at the film's opening and will remain insistent on linking the private with the public.

The erotic scene is a stark visual contrast to the repression and torture dance sequence that enacts the brutality of the Argentinian political regime as well as being reminiscent of the Spanish Civil War. The all-male group, dressed in military fatigues, marches in synchronized steps, disrupted by Elena's agonized close-up as prelude to the sound of a female choral group and intense drum beats.

Elena runs wildly from her aggressors, until she reaches a vision of the soldiers dumping bodies into a pit, framed by piled bodies. The camera also pans women herded at bayonet point by the torturers. The soldiers line both men and women against a wall and shoot, culminating in images of a plain chair for torture as a scene in stark red reveals the women's

FIGURE 4.4. The tango between women, *Tango*, Saura, 1998.

brutalization as they try to escape. The scene ends with a woman falling dead at the feet of her killers. A bell tolls as the screen becomes black, but the sight of women as the objects of violence and torture suggests a connection with the preceding torture scenes.

The subsequent episode reveals that the performance was designed for the principal investors who clap unenthusiastically. Instead of endorsing the performance, they echo Elena's earlier comments about the desirability of forgetting unpleasant things. One man asks, "Why bring up something that has been forgotten?" The investors' consensus is to eliminate a scene that "doesn't belong in a musical" neither in the theater nor cinema. Larroca says, "The generals won't like it," and Mario, citing Borges, responds: "The past is indestructible. Sooner or later things turn up again," and one of those indestructible things is "a plan to destroy the past." In a scene that rhymes with the initial scenes between Mario and Laura when he threatened her, Mario and Elena exchange angry words,

FIGURE 4.5. The tango dance of torture, *Tango*, Saura, 1998.

linking sexual violence to the earlier tango dance of torture, and so their private and public aspects.

An orchestra and chorus performing the Israelites' emotive aria "Va pensiero" from Verdi's *Nabucco* introduce the film's finale, the "immigration tango." *Tango*'s invoking Verdi's famed aria associated in people's minds with the Risorgimento suggests the years of Argentine exile referred to throughout the film. However, the dancers express the mixed population of Argentina, of ethnicities, races, genders, and generations. The group dances to "La cumparsita," the tango melody most familiar to international audiences, but the climax of the scene is not celebratory. Instead, it involves a repetition of violent eroticism. A renegade among the immigrants tries unsuccessfully to seduce the object of his desire played by Elena and, in rage, stabs her, again recalling Mario's fantasy of killing Laura and Larroca's physically threatening Elena. The performance ends with the woman falling to the ground to Larroca's resounding shout, "No." And the "live" Elena rises and leaves with Mario. With the characters offstage and with only an empty set, a movie camera fills the screen to create an unfinished counter-history that identifies the role of cinema to introduce "the labyrinthine game of time, of temporal leaps" to invent "a story that can exist or never did exist" (Ponga 2003, 153, 151).

This counter-history of political and sexual violence relies on the cinema as instrumental in injecting time and, hence, the potential of thinking connections between the real and imaginary through the power of the images to invoke memory. Through recollection and repetition, there is a reciprocal movement between the actual and the virtual so as to introduce attentiveness into habituation. The interplay of theater and cinema by way of visual and sound images is enacted through physical attitudes: gestures of bodies in motion to undermine habituated interpretations of the way things are through attentive memory. The spectacle creates a different order of sensation conducive to interrogating cinematic forms for revisioning contemporary history and art through the potential of music and dance. Through merging private and the political, the film, through the Argentinian tango, enacts "a juxtaposition or copenetration of the Old and the New" (Deleuze 1989a, 218) to create "a double impossibility, that of forming a group *and* that of not forming a group ... 'the impossibility of escaping from the group, and the impossibility of being satisfied with it'" (ibid., 219). As in minority expression, the film dramatizes how individual conflicts become political and possibly collective in enunciation. The film ends tentatively with a close-up of a camera, a major protagonist in the film.

BECOMING WOMAN: *THE TANGO LESSON*

The Tango Lesson, directed by and starring Sally Potter, is another expression of the tango as counter-history though an exploration of gendered sexual politics that entails a narrative of becoming-woman through its destabilization of the majoritarian and molar conceptions of the female body through an encounter with the dancing body as both constraint and possibility. The history and aesthetic form of tango plays a critical role in this film, as it does in the Solanas and Saura films, predicated on a conflict between conventional conceptions of tango as male dominance, if not violence, and a language of difference to portray what the body is capable of. Potter's film investigates the potential of cinema to enact this struggle through a position from which to overcome conventional conceptions of femininity.

Deleuze and Guattari's comments on the deterritorializing dimensions of minority expression are applicable to women in the following terms:

> How many people live today without a language that is not their own? Or no longer, or not yet, even know their own. And know poorly the language they are forced to serve? This is the problem of immigrants, and especially of their children, the problem of minorities, the problem of a minor literature, but also a problem for all of us: how to tear a minor literature away from its own language, allow it to challenge the language and making it follow a sober revolutionary path? (Deleuze and Guattari 1986, 19).

Potter's film, as the title suggests, is pedagogical and offers a lesson in challenging the visual and verbal language "that is not their own," but which "they are forced to serve." The overarching conception of the "tango lesson" breaks up into twelve lessons that connect Sally Potter as character, as dancer, as film director, and as spectator. The film involves a physical journey taken from Europe to Hollywood, Latin America, and back to Europe but also a mental journey of becoming for Sally in her attempts to escape "a static notion of identity" (Del Río 2008, 133). Sally's becoming is minoritarian, since

> all becoming is minoritarian. Women, regardless of their numbers, are a minority, definable as a state or subset; but they create only by making possible a becoming over which they do not have ownership, into which they must enter; this is a becoming-woman affecting all of human kind, men and women both. (Deleuze and Guattari 1987, 106)

The film begins with Sally's struggle to write a film script, titled "Rage," that evokes Potter's earlier *Thriller* (1979) with its ties to feminist theory and its focus on the gendered gaze, spectacle, and fetishism. Finding herself creatively blocked, she leaves her writing table and wanders into a tango performance where she becomes enthralled by Pablo Verón's (as himself) dancing. A close-up of her fascinated gazing at his movements frames her as a desiring spectator of his performance. Having succeeded in becoming his pupil, she undertakes the arduous task of learning the art of tango. Initially, Sally "seems entirely under his [Pablo's] spell—hanging on his every word, capitulating to his every chorographic command" (Fischer 2004, 50) but, as the drama unfolds, she gradually becomes aware of the constraining effects of this relationship as they expose increasing differences and obstacles to her creativity in her role as filmmaker and in her personal desire. She gains greater understanding of the tango and its relation to the history of minority subjection as she struggles to find an expressive voice.

As Sally immerses herself in the tango, she becomes competent enough to appear with Pablo in public. In his invitation to her to dance with him in a show, their relationship has entered a new phase, but, instead of becoming creatively productive, it generates a personal crisis. Having made a date for New Year's Eve with him, Sally dresses and comes to meet him at his apartment house only to be stood up. On the street, she waits in vain for him to appear and finally gives up and returns to her lodgings. He arrives much later at her lodging, repentant, and she informs him that she is not angry, merely sad, about his vulnerability to emotional attachments. Like a child, he drapes himself on her bed and sleeps as she turns out the light.

This episode opens up the terms of a profound difference between them. After their stage performance, she asks him "What did you think?" He sullenly responds, "You should just follow, do nothing, Otherwise you destroy my freedom to move. You destroy my liberty." She, in turn, informs him that he danced "as if I wasn't there, like a soloist." What stands in the way of reconfiguring their relationship is a power struggle that threatens her with becoming a submissive performer rather than a director, while Pablo discovers that cinema "acting is hard work, because it is collaborative and means following direction" (Mayer 2009, 127). After what appears to be a permanent rupture, she invites him to meet her at the Church of St. Sulpice where she stands before a painting of Jacob wrestling with the angel that, as Sally's interprets it to Pablo, might be considered as "Jacob simply wrestling with himself." The characters assume a tango pose similar to that of Jacob and the angel to acknowledge their contested relations. Following this moment, the two stand at a fountain where Pablo baptizes Sally with the water and where a shot of him swimming in the fountain signifies his own baptism. The scene culminates with the two exiting from a car and dancing the tango together in the pouring rain as a shift from reactive to active involvement in their relationship.

FIGURE 4.6. A lesson in vision, *The Tango Lesson*, Potter, 1997.

The scenes of the two in the synagogue evoke an earlier conversation between Sally and Pablo in which the latter wants to know if she believes in God; she answers that she does not believe that "our lives are written by a superior power controlling what we do." She declares that she is a "Jew," aligning herself with nomadic and marginalized people; he refers to himself also as a Jew. Problematic identity designations so central to the film are thus broadened to include the tango in a different political and spatial register allied to tango: Buenos Aires "not only sounds out the colonial origins of Buenos Aires, but the imperial legacy of slavery" (Mayer 2009, 134) to situate both artists in collective rather than individual positions. It also seems that the tango film with Sally as director can now proceed.

When Sally, along with Pablo and his tango colleagues Gustavo Naveira and Fabián Salas (as themselves), hunt for a film location, the film's investigation of sameness and difference deepens. This sequence involves a mirror shot of Pablo and then with Sally in which he vents his anxieties about her filmmaking.

Pablo now accuses Sally as a filmmaker of not being "here with me," reminiscent of her earlier complaint about his dancing with her. However, his complaints are transformed from judgment to investigation in his question: "I want to know why we met." This is where the film resists answers but remains open to an uncertain future. The film ends with their dancing to lyrics sung by Potter (from her film *Orlando*) that merges life with cinema through music and dance.

Thus, the unfolding tango lessons challenge the passive suffering of men and women under patriarchy and enact the possibility of becoming different by unsettling traditional bodily and mental investment in life and art (Mayer 2009, 134). Here collective memory comes into play through reconsideration of historical constraints to create new forms of expression of the body through dance and/as cinema. And, thus, this counter-history is not a clichéd "resolution" to reconcile antagonisms about identity, but a pedagogy that challenges prevailing forms of identity in which dance and cinema transform into a world that is not predetermined but open to the potential of difference. The pedagogical dimensions of the lessons involve a cinematic education for the spectator through Sally and Pablo's becoming as another reminder of the potential of counter-history to imagine a different future. According to Elena Del Rio, "The episodes of the film as they have involved Pablo and Sally's interactions seem also to enact the episodic character of the tango that call forth a range of affects expressed through the body of from rage, subjection, abjection, rejection to becoming: 'Where the body no longer is, but, more properly, *becomes*'" (2008, 133).

FABULATION, BECOMING MINORITARIAN, AND THE MISSING PEOPLE

The conception of a "becoming-minoritarian" in Deleuze and Guattari's *A Thousand Plateaus* (1987) and *Kafka: Toward a Minor Literature* (1986) investigates the dominant ways in which individuals and groups are defined and captured as identities belonging to the state. Kafka is an exemplar of an individual writer who is heir to a linguistic dispossession, making him a foreigner in his use of his language. Kafka's writing (as well as their own mode of analysis) is "rhizomatic," typically associated with numerous branching nodes, in contrast to the arborescent, tree structure "with its fixed points, localizable linkages between points and positions, centering and pre-established paths/maps, named by language and artistic form." The rhizome is "a model that is perpetually in construction or collapsing . . . a process that is perpetually prolonging itself, breaking off and starting up again" (Deleuze and Guattari 1986, 20).

These two models describe different processes of thinking as a way of passing through dualism to arrive at different organizations of power (Deleuze and Guattari 1986, 21). In the rhizomatic model of expression, the author "tinkers with the wheels and gears of the social machine and sets them into a delirious overload" (Bogue 1989, 108). This overload relates to considerations of territoriality and occurs when consistency is challenged either internally or externally, giving rise to variation, thereby deterritorializing the elements of composition and function of cinematic language and forms. Dispossession introduces catastrophe and chaos to deterritorialize the subject, but it "transforms grotesque absurdity into affirmation" (ibid., 120–22).

A key difference between majoritarian cinema and modern political cinema is the treatment of the private and the political. In the case of the former, a distinction between the two is apparent, whereas, in the latter, the private affair merges with the social or political and blurs the boundaries between them (Deleuze 1989a, 218).

Becoming minoritarian serves to undermine hierarchies, clichés, and myths belonging to an arborescent model of causality, teleology, and stratification to deform them in the interests of creating a form that speaks by and to a colonized minority. Minoritarian literature is not a literature that comes from a minor language but a literature that emerges "within a major language" (Deleuze and Guattari 1986, 16). As thinkers who are critical of the connection between identity and representation, Deleuze and Guattari's conception of minoritarian expression is not related to molar identities, nor to a politics that seeks representation or recognition through the law but through "acts of collective utterances capable of raising the misery into a strange positivity" (Deleuze 1989a, 222). "Every personal fiction," claims Deleuze, echoing Walter Benjamin "like every impersonal myth, is on the side of the 'masters.'" Hence, the author must not "make himself into the ethnologist of the people, nor invent a fiction which would be one more private story" (ibid., 222).

This process of the concept of "becoming-minor" converges with "becoming-woman," in which everyone has to "become-woman," even women by "becoming-animal," "becoming-molecular," "becoming-imperceptible," and, ultimately, "becoming revolutionary." Each type of affective becoming marks a new phase of deterritorialization that entails multiple entrances and exits in time and space, different layers of recollection in which, by storytelling, the author contributes to the invention of a people through "a production of collective utterances" that put into a crisis "the impossibility of living under these conditions" (Deleuze 1989a, 223). In the following discussion of the films of Ousmane Sembène and Djbril Diop Mambéty, I indicate a similar phenomenon in relation to their deployment of the languages of colonization and neocolonialism that reveal how the people are "colonized by stories that have come from elsewhere, but also by their own myths that become impersonal entities at the service of the colonizer" (Deleuze and Guattari 1986, 222).

PEDAGOGY AND FAILURE: *THE CAMP AT THIAROYE*

Sembène's *The Camp at Thiaroye* is pedagogical and allegorical in its treatment of history. However, this 1988 film does not offer itself as a voice of truth but an investigation of events that transpired during World War II with the return of African infantrymen and prisoners of war to Senegal where they were to await repatriation to their respective African states. The narrative of repatriation and its dire consequences are the basis of the film's storytelling, its pretext for investigating that event. Language has been a major concern in Sembène's novels, films, and critical writings. In the case of the films, the problematic of subaltern silence is painfully evident in both his earlier *Black Girl* (*La noire de . . .* 1966) and *The Camp at Thiaroye* but with different accents that attest to the multiple ways in which language functions for the subaltern. In the case of Diouana in *Black Girl*, her immigrant status in France renders her silent and the viewer attentive to the myriad ways in which this silencing functions as a medium for Sembène to dramatize its minoritarian dimensions. Significantly, an element of alienation is introduced, one that involves more than verbal misrecognition and leads to her suicide: Diouana—is doubly alienated, bodily isolated both from the world of her French employers and from her contacts in Senegal. Her narrative becomes not only that of an individual but emblematic of the colonized body of Senegal.

In *The Camp at Thiaroye*, the dual trajectory of the narrative involves a dramatization of cumulative events that lead inexorably to a brutal massacre on December 1, 1944, of returning African soldiers from the European theater during World War II. The film poses the issue of whose history is under investigation: the official history of French imperialism or a counter-history of African resistance. Its portrait of the French military, from the general down to the lieutenant, dramatizes the problematic of authority that can be characterized as not only being indifferent toward the African populace but actively and brutally repressive in relation to phases of both conquest and occupation (Murphy 2000, 154). The events in *The Camp*, while climaxing with massacre, extend beyond that time to address the "continuity in colonial practice" (ibid., 159) by the French, but also to address the forms of actual and potential resistance that are inherent to conceptions of counter-memory. *The Camp* dramatizes the failure of the infantrymen (*tirailleurs*) returning from World War II Fascism with its atrocities to confront similar carnage on the part of their colonial masters. A failure of recognition is central to the film's narration by bringing to the fore "narratives of the defeated rather than of the victor, narratives that have been effaced or misrecognized by official history" (Landy 1996, 39). However, through allegorizing and montage, "actual" events invoke familiar patterns of repetition drawing on forgotten or elided accounts relevant to past interactions between the African community and the French, and also fragments of folklore, myth, and ritual expressed through verbal and gestural language.

The film begins with the infantrymen returning from Europe, being greeted as they debark, entailing a ceremony of rousing music. The returnees march in military formation to a detention camp prior to repatriation to their homes. The view of the camp with its stark huts and barren landscape visually evokes European prison camps, a view reinforced in the indifferent welcome by the French officers. However, in keeping with the escalating drama of their now unceremonious return, a lengthy scene is inserted involving Pays, a traumatized soldier, presumably a victim of torture in a prison camp, who is unable to speak. He walks to the barbed-wire fence that surrounds the camp, looks up knowingly at one of the watchtowers that triggers a flashback of a German camp, reinforced by the sound of German folk music played on a harmonica. A close-up of his hand as he moves it along the barbed wire reinforces a connection between the German camp and the present one. His friend, Corporal Diarra, hands him a German helmet with a swastika, a reminder of the Nazi brutality that Pays refuses to part with, and reluctantly Pays allows Diarra to lead him to his assigned hut. Though capable only of grunting and pointing, Pays will not relinquish the memory of the war in Europe.

The disgraceful situation in which the men now find themselves is exacerbated further by the infantrymen's anger at the meager food they are being served, which they compare to food fit for prisoners in German camps. This episode sets off a series of events involving episodes in the town as one group goes for food and as another, Sergeant-Major Diatta, accepts a ride and goes to a bar/brothel where he is refused a drink because the madam does not serve "niggers." Further, since he is in the American uniform given the men by the French to replace their prison garb, he is mistaken, beaten, and arrested for not being dressed as an African. He is not freed until the African soldiers report his arrest, and he is freed then only through the intervention of Lieutenant Raymond who is impressed with Diatta's knowledge of French literature and classical music, and his ability to speak several languages.

Not only do these episodes underscore the pervasiveness of racism at home on the part of civilians and the French military, but they serve to develop the differences among the various Africans who are identified by their regions: Niger, Congo, Oubangui. They speak their regional languages but communicate with the French and with Africans from other regions through "Francite," a form of pidgin French. They are also identified with their occupations and skills, thus undermining the view articulated by the French officers that Africans are all the same—childlike, ignorant, incorrigible, lazy, and rebellious. The case of the Sergeant Major Diatta is somewhat different, since he has been assimilated into French culture. He is married to a French woman and distanced from his village, which had been a scene of an earlier massacre by the French in their efforts to recruit more men for the war, a story told to him by his family. He is multilingual, competent in Diola, French, and American English; a reader of French literature, including Jules Romains and Roger Martin du Gard among others; and versed in classical music as well as jazz. An intellectual and aesthete, he presents a problematic figure for the French officers with the exception of the liberal Captain Raymond, but both men, as intellectuals, are impotent in the face of the virulent racism that underpins the intractability and violence that supports the power of the colonial authorities.

The film is relentless in dramatizing the parallel between French colonialism and European Fascism. The culminating event of the brutal encounters of the Africans with the officers is their "offer" to pay the men what is due them for their service in the European theater of war at half the international rate of exchange; further, they are accused of having already stolen money from the dead on the battlefield. This announcement is preceded by another announcement: they will have to exchange their American uniforms for those of Senegalese infantrymen. Not only are they told to remove their American uniforms, but they are also told to place them on piles of discarded uniforms similar to the heaps of inmates' clothes associated with the German prison camps. As David Murphy comments, the American uniform had "become a sort of status symbol for the men, a badge that marks them as veterans of the war in Europe" and not as subjects colonized by the French (2000, 165). This episode deepens the affect associated with the progressive degradation of the situation. At the same time, the refusal to pay the soldiers for their wartime services is what finally bonds the men in their resistance to the colonial masters. They deliberate and, when their petition is fruitless, they take the general hostage until he agrees "on his honor as a General" to pay the men in full. The men release him on his word that he will pay them.

Captain Raymond has insisted to his fellow officers that the issue of paying the men the promised sum concerns the honor of a French officer, their word being their bond; by contrast, the general reenacts the fraudulence and force of colonial power, exposing the credibility of "any distinction between Free France and the fascist Vichy regime" (Murphy 2000, 159) in his duplicity, giving them a promise that he does not keep. The traumatized Pays's consistent gesticulations to indicate the duplicity of the officer are disregarded. After the men's victory celebrations, he stations himself on a watchtower as the others sleep, and, when the lights of the oncoming French tanks becomes visible, he rushes to awaken them, German helmet in hand—but he is once again ignored. In this context, the helmet takes on deeper significance. According to Murphy, it "becomes a sign of resistance" (ibid., 164) to the duplicitous language of the general, though the others fail to recognize Pays's warning, couched in a gestural, not verbal, language.

When asked in an interview with Murphy "to explain this paradox of silence and language in your art," Sembène responded, "Language is like that. Sometimes, you don't need to speak to explain something" (Murphy 2000, 233). This statement speaks to his conception of language and cinema, particularly in relation to using the "film medium, as a speaking voice of the people" (Ukadike 1994, 250) and by extension to capture "the muteness of Africa in the new world order" in the "political inertia, economic impotence, and dependency that has become part of Africa" (ibid., 296). Hence, the choice of Pays as the mute subaltern, whose name translates as "country," is symptomatic of this impotence in which resistance takes on a different conception of rethinking existing forms of language. In this sense, Pays's futile acts of resistance are a prod toward a rethinking of the nature minority speech as a form of stuttering, "a foreign language in a dominant language, in order to express the impossibility of living under domination" (Deleuze 1989a, 223). Thus, the film's pedagogy is directed toward a breakdown of the dominant language through excavating the multiple sites of domination through minoritarian forms of expression directed toward the viewer.

The film's counter-historicizing relies on a range of strategies characteristic of minoritarian forms. In its focus on bodies, it visualizes the dire effects of war and the legacy of colonialism that are tied to racism and its disregard for life. In Giorgio Agamben's terms, the men become exemplary of "bare life" in which life "becomes the project and calculation of State power" (Agamben 1998, 9). Not only are bodies portrayed as expendable, but the film catalogues the multiple ways in which this expendability is expressed: in the men's dress, the food they are given to eat, the ways in which they are addressed, and the illusion of choice they have over their lives and deaths. It does not stop on these external constraints: it presses on to dramatize how the internalization of racism clouds their

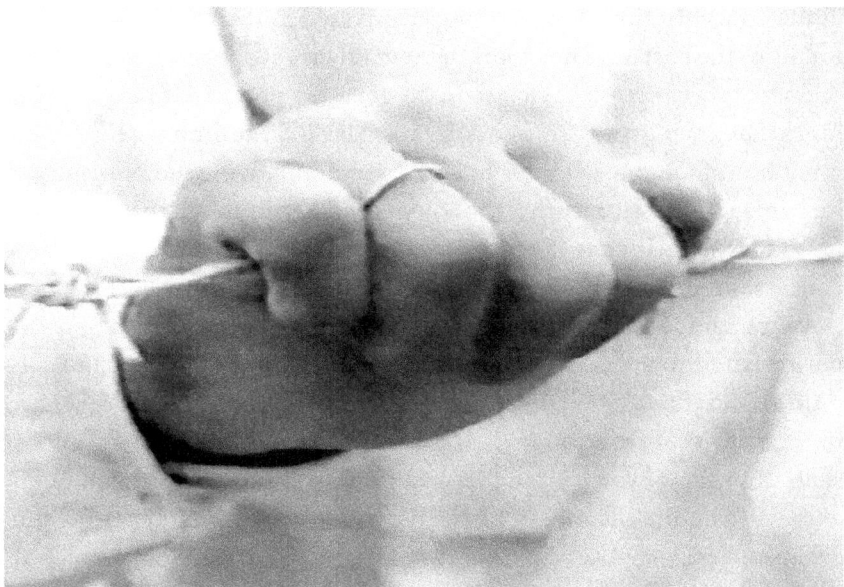

FIGURE 4.7. Pays's hand and the verbally inexpressible, *The Camp at Thiaroye*, Sembène, 1988.

ability to act in their own interest. In short, the film resists moral distinctions that produce stark contrasts concerning the perpetrators and the victims of war, by identifying and expressing the lack of principles, the false moral distinctions embodied in the myth of a "common language" that can be applied to justify actions in the name of discipline, order, and justice as articulated by the Frenchmen.

Sembène's film as expressive of a minoritarian position regards the role of the *tirailleurs* differently: his investigation involves a view of the silent subaltern through the character of Pays. Pays's inability to communicate verbally about torture is expressed in the language of his body and in his obsession with the Nazi helmet and the barbed wire that are displayed for the other African men to see the impossibility of their situations.

On the other side of the equation is the position of the men who do not perceive the untimeliness of their revolutionary actions. More than that, they cannot recollect the numerous betrayals that brought them into the war: being pressed into the European theater, being horribly treated in the concentration camps, all now expressed in their repatriation. The events of the past have not come to their aid via recollection, so that their premature celebration of victory in the general's promise to pay them signifies their inability to think counter-historically. The filmmaker's project is not one of judging the men, but rather of dramatizing their inability to recognize the possibility that the colonel will betray them; that his promise to give the Africans the proper exchange rate is merely a momentary concession to escape and prepare another attack.

What Sembène has dramatized is the quintessential dimension of minoritarian filmmaking in which the people are missing. Under the conditions presented, the outcome of the massacre appears inevitable: it is in the nature of repetition. The characters are positioned in an impossible situation, involving language, suggested by the verbally mute but expressive bodily gestures of Pays. His inability to communicate the dire events not only exposes the repetitive, predictable nature of betrayal, affirmed by the massacre at the end and by the repetitive ending with a new troop of soldiers on their way to France, but it expresses the men's inability or refusal to comprehend their situation—the memory of their past and present oppression imposed on them by the colonial masters. However, the film is more than an elegy for the dead infantrymen: it is a productive pedagogy of failure that resides in bringing the physical and the material (the massacre and the history) in which the misery of the people, expressed through the violence to their bodies, is transposed onto the possibility of thinking toward the future. The memorialization of the event is grafted onto a contemplation of the future invention of a people directed toward the spectator. Thus, minoritarian expression as counter-history evokes sensations involving cruelty, destruction, and betrayal as a form of pedagogy that brings the body into consideration of its potential to produce thinking and feeling through art.

A "DELIRIOUS OVERLOAD": UNSETTLING MYTH THROUGH THEATRICALITY FROM INSIDE OUT IN *HYENAS*

Djibril Diop Mambéty's 1992 *Hyenas* is a blend of different art forms, including theater, literature, folklore, and cinema, as well as different systems of knowledge. Though not described as a historical film, it is an instance of counter-history making through minoritarian expression. First by adapting *The Visit*, a play by Friedrich Dürrenmatt, a Swiss writer of an earlier generation, Mambéty departs from commercial cinematic forms to create a multifaceted version of marginalization and neocolonialism. Utilizing parable and allegory the film's narrative involves the return to the impoverished African village of Colobane by a woman, Linguère Ramatou, who had been betrayed by her lover Draman Drameh, forced to leave the village, and enter onto a life of prostitution, "a trope that has proven satirically powerful to portray a drama of marginalized people [and] bring a community into contact with a wider world" (Ukadike 1994, 1999). Now rich as the World Bank, the woman has the economic capital to exact revenge on Draman, a fairly prosperous grocer married to a well-to-do woman, Koudia Lo, and popular among the villagers. Linguère returns in regal style and offers the villagers the opportunity of becoming wealthy on the condition that Draman be tried and killed for his betrayal. The impoverished community is torn between the cruelty of her plan and the rewards that her wealth offers to them, which become increasingly visible in the commodities that they acquire as she finally turns them against Draman. The work is a fiction attuned to actual social, political, and economic events in postindependence Senegal, but, characteristic of satiric allegory, it blurs the line between the surreal and quotidian life, the actual and the conceptual.

Richard Porton (1995) has considered Mambéty's *Hyenas* as an allegory in the sense of Walter Benjamin's conception of allegory in his *Origin of German Tragic Drama*. The film has been described by Porton as a revelation of the ruins of the world, of its "decline." For Benjamin, modern allegory is a natural history in which history appears as "a petrified primordial landscape... a form in which man's subjection to nature is most obvious" (1998, 166). Porton regards the film—despite its apparently pessimistic ending—as not foreclosing on the possibility of a utopian reconciliation in its "tragicomic version of allegory" (1995, 97). While Porton reads the film as an allegory of neocolonialism via the World Bank's control of debtor nations, he asserts that it is rather to be regarded as "an intermittently comic dirge than a sermon" (ibid., 98). As allegory, the film is multilayered, orchestrating in complex terms the contradictory factors that contribute to a scenario of exploitation, decline, violence, and failure that, similar to Sembène's film, the people do not seem to notice.

According to Clyde Taylor, the film guides the viewer to a powerful engagement of its differing politics and aesthetics through its "tonal texture that exceeds a satiric portrait of corrupt bureaucrats" (2000, 142). The allegory identified by Porton via Benjamin not only turns on a line of inquiry that involves global capital but also ties the allegory to the complicity of the African figures. The inhabitants of Colobane from the mayor and his cohorts to the professor, the clergy, and the women, in Taylor's words, "become hyenas of greed, moral scavengers, eager to profit from Draman's demise" (ibid., 142). Fragments as a series or cycles of concepts serve to create the sensation of confronting the viewer with the possibility of contributing to the invention of a people by inventing "new conditions of struggle" in which the spectator is implicated (Deleuze 1989a, 217). Rather than regarding the film as a sentimental and pessimistic narrative in the "disappearance" of Draman at the end of the film, it seeks, through Draman's actual and virtual vanishing, to dismantle familiar forms of political cinema in its often cruel and parodic, and portrait of African subalternity and to undermine sentimental and reductive notions of passive victimhood.

The film's allegory operates through instances of doubling, in the animal human parallels, in folding between past and present time, and especially in its adaptation of Dürrenmatt's *The Visit*. Both *The Visit* and *Hyenas* dramatize the vengeful return of a woman who has been disgraced and forced to leave her home. Forced into prostitution, Linguère Ramatou, similar to Claire Zachanassian in *The Visit*, becomes the richest woman in the world, with the financial means to extract revenge on her betrayer. In the play and in Mambéty's version, the woman's revenge is based on the lover's disavowal of paternity, his libelous assertions about her sexual behavior, and his marriage of convenience to an affluent woman. Thus, in both the play and the film, aesthetics and politics involve the equation between sexual politics and economic exchange, since prostitution is at the basis of the wealth that enables the woman to capture the control of the community. Mambéty ties his film to the fate of Africa, and more particularly to consumer capitalism as a force that erodes the past and even more cogently the present and the future.

The position of women becomes critical to this scenario, since the portraits of the women involve unrealized desire, loss of youth, and consequent hardship until the opportunity arises for revenge. Despite Linguère Ramatou's harsh and cruel vindictiveness, the film presents her not as a melodramatic victim or villain but in strongly affective terms as a tragic figure who realizes that her victory is hollow. She has claimed that money would allow her to abolish time, to buy back the youth and love stolen from her, but her pursuit of power and possessions has left her cold and lifeless, "half-metal," as Draman rather ungallantly remarks when he sees her gold leg (Ukadike, n.d.). The film's other women include Draman's wife, Khoudia, and the mayor's wife, both of whom are antagonistic to their incompetent spouses. The women's commitment to status and money aligns them with the new order of commodities that inflects every aspect of this decomposing milieu, evident in the ironic praise by the mayor of Linguère Ramatou as a paragon of memory, honest and generous, who will finally act as a destroyer of this world.

Though women play a prominent role in focusing on the political corruption, so do the animals that are generously interspersed throughout to illuminate and complicate the relation between the organic and the inorganic in relation to the allegorical interpenetration of relations between nature and history. The women and the animals are prominent from the outset of the film, and both connect to the immanence of becoming-woman and also becoming-animal. Even before the viewer is confronted with human actors, she is introduced to images in lengthy takes in close-up of their feet and in middle distance of herds of elephants on the move, dissolving into herd of humans (in long shot and then in close-up of men's feet). An image of an elephant herd appears and recurs at the end of the film, and the image of a mangy monkey introduces the viewer to Draman's grocery store. The animal paces back and forth within its confines, to reinforce a parallel between humans and simians, especially identified with the penniless men who trick Draman into giving them drinks. Draman serves them in the expectation of payments "at sundown" to the disdainful look of his wife. Once again, this episode is interrupted by another image of the bound monkey, circling his "prison" and foreshadowing Draman's future "imprisonment" at the hands of the community.

The film distorts the characters and situations by enlarging the catastrophe in its cruelly comic treatment of the inhabitants and their affiliation with the ubiquitous animals. Indeed, the film explores the alignment of animal and human to invoke and question the characters' behavior and to account for the chaos that ultimately ensues after the arrival of Linguère Ramatou, whom Draman describes as his "little wildcat," while she describes him as her "black panther." The hyena signifies the inhabitants of Colobane, especially Draman. Linguère Ramatou (named for the Ramatou bird) also designates another threatening animal. Her litigious exposure of Draman's deceit to get rid of her and marry Khoudia Lo is exposed to the community in a highly stylized trial scene articulated through her lawyer to satisfy her past humiliation at his hands. Her cruel revenge is expressed in the castration of the slanderous men who falsely testified for Draman. Her revenge is designed to force the people to choose between Draman's life and the large economic reward she holds out. After Draman is publicly exposed for his actions toward Linguère Ramatou, the question arises about equivalence between his past actions and her demands for his death as satisfaction for his treatment of her. More images of packs of hovering hyenas come into prominence as he tries to escape is fate.

Seeking to save his threatened life, Draman appeals to the community for support, only to confront the complicity of the police, the mayor, and the priest. They have succumbed to the lure of money. When he observes their hypocritical acquisition of boots, typewriters, plans for a new village, a new chandelier for the church, he is told in uncertain terms that it would be best if he left the village. Though taunted into leaving the village, Draman is physically obstructed by the police and other members of the community from doing so. This scene intercuts numerous times with images of the restless hyenas waiting for their prey. According to the filmmaker,

> The hyena is an African animal—you know that. It never kills. The hyena is falsehood, a caricature of man. The hyena comes out only at night; he is afraid of daylight... he does not want to see daylight, he does not want to see himself by daylight, so he always travels at night. He is a liar, the hyena. The hyena is a permanent presence in humans, and that is why man will never be perfect. The hyena has no sense of shame, but it represents nudity, which is the shame of human beings. (Ukadike 1999, online)

FIGURE 4.8. Mission accomplished, *Hyenas*, Mambéty, 1992.

The opposite link between inorganic and organic in the human–animal relationship involves Ramatou's wearing of a gold prosthetic limb to replace her lost leg, which transforms her from an organic to a semi-artificial being, a hybrid. Similarly, the villagers, at a carnivalesque bazaar for the commodities now made available to the women (washers, television, and air-conditioners), are seduced by goods that are to be paid for by Draman's death. The ubiquity of the animals is reiterated in the final episodes that lead to his sham trial and physical disappearance. The film in allegorical fashion blurs the boundaries between the human and animal to pose the challenge of becoming-animal. The animals are inherent to the milieu, whereas the humans have become increasingly divorced from it, and, by the film's end, the bulldozers will level the landscape and herald the new order of power unleashed on the community.

The animals are a physical part of the landscape as well as allegorical emblems, a reminder of forms of human life that have been metamorphosed: in the case of Draman, obliterated in the disappearance of his body and in the coming of the machines of progress to replace the now-obsolete forms of sociability and interaction. The disappearance of his body reinforces the project of minoritarian film in the reminder that the people are missing and also of dreaming their invention through the magic of cinema. Mambéty has said, "For example, at the end of *Hyènes*, if you want to know where Draman Drameh's body has gone, you risk breaking the magic. Only magic knows where his body has gone. Cinema is magic in the service of dreams" (Ukadike 1999, online). Thus, Ukadike identifies the elusive pedagogy of Mambéty's film.

Hyenas is a political film that evokes the advent of global capital in its abstract and fetishistic character of credit. The pervasiveness of a climate of violence and death, the reign of the hyenas, is indicative of "a notoriously sleazy market and transit point on the edge of Dakar" (Ukadike 1994, 172–73. In this respect, the film is consonant with assessments of African culture and politics as exemplified in the films of Sembène. The theatrical, visual, and auditory strategies employed by Mambéty serve to complicate Deleuze's conception of minoritarian language. In its play with and transposition of the Dürrenmatt drama through the variants of return of the dispossessed and her revitalized economic position as an instrument of revenge, Mambéty's film makes inroads on the characterization of narratives of underdevelopment and subalternity, especially in relation to films that present the subaltern in sentimental and reductive terms as being a passive victim, thus obliterating recognition of the forms and history of exploitation and domination.

The particular stylistic resonances offer the spectator a multiplicity of fragmented relations rather than a unified and familiar interpretation of the position of the colonized in relation to neocolonialism and economical imperialism. The ceremonial moments—the arrival of Ramatou, her appearance before the assembled community, the carnivalesque fair in which the commodities are greedily appropriated by the women (including Khoudia Lo) to the accompaniment of music, dance, and fireworks, the frequent parallels with animals, and the ritualistic demise of Draman to the chanting of the assembled men—resists the "European gaze" as well as a strict binary distinction between the innocent and the guilty. Furthermore, in contrast to Ramatou's formal demand that the cost of justice is the demise of Draman, the interactions between the two are as restrained as are his own responses to his trial and subsequent disappearance. Thus, the film's form of minoritarian expression unsettles boundaries between

FIGURE 4.9. On the verge of disappearing, *Hyenas*, Mambéty, 1992.

past and present, inside and outside, private relations and politics to offer a collective form of storytelling that unflinchingly questions existing power and the shape of the African future.

Similar to the other films discussed in the chapter, Mambéty's film consists foremost in its proffering of "new strategies for dealing with the past that point toward new forms of historical thought" (Rosenstone 2006, 18). These films eschew melodrama through a stylized allegorical treatment and through language to create a collective identity crisis that cruelly narrates the disappearance of a people. In introducing a parabolic style, the films not only create a world vision pertaining to a past that has brutally been demolished, but they invent, fabulate, a form of pedagogy to think about the present. Similar to the other minoritarian narratives discussed in this chapter, this form of filmmaking is not a supplement to existing historical forms but a construction of a cinematic world that reimagines the real in its invitations to the spectator to think about "the future of our past" (ibid., 160). In their various forms for creating minoritarian cinema, these films require the spectator to see and contemplate what one "cannot assimilate or grasp" in how the eye and the ear are assaulted "by offering a hypertrophic surplus of irreconcilable passions and sensations" (Shaviro 1993, 259 that qualify as being historical but are counter to prevailing and dominant models of historical thinking as apocalyptic, cynical, and apolitical, if not dispassionate.

THE REAL AND THE IMAGINARY: TSAI MING-LIANG'S *THE HOLE*

Musicals, until recent decades, have been seen largely as being ahistorical, escapist, and nonserious. However, Rick Altman, Jane Feuer, and Richard Dyer undertook a revaluation of the musical's changing forms in the light of cinema history, social, and cultural history. Their work focused mainly on Hollywood and is largely silent on international expressions of musical (for example, Bollywood), though their observations are germane for understanding non-Hollywood expressions of the musical. For them, the musical is self-reflexive not only about its strategies but also about the changing nature of popular culture in its connections to dancing bodies, to the operations of the cinematic image, and to its designs on its viewers. In her discussion of the connections between the world and the stage, Feuer writes, "The ultimate synthesis of the musical consists in unifying what was initially imaginary with what initially was real. But in the film's unfolding, the boundary between real and imaginary may be blurred. Musicals may project the dream into the narrative, implying a similar relationship between film and viewer" (1982, 77). Further, her discussion of the relationship between the popular musical and modernist filmmaking in their uses of direct address, quotation, reflexivity, allusions to popular forms, and tensions between the virtual and the real inserts the musical into a different place in the history of cinema than the one it held previously.

More recently, Amy Herzog has written on the musical (2010), drawing on Deleuze's cinema books to expand on its heterogeneous worlds, exploring how the musical comedy "does not simply give a fluid world to images" but transports the viewer into a "plurality of worlds" in which one passes from one world to another, from the actual to dream (1989a, 63). Herzog's analysis of *The Hole* (1998) by Taiwanese filmmaker Tsai Ming-liang not only extends the reach of the musical transnationally but also explores how the "musical moment generates patterns of representational repetition that are, simultaneously and uniquely, open to the interventions of difference." Accordingly, Herzog explores how "the musical moment is unusual in its capacity to make this tension palpable; it is at once one of the most conservative and the most irreverent filmic phenomena" (2010, 8). Her analysis of *The Hole* plumbs this contradiction.

Tsai Ming-liang's films are no respecter of genre forms or of history proper (Hong 2011, 159–82). In my terms as counter-history, *The Hole* (1998) combines science fiction disaster film with musical interludes. The film presents a jarring contrast between a flooded, dreary, and decomposing world and the spectacular world of music and dance. Through the watery spectacle of Esther Williams's swimming in *Neptune's Daughter* (1949) and the musical interludes in *The Hole* (1998) starring Grace Chang, a popular Chinese film star and recording artist, Herzog undertakes an intricate examination of the fantasy worlds presented in both films. Herzog builds a case for a philosophic connection with the seeming disparate segments of the film through heretical conceptions of bodies, time, and history. What she demonstrates is how *The Hole* is a counter-history, that is, as "a stimulus that startles or unsettles us, making something that was previously imperceptible perceptible" (Herzog 2010, 159). What becomes perceptible is a cinematic approach that undermines determinist, clichéd, and reductive beliefs in history through dream.

In this regime, the character (and the viewer) is "no longer subject to the rules of response or action. He records rather than reacts. He is prey to a vision, pursued by it or pursuing it" (Deleuze 1989a, 3). Time is contracted into the smallest circuits through recollection, dream, or hallucination to render indiscernible the boundaries between the real and the imaginary: "the impossibility of decoding why the events are taking place calls into question and literally falsifies our standard means of apprehending them" (Buchanan 1998, 153). In his writings on the musical exemplified in the films of Vincente Minnelli, Stanley Donen, and Gene Kelly, as well as the burlesque of Jerry Lewis, Deleuze maps the passages from narrative to spectacle to connect the world of the real to that of recollection and dream. This passage occurs through dance and music, since the crystal image is both visual and optical. In relation to the music, Deleuze refers to the repetitive character of the ritornello and gallop as serving to define the crystal of time "in which time itself becomes a thing of sound" (Deleuze 1986, 94). As might be expected in his concern with difference and repetition, Deleuze reminds his reader, "Repetition is never a historical fact, but rather the conditions under which something new is effectively produced" (Deleuze 1994, 90).

The Hole was commissioned by French television as part of a world media project to usher in the millennium. Tsai's comedy takes place in the year 2000, and the film offers a bleak view of an apartment house where rain threatens the inhabitants with flooding, loss of power, cockroaches, and disease. A voice-over from a radio urges the inhabitants to abandon their residences and move to temporary housing. However, a young man (Lee Kang-sheng) from an upstairs apartment and the woman (Yang Kuei-mei) who lives in an apartment below remain and are brought into contact when a plumber knocks on the man's door, looking for the source of a leak that created a hole that leads from his apartment to that of the woman, which becomes a means for him to observe her.

The hole becomes a source of contention, each trying to cover it up. His apartment is untouched by the invasive waters, while the woman is frantically engaged in trying to stop the rising water, using rolls of paper towels that she has amassed to staunch the flow. Moreover, her tap water is affected. The man's life appears to follow a practical, seemingly indifferent routine, involving his cooking, eating, and resting; his forays to a ground-floor grocery where he works and where attention is focused on a stray cat that he feeds; and his tracking an incoherent man who has assumed the behavior of a cockroach crawling on all fours to find a place to avoid the light.

While the situation of the man on the upper floor remains unchanged, the woman continues to deteriorate in a fashion similar to the infected man in the basement. Though she attempts to maintain an everyday routine, she is frustrated in her attempts: the water from the spigot does not run to enable her to boil her noodles (though it does work for the man upstairs). When she tries to maintain her appearance by giving herself a facial, a cockroach invades her apartment and upsets her; and, finally, the water seeps from the entrance into her bedroom, and she is driven to find refuge on the bed. Her responses to her desperate and lonely situation are portrayed through her masturbating during an actual or imagined erotic phone call and as she bathes. Finally, when she displays the symptoms of the virus reported over the radio, the man reaches down through the hole and lifts her up to his apartment. Given her illness and the dire warnings and the episode with the infected man, it is likely that the woman will expire. However, this ending suggests the possibility of deliverance.

The narrow framing of the small apartments and the concrete corridors and stairways and the bleakness of the grimy ground floor visualize an enclosed, ugly, and stifling milieu. The sound track, too, with the incessant falling rain and the impersonal blaring radio with dire reports of the catastrophe, further reinforce the characters' isolation and entrapment, as does the camera work, with its extended long takes of the man stretched on the sofa in contrast to the repetitive shots of the woman vainly mopping her floor, sitting on the toilet with a dishpan over her head, lying on the bed as the rising waters invade her bedroom, or crawling on the floor like an insect in search of darkness. Similarly, the numerous long takes of the young man in his routine actions culminate in his sitting by the hole, crying until he reaches down to her through the opening and pulls her up. Acquarello (2001) compares Tsai's film to Antonioni's through its portrayal of ennui reminiscent of Deleuze's observations on Antonioni, in which the "idle periods of everyday banality . . . pushes them [the characters] to the point of dehumanized landscapes, of emptied spaces that might be seen as having absorbed character and actions" (Deleuze 1989a, 5). In Tsai, the style of long take and the framing of desolate, and intermittently empty, spaces are also indicative of a dehumanized landscape.

The ordinariness of the nameless characters, their inarticulateness, and the repetitive nature of their limited movements in the constraining areas of the apartment house are transformed into five musical song and dance spectacles that belong to a world of musical pleasures and bodily freedom through the songs of Grace Chang, lip-synched by the actress playing the woman downstairs. The first number takes place in an elevator featuring a calypso number, "Oh, Calypso." The woman appears in an elevator dressed in a red-feathered headdress and multicolored sequined sheath conforming tightly to her body as she gyrates to the music. Her movement is confined to the elevator, but the camera moves between proximity and distance. Her upstairs neighbor is revealed to be inebriated in the corner of the elevator.

The second number, "Tiger Lady," includes her with a chorus of three women. She is dressed in a flared red and white floral dress, dancing on stairs (with moldy walls in the background), the lyrics focusing angrily on the ineptness of men who should "take a hike." The third flamboyant number, reminiscent of a Hollywood musical, is more seductive, beginning with just her leg outstretched; then, she emerges in an amber-sequined, knee-length dress as she pursues the reluctant young man from upstairs, this time dressed in an iridescent pale blue silk suit, as she sings (in English) "I want you to care." The fourth number, a cha-cha musical moment, following her sneezing in the tub, is appropriately named "Achoo cha," and she appears in a short white dress trimmed in scarlet feathers, accompanied by four men and three women as a chorus. They dance on a long stairway moving through a bricolage of sheets of plastic.

The song and dance numbers also invoke geographic locations beyond Taipei such as Latin America, the U.S., and Hong Kong that are characteristic of the allusions to transnational cinematic landscapes in Tsai's other films (for example, *What Time Is It There?*). Furthermore, these sequences, including the final musical number, are tied to the sites of the apartment house—the elevators, stairs, and corridors—and the final sequence is in the man's apartment, rather than radically altering the milieu of the musical. Thus, the dream milieus reinforce the contrast between the woman's masquerading as popular performer and as infected inhabitant of a bleak world in the disorienting disjunctions and unstable boundaries between the actual and the fantastic. The film invokes different layers of time through the repetitive focus on liquids: the rain, running kitchen tap and the bath water, the characters' urinating, and the rising water in the woman's apartment. This emphasis on water is suggestive of Deleuze's discussion of the French pre–World War II cinema with its predilection for liquidity: "What the French school found in water was the promise or implication of another state of perception, a perception not tailored to solids, which no longer has the solid as object, as condition, as milieu," that evokes a "more delicate and vaster perception, a molecular perception, peculiar to a ciné-eye" (Deleuze 1986, 80).

Deleuze's regards cinematic movement as involving a state of liquid or "flowing" perception," as "the most perfect environment in which movement can be extracted from the thing moved, or mobility from movement itself. This is the origin of the visual and auditory importance of water" (Deleuze 1986, 77). This flowing perception is also central to both the watery world in which Tsai's characters are trapped and the song and dance numbers that hold out the tenuous promise of art as an affective force "to liberate the life that is trapped in man and his organs" (Goodchild 1996, 191). If the civilization of the image has produced a concerted organization of clichés, Deleuze ceaselessly explores whether it is possible to extract from this misery the possibility of thinking differently about the relation of cinema to thought through an expression of bodily sensation. Tsai's film, characterized by the musical episodes interspersed with the misery of the diseased and rain-sodden world, serves to connect the exhausted body to a virtual world of possibility.

Consonant with Deleuze's conception of the movement-image, its crisis, and the emergence of the time-image, Tsai's film engages with different orders of time: the first involving chronology relating to bodies subjected to the tyranny of measurable clock time and of natural exigency; the second engaging with a form of time associated with oneiric time, with art, and with mobile and affective bodies. The world generated by the musical episodes through the voice of Grace Chang and the bodily movements of the woman transport her and the spectator to another time, to a future and a becoming. The spectacle of music and dance does not cancel out the grotesqueness of the pestilence but projects the viewer into another world in which the familiar and repetitive drama of catastrophe is connected to the world of art. This has significance for thinking differently about history. As Herzog writes, "If Tsai's musical presents a historical-image, it can be located precisely within his reformulation of the body as open to the outside" (2010, 197). Participating in the struggle to become other is the basis for imagining and thinking counter-historically. It is "acting counter to the past," in the hope of entertaining "the present for the future" (Deleuze and Guattari 1994, 112).

Tsai describes himself as "somehow unsatisfied with the modern world. I don't really much like the world the way it is now, but I love these things from the past" (Rapfogel 2004, 28). In his focus on bodies, his characters struggle to maintain their routinized and circumscribed lives in their trapped bodies, but, through the cinematic, a world identified with music and dance is "the sole means of entry into another world, that is, into another's world, into another's dream or past" (Deleuze 1989a, 63). The final musical moment of the film, the man and woman dancing together after he has raised her body from the hole, suggests a vision of a release from history through "experimenting with something that escapes history" through history (Deleuze 1994, 112) in a future becoming that implicates the viewer in thinking counter-historically.

5

Memory, the Powers of the False, and Becoming

> History progresses not by negation and the negation of negation, but by deciding problems and affirming differences. It is no less bloody and brutal as a result. Only the shadows of history live by negation: the good enter into it with all the power of a posited differential or a difference affirmed; they repel shadows into the shadows, and deny only as the consequence of a primary positivity and affirmation.
>
> —Deleuze, *Difference and Repetition* (1994, 268)

COUNTER-HISTORY OVERTURNS classical conceptions of thought and practice by substituting for them a dynamic conception of connections between the body and social existence. In Deleuze's singly authored texts, he elaborated on a philosophy of difference that he finds affirmed through the writings of Spinoza that have implications for thinking counter-historically through the powers of the false. According to Deleuze, "Life is poisoned by the categories of Good and Evil, of blame and merit, of sin and redemption.... Before Nietzsche, he [Spinoza] denounces all the falsifications of life, all the values in the name of which we disparage life" (Deleuze 1988a, 26). Deleuze's engagement with these philosophers reveals how consistently he evolved concepts of affect, movement and time, virtual and actual space, and of relations between the true and the false by creating an ethic for thinking productively about becoming in the world through the body. Spinoza's writings on affect and power offer a "philosophy of 'life'" through which Deleuze explores the active and reactive powers of the body: its "capacity to affect is manifested as a *power of acting* insofar as it is assumed to be filled by passions" (ibid., 27, italics in original). According to him, when "we encounter a body that does not enter into composition with own... our power of acting is diminished or blocked, and that the corresponding passions are those of sadness" (ibid.). Deleuze further asserts that "only joy is worthwhile, joy remains, bringing us near to action and to the bliss of action" (ibid., 28). Joy is "inseparable from the creation of new modes of social existence" (Goodchild 1996, 41). Deleuze distinguishes between active and reactive forces. Becoming-active "presupposes the affinity of action and affirmation," whereas "reactive-force is negating and nihilistic" (Deleuze and Guattari, 1987 68). New modes of thinking emerge that "provoke undecidable alternatives and inexplicable differences between the true and the false as adequate to time" (Deleuze 1989a, 132).

The powers of the false expose how "the nature of knowledge qua science (*Wissenschaft*) has been dominated by a 'will to truth' that determines the basis for metaphysical representation and moral judgment by consigning the false to abnormality, immorality, and error" (Flaxman 2012, xiv). The power of the false is predicated on the proposition that truth has to be sensed through a series of falsifications. At stake in this falsifying narration is the indiscernibility between the real and the imaginary revealed through the changing crystal images of time. While truthful narration is developed organically, according to legal connections in space and chronological relations in time, "falsifying narration shatters the system of judgment" (Deleuze 1989a, 133) and thereby reigning claims to truth.

Deleuze's notion of becoming challenges common sense, identity, and resemblance by introducing biological, geological, and philosophical conceptions for thinking about development, creativity, and history. He introduces the concept of *incompossibility* (derived from Leibniz) to consider historical events that did not but might have happened, though in different worlds, to place truth into crisis and introduce new possibilities for thought and action. Deleuze entertains the possibility that events can occur in the same world through forking time that passes through incompossible presents to return to "not-necessarily true pasts" (1989a,

131) to release the potential for thinking counter-historically. In *The Fold*, Deleuze again refers to Leibniz, the baroque, and multiplicity to elaborate conditions of possibility within one (not different worlds) "transformed in a world built out of contingent propositions" (Rodowick 1997, 96).

Deleuze draws on the works of novelists, poets, and painters to exemplify the power of the false, though the cinema is for him a dominant medium for thinking aesthetically and philosophically about conceptions of movement and time. In thinking about Deleuze's time-image, the temptation is to regard the fragmented, molecular, antinarrative treatments of character, landscape, and affection as completely removed from forms of action and belief characteristic of the movement-image. However, the time-image introduces the conception of contingent transformations from negativity to positivity, from identity to difference, and from history to counter-history. If the world of the movement-image had affirmed moral efficacy, identity, and presence in the face of impossible odds, in the time-image there is less a break than a shift in belief. The direct image of time gives new expression to potentiality always present, always renewable though the cinematic image.

The movement-image exemplifies a conception of historicizing reliant on a conception of time that is linear and organic and that aspires to be universal. In its various affective connections between situation and action, the movement-image is one in which history is determined by a system of judgment based on the belief "that one party will ultimately—finally and teleologically—represent the right and the true" (ibid., 85). The injection of direct time is instrumental in the undoing of assigned meanings in relation to entrenched philosophical systems, socialized behaviors, and judgments of truth. In the cinema of the time-image, both character and spectator move from consideration of the content of the film to its formal constitution, where they "cease to judge in terms of true and false, real and possible" and where "the frame ensures a deterritorialization of the image" to create a different relation to the real that questions rules, judgments, and disciplinary responses. In chapter 4, I discussed forms of fabulation expressive of changing conceptions of narration in the interests of minoritarian thinking. In this chapter, I explore further the role of dynamic movement, images, and time through a discussion of films that exemplify the powers of the false.

To trace changes in cinematic form from the 1940s to the present, I examine Deleuze's return to postwar neorealism to track the genealogy of what he terms "the crisis of the movement-image" as initially expressed through neorealist practices. I refrain from privileging Italian neorealism and turn to the films of Indian filmmaker Satyajit Ray, first through a discussion of the Apu trilogy of the 1950s and his city films of the late 1960s and 1970s to examine how a crisis of the image is inherent in transnational neorealism at that time and of changing forms of cinema. David Cronenberg's *A History of Violence* (2005) is a more recent expression of falsifying narration that challenges belief in righteous moral action as being based on claims to truth through its focus on a protagonist who is a pretender. My discussion of *The Illusionist* (Sylvain Chomet, 2010) considers a work of animation: a magician, Tatischeff, the animated figure of the filmmaker Jacques Tati as double, becomes the film's strategy for invoking time and memory through cinema to offer a philosophic confrontation with orders of time that "pose inexplicable differences to the present and alternatives which are undecidable between true and false to the past" (Deleuze 1989a, 131).

Two films by Michael Haneke, *La pianiste* (2001) and *Das weisse Band* (*The White Ribbon*, 2009), are my opportunity to examine the filmmaker's treatments of violence and torture in which the spectator is implicated in a form of falsifying narration reminiscent of Artaud's theater of cruelty. Finally, three films by Aleksey Balabanov—*Trofim* (1996), *Of Freaks and Men* (1998), and *Morphia* (2008)—are further examples of falsifying narration that question reigning truths and unsettle habitual modes for addressing recollection, resemblance, and memory.

THE VOYAGES OF NEOREALISM AND BEYOND

In 1954, Roberto Rossellini mused, "The term neorealism was born with the success of *Open City*—a delayed-action success, like a time bomb. When the film was shown at Cannes in 1946, it went quite unnoticed. It was discovered much later and I am not yet sure the message has been fully understood" (Rossellini 1992, 44). Can his same observation be applied to Satyajit Ray's cinematic works? What are the obstacles that have stood in the way of a fuller understanding " of neorealism, and how are they connected to counter-history? To address these questions, I focus on three prevailing critical positions to challenge assessments of neorealism: (1) that it was a dramatic rupture from the cinema that preceded it; (2) that it was a short-lived movement that lost its momentum and died in the political events of the 1960 to the 1970s; and (3) that it was primarily an Italian phenomenon.

Neorealism in Italy did not erupt magically after the end of World War II. In Italy, it was the consequence of convergent factors arising from long-standing dissatisfactions with social, political, and aesthetic conditions existing even before the Fascist regime, dating back to the Risorgimento and the unification of Italy as a nation. The Fascist regime made attempts over twenty years to modernize the nation through enforced and manufactured consensus, colonialism, and war, in which the novel and cinema particularly were to play a critical, if contradictory, role not only under Fascism but after World War II especially as this involves conceptions of the practices of realism.

Initially, "realism" during the years of Fascism's ascent was mobilized by critics and ideologues determined "to portray the sufferings of the people" as a reaction against "decadent" Italian and foreign literature and films of the 1920s. By the late 1930s and into the 1940s, when dissatisfaction with the regime began to emerge, realism was still debated but with an emphasis on a return to "national traditions," in the interests of combating the effects of Fascism on politics and art. The writings of Cesare Zavattini and contributors to the journal *Cinema*, the novels and short stories of Giovanni Verga, as well as the writings of Americans such as John Dos Passos became the vehicle for this return (just as later in the 1950s so did the writings of the political philosopher Antonio Gramsci).

This "new" realism, identified with certain scriptwriters, directors, and cinematographers (putatively aligned to the Communist Party), involved location shooting (in unfamiliar lower-class urban and regional locales), nonprofessional actors, "casting professional actors against type," a documentary-like quality, a preference for natural lighting, loosely structured scripts, and a focus on marginalized social characters (Sheil 2006, 13) For many critics, these elements became the determining canonical features of the politics and aesthetics of neorealism. However, too often the restriction to these technical criteria occluded significant formal and conceptual characteristics that were to play a critical role in the evolution, not demise, of neorealism internationally.

The image brought into being by neorealism in Gilles Deleuze's view is characteristic of a cinema of elliptical events, empty spaces, and irrational intervals (gaps) between perception and action. An awareness of time emerges through "chopped-up encounters ... [a] cutting up of history ... [that] call into question the prefabricated roles which were imposed on it by a power which cannot be pinned down ... [and] only known by its effects" (Deleuze 1989a, 11–13). However, Deleuze's focus on Italy as the first and primary exemplar of neorealism indicates his focus on Europe to the detriment of global developments that play a concomitant role in the transformation of the cinematic image in its relation to time. Neorealism's encounters with time and space involve "deliberately weak links, the voyage form, the consciousness of clichés, and the condemnation of the plot to exchange and propagate clichés" (Deleuze 1986, 210). These elements introduced new relations to conceptions of history, memory, subjectivity, and politics that, while abandoning functional forms of realism, introduced a "mental image." Instead of representing an already deciphered real, neorealism was instrumental in altering cinema on a global scale.

GLOBAL NEOREALISM

Moinak Biswas' insights into Indian cinema's encounter with neorealism entail "an internally conflicted model of cultural modernity ... not in terms of a binary of West and non-West but in terms of a global movement that acts against the globalization of ossified commercial forms. As the Indian realists of the 1950s entered into a dialogue with Italian cinema they shared an internationalist project built on the basis of local enterprises" (Biswas 2007, 75). Biswas raises the stakes of neorealism by pointing out that realism in the Indian context, and particularly in Ray's films, necessitates a rethinking of neorealism by directing it conceptually to a global plane for a better understanding of its aesthetics and politics.

Biswas provides a map of the evolution of realism from the 1930s to Ray's films of the 1950s. The elements that he focuses on are as applicable to assessments of Italian neorealism as they are to identifying and differentiating the Indian encounter with realism. Most germane to his discussion of style is his elaboration on the "ramble" in the "discovery of the landscape principle" (Biswas 2006, 43) so critical to the development of this aesthetic, particularly in Ray's films. Indian cinematic social realism was to introduce, not without visible tensions, new modes of representation, involving also a fusion of novelist forms with perceived rhythms of live. In Biswas's terms, "the scope of reality had to be 'extended' to respond to a reality in visible ferment" (Biswas 2007, 79). It is this crisis to which the Indian cinema responded, as did the Italian, in their specific cultural, historical, and political manifestations. In the 1940s, a new set of imperatives was made manifest after struggles for independence, political unrest, and partition. Subsequent deep political and economic conflicts in the 1950s and 1960s interacted with cinematic expression, exemplified by distinctions in studio films and those of social realism that offer evidence of a contest between static and dynamic spatial relations between actors and milieu and documentary incursions. The films of Satyajit Ray belong to this milieu and characterize a crisis of representation.

Similar to responses to Rossellini's work, Ray's Apu trilogy has been subject to divergent assessments internationally. For many critics in Europe and the U.S., Ray's films are approached as auteurist with an emphasis on "lyricism, poetry, and humanism" as well as on their ethnographic and allegorical character, while the Indian response has connected it to "'the industrial program and to the theme of nation-building' closely aligned with the technological optimism and socialist ideals of India's first prime minister Jawaharlal Nehru" (Majumdar 2005, 515). Also disparaged or lauded are the "authentic" portrayals of poverty in the Apu trilogy. These disparate responses echo those on Italian neorealism as an ongoing site of critical, political, and aesthetic contention.

In each of the three Apu films, *Pather Panchali* (1955), *Aparajito* (1956), and *Apu Sansar* (*The World of Apu,* 1959), space-time is the protagonist, conveyed through a voyage form, especially through long tracking shots of the characters through changing landscapes from the village life to the metropolis. From my perspective, the trilogy can be viewed through its treatment of children, *mise-en-scène,* landscape, and everyday ordinariness dependent on the uses of framing, camera movement, visual image and sound, camera work, and music. The visual descriptions of everyday survival involve encounters with sustenance, birth, adolescence, marriage, illness, deterritorialization, and death. These underscore the tensions between an impoverished material world and natural plentitude, physical and psychic pain, and also stolen moments of pleasure. The style of the three Ray films alters functional (or sociological) forms of realism by offering perspectives through the characters. The children (or childlike characters like the aged Auntie) become critical to spectatorship. Being "affected by a certain motor helplessness" that makes them "all the more capable of seeing and hearing" (Deleuze 1989a, 3), these characters "invest the settings and the objects with their gaze.... [T]hey see and hear the things and the people ... before action takes shape in [the situation], and uses or confronts its elements" (ibid., 4).

Time, especially idle periods, is critical in this form of realism periods and introduces "an inexplicable break or emotion into daily banality" (Deleuze 1989a, 12). Such breaks are evident in the repetitive negligent treatment of elderly Auntie (Chunibala Devi) by Sarbojaya (Karuna Bannerjee) and observed by Durga (Uma Das Gupta) in *Pather Panchali*. Defeated in an attempt to escape, Auntie returns to die, is tended, then mourned by Durga. The film's uses of idle time as waiting become more pronounced in Sarbojaya's desperate waiting for her husband, who has gone to seek work in the city. Alone, she tries vainly to save the life of feverish and semi-conscious Durga. Her long waiting climaxes in a montage of a storm that rages loudly during the night of Durga's dying, with extended shots of Sarbojaya's frantic looking at the wildly blowing curtains and an image of the almost lifeless body of her young daughter intercut with images of a goddess. Both episodes reveal the emergence of time-images with their different affective impact on the viewer, calling attention to an altered link between passion and action and the impossibility of the characters' situation. If in neorealism the character becomes a seer, the viewer too has become a character (ibid., 3).

Similarly, objects in *Pather Panchali*—a stolen guava, Durga's treasure box, a diminishing rice container, Auntie's threadbare shawl and her new one, a necklace stolen by Durga and thrown into the water by Apu after her death—are not symbols. They are inherent to the film's engagement with things that bear the imprint of material history and memory as fragments, or ciphers, that communicate the transience of things through the introduction of banal, everyday events, objects, attitudes, and descriptions. This form of narrative has been enhanced by a plurilingualism, introducing a free indirect vision (Pasolini 1988, 148) that expresses the multifaceted visions of the characters and of the author as expressed in *Aparajito*. The images of space in term of objects and of time as relating to Apu's mother and Apu as they leave Benares by train for him to enter school capture the layered ways in which Ray brings together the film as journey, the author, his characters, and the landscape, not toward the ends of advancing narrative action but to disrupt it on behalf of introducing problematic situations that are not reducible to the "exteriority of the physical world any more than to the psychological interiority of the thinking ego" (Deleuze 1989a, 175).

The lengthy sequence alternates between shots of the exterior urban, then rural landscape and lengthy enigmatic close-ups of Sarbojaya's face framed by the train's window. The "blurring of the boundaries induced by sociological vision and their background shows how important it was for the film to create a sensate space, a space imbued with intelligence and feeling to enhance a "new mode of construction" (Biswas 2006, 45). Ravi Vasudevan, writing on the final sequences in *Aparajito*, finds that "here, in a very distinctive way, Ray conveys not only a passage within the protagonist, but a nurturing and cultivation of memory against the process of modern processes and subjectivities" (2006, 91), an indication of counter-history.

Ray's films from the 1970s are a further instance of the evolution of neorealism as exemplified in his Calcutta trilogy (*The Adversary*, 1970; *Company Limited*, 1974; *The Middleman*, 1976). These films are exemplary of transformations in this form of filmmaking transpiring in the 1960s and 1970s. If the Italian cinema of the 1960s, as in Antonioni's *Red Desert*, is an instance of "bicycle-less neorealism," in terms of the description of space, mobility, and subjectivity in post–World War II cinema, Ray's films involve "movement (the trip ballad) with a specific weight of time operating inside the character and excavating them from within the chronicle" (Deleuze 1989a, 23). If *Red Desert* is a portrait of a sick Eros, "sick not just because he is old and worn-out in his content, but because he is caught in the pure form of a time which is torn between an already-determined past and a dead-end future" (ibid., 24), Ray's Calcutta trilogy can also be said to be his "portrait of a sick Eros." This transformation is not a derivative form of Italian filmmaking so much as an illustration of a global condition.

In Ray's city films, space–time takes on a different valence from the Apu trilogy, as described by Supriya Chaudhuri. In her words, the city films are

> not free of the pressures of time; [they] cannot stand back and view them objectively. These are driven, haunted films; films recording the spectrality of the modern city, a place of memories, desires, ghosts. This quality, a quality of being intensely present, located in the material world, and for that very reason, being an aspect of unreality, its relegation of existence to nonexistence, distinguishes all the films in the Calcutta trilogy. (2006, 254)

The protagonist in these films is the modern city, and the dominant characters are young unemployed men immersed in this urban milieu. The characters and the viewer share, in ways reminiscent of Antonioni's and Akira Kurosawa's contemporary films, a confrontation with "limit situations . . . dehumanized landscapes, of emptied spaces that might seem as having absorbed characters and action, retaining only a physical description, an abstract inventory of them" (Deleuze 1989a, 5). And as inherited from earlier explorations of neorealism but modified to the changing Indian milieu of the 1970s, the distinction between subjective and objective in the Ray city films seems "to lose its importance. . . . [W]e no longer know what is real and imaginary, not because they are confused, but because we do not have to know and because there is no longer even a place from which to ask" (ibid., 7). The space of the city becomes a space that "refers back again to the lost gaze of being who is absent from the world as much as from himself" and "the imaginary gaze makes the real something imaginary" (ibid., 9).

The city in all three films is conveyed through the movement of characters through the urban landscape, and they, like the viewers, are privy to the sights of the shots of high-rise buildings, street traffic, advertisements, and jarring noises on the sound track. In the case of *Pratidwandi* (*The Adversary*, 1972), Siddhartha's cinematic strolls confound their point of view; the domestic scenes do not link seamlessly to the milieu, and they do not "explain" the character's interior state. What we are given instead is a problematic relation between subjective and objective perception, allowing

FIGURE 5.1. Calcutta urban space, *The Adversary*, Ray, 1970.

for an evocation of genre (and documentary-like moments) that frustrate reductive political judgments on how to assess the different planes of time with their visible and auditory discordant elements. The problematic nature of these characters and their relation to the cityscape, in particular, are further compounded by the recourse to repeated flashback and dream states, constituting another layer and order of signs that further complicate an assessment of the films' evocations of time and of memory. For example, in *Pratidwandi*, the father's dead body, intercut with images of the dead father, young Siddhartha and his mother filmed in negative, projects the viewer in *medias res* into the past, then abruptly thrusts the spectator into the film's present moment with its montage of images of urban life.

Siddhartha's "stroll" encompasses a number of incidents that include his visit to the tailor to repair his pants, his unsuccessful interview for a job, flashbacks from his childhood, reiterated recollections of a medical lecture from his studies, and his two visits to the cinema. These episodes are characterized by different registers of time (evoked by chronology and through visual allusions to clock time via his watch and those of memory). What is striking is how these variegated episodes are not "irrelevant" to the film but related to his position as a "sleepwalker," rather than his being a character engaged in action. His "motor helplessness" enhances further the gap between the character and his milieu. Thus, to posit a consonance between them is to ignore their incommensurability and especially to violate the film's immersion in the time-image that invokes different peaks of past and present and invites the viewer to contemplate relations between past and present, actual and virtual time.

At the end of *Pratidwandi,* Siddhartha, having left Calcutta for the country, gazes wordlessly on his new surroundings. The sight and sound of a bird evoke earlier flashbacks to his youth. He hears again the sound of a bird from his childhood, and his gaze is drawn toward the provincial landscape, toward an ending that Supriya Chaudhuri identifies as possibly both "redeem and nostalgic" (2006, 268–69). More provocative and more relevant to Ray's treatment of this character is Chaudhuri's description of Siddhartha as "not so much a body as a sensibility" (ibid., 269). And this sensibility illuminates the film's opening and its ending. I regard the film's closure as projecting the spectator into the future and onto an experience of duration, not in terms of the pain of loss but as an encounter with "a suspension of the world... which far from making thought visible ... [reveals a] cinema concerned with a thought whose essential character is not yet to be" (Deleuze 1989a, 168), a characteristic of counter-history that evokes the real as virtual.

The other two films of the trilogy, *Seemabaddha* (*Company Limited,* 1972) and *Jana Aranya* (*The Middleman,* 1976), present male protagonists mired in time that threatens to devour them. In the case of both Somnath and Shymalendu, their actions drive them to inhabit the position of opportunist. They begin as truth seekers but end as deceivers. Somnath finally sees that his position has led him to the darkest dimension of city life when, as "middleman," he delivers a young woman to prostitution. If in *Pratidwandi* time as duration and space as increasingly deterritorializing become the disorienting forces that drive Siddhartha away from the city, in *Jana Aranya,* Somnath (Pradip Mukherjee) becomes a denizen of the metropole and an incarnation of the powers of the false. Starting as a naïve initiate to the business world, he ends as a pimp for his employer in delivering a young woman to a hotel room where a client awaits her and as a liar to his father. In a darkly lit and claustrophobic sequence, he returns home where his shadowy image is followed by a close-up of his father's face as Somnath tells the old man what he wants to hear. The dialogue is simple: "I've got it [a job] father." The final image is of the father shot in close-up as he wipes his brow and the scene darkens. The film is not without humor, though grim humor.

The final moments of *Seemabaddha* occur after Shyamalendu (Barun Chandra) has betrayed the striking workers at his work place, as well as approving the sale of damaged commodities. The ultimate sequence of the film is an encounter between himself and his sister-in-law Tutul (Sharmila Tagore) whom he prefers to the company of his wife. Tutul is the window to the spectator, offering a critical view on the company and on Shyamalendu's marriage. There is a cut to her seated diagonally across from him. After several intercuts between the two, she wordlessly returns a watch that he had loaned her and goes to stand at the window, looking out on the city. The music rises: he covers his face, and there is a cut to the fan and to her empty seat, leaving the viewer burdened with this silent ending and by its problematic connections to the future through a form of filmmaking different from functional forms of realism but offering an encounter with the real.

The film movement initiated by realism in literature and cinema with their ties to changing historical, national, and international contexts was to have an impact on the character of noncommercial and experimental cinema evident also in the films of Ritwik Ghatak and Mrinal Sen. The spectator is drawn into engagement with increasingly contested terrains involving the character of the viewing subject; the world viewed; different encounters with history, memory, fantasy and dream; and conceptions of politics. Ray's cinema of the 1970s entails "a conception of history that simultaneously calls up the comic and the dramatic, the extraordinary and the everyday: new types of speech acts and new structurations of space ... constructed on a pedagogical base" (Deleuze 1989a, 246). This pedagogy works differently from conventional forms of realism in its address to its spectator. Ray's characters have shed their reverence for the truthful protagonist and instead foreground the forger and deceiver as guides to the powers of the false and, as such, the crisis of truth.

THE POWERS OF THE FALSE: CRONENBERG'S *A HISTORY OF VIOLENCE*

David Cronenberg's *A History of Violence* (2005) is a counter-historical investigation of violence that operates on philosophic, historical, aesthetic, and psychological planes. At its core is a scenario relating to the private affective realm in the guise of a family melodrama that exposes contradictions between the private and the public through the powers of the false. As Adam Lowenstein has argued, "Cronenberg's cinema crystallizes the fraught translation of an embodied self into a public, abstracted social body.... His films insist that the traumatized body cannot be explained simply as a diseased self in need of reintegration with a healthy public body" (2005, 146). Instead, his films have focused on the powers of the false to convey at their most extreme a process of becoming-other that emerges "from a countervailing desire to evade ... limits, to find lines of flight wherein new potentialities for desire and identity can be expressed" (Rodowick 1997, 155). The sites for Cronenberg's cinematic explorations have been horrific transformations that dramatize in excess these lines of flight. *A History of Violence* focuses on the ubiquitous sense in which these lines are implicated in the powers of the false that exposes the lies, the forgeries, and the judgments on which violence is justified in the name of truth.

Canadian David Cronenberg is known for his prolific output of popular feature films, TV series, and art house films. He has worked in a variety of genre forms—science fiction, horror, biography, and melodrama—and his films have been exemplary for their remarkable ability to cross many boundaries involving national identity (especially Canadian and American), popular genres, experimental, and avant-garde forms, and scientific and philosophical concerns. Presumably, derived from a graphic novel by the same name, *A History of Violence* raises the vast and problematic subject of violence through the apparent form of family melodrama. Given Cronenberg's engagement with the pervasive and distinctive forms of violence, it becomes evident that *A History of Violence* undermines the classical treatment of linkages between the private and the political through eroding conventional boundaries between the two. *A History of Violence* "acknowledges the painful inextricability of public and private, and demands that spectators inhabit it as a complex, endless moment of ambivalent transformation" (Lowenstein 2005, 158). I interpret this transformation to Cronenberg's orchestrating of bodily states, violence, and the impossibility of arriving at a reconciliation between personal desire and moral action as provocation for the viewer to contemplate given forms of representation so as to solicit thinking about resemblance, identity, the body, and conceptions of community. These deeply philosophical and political issues are intimately tied to a connection between cinema and truth seeking.

The form of this film is embedded in the history of cinematic culture and in the historical imaginary that Deleuze has elaborated in his works *Difference and Repetition, The Logic of Sensation,* and the two cinema books. The narration and style of the film enacts an encounter between the classical movement-image and that of the time-image; hence, my understanding of the title as a "history" involves a complex transformation from academic considerations of history to one that evokes the potential for counter-historicizing through falsification. As in Deleuze's examination of the movement-image, this film is a repudiation of the cinema of affection and action that produces a sense of confidence and belief in violence as redemptive. Rather, the film is engaged in examining the constituents of modern political cinema through an invocation of an ahistorical imaginary that questions the organic image of the world based on an affective belief in the certainty of moral action. Cronenberg's "history," through its focus on the legacy of western legends, challenges narratives of the exceptional individual who by his actions brings into being a new moral order.

The film takes another direction to undermine belief in the truthful hero and offers instead an effective history that animates both Foucault's and Deleuze's writings on historicizing. Rather than approaching the film's form of history from the standpoint of conventional melodrama as exemplified in its penchant for violence, I regard it from the vantage point of its exposing inherited and sanctimonious values about historically justified violence. By introducing a falsifying narration that inverts stark distinctions between the truthful man and the liar, the film challenges the binary logic of common sense that serves to separate them. Derived from Nietzschean thinking, the false is not the obverse of the true but one that places notions of reigning truth into crisis characteristic of these films.

Deleuze's cinema books are for recognizing and identifying different practices in writing cinema history. He prefaces his first volume, *Cinema 1: The Movement-Image*, with this assertion: "This study is not a history of cinema. It is a taxonomy, an attempt at the classification of images and signs" (1986, 7). In his seeming dismissal of existing historiography, his observations on the power of the false are not an abandonment of history but an attempt to arrive at a different understanding of the modern cinematic image in its past incarnations, its status in the present, and its future possibilities through cinema. His distinction between the movement-image and the time-image refers to particular moments in cinema history as a way of mapping new conceptions of creation and reception that are philosophical and political in a sense that they differ from earlier and prevailing conceptions of politics through films that are dependent on interpretation, judgment, and ideology.

In its episodes, Cronenberg's film offers the viewer a reenactment of the cinema of action characteristic of the western and crime genres where the protagonist confronts situations and becomes capable of action to restore or at least stabilize threats to its well-being, but the film reverses this direction to enact a loss of belief "in the capacity of a community to have hopes and dreams powerful enough to bring about the confidence necessary to reform itself" (Marrati 2008, 105). In its foregrounding of violence through the exposure of the true exposed as false, the film passes from a belief in the power of righteous action to a reconsideration of the uncertainties but also possibilities of memory, identity, and belief. The film subjects the affective power of righteous action, law, and judgment in the name of community and national survival to an intense interrogation.

The world of the movement-image as expressed by Deleuze in the early western is largely deterministic, behavioral, and judgmental in its adherence to legality, faith in reason, reliance on a great man, the family, and community (see chapter 1) and predicated on a conception of the image as primitive. Protagonist Tom Stall's (Viggo Mortensen) elimination of the destructive forces that threaten the lives of his family and his peers raises the troubling question of violence in relation to the survival the body of the community: namely, whether one is commanded to attack destroyers of the peace in the name of personal or group survival.

The large form of the movement-image as exemplified in historical, psychosocial, and western films is dependent on a character in an antagonistic situation to foresee a challenging force (Deleuze 1986, 142), anticipate the moves of that force, and exercise counter-force to create a restored or new situation. Deleuze's analysis of the movement-image captures the historical role of a defense of the nation, community, family, and self that involves violence in the name of morality. This is a cinema of behaviorism and realist violence in which the action must permeate the character deeply and continuously, a realism that entails "an explosive acting out in relation to fictitious objects that incite an affective memory and give rise to emotion that connects the permeating situation and the explosive action" (ibid., 159). While Deleuze's movement-image is sensitive to forms of narration conveyed through montage, his mapping of cinematic forms is not sufficiently attentive to the cinema of attractions and spectacle (Gunning 2007) conveyed in such films as the spaghetti western or the cinema horror that are episodic, do not resolve conflict, or create a new order. According to David Martin-Jones (2011, 41–65), Deleuze's analysis of the silent film is cinema based on thinking of this cinema as exemplifying primitive narration, a form of realism, that does not take account of images exemplary of a noncontinuous temporality such as the use of tricks and other visual effects that already reveal the presence of montage, discontinuity, and an introduction of, temporality.

In *A History of Violence,* situation and action open onto another terrain, a falsifying terrain that places them into crisis by rendering the "true" identity of the character and of situations undecidable and unresolved. Tom gradually emerges as someone else, another identity, related to Leland, Billy, Fogarty and his thugs; and his natural brother, Richie, is the instrument of his transformation in a scene of revenge. One might assume that this "transformation" places him on the other side of the divide between protector and perpetrator. Yet the question of his identity is not resolved merely because of the discovery of Tom Stall's prior identity as mobster Joey Cusack. Rather, the film has introduced another scenario of violence in a different milieu, thus moving from the ethos of the historical film or pre–World War II western into the domain of the gangster film, though once again, through parody, he is confronted with self-defense and survival. What has been complicated is that his transformation has placed Tom/Joey in a different milieu as an embodiment of the power of the false that ties it to other film forms, including the gangster film, the western, melodrama, and film noir.

This hybrid tendency to evoke cinematic recollections of these genres' shared involvement in violence and their connection to social and political thought are embodied in cinema history and in the conceptual and aesthetic transformations to which it has given rise. As J. Hoberman comments, "*A History of Violence* is a hyper-real version of an early-'50s B-movie nightmare—albeit one where the narrative delicately blurs dream and reality, the performances slyly merge acting with role-playing, the location feels like a set, and blood always splatters from lovingly contrived prosthetic injuries" (2005a). To describe the film's highlighting of media as merely a form of self-reflexivity is to lose the film's complex treatment of history in and of film through different evocations of affect that unsettle conventional expectations of an action-oriented genre through the qualities of allusion, dysnarrativity, and slight deformations in the landscape and in the character's appearance.

From the opening of *A History of Violence* (evoking David Lynch's *Blue Velvet*), the viewer is offered a clichéd image of small-town life drawn from idealized inherited portraits of community. Whereas in Lynch's film the town of Lumberton is steeped in bright colors to conjure momentarily the innocence and normality of a landscape that will shortly undergo transformation, color and landscape in Cronenberg's Millbrook, Indiana, are visually somber and ostensibly less surreal. However, a similarity exists in the two films in their focus on probing links between the surface of normality and the gradual emergence of violence.

The initial shots of a banal motel in a rundown part of town offer a brief respite from the brutal action to come—until the appearance of two thugs, Leland and Billy, who prefigure the enigma of brutality that the film explores and that runs counter to sentimental portraits of small-town American life. Their unprepossessing presence slowly is revealed in their unkempt appearance, exhaustion, and hostile relations with each other. When it is time to leave the premises, Leland, the dominant figure of the two, goes to the office to pay the bill, the sound of gunshots are heard, and he exits. Billy then enters to get water for the trip to come. Indifferent or blind to the sight of multiple dead bodies lying on the floor (presumably, shot by Leland), he obtains the desired water only to confront a survivor of the carnage. At the sight of a young child holding her doll and crying, Billy coolly pulls out his gun, puts his finger to his lips to silence her, and shoots her. (Once is reminded of the killing of the McBain boy in Sergio Leone's 1968 *C'era una volta il West* [*Once Upon a Time in the West*].) The scene cuts abruptly to the sound and then images of a child screaming that turn out to be those of another child awakening from a nightmare. The "protected" child is Sarah (Heidi Hayes), the offspring of Tom and Edie (Maria Bello) respectable members of the community, comforted by her parents and her brother Jack (Ashton Holmes) after a nightmare.

The contrast between worlds is now stark: that of the nomadic, exhausted, and bored gangsters and that of the iconic middle-class family huddled together to comfort their distraught child. Yet the two scenes pose the problematic of their connection with dreaming that will intensify through the further development of the Stall family. Cronenberg's film makes repetition and difference hang on unexpected and almost indiscernible transformations. The repetitive and clichéd dimensions of apparently monstrous and everyday existence, despite differences in locale and affect, are introduced in a brief and seemingly banal contretemps at breakfast between Tom and his son, Jack, who rejects his father's offer to serve him cereal, preferring to serve himself. The familiar domestic milieu is further developed in the repetitive, pacific, everyday rituals that mark their lives. A sense of sameness is enhanced through the reassuringly familiar shots of a small-town Main Street, reinforced by an image of the post office with its prominent clock, its time stopped at 1:15 (a shot repeated later).

Tom's arrival at his diner is introduced, again with a reference to dreaming (or nightmare?) by the short-order cook who recounts an amusing story to Tom of having sex with a woman who tells him that she had dreamed that he threatened her life and that he awakened her, and she stabbed him. When asked by Tom what the dreaming man did with this episode, he quips that he married her. Slight aberrations in episodes relating to dreaming and sexuality are treated humorously as part of everyday interactions but are central to the film's insistent emphasis on forms of sexuality and their evocation of forms of violence presented, as in this case, as "entertaining" and "normal." Tom and Edie's sex life will evoke aggression treated as playfulness. Indeed, the film's probing of sexuality permeates many episodes and their connections to violence; the psychosexual allusions from the diner shift to Jack at a gym-class baseball practice where Jack successfully catches a fly ball that classmate Bobby had hit, thwarting Bobby's effort to appear dominant and in control before his peers. Jack is then confronted in the gym locker room by an enraged and defeated Bobby, who is determined to goad Jack to fight and provocatively taunts him about being a "faggot." Other names that Bobby will throw at Jack involve the same sexual and queer connotation. This encounter injects another queer competitive expression in relation to male hierarchies involving body sports, the masculine body, and sexuality aligned to aggression and its climax in violence when Jack later abandons his verbally pacific response and reacts physically to Bobby's provocation.

The film turns to Tom's identity as exemplary citizen, a character that will seem to be the least disturbed in his identity as both father and as citizen. A scene of sex between Edie and him suggests another possibility. In a darkly lit room, Tom waits on their bed for a "surprise" planned by Edie, as she emerges from the bathroom dressed as a school cheerleader. She aggressively falls on him. They tussle on the bed, she playfully assuming the dominant position, which elicits from Tom the description of her as being "naughty" and she of him as a "a bad boy." After their sexual encounter, they reminisce about their fortunate relationship in which Tom describes himself as a lucky man and she praises him for being the "best man" she has known, another dimension of the powers of the false as appearances.

This scene will compare grotesquely with the later violent rape scene on the stairs, after Tom has been exposed as gangster Joey Cusack. After slapping Edie, he imprisons her in his grasp and overcomes her, no longer the playful and gentle lover. She, however, wavers between resistance and response, suggesting that the previous sexual games between them were indicative of the limitations of their sexual life, while the later ones, as Bart Beaty has indicated, are reminiscent of scenes in such films as *The Fountainhead*, in which "powerful men ravish the women that they love" (Beaty 208). Once again, the Cronenberg film has drawn on another popular cinematic form to link the characters to forms of violence embedded in gendered fantasies of desire.

When the two hired killers, Leland and Billy, finally arrive at the diner and threaten Tom and his hired help, Tom pulls out a gun, and, in few minutes, Tom has killed the two gunmen as in a western, to enhance the film's play on repetition and to allow the problematic of Tom's assumed identity to emerge. Tom stares at the instrument of his violence, as if an alien object or as the first indication of his recollection of another life and another identity. Hoberman writes that the film impersonates "an action flick in its staccato mayhem while questioning these violent attractions every step of the way" (2005b). His comments bear further examination in the light of Deleuze's examination of the crisis of the movement-image that, through the power of the false, are identified by Hoberman as "role-playing" to undermine clear-cult demarcations between the film and reality. By invoking "a hyper-real version of an early-'50s B-movie nightmare—albeit one where the narrative delicately blurs dream and reality" (ibid.), *A History of Violence* induces indiscernibility between cinematic action forms and their power, dismissed to entertainment rather than forms for thinking about their pretensions to truth. Such a blurring of boundaries has the potential for creating the possibility of mental images to emerge based on the uncertainties and deformations about identity and resemblance raised also by Edie's comments later about the possibility of Tom having multiple personalities. The film's emphasis on falsification of identities, inherent in Tom's metamorphosis into Joey, is his identity dissolution and with it a decentering of any privileged position in relation to resemblance and judgment.

Uncomfortable with the media hype that follows the killing of the hired gunmen, Tom confronts the media that is determined to interview the local hero, parodying the voyeurism of the media (reminiscent of the final moments of Martin Scorsese's *Taxi Driver* in relation to Travis's incarnation from killer into local hero). In the modest glare of celebrity, Tom appears not only uncomfortable but also angry and tries to return to normality, "to be with his family." However, his stance as a normal man of justice and truth is quickly challenged by the arrival of Fogarty (Ed Harris), the brutal instrument of unraveling the image and identity of Tom as a man of truth, exposing what Deleuze describes as the powers of the false that are realized in a different space to organic narration, one identified as crystalline in its breaking into fragments of time (Deleuze 1989a, 69). This form of narration is enhanced in the film by its unsettling indeterminacy involving characters, place, and the time of events. The present has bifurcated, and recollection in the form of dream-like images begins to pose a dilemma between the image of moral righteousness and its obscure sides through the figure of a man who has metamorphosed from a normal, if nondescript but upright, figure and will soon assume emerge as the deceiver. As Sheriff Sam Carney notes, "We take care of our own"; but Tom revealed as Joey displays a different relation to that unified community.

While Tom as hero seemed initially to embody the role of restoring order to the community, the film reinforces uncertainty in relation to his "authentic" embodiment of the values of the community and especially of the family. Gradually, Tom is transformed into killer Joey Cusack from Philadelphia. Confronted by his wife who asks him to tell her "the truth," she claims that she saw in her husband "the killer Fogarty tried to warn me about." He confesses how in the desert he had killed Joey the killer and become Tom Stall. Tom is thus exposed as a bearer of counterfeit identity, and this falsification is at the heart of the film's enigmas that encompass all the characters, the townsmen and the gangsters: the issue of the various forces that remain chained to judgments and appearances.

Edie's response is disbelief, but she expresses concern about the legitimacy of their family name, asking him, "Did you just make that up?" Expressing physical disgust at this new identity, she repudiates him. His son also similarly repudiates him. Both son and wife operate within the realm of resemblance and identity in wanting to be reassured about who Tom really is and of what he is capable. Theatricality emerges in the scene where Edie supports her husband to deflect the sheriff's question about Tom's identity, despite what she has seen. Her momentary metamorphosis into the dutiful evaporates in the sheriff's departure giving way to a violent scene of sex and then her repudiation, both inherent to a rapidly mutating scenario. Edie's allusion to multiple personality exposes the schizoid dimension that the film exposes that infects the other characters and creates a counter-history of violence. The variant expressions of violence that emerge from the discovery of Tom/Joey's identity are central to thinking counter-historically about conceptions of self, family, the sexual body, naming, and justice.

A History of Violence's attraction to the powers of the false implicates the dominant character's "truthfulness" expressed in their *ressentiment* and self-justification and exposed through the scenarios in which they are implicated. In moving away from the binary moral values in early westerns and casting doubt on justice, the film comes closer to the transnational western in its probing of violence through cinema. Joey's return to his brother Richie's (William Hurt) mansion also involves family, underscoring Richie's ambiguous relations to women, homosocial bonding with his men, and prurience about Joey's marriage and sex life. The episode reenacts Joey's facility with his body and with weapons as he shoots Richie and his men, thus completing this chapter in the *History of Violence*. He leaves his brother's house and walks to a pond on the premises where he throws the gun into the water and cleanses his body while the camera focuses on the dangling cross he wears around his neck.

This scene and the brief one that follows it with Joey's return to Millbrook and home, in Cronenberg's terms, suggest the "mask of a hopeful ending even for an audience accustomed to his manipulations of convention" (Beaty 2008, 82). This notion of "hopefulness" is ambiguous: either it ironically refers to generic conventions and the possibility of regarding the ending as restoration of the normal or, given the strategies of disturbing the narration, hints at a potential to think otherwise about restoration to the status quo. To think otherwise entails passage from the passive dimensions of habitual recognition to attentive recognition that arises from a different relation to time, bringing circuits of the past and memory into a different relation, so that the passing present has become virtual.

Since image production is "not a simple reproduction of images or of becoming aware . . . [the] images must be produced in such a way that that the past is not necessarily true, or that the impossible comes from the possible" (Deleuze 1989a, 131). In relation to the forger, for example, where earlier he could exist in a determinate form, he now "provokes undecidable alternatives and inexplicable differences between the true and the false" (ibid., 132). However, it is clear that the film evokes a crisis of the movement-image through this transformation into another, presumably monstrous form, in the encounter between Joey and his brother that unravels the nature of doubled identity but significantly does not radically alter Joey's appearance except for the clichéd shots that repeat his image as the man with the gun. It is at this point that Cronenberg's film transforms the true into the power of the false: namely, that truth is appearance. Looking at the film from its ending to its beginning, the initial shots, if not the whole film undergoes a transformation that allows for a multiply inflected (rhizomatic) understanding of its investigative character relation to historical documents.

As is characteristic of the time-image, the film offers no narrative closure despite the return home as Tom or Joey. Instead, the film has surpassed the genre forms invoked throughout in its refusal to fall back on the commonsense visualization of the *History of Violence* involving different embodiments of relationships between father and son, husband and wife, fraternal relations, and other versions of social bonding. Beyond its various presentations of the media as object of reflection concerning the expression of connections between the private and the social, the film appears to offer, in Deleuze's terms following Nietzsche, a derailing of judgment, whereby life is able to free itself of both appearance and truth in which both the man of truth as well as the forger become problematic. They "have neither the sense nor the power of metamorphosis.... [T]hey reveal an impoverishment of a vital force (*élan vital*), of an already exhausted life" (Deleuze 1989a, 146). However, the artist is different through creating forms and shapes that can reveal an "outpouring of life" (ibid., 147) rather than violence and death.

Thus, Cronenberg's film is not a litigious judgment of violence but a philosophic and biological exploration of forces that either obstruct or overcome exhausted life and the forms in which it is projected. Hence, the ending implicates the viewer in a position of thinking differently, not by reinforcing belief in the protagonist's "purification" but by situating the viewer in a different relation to the role of art as capable of transforming the already known into a point of view on creativity. The final silent moments of the film are significant for their use of close-up without dialogue, though with musical overlay and with several close-ups of Tom that resolve into a group picture of the silent family. The vignettes of the family are enigmatic insofar as they raise uncertainty about their signification. They are either indicative of a potential reconsolidation of power or

FIGURE 5.2. The rest is silence, *A History of Violence,* Cronenberg, 2005.

a transformation into a different form of engagement and belief in a life as yet unrealized.

By introducing and slightly disfiguring conventional scenes derived from other genres that involve the reconciliation of family, community, and even necessary violence and by defacing the "real" image to jam clichés, thereby falsifying their content and form, *A History of Violence* performs a philosophical theater for the future. As a counter-history of violence, Cronenberg's film has offered a diagram of the everyday body and its connections to organicist views of history by subjecting them to the deformations of the time-image that include different sheets of time, passages between the organic and the crystalline, through a falsifying narration that calls identities, judgments, and resemblances into question. The film is an exceptional cinematic foray in philosophical and aesthetic to create a counter-history as a process that bypasses the apocalyptic and the utopian versions of the world as through invoking the false to investigate and undermine historical clichés and confront alternative possibilities of political life.

ANIMATION AND FALSIFYING NARRATION: *THE ILLUSIONIST*

The powers of the false inherent to the time-image has "topology and time" as a primary characteristic (Deleuze 1989a, 125). Though Deleuze does not discuss animation, his comments on crystalline narration as different expressions of time are central to his conception of falsifying in which "the virtual detaches itself from its actualizations [and] starts to be valid for itself" (ibid., 127). The actual image coalesces with the virtual, making them indiscernible from each other by giving way to "a multiplicity of movements on different scales" (ibid., 126) in which the artist becomes a forger, a deceiver who injects forms of time and treatment of visual and sound image that put truth into crisis. However, perception is not a consciousness of an actual image but part of an incomplete process that relies on an interval in which selection takes place "to direct movement in relation to a discernible cause" (Rodowick 1997, 36). In the case of the movement-image, this process involves a passage from perception to affection and to action, reliant on an indirect image of time. A different relation to subjectivity is constituted in the case of the time-image. Perception breaks with action to produce a dispersive reality that projects different circuits of time whereby the present is inflected by different orders of time.

In my discussion of *The Illusionist*, I follow Thomas Lamarre's discussion of animation as a process of injecting the role of the machine as technology onto an "abstract, multiplanar machine—that is at once technical/material and abstract/immaterial," since "the stacking of sheets or planes of the image (and thus compositing) happens in concert with the mechanical succession of the images" (2009, xxvi). This succession does not imply a totalizing structure but is rather the outcome of a multiplicity of forces: the creators, a play with realism, and a reliance on other machines, (such as trains, automobiles, printing presses, and cameras) that alter the spectator's perception and affect. Lamarre's concern is how to assess theories of animation as they connect to the character of cinema. In the context of Deleuze's movement-image, full animation strives "to produce the illusion of movement into depth, of travel into a world, thus suppressing the sense of movement between layers of the image" (Lamarre 2009, 10).

Cinematicism, a fusion of "cinema" and "animetism," is Lamarre's term for thinking about animation as addressing the overlap between movie and machines in relation to altering human perception.

Animetism, the process of aesthetically creating an animated image through multiple, more independent layers—also called flat or open compositing, versus the movement-into-depth of the closed compositing of Disney animation—is removed from the organicity of the movement-image in terms of the creation of characters, space, movement, and spectatorship on the basis of "affective responses, mood swings, and emotional values" (Lamarre 2009, 199) that provoke thinking and remembering, by "leaping across media"—involving cinema, television, cartoons—to revaluate the specific potential of the animated image to invoke its becoming "the soul and brain of cinema" (ibid., 198), Lamarre offers a series of postulations that help guide thinking along these lines that assist me in my discussion of *The Illusionist* as an animation text. First of all, he insists on cinema's technological determinations that self-consciously involve "its thinking about technology" (ibid., xxx), its character, and effects. Further, he subordinates a discussion of themes and stories as well as reflection theory concerning the film's role as representation of a national allegory (ibid., xxxi). While not rejecting other technologies (for example, live-action film), Lamarre insists on attending to animation's materiality and concomitant immateriality, its actual and virtual character. He also regards the animetic machine as an ensemble that straddles a middle course (via Henri Bergson and Gilbert Simondon) that is neither idealism nor realism but characteristic of image composition that arises from a center of indetermination "where delay or duration arises, and with it thoughts, emotions and affective responses" (ibid., xxxii). Thus, following the tenuous relations between the movement and time-image in Deleuze, Lamarre places the animetic image at a crisis of the organic movement-image that suggests a veering toward the time-image.

My discussion of *The Illusionist* (2010) underplays thematic and narrative analysis and stresses its metacritical dimensions that complicate the animated body through awareness of cinema history and technology. Certain reviewers interpret the film (for example, Ebert, 2011) as a nostalgic narrative, but this is only a partial view. Indeed, the professional failure of the magician and the film, as well as the filmmaker Jacque Tati, has been seen as yearning for a lost world. The film has been accused (even more than *The Triplets of Belleville*, 2003) of sentimentality, thus aligning the narration with the movement-image and its organic, linear narration. The significant role of animation is neglected when the film is treated as a straightforward narrative. *The Illusionist*'s treatments of the animated image suggest that another form of affect emerges, belonging to sensation and thought, rather than sentiment. Tatischeff's animated figure belongs to the power of the false. His role as illusionist inflects the entire film to become a medium for challenging long-standing binary distinctions between the real and imaginary, between film and the art of animation.

The film depends on a form of compositing that creates the illusion of movement on the part of the characters in landscape drawings that enhance their mobility through the simulation of depth. The compositing produces effects of live action, but the characters disrupt the spectator's total affective immersion in the scenes through the detailed creation of their forms, gestures, and mechanical behavior enhanced through caricature of the figures. The compositing of the "characters" invokes a multiply determined sense of their connections to clichéd attitudes associated with appearance and behavior though animation derived from multiple sources (burlesque, comic strip, and cinema). On the one hand, the work of animation seems to chart a linear downward journey from popular cinematic to mass commercial forms through the figure of the titular illusionist Tatischeff. On the other hand, the conspicuousness of transformation from animation to live action via cinema in the film clip of Tati (*né* Tatischeff) underpins the metacritical aspect of the film by self-consciously invoking technological/aesthetic investments that focus on a counter-history of animation technology. The figure of Tatischeff invites reflection on the relation of forms of animation via cinema that relate to connections between cinematicity and magic as integral to the evolution of the cinematic medium.

The initial sequence of the Music Hall, where Tatischeff repeats his classic tricks to an indifferent and booing audience, as well as to hostile co-workers, suggests the multiple planes in which the animation operates, offering a context for this changing culture through shifting views of the orchestra, the quality of other performers, views from offstage and onstage, and the positioning of Tatischeff within these different frames.

Similarly, the ensuing scenes involving the instruments of his profession are developed through the introduction of an unruly rabbit (the stock of his trade) that is pejoratively likened by the workman to a rat. This points to the use of animals inherent not only in the magic profession but in the history of animation, and references the contemplation of powers of the false through mutating relations between human and animal.

Tatischeff exits the theater where his act has bombed, gazes at his poster, goes to a train station, and finally to a boat, thus constituting the next phase of his and the spectator's journey essential to *The Illusionist*'s treatment of time as animated movement. The trip has now brought him to London where, like a somnambulist, he walks to his next place of employment. In a rather lengthy sequence in which he becomes a spectator to the performance of a rock group, "The Britoons," the editing becomes more complex, intercut as it is with different perspectives—his from offstage on the performers, the rock performers, and the teen audience that screams hysterically at the group, seen from Tatischeff's position. He is finally allowed to appear for an audience of two, an old woman and a young boy, the latter of whom exposes the magic tricks. On the street again, he removes the poster advertising his performance and is next seen at a carnival along with a heavy-set opera singer whose act he follows, though a staggering drunk interrupts his act. The cinematic journey has taken him and the spectator through the vicissitudes of performance and also through a range of animation techniques employed to enhance and to create curiosity, wonder, and thought about the film's animation techniques.

While repetition manifests itself in Tatischeff's return to the train station to visualize the futility of his attempts to survive, the viewer is astounded by the changing treatment of landscape that produces a sensation of awe in how the compositing characteristic of multiplanar animation shifts from the cityscape to the mountains and then to the sea to create a dizzying sense of place, perspective, and the perception of movement. The various journeys in the film undertaken by Tatischeff highlight the role of travel and of sameness and difference so central to the film's narration that connects technology and animation. Lamarre's study of animation introduces cinematic connections between trains and modern perception derived from Wolfgang Schivelbusch (1986) that coincide with the effect of traveling at speed to emphasize modern modes of perception. The perspectives created by *The Illusionist*'s focus on trains and other forms of travel through animation are an invitation to the spectator to appreciate animation as having a stake in broadening perceptions of the composited image.

Tatischeff's arrival in a Scottish village appears initially to carry the viewer back in time to a pastoral idyll through the images of the animals, shop, location by the water, and the period character of the inn where Tatischeff will remain and work for a short while. Once again, after the traditional dancing and his mildly received performance, a jukebox is brought in, the inhabitants dance to the music generated by the mechanical instrument; thus, another stage in the downward trajectory of the magician is figured. However, Tatischeff does have an admirer in Alice, a young woman, who works at the inn and believes in his magic. The animation takes on a different cast in the enigmatic and nonverbal encounters between Tatischeff and Alice that depend on the role of objects. Curiously, his magic is connected to his buying her red shoes, an allusion perhaps to the Michael Powell film about dance art (*The Red Shoes*, 1948). Thus, another journey finds him no longer alone as Alice emerges at the station having followed him, and the two figures are connected to various perspectives of Edinburgh: the castle, modern shops, the streets, and the hotel in which the two live.

The incongruity of the aging man and the young girl evokes Chaplin's *Modern Times* (1936), since that film, Tati's *Mon oncle* (1958), and Chomet's film all involve technology and modernity. In short, the analogy between animation and cultural history continues to play a prominent role throughout the film. The scene where Tatischeff spies Alice with the young man and hides only to find himself in a theater ("The Cameo") where Tati's *Mon oncle* is showing complicates the question of the technologies portrayed throughout by juxtaposing live action film to animation. Tatischeff stands, looks at the image, and then runs out of the theater. The significance of Tati's image is not mere homage: It is central to the "peaks of present and the past" that the film invokes through the insertion of this clip, with Tati viewed on the screen and Tatischeff seen from the rear. Says Chomet of this brief encounter, "I wanted to experiment in this confrontation to see if in this confrontation the animated drawing of Tati doesn't appear truer than the 'true' Tati filmed in *Mon oncle*. How at this moment

FIGURE 5.3. Tatischeff meets Tati in *Mon Oncle*, *The Illusionist*, Chomet, 2010.

can one weigh this film from the other side when the moment where the true Tati meets the false?" (Genin and Goudet 2010, 101).

The doubled image of Tatischeff and Tati raises the question of whether or how it matters which image is the false and which the true, the animated or the film image, the past or the present. The Edinburgh segment of *The Illusionist* best orchestrates the multiplanar dimensions of the film's animation revealing different visual and conceptual planes. Among these is the homage to filmmaker Jacques Tati through the brief film clip from *Mon oncle*, evoking Tati's cinematic persona in that and such other films as *Jour de fête* (1949) and *Les vacances de Monsieur Hulot* (*Mr. Hulot's Holiday*, 1953). While the inclusion of the film clip invokes the cinematic medium, it exceeds it by introducing different dimensions through tying the cinematic image to an animated form and so raising the issue of the connections between the real and the virtual as against conceptions of true and false. Tatischeff is not a mere copy of his filmic namesake any more than Tati's cinematic image is false in relation to his actual image in life. Through translating the figure of Tati into the real Tatischeff by way of animation, the Chomet film foregrounds the element of time, its relation to different visual forms, cinema and animation, not as antagonists but as the problematic of virtual as it relates to animation and by extension to counter-history as a multifaceted encounter with representation and meaning.

The film might also be considered as an animated version of a biopic on Tati, involving aspects of his life and work. The introduction of Alice conveys not only generational but also biographical and cultural difference. It also compels a shift into an affective register that reinforces significant differences between the young girl and the considerably older Tatischeff. While from an interpretive reading this difference can be considered an Oedipal relationship, the animation leads elsewhere: beyond theatricality, beyond nostalgia for the past, and especially beyond the sentiment of loss attributed to it, and to a confrontation with the power of animation.

Full or complete animation is most often articulated as a closed system and presumes a relationship to a theory of representation and time closely allied to conventional historicizing, while limited animation as referred by animation theorists such as Thomas Lamarre emphasizes uncertainty and indeterminacy as enabling investigation to consider the unthought involved in the medium. Lamarre suggests that full composition is closer to the action-image "through 'closed' compositing and through the production of action-images that serve to mask the gap that cannot be entirely closed." The tendency of full animation, therefore, is to "'step on the gas' or to pour on the sentiment" (ibid., 200), and Chomet's film does indeed present situations that are potentially melodramatic; but the attraction of the text resides in its preoccupation with form. In the case of *The Illusionist*, the element of time works through sensations of movement, color, and landscape to shift attention onto technique. The "pouring on" of sentiment alluded to operates differently in *The Illusionist*. Its composition resonates with Deleuze's descriptions of the time-image in terms of its creation of characters and actors as "see-ers," forgers in the interest of the creative power of the false via illusion.

The film's sensitivity to the passage of time, especially in relation to memory and to the different regions or circuits that enable movement between past and present and the role of visual and aural images to unsettle the old forms of realism through different sensations, injects thinking into the image. The passage through the organic to the mental is carried through the baroque character of the animation in which past and present interact and memory holds out the potential of difference. By examining the film solely in terms of its narrative, its drawing on clichés, its homage to Tati in the spirit of a biopic based on content and limited sense of generic form, it could be considered a throwback to the movement-image. However, the difference introduced by the union of hand and digital creation and the differences developed in the parallel between the death of live performance and the triumph of digital animation enact a concern with an alternative counter-history that is sensitive to the relations between cinema, animation, and technology. The prominent uses of color in the film are another instance of the signifying dimensions of animation.

The techniques of animation invoke the perennial issue of illusion and magic as inherent in the real. The animated reincarnation of Tati serves as reminder of earlier cinematic forms of thinking on media and on animation in particular. Rather than reinforcing rigid distinctions between live action and animation, *The Illusionist* connects past forms of cinematic art through cinema onto animation to explore productive ways of seeing and hearing through realizing different ways of seeing. The powers of the false in relation to the real and the imaginary become indiscernible, though not confused. The introduction of time involves reconsiderations of falsity and truth to invoke thinking sameness and difference, identity and representation, in the interests of thinking differently. Thus, *The Illusionist* is, as its title suggests, concerned with the nature and machinery of illusion in relation to history and memory, placing the viewer in a position in which the film becomes more than a story, even more than a formal exploration of animation; it becomes hybrid form for staging an encounter with the power of animation for thinking counter-historically as difference.

VIOLENCE AND PEDAGOGY: COLDNESS AND CRUELTY IN MICHAEL HANEKE'S FILMS

Michael Haneke is a filmmaker whose work is also vitally concerned with media history and spectatorship through scenarios concerned with performativity, illusion, and the nature and consumption of media images.

His films create uncertainty in discerning relations between the real and illusory that "ask for a different concept of history that seems to be inspired by Walter Benjamin" (Speck 2010, 60). Much has been written about Haneke's "perverse but insistent dramatization of violence and brutality, affected not only on the characters in his films but on the spectator as well" (Martig 2010, 34). My discussion of *Das weisse Band: Einer Deutsche Kindersgeschichte* (*The White Ribbon: A Child's Story*, 2009) and of *La pianiste* (2001) confront this filmmaker's reputation for coldness and cruelty by examining the films' treatment of violence from a philosophical/aesthetic position that resists familiar forms of explanation and a litigious verdict of assignable guilt to characters.

The treatment of violence functions in investigative fashion as a perplexing parable that demands that "what may seem deceptively clear at the time" (Stewart 2010, 42) must be regarded as problematic rather than an accurate accounting of past and future. The problematic posed by see Haneke's film can be related to Pasolini's film *Salo*, "haunted by a question to which ... [it] cannot reply" (Deleuze 1989a, 175). In other words, it is not the filmmaker who is cruel but the intolerable cruelty of the world. Haneke's two films rehearse a familiar scenario of violence but resist a familiar historical interpretation in relation to Nazism through an enigmatic, if not allegorical, treatment of characters and situations that have a broader implication connecting past and present in relation to conceptions of history as theater. Nietzsche's writing is critical to conceptions of the theater of history. As we have seen in my previous chapters, this form of theater is "a theater of unbelief, of movement, as Physis, already a theater of cruelty," and, invoking Nietzsche's version of this form of theatricality, Deleuze writes,

> We experience pure forces, dynamic lines in space which act without intermediary upon the spirit and link it directly with nature and history with a language that speaks before words, with words which develop before organized bodies with masks before faces, with spectres and phantoms before characters—the whole apparatus of repetition as a terrible power. (Deleuze 1994, 10)

It is this terrible power of repetition that Haneke's films explore through his creation of counter-history by invoking the masks, specters, and phantoms that are attached to actual places and events and, through fiction, render a cruel, often surreal, world that entails violence in its focus on children, pedagogy, the family, the church, and art as well. My particular focus in the discussion of the two Haneke films is to examine how violence, as in the Cronenberg film, is connected to the power of the false—not as error or immorality—but as indicative of revealing truth as the ultimate falsifier, since "the power of falsity is time itself, not because time has changing concepts, but because the form of time as becoming brings into questions any formal model of truth" (Deleuze 1995, 66). Thus, expressions of violence are to be regarded as suspect when they purport to offer models of pathological explanations for their existence.

THE WHITE RIBBON

The White Ribbon is a film situated in late nineteenth- and early twentieth-century Wilhelmine, Germany, whose "historical" dimension, as is so often the case with Haneke, portrays and investigates powerful institutions, ideologies, and cultural norms through a combination of authoritarianism, nationalism, and Protestantism (Grundmann 2010b, 38). However, in relation to its treatment of the past, "the film is not a document but a metaphor. The education metaphor works everywhere and, according to Haneke, implicates the spectator as well" (Grundmann 2010c, 598, 605–606). It would not be unreasonable to consider the film a variant of the crime film, with the spectator in the role of a detective concerned with unraveling the mysterious commission of violent crimes in a small village, crimes that are both physical and also epistemological. In keeping with his other films, this art film has a philosophical, aesthetic, and ethical design on its viewers.

In the conventional crime film, a solution to a criminal act in the past is sought, and the perpetrator is exposed and punished. Domietta Torlasco's interrogation of Antonioni's *L'avventura* (1960) is applicable to Haneke's film:

> What happens, then, when the investigative paradigm deteriorates . . . ? What happens not only to our desire to see into the past but also to the very possibility of isolating the past from the present and the future, locating the detective and ourselves, the spectators, in a time that is successive to the time of the crime? (2008, 3)

In other words, does *The White Ribbon* implicate the spectator in a form of narration that upsets certainty about the criminals' identity, though there is certain knowledge of the crimes? The film thus becomes a form of counter-history in its refusal to connect the crimes directly to Nazism and to the violence enacted as a document of the past but as an exploration of the present and future that invokes an unsettling perspective as to its focus on violence, secrecy, and resentment.

Haneke's film assaults the viewers with portraits of cruel and violent acts. The town's physician survives a brutal accident; however, his incestuous relations with his daughter, indifference to his younger male child, and contempt toward their governess whom he has also sexually exploited are inherent in the enigmatic world the film presents, Among other victims are a carpenter's wife, a steward's baby, and two young boys, Karli and Sigi; the physical violence of these crimes is largely relegated to off-screen, but not the affect they evoke. Haneke's *Deutsche kindergeschichte* (a German children's story) has the cruelty characteristic of fairy tales in which the cruelty is identified with both children and adults. In Haneke's film, the children are also investigated since they too are implicated as victims and as perpetrators.

The film begs to be considered as a form of realism that pertains to the landscape and events portrayed for their fidelity to reproduce the way things were, through a scholarly reconstruction and recounting of the pre–World War I era. The film, in its emphasis on verbal and physical violence, withholds the most graphic images of physical cruelty perpetrated on and by children. The narrated and partially visible acts of violence and their aftereffects produce a discomfort between what is narrated and what is seen. With only a partial perspective, often through door frames, as with Rudi looking at his sister Anna on the surgical table when the doctor performs the ambiguous ear piercing, or behind closed doors when the Pastor beats his errant children, the emphasis shifts from familiar to confusing, if not unsettling, responses.

Furthermore, the adults are treated obliquely, largely identified by their social class and profession but not given fictional names: the upper class Baron and Baroness, the professional physician, the Pastor, the Steward and his wife, and the Teacher. Significantly, the Teacher as nameless narrator (through the voice-over by Ernst Jacobi) is not the voice of the actor Christian Friedel who plays him. His incomplete knowledge of events, limited if not unreliable narration, serve to reduce his authority. Though an outsider to most of the events along with the viewer, he does assume a position of detective in trying to identify the perpetrator of Sigi's mutilation. When the Teacher confronts the vulnerable Erna, who indicates some knowledge of what has transpired but passes it off as a dream, he actively undertakes to investigate the children's role, only to be silenced by the Pastor when he comes to inform him of what he has learned. However, his treatment of Erna leads to her rough treatment at the hands of the police and to an unresolved outcome to this investigation of the crimes. As for the Pastor, who plays a critical role in the film in relation to his harsh disciplinary treatment of his own children, Haneke regards him

> not as evil . . . he's really convinced of what he does. He really loves his children. That's the horror of it. It was normal to beat one's kids. . . . It's not very interesting to see him as a sadist or as a grotesque mental case. If these people had just been perverts this kind of behavior wouldn't have such broad effects. (Horwath 2009, 29)

When Haneke claims that "there are no completely positive or negative characters in the film" we must either regard this comment as misleading or as corroboration of another position on ethics in relation to the cruel events presented. The crimes of violence that have been committed belong to another order of thinking that remains masked in silence and uncertainty. In Haneke's case, "questions get posed but not answered" (Grundmann 2010c, 606). These questions are related to the power of the false that eschews judgment insofar as the question of truth, as I have indicated, rests on the problematic belief in truth telling and of falsification as revelatory of how judgment impedes recognition of life. Thus, "it is not a matter of judging life in the name of a higher authority which would be the good, the true; it is a matter on the contrary, of evaluating every being, every action and passion, even every value in relation to the life they involve" (Deleuze 1989a, 141). Hence, Haneke's endorsement of Goethe's statement "I have never heard of any crime which I might not have committed" (Horwath 2009, 30) is applicable to his treatment of the characters in *The White Ribbon*—both adults and children.

The children are not treated sentimentally. They are given names and assigned positions in relation to the family. What is significant is that they are portrayed as sleepwalkers, dreamers (for example, the case of Erna) as hallucinatory, or as unwilling to reveal what they know. Children or childlike characters play a critical role in Haneke's films but especially in this film. In his discussion of the time-image and its relation to neorealism, Deleuze highlights the role of children (as well as childlike characters "prey to a vision") in the world of adults: "The child is affected by a certain motor helplessness, but one which makes him all the more capable of seeing and hearing . . . subject to sensory-motor schemata which are automatic and pre-established . . . all the more liable on the least disturbance of equilibrium . . . to free itself from the laws of this schemata and reveal itself in a visual and sound nakedness, crudeness and brutality, which make it unbearable" (Deleuze 1989a, 3).

Here, as in Deleuze's view of neorealism, the children are witnesses through the film's elliptical and enigmatic treatment of surveying and also of silence and withholding. Their refusal to say what they know is matched by the reiterated visual play on closed doors, shrouded events, and scenes that reinforce their inability to speak for fear of disciplinary consequence, so that the film as a form of counter-history demands more of a viewer who cannot remain comfortable in a belief in the German past as "aberrant" or "monstrous." According to Grundmann, the world of *The White Ribbon* is symptomatic of a familiar, almost everyday, world in which the young individual is broken so that he and she "become tolerable for society" (2010c, 599).

This observation is comforting and familiar to those in search of a description and causal explanation for the negative effects of discipline and punishment as social controls that suggest social amelioration. However, Brian Price and John David Rhodes remark, "If this is what Haneke's films do, ask, ask us to think about, or ask us to do, then we shouldn't need Haneke at all" (2010, 4). Haneke's films are not reassuring in their exploration of power. *The White Ribbon*, in its reliance on the power of the false, challenges the spectator to confront a world that, in Deleuze's terms, enacts the "will to power," the will to dominate through the agency of "higher men who claim to judge life by their own standards, by their own authority" (Deleuze 1989a, 140). Deleuze resists judgment

FIGURE 5.4. The Pastor and the united community, *The White Ribbon*, Haneke, 2009.

about these higher men in terms that I believe are applicable to *The White Ribbon*; the film seems to be concerned with undermining distinctions between of truth and falsity as they offer shocking and difficult images to contemplate outside familiar forms of historical representation.

In *The White Ribbon*, violence is inherent in the events dramatized or alluded to in the film, but with a difference. While, in mainstream film, sympathetic identification is achieved through an exaggeration or aestheticization of the violent actions to create empathy and fascination with or repulsion to the gruesome images of blood and mutilation (Mattias Frey, in Price and Rhodes 2010, 155), Haneke's film eschews rhetorical and stylistic strategies that frustrate identification with either the perpetrators or the victims. Haneke's restrained and elliptical portraits of the affected characters are only one clue to his resistance to classical horror forms; another resides in his treatments of the characters that avoid reductive notions of them as mere victims or monsters. The cruelty of his film resides in his refusal to pass moral judgment on them. He prods his spectators not only to confront the familiar forms that have been adopted to account for historical violence but to contemplate their imprisonment in the power of repetition without the comfort of thinking differently.

The film does not "resolve" the investigation of the crimes perpetrated but culminates in another scenario of violence and cruelty to come by abruptly shifting to the coming of the war that blocks further exploration of the previous events and leaves the viewer with still more questions about their meaning. The communal service for the coming of World War I visually and aurally corroborates what Garrett Stewart has described as "a darkness at noon" anticipatory of the greater violence to come (2010, 47) in the advent of World War I.

The counterintuitive factor entails the pedagogical possibility, however slight, for the spectator of breaking with the past, with repetition through rethinking the nature and effects of powerlessness. Herein lies counter-history in this ostensible historical film as a pedagogical exercise on historicizing, an exercise that demands thinking an engagement with "philosophic questions concerning structure and the ways in which structures produce different kinds of violence" (Price and Rhodes, 2010, 36). The violence enacted in the film is not temporized, explained or, offered as reassurance, and the abrupt ending with the coming of the war in the anticipation of more violence leaves the viewer bereft of explanation but with invitation to "step into the unknown" (Orr, 263).

A DIFFERENT PEDAGOGY OF COUNTER-HISTORY: HANEKE'S *THE PIANO TEACHER*

La pianiste (*The Piano Teacher*, 2001) offers a different, though equally disturbing form of counter-history to that of *The White Ribbon*. This film also invokes familial and pedagogical relationships through an investigation of the cruelty and effects of the struggle over power and domination that infect every aspect of personal and social existence. Adapting elements of Elfriede Jelinek's novel *Die Klavierspielerin* (*The Piano Player*), Haneke extracts from her literary text a mother–daughter drama that focuses on a psychocultural portrayal of masochism and its relation to power, not as a clinical or pathological treatment or even as pornography but as storytelling built on the unmistakable ruins of modern European culture conveyed through music and pedagogy.

Critics of *La pianiste* have described the film as highlighting a "sadomasochistic" and/or masochistic scenario (Peucker, in Grundmann, 2010, 143–44). In its focus on the desiring body, the film subjects the viewer to painful encounters with physical mutilation and cruelty. As in Haneke's other films, these images serve not as an incitement to pleasure so much as a prod to think about philosophical, aesthetic, and historical reflections on pleasure and pain (Freud, Deleuze, Lacan). Deleuze's writings on the powers of the false are revealed in his reworking of psychoanalytic concepts concerning aggression germane to Haneke's spectacles of cruelty and torture. Deleuze's *Masochism: Coldness and Cruelty* (1989b) addresses power and sexuality through a critique of the long-standing fusion of sadism and masochism, termed sadomasochism. Deleuze delinks their familiar fusion and situates each as offering different regimes of power that *The Piano Teacher* enacts in the multiple levels of interaction. The basis of the film's counter-history is related to *The White Ribbon* and relies on a form of narration that treats multiple viewpoints to produce doubt about the status of the image especially as this concerns the nature of counter-history and memory. This process relies on doubling and splitting, on enigmatic events, and a challenging of personal and national identity. Torture and violence are the basis for moving the viewer beyond cliché into thinking about relations between sexuality and power.

The film's abrupt opening intersperses the viewer and its credits to a quasi-comic scene of a mother's (Annie Girardot) aggression toward her daughter Erika (Isabelle Huppert) as the mother opens their apartment door and immediately seizes Erika's purse and scatters its contents. The women fight over Erika's purchase of a frivolous dress, and the mother calls her daughter a bitch (accompanied by the sounds of television that will come to be associated throughout with the mother). Haneke introduces a familiar cinematic image of a mother and daughter relationship that provokes escalating violence on the part of each figure. This segment is interrupted by a news report that highlights an image of a man wounded for loudly advocating women's inferiority, interrupted by yet another film credit. And the mother complains about money saved by both for a new lodging and spent frivolously by her daughter on a new dress.

A bedroom scene with the two in bed prolongs the conflict with the mother's complaints now about her daughter's professional identity, to admonish Erika that "no one must surpass you" as a pianist. This scene too is interrupted by a credit. The next sequence portrays Erika listening to a student of whom she is critical for the student's sloppy playing. Again, after another interruption by credits, Erika's style of teaching piano is further foregrounded as she observes a young man, who, in her words, can "play only phrases," but the scene is again aborted by a title. Erika, alone, reaches for her coat and gloves, dresses, takes her purse, and exits from the practice room as the scene cuts to the final title that credits Haneke as the director. The numerous credits that disrupt the events are an integral part of the film's narration that will inhibit continuity and foreshadow the enigmatic mother/daughter relationship, the daughter's interaction with her students, and oblique fragments of the world that the characters and the spectator will inhabit.

Further problematic relations between Erika and her mother via their exemplification of European bourgeois culture are manifest when the two attend a musical recital in a private home. As they ride an elevator, a young man races up the stairs to keep up with them. On arrival, they are introduced to the breathless young man as the hosts' nephew, Walter Klemmer (Benoît Magimel). Before the assembled guests, Erika plays the piano. The scene cuts from her hands on the keys to her impassive face and to close-ups of Walter gazing at her in rapt attention. At a buffet dinner, Walter approaches Erika enthusiastically and praises her for keeping classical music alive, though Erika assumes a superior and arrogant stance toward him. She makes a point of alluding to the writings of Theodor Adorno, commenting on Schumann's Fantasia in C Major as a "twilight work" in which the composer felt threatened by mortality and loss of sanity. Her comments are exemplary of her pedagogical, if not derivative, stance toward music, despite her competence as a performer/accompanist. Her presentation of herself to Walter is as a purveyor of superior insight and knowledge about music.

Fascinated by her insights on music and on her performance, Walter naïvely praises her for being "a good teacher," and, based on her comments, he changes his plans to play Schumann and instead performs Schubert's Scherzo in E Major. Thus, in her teaching, Erika presents herself as a paragon of icy commitment to her art, and the interactions with her students are emotionally cold, precise, and pitiless, symptomatic of her persona as one of discipline and control. These interactions, bordering on cruelty, will animate a masochistic scenario in which the mother/daughter relationship plays a determining role in relation to Erika's secret life of desire.

In relation to Mrs. Kohut's tyrannical insistence that Erika always be home promptly from work, indicative of the fusion with her daughter, Erika reveals a hidden and counter dimension in her constraining life through her visit to a porn parlor. In a private compartment, she looks at videos of nude women and men in various acts of sexual intercourse. Leaning over and picking up a discarded paper with stained seminal fluid from a waste paper basket, she holds it to her nose. This striking contrast between her professional demeanor and her leisure inclinations are prelude to the revelation of a persona "incommensurable with her facade of respectability" (Ma, in Grundmann, 2010c, 512).The other side to her autocratic persona emerges in her somnambulistic wanderings that take her not only to the porn parlor but to a drive-in theater where she is aroused to masturbation at the sight of a young couple in the throes of intercourse. Caught in the act, she is angrily chased away by them, punished for her vicarious participation in their sexuality.

This scene in inverted fashion mirrors her peremptory treatment of the students at the porn parlor, whom she calls "pigs" and threatens to inform on them to their mothers. Both scenes concern a fusion of the anticipation of sexual pleasure and its punishment that will emerge in more specific situations and images through her relationship with Walter. Her resistance to taking him on as a student is prelude to enigmatic expressions of cruelty that she will exercise on him and also on her student Anna, and, finally, in self-destructive fashion on herself. We learn more about her penchant for self-punishment through her mutilating her sexual organs as well as observing the bleeding wound. Thus, the viewer is confronted with the fusion of pleasure and pain involving her sexualized body, raising questions about how to understand these seemingly disjunctive and uncertain aspects of her behavior.

In an effort to avoid reductive sociological, judgmental, and narrowly psychological explanations for the film's explorations of Erika's position as both torturer and victim, I submit Deleuze's complex text on masochism as germane to the film's emphasis on cruelty power, in which he is critical of the frequent conventional conflation of sadism and masochism under the rubric of sadomasochism. In his analysis, sadism and masochism are different psychocultural expressions of violence and eroticism. In sadism, the emphasis is on an alliance in cruelty between father and daughter, and it is he who incites the daughter to torture and murder the mother (Deleuze 1989b, 57–69,). The distinctive dimension of sadism resides in its repetition of cold-blooded, depersonalizing crimes of violence that negate nature.

No less cruel but more aesthetic, the masochistic fantasy is aligned with the mother, involving the "administration of cruelty" in which the masochist "idealize[s] the functions of the bad mother and transfers them onto the good mother" (Deleuze 1989b, 62), as would seem to apply to the oscillating affect that characterizes Erika's relations with her mother, involving buried family, if not political history. Masochism founded on fetishism, suspense, and the elevation of the ideal against the real remains suspended or neutralized in the ideal, the better to shield itself against the painful awareness of reality (ibid., 32). In masochism, punishment and humiliation serve "as prerequisites for obtaining gratification" (ibid., 71). Masochism is predominantly an aesthetic phenomenon, involving disavowal and deferral in the perverse anticipation of pleasure to come. A critical distinction between the sadist and the masochist is the significance of the contractual and instructional relation between the torturer and the victim that "presupposes in principle the free consent of the contracting parties and determines between them a system of the reciprocal rights and duties . . . ; it cannot affect a third party" (ibid., 77). If Erika's behavior in *The Piano Teacher* seems to evoke a portrait of a masochist, this is not to conclude that Haneke's exploration of her persona as contained in masochism is reduced to univalent explanation of the film's explorations of cruelty and violence.

The most prolonged episode of Erika's cruelty is the scene in the school lavatory where Walter finds her and seeks to consummate his desire for her in this unromantic space of bodily wastes, similar to her frequenting the porn parlors. He kisses her and picks up her skirt to penetrate her, and she seems at first responsive. Then she becomes resistant, keeping him at bay, and repeating for him, in the language of Deleuze's masochist to "wait." When eager to relieve himself even if without her, she further orders him not to look at his penis, refusing him the gratification of an orgasm though she insists on his facing her, so she can see "it." Unrelenting, and in the spirit of a masochistic contract, she tells him that she will send him a letter telling him what it is she wants. When he comes to the house, she refuses to yield until he reads the letter with her "instructions" about sex and agrees to its contents. Walter at this point is still acting love-struck but increasingly impatient about ejaculation; however, Erika's refuses to grant him gratification.

Erika's behavior is, however, not that of the sadist who requires total domination for purposes of destruction but of a female masochist in which the victim, a man, is to be "educated and fashioned by the authoritarian woman" (Deleuze 1989b, 22). The teacher seeks to educate the young man through a contract that depends on Walter's consent to the terms once he learns of its contents. Walter, for a time in his enamored and idealistic fantasy of his teacher, first occupies a position of submissive waiting but later takes on the sadistic position of the degraded and degrading role of rapist. The relationship between Erika and Walter exposes instruction as an imposed power dependent on the student's subservience and introduces eroticism as intrinsic to instruction inherent to cultural, subcultural, familial social, and political forms of expression. Erika's behavior repeats her abject relationship to her demanding and withholding mother, but also undermines it through seeking perverse gratification for her desire. The film pedagogical dimensions also extend to the film's spectator, who occupies a contractual position that includes acceptance in the encounter with the spectacle of pain.

We learn through her contract with Walter how Erika articulates for him the stages of a sexual encounter that involve gagging, blindfolding, whipping, rimming to place her tongue into his buttocks, and the requirement that she and Walter perform sex outside the mother's door. And in the spirit of a masochistic contract, she insists that his assent is voluntary. This scenario takes place in Erika's locked room as Erika's mother bangs loudly on the locked door. Pacing frantically as the ubiquitous TV plays, her mother turns down the sound to eavesdrop on what is transpiring beyond the locked door, rhyming Erika's own voyeurism at the porn house. Walter's response, after Erika's demands are exposed, is, "You're sick. You need treatment. I don't want to soil my hands . . . on your sort," and he leaves the apartment. The falsification of Erika's identity produces uncertainty as her character shifts from chaste respectability to forms of sexuality that lead to self-injury.

The motif of madness comes into play, identified earlier in her predilection for Schumann and Schubert in her unconventional pursuit of pleasure. A second time, Erika is told, this time by her mother, that she is mad when Erika climbs on top of her in bed, seeking physical contact that seems less a movement toward a sexual encounter and more a desire for incorporation. Nonetheless, in the film, following the masochist scenario, Erika becomes the embodiment of the despotic matriarch (Deleuze 1989b, 67). It is evident that Deleuze focuses on the male figure as the recipient of an encounter that "fashion[s] the woman into a despot" in which "the masochistic experience involves the putative education on the part of the victim who speaks through the mouth of the torturer, and through whom there are a reversal and reduplications in the allocations of roles and discourses" (ibid., 22). Significantly, physical violence is reserved for her own body: in the bathroom scene where she cuts her labia, in her final sexual encounter with Walter, and when she stabs herself in the final moments of the film.

This holding up of a mirror to nature and history is, however, shared by both the sadist and masochist, but, in the case of the masochist, the female torturer "escapes from her own masochism by assuming the active role contrary to sadism that entails submission. The proud and imperious masochistic heroine disavows sensuality but not feeling" (Deleuze 1989b, 52). It is critical that the father is absent and that Erika and her mother contest finally for the role of dominance in a scenario different from the Oedipal one. This reading of masochism foregrounds the mother over the father (the father is absent and alluded to briefly and ambiguously) to give rise to an expressions of cruelty characterized by the mother's treatment of her daughter and mirrored in Erika's abjection to and fusion with her to alter and expand reigning Oedipal presuppositions of the familial order.

The scene that enhances the scenario of cruelty involves the sexual encounters between Erika and Walter in her own apartment and with the mother locked in her room, per Erika's instructions to Walter. Erika has engineered this scenario, in contradictory fashion, to realize pleasure that

FIGURE 5.5. Repetition or difference? Closure in
The Piano Teacher, Haneke, 2001.

ends in real rape. This scene of the crime in the familial space becomes the realization of Erika's attempts to free herself from the imprisonment of her milieu or perhaps suggests "a more radical solution ... [through] an event that would alter the very sense of what constitutes the parameters of being" (Coulthard 2011, 73). Walter or Erika appear to be symptomatic of a culture that contains romantic, idealized, and historically sanctioned conceptions of the role of art, and the film locates them in the heart of a culture that exerts a terrible power over others and inhibits their capacity to think and believe in the world. As Deleuze has written about modern cinema: "What is certain is that believing is no longer believing in another world, or in a transformed world. . . . I am the man who has lost his life and searching by all means possible to make it regain its place "(Deleuze 1989a, 173).

At the end of the film, Erika abandons her performance, stabs herself in the chest, though not fatally, with the kitchen knife she has brought from home and hidden on her person. She leaves the concert hall and vanishes into the landscape. This enigmatic closure suggests several possibilities characteristic of Haneke's form of closure to his films that transfer the burden of the film onto the spectator. To contemplate Erika's oscillation between dominating and being dominated, pleasure and punishment, is only one side of the struggle over domination that the film presents; the other involves Walter's jejune and clichéd romanticism, revealing the darker side of romantic love that emerges through his *ressentiment* expressed in his humiliation and degradation of her body.

Haneke's counter-history explores the persistence and effects of sexualized power relations as they exemplify not Erika's dilemma as symptomatic of exhausted discourses that underpin modern cinema and art but expose another face to the world in relation to the potential of becoming-other. The film is not invested in judgment but in an exploration of the power of the false exemplified in Erika's divided persona that challenges the spectator cruelly with the possibility that they have not yet confronted the "limit between knowledge and enjoyment" (Thakur 2007, 149). The film's viewers are confronted with a heretical view of cinema. Its counter-history is not an appeal for redemption through prevailing forms of art but an interrogation through the powers of the false produced through art that reveal alternative forces in the interests of producing something new through seeing the world differently, namely, less nostalgically, reductively, and judgmentally (Speck 2010).

FALSIFIED NARRATION IN THE FILMS OF ALEXEI BALABANOV: FREAKS IN COUNTER-HISTORY

Alexei Balabanov's *Of Freaks and Men* (1998) has properly provoked conflicting critical responses about its character and effects: Is it a historical film? Is it a commentary on post-Soviet culture and society? Is it an essay on the history of cinema? All three? None of the above? The discussion that follows regards this film and *Morphia* as productive instances of counter-history. The assemblage of myriad layers of time complicates a reductive answer to these questions particularly in relation to Balabanov's treatments of historicity. In addressing the issue of historicity during the Khrushchev Thaw (1956–67), Peter Petrov (2005) writes,

> During the Thaw, historicity ceases to be a viable category for understanding individual and social being. The dynamics of existence and, consequently, the dynamics of narrative are made sense of not in terms of successive stages, but in terms of co-present states. The energetic

principle behind narrative movement is no longer that of linear progress, but that of transcendence. In order to make this movement possible, space must somehow eschew its horizontality.

Petrov's comments on historicity share affinity with those of Deleuze who, in *Cinema 2*, views the post–World War II cinema as reliant on the time-image with its rejection of narrative continuity as linear progress as well as its treatment of characters who are somnambulistic, placing them in a position of being "see-ers." History becomes a coexistence of different orders of time to give narration a new value "irreducible to the dimensions of space" (Deleuze 1989a, 108). Nonlocalizable connections shift from one plane to another, from horizontal to vertical, present to past to future, frustrating chronology and serving to introduce a conception of simultaneity.

Of Freaks and Men offers a view of the early twentieth century through a focus on two families that fall prey to the machinations of three unscrupulous pornographers. The film begins with the title "Present" and slips into the past with Doctor Stasov's adoption of Siamese twins who are photographed as infants, introducing falsification through time. The light of a flashbulb fuses this episode with other images, this time of Engineer Radlov's family; his daughter, Liza, seated before an early twentieth-century portrait camera, is photographed as her father gazes longingly at the young girl bereft of a mother. Having initiated a connection between the domestic arena with the photographic medium, a title announces that "Years Passed," and, with the passing time, the situation of the families has changed but also has that of the photographers, Iogan (Sergei Makovetskii), Viktor Ivanovich (Viktor Sukhorukov), and Putilov (Vadim Prokhorov) who are now actively running a pornographic business featuring photos of nude women being beaten.

Iogan gains entry to the Radlov's house through his sister Grunia, Radlov's servant. While ejected by the engineer, the influence of the pornographers has its pernicious effects on the fate of the family. Engineer Radlov, being shown the photos of his daughter by his paramour, the maid Grunia, succumbs to a heart attack and dies, leaving the control of his will to Grunia under the guise of her serving in the role of mother to Liza, now a young woman (Dinara Drukarova). After Radlov's death, Iogan gains free access to the house, now also including Iogan's grandmother, and enlists Grunia and Putilov to coerce Liza into conforming to their "professional" demands. Thus, the viewer is given one of the two most publicized scenes of the film in which Liza, like the nude women in Iogan's clandestine basement establishment, is brought into a room nude and forced to crouch so that her buttocks are exposed to the camera that has been set up to film her, and she is whipped. Iogan will have the photo developed, and it will be sold to willing customers.

These episodes are intercut with scenes of the Stasov family with the male Siamese twins and doctor's blind wife, Ekaterina (Anzhelika Nevolina) who has showered the boys with attention and introduced them to music, piano playing, and singing, while she refuses sexual contact with her husband. In the case of both families, the one a widower, the other a sexually frustrated husband, the way is clear for the pornographers to film private acts of sexuality and deformity. The Stasov twins are a far greater commercial coup for Viktor Ivanovich, who sees their profitability for exploiting them as "freaks." Not only are they forced to perform sexual acts domestically but also they are lucrative in the theater. The pornographers consolidate the two households, bringing Liza and the twins, Tolya and Kolya, and later Ekaterina into the forefront as actors in this drama of sadism and masochism to titillate viewers though the photographic medium.

The presentation favors cinematic techniques that permit the viewer to confront events without the intervention of rhetorical strategies that would accentuate and reinforce morally judgmental responses to the world viewed. Instead, the sight of the bodies and the accompanying sights and sounds of whipped, humiliated, deformed, and exposed bodies coercively administered by the pornographers are better viewed through the lens of a grotesque, dark humor that elicits different, uncomfortable sensations that underplay the erotic dimensions of what is being shown and cast them into an enigmatic mode unsettling for the viewer. More to the point of the film's address of sexuality and deviance are the ways it self-consciously highlights the cinematic apparatus, focusing on photography, filmmaking, visual and auditory composition, and emphasis on intra- and extradiegetic spectators, thus creating indeterminacy about generic form, aesthetics, and particularly discursive investments in pornographic voyeurism. The problem posed by the film is how to view and understand the film's political and aesthetic investment in the context of the historical milieu of early cinema it has selected to investigate.

The critical literature on this film, as well as on Balabanov's other films (for example, *Trofim* [1996]; *Brat* [*Brother*, 1997]; *Brat 2* [*Brother 2*, 2000]; *Gruz 200* [*Cargo 200*, 2007]; and *Morfiy* [*Morphia*, 2008], focuses on the historical and political dimensions of this director's attention to embodiment, if not on its integral connection to his experimentation with cinematic practices. As Nancy Condee has commented, the city in Balabanov is "typically a dynamic, modern ironworks of unrelenting repetition, of aggressive and mechanized return . . . the metal id, amoral, primal, compelled toward acquisition and gratification" (2009, 223). And Frederick White, focusing particularly on the city of St. Petersburg, cites the writings of Pushkin, Gogol, and Dostoevsky that portray that city as an uncivilized space with inhabitants "haunted by demons and devils" (2008, 285) in relation to nineteenth- and early twentieth-century popular theories of degeneration, a view that has resonance in Balabanov's portrayal of the city in his film. White invokes the concept of degeneration, a concept traced to such figures as Cesare Lambroso whose writings focused on physical characteristics, heredity, and environment as a discourse that connected urban groups to a climate of criminality and pathology among whom were women, Jews, southern Italians, and physically deformed individuals. The concept of degeneracy was tied to the emergence of industrialization and urban life and was considered responsible for the degeneration of social life; White regards this as applicable to an understanding of the film. Pornography is, in his view, tied to a moral crisis, in which "deviant sexual pathology is indicative of a generalized economic malaise resulting in the ubiquitous devolution of post-Soviet Russia" (2008, 294).

The wealth of social and literary information that White brings to bear on the subject of degeneration and its connections to urban life and crime applies not only to *Of Freaks and Men* but to other Balabanov films. However, White's reading of the film is suggestive of a form of reflection theory that sees external events as reductively determining art, exemplifying social realism and familiar forms of historicism. Interesting and formative as this information is about context and time, it does not take into account the polysemic character of the cinematic image that has in its arsenal dynamic and complex relations to space and time, the real and the fantastic, that are not merely a dimension of modernism but are inherent to questions of what cinema is, how it evolved, and how it functions beyond information.

My focus on Balabanov's uses of the moving image moves in another direction. I regard his focus on suffering bodies not merely as a reflection of a doomed environment but as an inquiry into the ways in which embodiment has links to what Michel Foucault, in *The History of Sexuality* (1980), has identified as exemplary of the transformation of sex into a discourse disseminated through medicine, psychiatry, and science. It is hardly accidental that one of the characters in *Of Freaks and Men* is Stasov, a physician, and the other, Radlov, an engineer, thus, tying the film to science and technology. The doctor's adoption of the twins is ambiguous, related perhaps to his having helped deliver them and to his voyeurism as he views their fused bodies. Or perhaps his adopting the boys is connected to his marriage to a woman who rejects his sexual advances and his attempts to revivify their moribund relationship. Radlov, the engineer, is equally enigmatic. He is enamored of the technological promises held forth by cinema as a coming art form to "reveal truth." While Stasov's view of the cinematic body emerges from the desire to ameliorate his barren life, Radlov's euphoric and utopian view of the camera is expressed in his expectation of enrichment and social advancement through the new art.

Of Freaks and Men in certain ways bears reference to another earlier collaborative short film by Balabanov and other Russian filmmakers, *Pribytiye poyezda* (1996), which challenges Radlov's utopian view of motion pictures, focusing on a peasant, Trofim, who has murdered his brother and escapes by train to the city. On arrival, a movie cameraman taking shots of the train and of the passengers captures his image. Trofim is another of Balabanov's naïve and doomed male characters; his brief life in St. Petersburg ends with his being arrested for associating with criminal types and with his image excised from the alleged Pathé film "Russian Train Arriving." Reflexively, invoking the Lumières' *L'Arrivée d'un train à La Ciotat* (Arrival of a Train at La Ciotat, 1896), Balabanov's brief film offers a pessimistic view of the medium.

The repetitive and incremental presence of trains, along with boats, trolleys, and other forms of mobility, accompanied by classical music, is juxtaposed to interior shots of the Radlov house, creating disturbing

FIGURE 5.6a and b. Title and image from *Trofim*, Balabanov, 1996.

connections between interiority and exteriority. The ominous recurrence of the train in *Of Freaks and Men* is often viewed by the characters through a window or heard off-screen. In short, the film relentlessly explores a pessimistic, or at least inquisitorial, position about the character and fate of cinema, involving a blurring of boundaries between the private and public.

If *Of Freaks and Men* invokes a world self-consciously communicated through the cinematic apparatus that has fallen prey to bodily images of cruelty, violence, and torture situated within a decadent milieu, the film pays scrupulous attention to a technology of vision that both constructs and disseminates these images; it thus explicitly and implicitly situates itself as a media text obsessed with the exploited, if not doomed, nature and effects of cinema. The ironic emphasis on the visual is captured in the character of Ekaterina Kirillovna, whose blindness implicates other sensory responses, especially the aural in the uses of music that are evident throughout this film: for example, the reiterated music on the phonograph, her teaching music to the twins, the twins' performances as singers, the boat journey by Iogan rhythmically accompanied by the music of Mussorgsky and reiterated later in Liza's train journey west, as well as in the uses of Prokofiev that accompanies the viewings of the postcards. The classical music on the soundtrack in relation to the visual image is unsettling: it is evocative of the dissonant relation between sound and image throughout the film.

In the final scenes (minus dialogue) pornography and sexual commodities are displayed in shops, beckoning streetwalkers and flâneurs, including Liza and Iogan, into the perverse pleasures of cruelty, torture, and prostitution. And, after a lively demonstration on the street by an enthusiastic crowd chasing Putilov, now a celebrity, in an automobile, the victory of pornography is finally made manifest through a visit by Iogan to a movie house screening the film *Punishment for a Crime*. The film within the film replays the earlier scenes exposing images of bodily whipping that Iogan had helped create but that are now disseminated by Putilov. Iogan is the last to exit the screening. The film reaches its ambiguous closure in Iogan's suicide in the icy waters of the Neva. His disappearance in the river raises questions about the director's rationale for this enigmatic ending. Is Balabanov mocking this unattractive figure,

FIGURE 5.7. The *flâneuse* on the street of pornographic shops, *Of Freaks and Men*, Balabanov, 1998.

or portraying the death as "righteous punishment of Iogan for the trouble he has caused" (Condee 2009, 232)? Given Balabanov's self-conscious focus on cinema in this film (and briefly in *Trofim*), this ending suggests another order of analysis.

In the spirit of the powers of the false that have undergirded Balabanov's investigative treatment of cinema, *Trofim* and *Of Freaks and Men* focus on cinema as posing provocative questions about the "truth" of cinema in its recounted histories. Contrary to the movement image that relies on a belief in truth through action, the powers of the false exemplify the postwar crisis of truth through liars and exploiters such as Iogan and his cohorts and uses the cinema to extend beyond the characters in Balabanov's film to address the falsifying character of cinema, as in the removal of Trofim's image from the film *Trofim*. Hence, while the viewer can be dismayed or disgusted about the visions of cruel voyeurism offered them, the film appears to invoke a different set of concerns that exceed the abolition of the pornographer and punishment for his exploitation, to invoke the more difficult and impossible question about the film's dramatization of what cinema was and how it evolved, and rather situating it as an interrogation of vision and hearing,

The counter-historical character of this film resides in its flouting of classical forms of presenting history that paradoxically extend beyond the boundaries of Russia to share similar concerns with such filmmakers as Michael Haneke who also appear to be "antagonistic to the intelligentsia" (Condee 2009, 231). Its reflections on cinema are not narrowly medium specific but invite a rethinking of the image and its aesthetic and ethical dimensions in the present and for the future. This counter-history rejects linear and facile explanations both of history on film and the history of cinema to offer access not only to the visible and articulable but to a "reality not merely described or represented," one that raises the image to a "dissociative force which would introduce ... 'a hole in appearances'" (Deleuze 1989a, 16). What has inspired philosophic thinkers on cinema, such as André Bazin, Stanley Cavell, and Gilles Deleuze, is the search to find a language to entertain the invisible and unthinkable through the image. Hence, I regard Balabanov's film as producing an unsettling form of historicizing in addressing cinema through bringing its past and present, if not future, into coexistence to solicit thinking through forms for unsettling historical and aesthetic claims to truth.

BODIES IN PAIN: THE COUNTER-HISTORY OF *MORPHIA*

Sharing a similar cavalier attitude toward historicity, *Morphia* (2008) poses similar problems in relation to the world viewed, especially in its treatment of landscape and character. The temptation to regard the film as a reflection of the 1917 revolution through the crazed vision of a physician is perplexing, if interpreted as providing an explanatory consideration of Russian history. Balabanov's singular and elusive vision, described as demonstrating "the absence of a stable world" (cited in Condee 2009, 231), is congruent with film's treatment of time as crystalline, nonorganic, arising from post–World War II thinking from science and mathematics, as well as historical revisionism, to inject undecidable relations about "a sense of history as unpredictable change" (ibid.) in which events are unmoored from deterministic thinking. Through injecting images of direct time that falsify truth, the presentation of events becomes a "ceaseless opening ... where unforeseen and unpredictable events may occur" (Rodowick 1997, 17). *Morphia* inserts the viewer into a cinematic world that becomes an analysis of the image by "subordinating description of a space to the functions of thought" (Deleuze 1989a, 22–23). This process is central to Balabanov's films that solicit answers to impossible situations that are counter to formal historical analysis, in this case, involving the Russian Revolution.

Morphia opens onto an image of a hurtling train with one passenger, young Dr. Mikhail Poliakov (Leonid Bichevin). Poliakov is met by an orderly who transfers him to a horse-drawn sleigh to be delivered to the rural hospital where he is to assume his duties as physician. Overlaid on the sound track is a song by Alexander Vertinsky, a popular poet/singer (1889–1957). The viewer is proffered alternate shots of the doctor and of a vast and wintry landscape that assumes the aura of a dream that will later become a nightmare, as the viewer is treated to visions of amputations, burning bodies, physical deterioration, and social chaos.

Adapted from Mikhail Bulgakov's *A Country Doctor's Notebook,* the film selects episodes from the doctor's arrival that involve critical encounters with patients who are of "an unassuming surface and an elusive import" (Milne 1990, 127) from the perspective of Poliakov. Balabanov alters not only the order of the stories in the Bulgakov novel but particularly interjects elements throughout the film derived from the last story, "Morphine," appended to the *Notebook*. Particularly critical is the doctor's first encounter soon after his arrival with a patient suffering from diphtheria, his unsettled viewing of the man's death, and thereafter his first injection of morphine. The film eschews a continuous narration, introducing titles perhaps as a nod to the literary text on which it relies, perhaps as allusions to silent cinema or as an allusion to the diary style characteristic of Bulgakov's "Morphine."

Balabanov's film has been accused of lacking structure, "making it hard to measure historical time [chronology] in relation to the characters' life" (Salazkina 2009). However, its very looseness and discontinuities mark the film's address of time, especially as they create a series of encounters that juxtapose perceptions of the doctor from shifting angles in which clouded vision becomes uncertain and indiscernible for the viewer, transforming connections between the real and the imaginary and the actual and the virtual. Poliakov becomes a figure who is "prey to a vision, pursued by it or pursuing it, rather than engaged in an action"

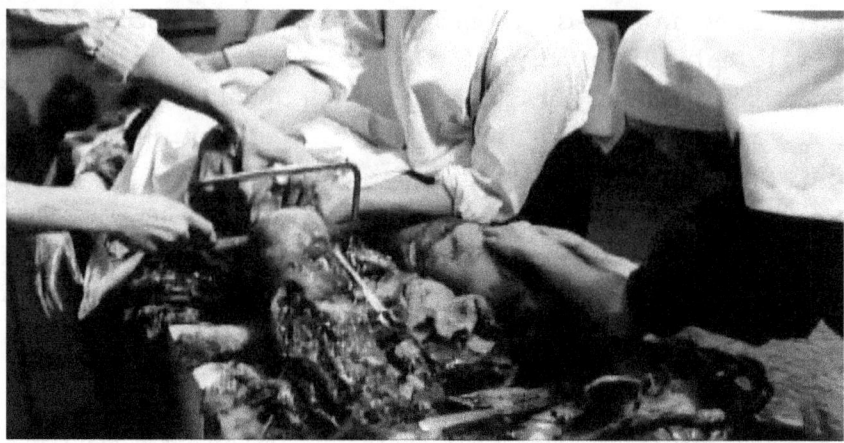

FIGURE 5.8. No respite for the doctor or film viewer, *Morphia*, Balabanov, 2008.

(Deleuze 1989a, 3). He records rather than reacts, and the spectator occupies an unsettling position in evaluating an unfamiliar rendition of history through the eyes of a drug addict, another instance of fabulation as counter-history

The film's multiple textures confound linearity through its treatment of bodily and mental responses to the situations it selects to portray. For example, to ask for an "explanation" for Poliakov's addiction runs counter to the film's strategies. The film is not a seamless narrative but a composite of elliptical and affective episodes, involving visual, aural, and kinesthetic reactions to events that implicate the diegetic and extradiegetic spectators in viewing mutilation and suffering in the various episodes that concern bodies in pain, the most notable being the graphic amputation of a young woman's leg.

Also visibly foregrounded are a tracheotomy for another woman, the sight of the horribly burned bodies of Vasily Osipovich and his daughter Tanya, and repeated incidents of Poliakov's responses to his unrestrained overdoses of morphine that include scenes of his experiencing delirium tremens and convulsive vomiting. The film does not spare the viewer the sight of his flesh, multiply punctured from needle shots, linking him to the wounded, addicted, and moribund bodies of his patients. Poliakov's addiction is enacted in his sexual relationship with Nurse Anna Nikolayevna (Ingeborg Dapkunaite), in which both share an addiction to become gradually lost in their separate hallucinatory worlds.

The doctor becomes a sleepwalker when he sees the charred victims of the fire, and, as a somnambulist, he wanders aimlessly through the corridors of the dispensary. This reaction is further intensified through images of him strolling through the streets of the city after escaping from the hospital for the treatment of drug addiction, where he had committed himself at the counsel of Anna Nikolayevna. In his perambulations, he encounters her crazed figure and that of Lev Gorenburg (Yuri Gertsman), a Jew and a militant member of the Revolutionary Committee whom he met when he tended to a servant of the landholding Osipovich family. From the first injection to film's final moments in his self-inflicted pistol shot that leads to his death, morphine becomes the instrument through which he joins a host of contemporary film characters "suffering less from the absence of another than from their absence from themselves" (ibid., 9). He becomes a character who escapes history to leave its devastation and its significance to the living.

The viewer is not spared the disorientating events that lead to Poliakov's demise, involving his encounter with the drug-wasted Anna Nicoleyvna and the "revolutionary" Gorenberg, in which the physician shoots Gorenberg and becomes a killer. This theater of cruelty culminates in the final moments of *Morphia* in a darkened cinema where, in viewing of the comedy, *Romance in Double Bass* (1911) based on a Chekhov story, Poliakov gazes at the screen, laughing with the other men in the audience, and then reaches for his revolver and shoots himself. This enigmatic ending evokes the writings of Antonin Artaud on the theater of cruelty "blood," but it is a "theater that is difficult ... on the level of representation.... Its objective is not of that of the cruelty that we can practice by cutting up each other's bodies, by sawing away at our personal anatomies ... but of that much more terrible and cruel necessity which things (images as ideas) can practice on us" (Artaud 1976, 256). This cruel necessity involves a confrontation with a life exhausted (Deleuze 1989a, 146) in the service of *ressentiment,* nihilism, and a negative will to power. Among the figures that populate the powers of the false, Poliakov may exemplify resentment and nihilism, but Balabanov's shocking film may be a generous act in which the artist is a physician of culture and offers the gift, though painful,

FIGURE 5.9. Melodrama as comedy? *Morphia,* Balabanov, 2008.

of confronting the spectator with images of addiction to truths that are destructive. About this film (and others he has directed), Balabanov has said, "I am not a teacher and it is not my task to teach people any lessons" (Anemone 2007). However, this statement does not negate his attempt to arouse, even to shock, his audience with the conditions of life and death through his bodily cinema and especially through the film's visual reflections on the connections between sensation and mentation.

I am reminded of the multiple ways in which the film invokes spectatorship through the reiterated window shots that portray Poliakov gazing out a window, the mirror shots in which he examines his body, the framing of shots that render the screen as a window or mirror for the external viewer, and of the sequences that involve his dissociation from the *mise-en-scène* in the interiors of the hospitals and in his strolls through the urban milieu that undo narrative and the old realism, inviting amelioration, which are also characteristic of Balabanov's reiterated concerns with cinema. Similarly, the insistent presence of Vertinskii and Panina's popular music and songs played by Poliakov on his gramophone serves to enhance the film's repetitive concern with escapism through popular art forms. The film makes reference not only to music but also to books, especially in the links to the Bulgakov novel, and, finally, as in *Of Freaks and Men,* to the film within the film that creates closure to *Morphia*.

These allusions function to incite the spectator's attention about their uncertain, but critical, relation to the film's multifaceted and complex presentation of the Russian past as enacted through Poliakov's perspective. Hence, without slighting negative responses to the film's history of the Russian Revolution and its consequences, I would argue that the film functions as a counter-history through memory and imagination to investigate the putative connections between past and present, proffering instead different critical conceptions on the already known that pertain to questions of life in the body that the film investigates.

The film is based on different paradigms and clues (Ginzburg 1992, 124–25) than those for unearthing, interpreting, and adjudicating a crime. *Morphia* is an example of falsifying narration in which time becomes a force for undoing expectations of clarification according to familiar forms of description and interpretation. Masha Salazkina (2009) offers a most intriguing comparison between Balabanov and Kafka in her assertion that Balabanov's "philosophical vision extends beyond political allegories, being more akin to Kafka's." (Salazkina). Her reference to Balabanov as a philosophical allegorist akin to Kafka regards *Morphia* as more elusive than political allegory, focusing rather on the possibility of finding an escape out of a machine that reveals "physical and moral decline" in relation to a decadent, smug, and oversexed aristocracy; an ignorant peasant class; and a problematic cinema history as exemplified by *Of Freaks and Men.*

Thus, Balabanov's falsification of the conventionally held truths of the past can be seen as a form of allegory that resists one-to-one correspondences but introduces multilayered and "dys-narrative" forms for challenging conventional meaning making in film. Experimentation is central to the process of narration as an escape from repetition. This contemporary and experimental form of allegorizing is reminiscent of Walter Benjamin's *Arcades Project* and *The Origin of German Tragic Drama* for an understanding of the character of films in which images of the past are scattered throughout the natural and social landscape, emblematic of the past but redolent of the possibility to blast open time's continuum.

Benjamin wrote, "Allegories are, in the realm of thoughts, what ruins are in the realm of things. . . . The quintessence of these decaying objects is the polar opposite to the idea of transfigured nature. . . . But it is as something incomplete and imperfect that objects stare out from the allegorical structure" (1998, 178–79, 186).

Balabanov's philosophic vision resides in these fragments of the past that resist labeling the protagonist Poliakov—along with Balabanov, his creator—for their imperfect, irrational, or ultimately nihilistic perspectives. *Morphia* is a counter-history in its challenge to how meanings are made and perpetuated. Its unsettling sensations and bizarre figures to enable thought and belief can be identified with the filmmakers discussed above—Cronenberg, Haneke, and Balabanov, particularly—who are committed to a shocking and radical investigation of cinema that creates categories of problems that introduce reflection into the cinema itself and its relation to truth seeking. This reflection on the cinematic (and televisual) image is not mere reference to itself or simply a catalogue of the formal features of artistic production but constitutes a larger essay into the conditions of possibility, if any, for a cinema of thought, belief, and action that retains a hold on the real. Or perhaps, as in the view of some, their films are redolent of the death of cinema in the age of digital reproduction, but certainly consonant with the strategies of counter-historicizing, since the historical positions portrayed are contentious, often inflammatory, and even sufficiently shocking to question received conceptions of the past.

Epilogue

Vitaly, in *For Ever Mozart,* says to Camille, the young enthusiast, "Perhaps the universe was once young like you and the sky was all ablaze. As the world grew older, it grew farther away. When I look at the sky through the stars, I can only see what has disappeared."

IN THE WAKE of the oft-proclaimed "death of cinema," writers on media and certain media artists have either lamented or celebrated this demise (Usai 2001). For still others, the advent of digitalization has made them cautious and productive in their rethinking of what cinema is. For example, in his essay "Moving Away from the Index: Cinema and the Impression of Reality" (2007), Tom Gunning raises unsettling questions concerning film's relation to photography and, hence, to conceptions of realism. Instead of succumbing to the view that computer-generated images have replaced cinematic realism, Gunning undertakes to revalue the status of the real by challenging the view that the basis of cinema is its reliance on the index, on recording, reproduction, and resemblance to the external world. He indicates how the notion of indexicality misrecognizes the genealogy of cinema, its medium promiscuity, its dependence on movement and time, and its penchant for the fantastic.

What is significant in his multiply inflected examination of arguments on the cinema to reassess its past as well as its contemporary incarnation is the necessity of identifying what has "disappeared" and what persists, what is the same and what is different. For example, "as a new technology at the end of the nineteenth century, cinema did not appear with a defined essence as a medium, but rather, displayed an amazing promiscuity (if not polymorphic promiscuity) in both its models and its uses." Historical research "uncovers a genealogy of cinema, a process of emergence and competition yielding the complex formation of an identity" (Gunning 2007, 35), a situation amenable to thinking of the emergence of not only older but of current technologies of vision.

In relation to the present moment, recognition of interrelations to other media, including cinema, would seem to be in order as opposed to clearly demarcated differences that entail the problematic issue of cinema's dependence on reproducing the photographic image. Another consideration is equally, if not more, significant in relation to formulations on the nature of the then-new medium that concerned early theorists: namely, was their attention to considerations of movement and their effect on the sensations of the spectator to produce the "impression of the real if not its materiality" (Gunning 2007, 44)? Gunning's views are counter-historical in their challenge to reductive, linear, and teleological thinking about new technologies as displacing and replacing a moribund cinema. The death of cinematic realism and of Bazinian thinking on the medium are not only premature but based on a conceptual failure to understand the real as "impression" as created in both cinema and digital computer technologies identified as "new media" (for example, Manovich 2001). Gunning's position is an invitation to reconsider the hold of conceptions of indexicality for reproducing a semblance of the world as it really was and instead to consider the real as an aesthetic and ontological encounter with ambiguity and multiplicity based on image facts that are to be deciphered rather than pregiven.

When it comes to considerations of cinema as developed in his two cinema books, and even more in his more philosophical writings, Deleuze's concerns are directed toward the past and the future of image culture. His *Cinema 2*, both in relation to his comments on the time-image and in his ambivalent explorations of future forms involving digital media, raises questions about the past *and* the future of visual media from a philosophical, aesthetic, and ethical position. And a reader of Deleuze's books "confronts something greater in mind than the simple preservation of the historical promise of temporal montage" (Murray 2010, 358). Rather than falling into an elegiac position on the passing of history and of cinema, Deleuze recognizes the appearance of new digital forms but refrains from a nostalgic or celebratory position on the passing of the time-image. However, in projecting tentative responses to the future of cinema, he is particularly concerned, if not pessimistic, about the proliferation of "informatics" where "information replaces nature" (Deleuze 1989a, 269). On the electronic "automata," Deleuze writes,

> The electronic image, that is the tele and video image, the numerical image coming into being, either had to transform cinema or to replace it, to mark its death. We do not claim to be producing an analysis of the new images, which would be beyond our claims, but only to indicate certain effects whose relation to the cinematic image remains to be determined. The new images no longer have any outside (out-of-field) any more than they are internalized in a whole; rather they have a right side and a reverse, reversible and non-super-imposable, like a power to turn back on themselves. (1986, 65)

For a growing number of writers on digital media, Deleuze's work beckons toward an exploration of projects that "respond to the virtual as an energetic field of what has to be thought or registered" (Murray 2008 360). Instances of contemporary avant-garde digital art in their integration into cinema create a possibility, if tenuous, for launching the time-image into the future. The "digital baroque," in Timothy Murray's terms, offers productive ways of thinking and producing works that address Deleuze's concern that "the new automatism in itself is worthless in itself if it is not put in the service of a powerful, obscure, condensed will to art, aspiring to deploy itself through involuntary movements which nonetheless do not restrict it. . . . So that electronic images will have to be based, on still another will to art, or on as yet unknown aspects of the time-image" (Deleuze 1989a, 266).

According to Timothy Murray, the time-image "carries both its passing and also its future" (2010, 353), and he further argues that a connection between the Baroque and images of temporality are exemplified in the storage of artifacts and "their transposition of the originally temporal data into a figurative spatial simultaneity" (Murray 2008). Thus, in the context of the digital baroque, its archival bent is toward accumulation in its drawing on this simultaneity by drawing on "historical methods, literary authorship, artistic icons, cinematic memories, and, most of all new world communities ... addressing the paradigm shift away from the remnants of humanist visions of subjectivity and projection toward reflections on a baroque model of the folds of intersubjective and cross-cultural knowledge" (ibid., 8, 9).

However, despite Murray's derivation of a digital baroque from Deleuze's time-image, Deleuze was tentative toward the "new technology." For example, Deleuze asserts that the cinema of Robert Bresson had "no need of computing or cybernetic machines; yet the 'model' for the film is a modern psychological automaton, because it is defined in relation to the speech-act and no longer, as before, by motor action" (Deleuze 1989a, 266). Deleuze argues that Bresson's filmmaking, as well as that of Alain Resnais and Jean-Luc Godard, are dependent on an aesthetic instead of calling on new technologies. Following Antonin Artaud, Deleuze credits cinema not with the power of making us think the whole but with a "dissociative force" that would introduce a "figure of nothingness," "a hole in appearances" (ibid., 170). What is needed, therefore, is something more than "media" or technical supports as modes of transmitting and receiving information" but ways of "disposing our senses ... so as to enable thinking or to make ideas possible" (Rajchman 2010, 301). Deleuze remained insistent on overturning "the totality of cinema-thought relations" (1989a, 167) not as technique but as compositional and conceptual. He cautioned,

> A theory of cinema is not "about" cinema, but about the concepts that cinema gives rise to and which are themselves related to other concepts corresponding to other practices, the practice of concepts in general having no privilege over others, any more than one object has over others. It is at the level of the interference of many practices that things happen, beings, images, concepts, all the kinds of events. (1998a, 280)

If a theory of cinema is not about cinema but about concepts to which cinema gives rise, then theories of history are not "about" history but about concepts of which History gives rise, and these concepts are related to other concepts and practices. In *What Is Philosophy*, Deleuze and Guattari write, "History is only the set of negative conditions that make possible the experimentation of something that escapes history. Without history experimentation would remain indeterminate and unconditioned, but experimentation is not historical. It is philosophical" (1994, 111). It is in this sense that my study has sought by way of cinema to think counter-historically: that is, to see how cinema has made it possible to escape history through experimentation, to go up the path that History descends to arrive "at the unhistorical vapor that goes beyond actual factors to something new" (ibid., 140).

Cinema and Counter-History has sought to locate that "unhistorical vapor" though examining certain moments related to the creation of something new, involved in concepts of movement, the body, minorizing conceptions, the powers of the false, and of becoming, expressed through different film forms and to changing times and of time as change. Hence, predictions about the death of cinema similar to prognostications about an end to history are prods to thinking counter-historically that entail consideration of connections between fiction and invention as purveyed through cinema's capacity to engender affects, emotion, and thought as encounters with the force of time and its ethical dimensions.

BIBLIOGRAPHY

Abel, Richard. 1984. *French Cinema: The First Wave, 1915–1929.* Princeton, NJ: Princeton University Press.

———. 1988. *French Film Theory and Criticism: A History/Anthology, 1907–1939.* 2 vols. Princeton, NJ: Princeton University Press.

———. 1999. *The Red Rooster Scare: Making Cinema American, 1900–1910.* Berkeley: University of California Press.

Acquarello. 2001. Review of "*Dong*, 1998 [The Hole]." *Strictly Film School.* http://www.filmref.com/directors/dirpages/tsai.html#hole. Accessed July 2, 2014.

———. 2010. Review of "*Morfia* 2008." *Strictly Film School.* Accessed August 25, 2014.

Agamben, Giorgio. 1998. *Homo Sacer: Sovereign Power and Bare Life.* Translated by Daniel Heller-Roazen. Stanford, CA: Stanford University Press.

Amad, Paula. 2010. *Counter-Archive: Film, the Everyday, and Albert Kahn's Archives de la Planète.* New York: Columbia University Press.

Andrew, Geoff. 2009. "The Revenge of Children." *Sight and Sound* 19 (12): 14–17.

Anemone, Tony. 2007. Review of "Aleksei Balabanov, *Cargo 200* (*Gruz 200*, 2007)." *KinoKultura.* http://www.kinokultura.com/2007/18r-gruz.shtml. Accessed July 2, 2014.

Aprà, Adriano. 2000. "Rossellini's Historical Encyclopedia." In *Roberto Rossellini: Magician of the Real,* edited by David Forgacs, Sarah Lutton, and Geoffrey Nowell-Smith, 126–48. London: BFI.

Artaud, Antonin. 1976. *Antonin Artaud: Selected Writings.* Translated by Helen Weaver. Berkeley: University of California Press.

Bakhtin, Mikhail. 1981. *Four Essays.* Edited by Michael Holquist. Translated by Caryl Emerson and Michael Holquist. Austin: University of Texas Press.

———. 1984. *Rabelais and His World.* Translated by Hélène Iswolsky. Bloomington: Indiana University Press.

Barber, Stephen, 2004. *Artaud: The Screaming Body.* London: Creation Books.

Barroso, Millán, and Pedro Javier. 2011. "*Tango*: Estética del límite y poetica tragica." In *Carlos Saura: Una trayectoria ejemplar,* edited by Robin Lefere, 113–38. Madrid: Visor Libros.

Barthes, Roland. 1981. *Camera Lucida: Reflections on Photography.* Translated by Richard Howard. New York: Hill & Wang.

Barton, David. 2008. "Clepsydra: The Fluid Melancholy of *What Time Is It There?*" *Asian Cinema* 19 (2): 281–91.

Bazin, André. 2005. *What Is Cinema?*, vols. 1 and 2. Rev. ed. Translated by Hugh Gray. Berkeley: University of California Press.

Beaty, Bart. 2008. *David Cronenberg's "A History of Violence."* Toronto: University of Toronto Press.

Bell, James. 2009. "A Stake through the Heart." *Sight and Sound* 19 (11): 43.

Benjamin, Walter. 1969. *Illuminations.* Edited by Hannah Arendt. Translated by Harry Zohn. New York: Schocken Books.

———. 1998. *The Origin of German Tragic Drama.* Translated by John Osborne. London: Verso.

———. 2002. *The Arcades Project.* Edited by Rolf Tiedemann. Translated by Howard Eiland and Kevin McLaughlin. Cambridge, MA: Belknap Press of Harvard University Press.

Bentley, Eric. 1965. *The Life of the Drama.* London: Methuen & Co.

Bergson, Henri. 1983. *Laughter: An Essay on the Meaning of the Comic.* Translated by Cloudesley Brereton and Fred Rothwell. In *Comedy: George Meredith's "An Essay on Comedy" and Henri Bergson's "Laughter,"* edited by Wylie Sypher, 59–190. Baltimore, MD: Johns Hopkins University Press.

———. 1988. *Matter and Memory.* Translated by Nancy Margaret Paul and W. Scott Palmer. New York: Zone Books.

———. 1998. *Creative Evolution.* Edited by Arthur Mitchell. Mineola, NY: Dover Publications.

Berressem, Hanjo. 2012. "Crystal History: 'You Pick Up the Pieces, You Connect the Dots.'" In *Time and History in Deleuze and Serres,* edited by Bernd Herzogenrath, 203–28. London: Continuum.

Bildhauer, Bettina, and Robert Mills, eds. 2003. *The Monstrous Middle Ages.* Toronto: University of Toronto Press.

Bingham, Dennis. 2010. *Whose Lives Are They Anyway? The Biopic as Contemporary Film Genre.* New Brunswick, NJ: Rutgers University Press.

Biswas, Moinak. 2006. "Early Films: The Novel and Other Horizons." In *Apu and After,* edited by Moinak Biswas, 37–80. Oxford: Seagull Books.

———. 2007. "In the Mirror of an Alternative Globalism: The Neorealist Encounter in India." In *Italian Neorealism and Global Cinema,* edited by Laura E. Ruberto and Kristi M. Wilson, 72–90. Detroit: Wayne State University Press.

Bloom, Michele E. 2005. "Contemporary Franco-Chinese Cinema: Translation, Citation and Imitation in Dai Sijie's *Balzac and the Little Chinese Seamstress* and Tsai Ming-Liang's *What Time Is It There?*" *Quarterly Review of Film and Video* 22 (4): 311–25.

Bogue, Ronald. 1989. *Deleuze and Guattari.* London: Routledge.

Bondanella, Peter. 2001. *Italian Cinema: From Neorealism to the Present.* 3rd ed. New York: Continuum.

———. 2009. *A History of Italian Cinema.* New York: Continuum.

Bonsaver, Guido. 2009. "Dall'uomo al divo: Un'intervista con Paolo Sorrentino." *The Italianist* 29 (2): 325–37.

Boundas, Constantin V. 1996. "Deleuze-Bergson: An Ontology of the Virtual." In *Deleuze: A Critical Reader*, edited by Paul Patton, 81–106. Oxford: Blackwell Publishers.
Boundas, Constantin V., and Dorothea Olkowski, eds. 1994. *Gilles Deleuze and the Theater of Philosophy*. New York: Routledge.
Brooke, Michael. 1970. DVD video review of *"Of Freaks and Men."* The Digital Fix. http://film.thedigitalfix.com/content/id/3496/of-freaks-and-men.html. Accessed July 2, 2014.
Brownlow, Kevin. 1997. *The War, the West, and the Wilderness*. London: Martin Secker & Warburg.
Brunetta, Gian Piero. 2001a. *Storia del cinema italiano*. Vol. 3, *Dal neorealismo al Miracolo economico*. Rome: Riuniti.
———. 2001b. *Storia del cinema italiano*. Vol. 4, *Dal miracolo economico agli anni novanta 1960–1993*. Rome: Riuniti.
Brunette, Peter. 1987. *Roberto Rossellini*. New York: Oxford University Press.
Buchanan, Ian, ed. 1998. *A Deleuzian Century?* Durham, NC: Duke University Press.
Buck-Morss, Susan. 1997. *The Dialectics of Seeing: Walter Benjamin and the Arcades Project*. Cambridge, MA: MIT Press.
Bulgakov, Mikhail. 1995. *A Country Doctor's Notebook*. Translated by Michael Glenny. London: Harvill Press.
Burgoyne, Robert. 2008. *The Hollywood Historical Film*. Malden, MA, and Oxford: Wiley–Blackwell.
———, ed. 2010a. *The Epic Film in World Culture*. New York and London: Routledge.
———. 2010b. *Film Nation: Hollywood Looks at U.S. History*. Rev. ed. Minneapolis: University of Minnesota Press.
Caine, Barbara. 2010. *Biography and History*. Houndmills, Hampshire, GB: Palgrave Macmillan.
Caldiron, Orio. 1998. *Mario Monicelli*. Rome: National Association of Motion Pictures and Affiliated Industries (ANICA).
Calhoun, John. 2004. "The Ox-Bow Incident." *Cineaste* 29 (3): 55–56.
Cameron, Ian, and Douglas Pye, eds. 1996. *The Book of Westerns*. New York: Continuum.
Canova, Gianni. 2003. "La sindrome del sublime: Poetica dell'eccesso e deriva del sguardo—L'ultimo Argento." In *L'eccesso della visione: Il cinema di Dario Argento*, edited by Giulia Carluccio, Giacomo Manzoli, and Roy Menarini, 105. Turin: Lindau.
Carlson, Eric T. 1985. "Medicine and Degeneration: Theory and Praxis." In *Degeneration: The Dark Side of Progress*, edited by J. Edward Chamberlin and Sander L. Gilman, 121–44. New York: Columbia University Press.
Casetti, Francesco. 2005. *L'occhio del novecento: Cinema, esperienza, modernità*. Milan: Bompiani.
Castro, Donald S. 1991. *The Argentine as Social History, 1880–1955: The Soul of the People*. Lewiston, NY: Edwin Mellen Press.
Cavalier, Stephen. *The World History of Animation*. Berkeley and Los Angeles: University of California Press, 2011.
Cavell, Stanley. 1979. *The World Viewed: Reflections on the Ontology of Film*. Enlarged ed. Cambridge, MA: Harvard University Press.
Charney, Maurice, ed. 1978. *Comedy: New Perspectives*. New York: New York Literary Forum.
———. 1991. *Comedy High and Low: An Introduction to the Experience of Comedy*. New York: Peter Lang.

Chamberlin, J. Edward, and Sander L. Gilman. 1985. "Introduction." In *Degeneration: The Dark Side of Progress*, edited by J. Edward Chamberlin and Sander L. Gilman, ix–xiv. New York: Columbia University Press.

Chapman, James, Mark Glancy, and Sue Harper, eds. 2007. *The New Film History: Sources, Methods, Approaches*. New York: Palgrave Macmillan.

Chaudhuri, Supriya. 2006. "In the City." In *Apu and After*, edited by Moinak Biswas, 251–77. Oxford: Seagull Books.

———. 2007. "Space, Interiority and Affect in *Charulata* and *Ghare Baire*." *Journal of the Moving Image* 6. http://www.jmionline.org/film_journal/jmi_06/article_09.php. Accessed accessed 2007.

Choi, Jinhee. 2011. *The South Korean Film Renaissance: Local Hitmakers, Global Provocateurs*. Middletown, CT: Wesleyan University Press.

Chomet, Sylvain. 2011. "Foreword." In *The World History of Animation*, edited by Stephen Cavalier, 6–9. Berkeley and Los Angeles: University of California Press.

Chopra-Gant, Mike. 2008. *Cinema and History: The Telling of Stories*. London: Wallflower Press.

Cieutat, Michel, and Philippe Rouyer. 2009. "Entretien avec Michael Haneke: Le plus insupportable, c'est la violence mentale." *Positif* 584: 17–21.

Cohen, Sande. 2006. *History Out of Joint: Essays on the Use and Abuse of History*. Baltimore, MD: Johns Hopkins University Press.

Condee, Nancy. 2009. *The Imperial Trace: Recent Russian Cinema*. Oxford: Oxford University Press.

Conley, Tom. 2003. "Afterword: A Politics of Fact and Figure." In *Francis Bacon: The Logic of Sensation*, translated by Daniel W. Smith, 130–49. Minneapolis: University of Minnesota Press.

Cooper, L. Andrew. 2012. *Dario Argento*. Urbana: University of Illinois Press.

Corrigan, Robert W., ed. 1965. *Comedy: Meaning and Form*. San Francisco: Chandler Publishing Company.

Coulthard, Lisa. 2011. "Negative Ethics: The Missed Event in the French Films of Michael Haneke." *Studies in French Cinema* 11 (1): 71–82.

"*The Covered Wagon:* A James Cruze Production." 1923. Publicity booklet. Hollywood: Paramount Pictures.

Cowie, Peter. 2004. *John Ford and the American West*. New York: Harry N. Abrams, Inc., Publishers.

Crain, Mary Beth. 1976. "*The Ox-Bow Incident* Revisited." *Literature Film Quarterly* 4 (3): 240–48.

Crowdus, Gary. 2008. "Exposing the Dark Secrets of Italian Political History: An Interview with Paolo Sorrentino." *Cineaste* 34 (3): 32–37.

Custen, George F. 1992. *Bio/Pics: How Hollywood Constructed Public History*. New Brunswick, NJ.: Rutgers University Press.

Dargis, Manohla. 2005. "Once Disaster Hits, It Seems Never to End." *New York Times*, September 23, Movies section, 1–2. http://movies.nytimes.com/2005/09/23/movies/23viol.html. Accessed July 2, 2014.

Deamer, David. 2009. "Cinema, Chronos/Cronos: Becoming an Accomplice to the Impasse of History." In *Deleuze and History*, edited by Jeffrey A. Bell and Claire Colebrook, 161–87. Edinburgh: Edinburgh University Press.

Debord, Guy. 1983. *Society of the Spectacle*. 3rd ed. Translated by Fredy Perlman and John Supak. Detroit: Black and Red Press.
de Certeau, Michel. 1988. *The Practice of Everyday Life*. Translated by Steven Rendall. Berkeley: University of California Press.
DeLanda, Manuel. 2009. *Intensive Science and Virtual Philosophy*. New York: Continuum.
Delanty, Gerard. 2009. *The Cosmopolitan Imagination: The Renewal of Critical Theory*. Cambridge: Cambridge University Press.
Deleuze, Gilles. 1986. *Cinema 1: The Movement-Image*. Translated by Hugh Tomlinson and Barbara Habberjam. Minneapolis: University of Minnesota Press.
———. 1988a. *Nietzsche and Philosophy*. Translated by Hugh Tomlinson. New York: Columbia University Press.
———. 1988b. *Spinoza: Practical Philosophy*. Translated by Robert Hurley. San Francisco: City Light Books.
———. 1989a. *Cinema 2: The Time-Image*. Translated by Hugh Tomlinson and Robert Galeta. Minneapolis: University of Minnesota Press.
———. 1989b. *Masochism: Coldness and Cruelty*. Translated by Jean McNeil, New York: Zone Books.
———. 1990. *The Logic of Sense*. Translated by Mark Lester with Charles Stivale. Edited by Constantine V. Boundas. New York: Columbia University Press.
———. 1993a. *Essays Critical and Clinical*. Translated by Daniel W. Smith and Michael A. Greco. Minneapolis: University of Minnesota Press.
———. 1993b. *The Fold: Leibniz and the Baroque*. Translated by Tom Conley. Minneapolis: University of Minnesota Press.
———. 1994. *Difference and Repetition*. Translated by Paul Patton. New York: Columbia University Press.
———. 1995. *Negotiations, 1972–1990*. Translated by Martin Joughin. New York: Columbia University Press.
———. 2003. *Francis Bacon: The Logic of Sensation*. Translated by Daniel W. Smith. Minneapolis: University of Minnesota Press.
Deleuze, Gilles, and Félix Guattari. 1986. *Kafka: Toward a Minor Literature*. Translated by Dana Polan. Minneapolis: University of Minnesota Press.
———. 1987. *A Thousand Plateaus: Capitalism and Schizophrenia*. Translated by Brian Massumi. Minneapolis: University of Minnesota Press.
———. 1994. *What Is Philosophy?* Translated by Hugh Tomlinson and Graham Burchell. New York: Columbia University Press.
———. 1977. *Anti-Oedipus: Capitalism and Schizophrenia*. Translated by Robert Hurley, Mark Seem, and Helen R. Lane. Minneapolis: University of Minnesota Press.
Del Río, Elena. 2008. *Deleuze and the Cinemas of Performance: Powers of Affection*. Edinburgh: Edinburgh University Press.
"Destry Rides Again." 1932. Review of Ben Stoloff film. *Variety*, June 21. Reprinted in *Variety Film Reviews 1907–1980*, vol. 4: *1930–1933*. New York: Garland Publishing, Inc. 1983.
"Destry Rides Again." 1939a. Review of George Marshall film. *Film Daily*, November 30 [76 (106)], 10.
"Destry Rides Again." 1939b. Review of George Marshall film. *Variety*, December 6. Reprinted in *Variety Film Reviews 1907–1980*, vol. 6: *1938–1942*, New York: Garland Publishing, Inc., 1983.

Dixon, Wheeler Winston, ed. 2005. *American Cinema of the 1940s: Themes and Variations.* New Brunswick, NJ: Rutgers University Press.

Doane, Mary Anne. 2002. *The Emergence of Cinematic Time: Modernity, Contingency, the Archive.* Cambridge, MA: Harvard University Press.

Dürrenmatt, Friedrich. 1990. *The Visit: A Tragi-comedy.* Translated by Patrick Bowles. New York: Grove Press.

Ebert, Roger. 1998. Review of [Arturo Ripstein's] "*Deep Crimson.*" *Chicago Sun Times,* January 16. http://www.rogerebert.com/reviews/deep-crimson-1998. Accessed July 2, 2014.

———. 2009. Review of [Park Chan-wook's] "*Thirst.*" *Chicago Sun Times,* August 12. http://www.rogerebert.com/reviews/thirst-2009. Accessed July 2, 2014.

———. 2011. Review of [Sylvain Chomet's] "*The Illusionist.*" *Chicago Sun Times,* January 12. http://www.rogerebert.com/reviews/the-illusionist-2011. Accessed July 2, 2014.

Ecksteins, Morris. 1985. "History and Degeneration: Of Birds and Cages." In *Degeneration: The Dark Side of Progress,* edited by J. Edward Chamberlin and Sander L. Gilman, 1–23. New York: Columbia University Press.

Fabian, Johannes. 2007. *Memory against Culture: Arguments and Reminders.* Durham, NC: Duke University Press.

Falsetto, Mario. 2001. *Stanley Kubrick: A Narrative and Stylistic Analysis.* Westport, CT: Praeger.

Fenin, George N., and William K. Everson. 1962. *The Western: From Silents to Cinerama.* New York: Bonanza Books.

Feuer, Jane. 1982. *The Hollywood Musical.* Bloomington: Indiana University Press.

Fischer, Lucy. 2004. "'Dancing through the Minefield': Passion, Pedagogy, Politics, and Production in *The Tango Lesson.*" *Cinema Journal* 43 (3): 42–58.

Fisher, Jaimey. 2007. "On the Ruins of Masculinity: The Figure of the Child in Italian Neorealism and the German Rubble-Film." In *Italian Neorealism and Global Cinema,* edited by Laura E. Ruberto and Kristi M. Wilson, 25–54. Detroit: Wayne State University Press.

Flaxman, Gregory, ed. 2000. *The Brain Is the Screen: Deleuze and the Philosophy of Cinema.* Minneapolis: University of Minnesota Press.

———. 2012. *Gilles Deleuze and the Fabulation of Philosophy.* Minneapolis: University of Minnesota Press.

Forgacs, David, Sarah Lutton, and Geoffrey Nowell-Smith, eds. 2000. *Roberto Rossellini: Magician of the Real.* London: BFI Publishing.

Foucault, Michel. 1977. *Language, Counter-Memory, Practice: Selected Essays and Interviews.* Translated by Donald F. Bouchard and Sherry Simon. Ithaca, NY: Cornell University Press.

———. 1980. *The History of Sexuality.* Vol. 1, *An Introduction.* 2nd U.S. ed. Translated by Robert Hurley. New York: Vintage Books.

Fowler, Catherine. 2009. *Sally Potter.* Urbana: University of Illinois Press.

Frame, Janet. 1991. *An Autobiography.* New York: George Braziller.

Frappat, Hélène. 2008. *Roberto Rossellini.* Paris: Cahiers du cinema.

Frayling, Christopher, 2000. *Spaghetti Westerns: Cowboys and Europeans from, Karl May to Sergio Leone.* London: I.B. Tauris Publishers.

Frey, Mattias. 2010. "The Message and the Medium: Haneke's Film Theory and Digital Praxis." In *On Michael Haneke,* edited by Brian Price and John David Rhodes, 153–65. Detroit: Wayne State University Press.

Fuller, Graham. 2005. "Good Guy, Bad Guy." *Sight and Sound* 15 (10): 12–16.
Furstenau, Marc. 2010. *The Film Theory Reader: Debates and Arguments*. London: Routledge.
Fusco, Coco. 1987–88. "The Tango of Esthetics and Politics: An Interview with Fernando Solanas." *Cineaste* 16 (1–2): 57–59.
Gadjigo, Samba, Ralph Faulkingham, Thomas Cassirer, and Reinhard Sander, eds. 1993. *Ousmane Sembène: Dialogues with Critics and Writers*. Amherst: University of Massachusetts Press.
Gallagher, Tag. 1998. *The Adventures of Roberto Rossellini: His Life and Times*. New York: Da Capo Press.
Gallant, Chris. 2001. *Art of Darkness: The Cinema of Dario Argento*. Surrey: FAB Press.
Galt, Rosalind, and Karl Schoonover, eds. 2010. *Global Art Cinema: New Theories and Histories*. Oxford: Oxford University Press.
Ganguly, Suranjan. 2012. "Becoming Father: The Politics of Succession in Satyajit Ray's *Pratidwandi (The Adversary)*." *Quarterly Review of Film and Video* 29 (4): 320–28.
Garcia, Jesús Rodrigo, ed. 1998. *El cine de Arturo Ripstein: La solución del bárbaro*. Valencia: Ediciones de la Mirada.
Génin, Bernard, and Stéphane Goudet. 2010. "Entretien avec Sylvain Chomet: De la chrysalide au papillon." *Positif* 592: 98–102.
Gilman, Sander L. 1985. "Sexology, Psychoanalysis, and Degeneration: From a Theory of Race to a Race to Theory." In *Degeneration: The Dark Side of Progress*, edited by J. Edward Chamberlin and Sander L. Gilman, 72–96. New York: Columbia University Press.
Ginzburg, Carlo. 1989. *The Cheese and the Worms: The Cosmos of a Sixteenth-Century Miller*. Translated by John Tedeschi and Anne Tedeschi. New York: Dorset Press.
———. 1992. *Clues, Myths, and the Historical Method*. Translated by John Tedeschi and Anne Tedeschi. Baltimore, MD: Johns Hopkins University Press.
———. 2012. *Threads and Traces: True False Fictive*. Translated by Anne C. Tedeschi and John Tedeschi. Berkeley: University of California Press.
Giovacchini, Saverio, and Robert Sklar, eds. 2012. *Global Neorealism: The Transnational History of a Film Style*. Jackson: University Press of Mississippi.
Girard, René. 1977. *Violence and the Sacred*. Translated by Patrick Gregor. Baltimore, MD: Johns Hopkins University Press.
Givanni, June, ed. 2000. *Symbolic Narratives/African Cinema: Audiences, Theory and the Moving Image*. London: BFI Publishing.
Godard, Jean-Luc, and Youssef Ishaghpour. 2005. *Cinema: The Archeology of Film and the Memory of a Century*. Translated by John Howe. Oxford: Berg.
Goodchild, Philip. 1996. *Deleuze and Guattari: An Introduction to the Politics of Desire*. London: Sage Publications.
Grabner, Franz. 2010. "'We Live in a Permanent State of War': An Interview with Michael Haneke." In *Fascinatingly Disturbing: Interdisciplinary Perspectives on Michael Haneke's Cinema*, edited by Alexander D. Ornella and Stefanie Knauss, 13–33. Translated by James T. Koranyi. Eugene, OR: Pickwick Publications.
Gramsci, Antonio. 1999. *Selections from "The Prison Notebooks."* Edited and translated by Quintin Hoare and Geoffrey Nowell Smith. New York: International Publishers.
Graulich, Melody, and Stephen Tatum, eds. 2003. *Reading "The Virginian" in the New West*. Lincoln: University of Nebraska Press.

Grayson, Sandra M. 2001. "Djibril Diop Mambéty: A Retrospective," *Research in African Literatures* 32 (4): 136–39.
Grundmann, Roy. 2010a. "Between Adorno and Lyotard: Michael Haneke's Aesthetic of Fragmentation." In *A Companion to Michael Haneke*, edited by Roy Grundmann, 371–419. Chichester, West Sussex, GB: Wiley-Blackwell.
———. 2010b. "Introduction: Haneke's Anachronism." In *A Companion to Michael Haneke*, edited by Roy Grundmann, 1–50. Chichester, West Sussex, GB: Wiley-Blackwell.
———. 2010c. "Unsentimental Education: An Interview with Michael Haneke." In *A Companion to Michael Haneke*, edited by Roy Grundmann, 591–606. Chichester, West Sussex, GB: Wiley-Blackwell.
Gunning, Tom. 2007. "Moving Away from the Index: Cinema and the Impression of Reality." *differences: A Journal of Feminist Cultural Studies* 18 (1): 29–52.
Günsberg, Maggie. 2005. *Italian Cinema: Gender and Genre*. Basingstoke and New York: Palgrave Macmillan.
Gural-Migdal, Anna, and Romain Chareyon. 2011. "The 'Ghost' Image of Horror and Pornography in Michael Haneke's *La Pianiste* (2001)." *Studies in French Cinema* 11 (1): 57–69.
Hamilton, Nigel. 2007. *Biography: A Brief History*. Cambridge, MA: Harvard University Press.
Hawkins, Joan. 2000. *Cutting Edge: Art Horror and the Horrific Avant-Garde*. Minneapolis: University of Minnesota Press.
Herzog, Amy. 2010. *Dreams of Difference, Songs of the Same: The Musical Moment in Film*. Minneapolis: University of Minnesota Press.
Herzogenrath, Bernd. 2012. *Time and History in Deleuze and Serres*. London: Continuum.
Hoberman, J. 2005a. "Historical Oversight: Desensitized to Cronenberg's 'Violence', Jury Anoints Dardennes over Jarmusch and von Trier." *Village Voice*, May 17. http://www.villagevoice.com/2005-05-17/film/historical-oversight/. Accessed July 2, 2014.
———. 2005b. "The Last Action Hero." Review of Cronenberg's *A History of Violence*. *Village Voice*, September 13. http://www.villagevoice.com/2005-09-13/film/the-last-action-hero/full/. Accessed July 2, 2014.
Hong, Guo-Juin. 2011. *Taiwan Cinema: A Contested Nation on Screen*. New York: Palgrave Macmillan.
Horwath, Alexander. 2009. "The Haneke Code: Talking Shop, Theory, and Practice with the Director of *The White Ribbon*." *Film Comment* 45 (6): 26–31. [Online version, "Michael Haneke Uncut," http://filminccom.siteprotect.net/fcm/nd09/haneke.htm.]
Howie, Gillian. 2002. *Deleuze and Spinoza: Aura of Expressionism*. London and Basingstoke: Palgrave Macmillan.
Hu, Brian. 2009. "Park Chan-wook's Insatiable *Thirst*." *Asia Pacific Arts*, July 17. http://www.asiaarts.ucla.edu/090717/article.asp?parentID=110445.
Hughes-Warrington, Marnie. 2007. *History Goes to the Movies: Studying History on Film*. London: Routledge.
Jackson, Kevin. 2009. "The Vampire Next Door." *Sight and Sound* 19 (11): 40–42, 44.
Jacobowitz, Florence. 1996. "The Dietrich Westerns: *Destry Rides Again* and *Rancho Notorious*." In *The Book of Westerns*, edited by Ian Cameron and Douglas Pye, 88–98. New York: Continuum.
James, David. 2009. Review of [Park Chan-wook's] "*Thirst*." *Film Comment* 45 (4): 70.

Jelinek, Elfriede. *The Piano Teacher*. Translated by Joachim Neugroschel. New York: Weidenfeld & Nicolson.
Jones, Alan. 2004. *Profondo Argento: The Man, the Myths and the Magic*. Surrey: FAB Press.
Jordan, Marion. 1983. "Carry On . . . Follow That Stereotype." In *British Cinema History*, edited by James Curran and Vincent Porter, 312–27. London: Wiedenfield & Nicolson.
Kaarsholm, Preben, ed. 2007. *City Flicks: Indian Cinema and the Urban Experience*. London: Seagull Books.
Kaufman, Eleanor, 2012. *Deleuze, the Dark Precursor: Dialectic, Structure, Being*. Baltimore, MD: The Johns Hopkins Press.
Kennedy, Barbara M. 2002. *Deleuze and Cinema: The Aesthetics of Sensation*. Edinburgh: Edinburgh University Press.
Kermode, Frank. 2000. *The Sense of an Ending: Studies in the Theory of Fiction, with a New Epilogue*. New York: Oxford University Press.
King, Norman. 1984. *Abel Gance: A Politics of Spectacle*. London: BFI Publishing.
Kitses, Jim, and Gregg Rickman. 1998. *The Western Reader*. New York: Limelight Editions.
Koc, Aysegul. 2003. "Vive le Cinema: A Reading of *What Time Is It There*?" *CineAction* 62: 54–57.
Kolker, Robert. 2000. *A Cinema of Loneliness: Penn, Stone, Kubrick, Scorsese, Spielberg, Altman*. New York: Oxford.
Koven, Mikel J. 2006. *La dolce morte: Vernacular Cinema and the Italian Giallo Film*. Lanham, MD: Scarecrow Press.
Kunzle, David. 1982. *Fashion and Fetishism: A Social History of the Corset, Tight-Lacing and Other Forms of Body-Sculpture in the West*. Totowa, NJ: Rowan & Littlefield.
Lamarre, Thomas. 2009. *The Anime Machine: A Media Theory of Animation*. Minneapolis: University of Minnesota Press.
Lamoureux, Serge. 2003. "Le Parcours des *Triplettes de Belleville*," *Ciné-Bulles* 21 (4): 2–7. http://id.erudit.org/iderudit/26507ac.
Lampert, Jay. 2006. *Deleuze and Guattari's Philosophy of History*. London: Continuum.
Landy, Marcia. 1996. *Cinematic Uses of the Past*. Minneapolis: University of Minnesota Press.
———. 2000. *Italian Film*. Cambridge: Cambridge University Press.
———. 2005a. *Monty Python's Flying Circus*. Detroit: Wayne State University Press.
———. 2005b. "Movies and the Fate of Genre." In *American Cinema of the 1940s: Themes and Variations*, edited by Wheeler Winston Dixon, 222–43. New Brunswick, NJ: Rutgers University Press.
Lanzoni, Rémi Fournier. 2008. *Comedy Italian Style: The Golden Age of Italian Film Comedies*. New York: Continuum.
Lefere, Robin, ed. 2011. *Carlos Saura: Una trayectoria ejemplar*. Madrid: Visor Libros.
Le Goff, Jacques. 1992. *The Medieval Imagination*. Translated by Arthur Goldhammer. Chicago: University of Chicago Press.
Levin, Harry. 1987. *Playboys and Killjoys: An Essay on the Theory and Practice of Comedy*. New York: Oxford University Press.
Levy, Brian, and Lesley Coote. 2005. "The Subversion of Medievalism in *Lancelot du lac* and *Monty Python and the Holy Grail*." In *Postmodern Medievalisms*, edited by Richard Utz and Jesse G. Swan, 99–126. Cambridge: D.S. Brewer.
Lim, Bliss Cua. 2009. *Translating Time: Cinema, the Fantastic, and Temporal Critique*. Durham, NC: Duke University Press.

Loiselle, André, and Jeremy Maron, eds. 2012. *Stages of Reality: Theatricality in Cinema.* Toronto: University of Toronto Press.

Long, Christopher. 2008. "*Camp de Thiaroye*—DVD Review." *Movie Metropolis,* November 19. http://moviemet.com/review/camp-de-thiaroye-dvd-review#.Uh-8Krylhcw. Accessed July 2, 2014.

Louvish, Simon. 2007. *Cecil B. DeMille: A Life in Art.* New York: Thomas Dunne Books.

Lowenstein, Adam. 2005. *Shocking Representations: Historical Traumas, National Cinema, and the Modern Horror Film.* New York: Columbia University Press.

Lusted, David. 2003. *The Western.* Harlow, Essex, GB: Longman Publishing.

Ma, Jean. 2010. "Discordant Desires, Violent Refrains: *La Pianiste* (*The Piano Teacher*)." In *A Companion to Michael Haneke,* edited by Roy Grundmann, 511–31. Chichester, West Sussex, GB: Wiley–Blackwell.

MacBean, James Roy. 1975. *Film and Revolution.* Bloomington: Indiana University Press.

Maciel, David R. 1997. "Serpientes y escaleras: The Contemporary Cinema of Mexico, 1976–1994." In *New Latin American Cinema,* vol. 2: *Studies of National Cinemas,* edited by Michael T. Martin, 94–120. Detroit: Wayne State University Press.

Majumdar, Neepa. 2005. "*Pather Panchali* (1955), Satyajit Ray." In *Film Analysis: A Norton Reader,* edited by Jeffrey Geiger and R. L. Rutsky, 510–27. New York: W.W. Norton Company.

Manovich, Lev. 2001. *The Language of New Media.* Cambridge, MA: MIT Press.

Manvel, Sarah. 2009. "Just What the Doctor Disordered: *Morphia* (2008)." *Critic's Notebook.* http://www.criticsnotebook.com/2009/12/morphia.html. Accessed July 2, 2014.

Marcus, Millicent. 2010. "The Ironist and the Auteur: Post-realism in Paolo Sorrentino's *Il divo*." *The Italianist* 30 (2): 245–57.

Marrati, Paola. 2008. *Gilles Deleuze: Cinema and Philosophy.* Translated by Alisa Hartz. Baltimore, MD: Johns Hopkins University Press.

Martig, Charles. 2010. "How Much Haneke Do We Deserve? Against Sadistic-Philosophical Tendencies in Filmmaking." In *Fascinatingly Disturbing: Interdisciplinary Perspectives on Michael Haneke's Cinema,* edited by Alexander D. Ornella and Stefanie Knauss, 34–39. Eugene, OR: Pickwick Publications.

Martin, Adrian, *Last Day before Every Day: Figural Thinking from Auerbach and Kracauer to Agamben and Brenez.* Brooklyn, NY: Punctum Books, 2012.

Martin-Jones, David. 2008. *Deleuze, Cinema and National Identity: Narrative Time in National Contexts.* Edinburgh: Edinburgh University Press.

———. 2011. *Deleuze and World Cinemas.* London: Continuum.

Martin-Jones, David, and William Brown, eds. 2012. *Deleuze and Film.* Edinburgh: Edinburgh University Press.

Marx, Karl. 1990. *The Eighteenth Brumaire of Louis Bonaparte.* Translated by Robert Browning et al. New York: International Publishers.

Mathijs, Ernest. 2008. *The Cinema of David Cronenberg: From Baron of Blood to Cultural Hero.* London: Wallflower Press.

Mayer, Sophie. 2009. *The Cinema of Sally Potter: A Politics of Love.* London: Wallflower Press.

McDonagh, Maitland. 2010. *Broken Mirrors/Broken Minds: The Dark Dreams of Dario Argento.* Expanded ed. Minneapolis: University of Minnesota.

McGee, Patrick. 2007. *From "Shane" to "Kill Bill": Rethinking the Western.* Oxford: Blackwell Publishing.

McGillis, Roderick. 2009. *He Was Some Kind of Man: Masculinities in the B Western.* Waterloo, ON: Wilfrid Laurier University Press.
McHugh, Kathleen. 2007. *Jane Campion.* Urbana: University of Illinois Press.
McLean, Adrienne L. *Being Rita Hayworth: Labor, Identity, and Holywood Stardom.* New Brunswick, NJ: Rutgers University Press, 2004.
Millán Barroso, Pedro Javier. 2011. "*Tango*: Estética del límite y poetica tragica." In *Carlos Saura: Una trayectoria ejemplar,* edited by Robin Lefere, 113–38. Madrid: Visor Libros.
Milne, Lesley. 1990. *Mikhail Bulgakov: A Critical Biography.* Cambridge: Cambridge University Press.
Mitchell, Lee Clark. 1996. *Westerns: Making the Man in Fiction and Film.* Chicago: University of Chicago Press.
Monod, Jacques. 1971. *Chance and Necessity: An Essay on the Natural Philosophy of Biology.* Translated by Austryn Wainhouse. New York: Alfred A. Knopf.
Monteagudo, Luciano. 1993. *Fernando Solanas.* Buenos Aires: Centro Editor de América Latina.
Morgan, Daniel. 2006. "Rethinking Bazin: Ontology and Realist Aesthetics." *Critical Inquiry* 32 (3): 443–81.
Murphy, David. 2000. *Sembène: Imagining Alternatives in Film and Fiction.* Oxford: James Currey.
Murray, Timothy. 2008. *Digital Baroque: New Media Art and Cinematic Folds.* Minneapolis: University of Minnesota Press.
———. 2010. "Time @ Cinema's Future: New Media Art and the Thought of Temporality." In *Afterimages of Gilles Deleuze's Film Philosophy,* edited by D. N. Rodowick, 353–72. Minneapolis: University of Minnesota Press.
Navitski, Rielle. 2011. "The Tango on Broadway: Carlos Gardel's International Stardom and the Transition to Sound in Argentina." *Cinema Journal* 51 (1): 26–49.
Neale, Steve. 2000. *Genre and Hollywood.* London: Routledge.
Nelson, T. G. A. 1990. *Comedy: An Introduction to Comedy in Literature, Drama, and Cinema.* Oxford: Oxford University Press.
Nelson, Thomas Allen. 2000. *Kubrick: Inside a Film Artist's Maze.* New and expanded ed. Bloomington: Indiana University Press.
Nerenberg, Ellen. 2012. *Murder Made in Italy: Homicide, Media, and Contemporary Italian Culture.* Bloomington: Indiana University Press.
Neri, Corrado. 2008. "Tsai Ming-Liang and the Lost Emotions of the Flesh." *Positions: Asia Critique* 16 (2): 389–407.
Newman, Kathleen. 1993. "National Cinema after Globalization: Fernando E. Solanas' *Sur* and the Exiled Nation." *Quarterly Review of Film and Video* 14 (3): 69–83.
Newman, Kim. 1988. *Nightmare Movies: A Critical History of the Horror Film, 1968–88.* London: Bloomsbury.
Nicoll, Allardyce. 1963. *Masks, Mimes and Miracles: Studies in the Popular Theater.* New York: Cooper Square Publishers.
Nietzsche, Friedrich. 1991. "On the Uses and Disadvantages of History for Life." In *Untimely Meditations.* Translated by R. J. Hollingdale, 57–124. Cambridge: Cambridge University Press.
———. 2001. *The Gay Science.* Edited by Bernard Williams. Translated by Josefine Nauckhoff and Adrian Del Caro. Cambridge: Cambridge University Press.

———. 2002. *Beyond Good and Evil.* Edited by Rolf-Peter Horstmann and Judith Norman. Translated by Judith Norman. Cambridge: Cambridge University Press.

———. 2007. *On the Genealogy of Morality.* Revised student ed. Edited by Keith Ansell-Pearson. Translated by Carol Diethe. Cambridge: Cambridge University Press.

Niogret, Hubert. 2009. "Entretien avec Park Chan-wook: Un changement de perspective." *Positif* 584: 25–29.

Olkowski, Dorothea. 1999. *Gilles Deleuze and the Ruin of Representation.* Berkeley: University of California Press.

Ornella, Alexander D., and Stefanie Knauss, eds. 2010. *Fascinatingly Disturbing: Interdisciplinary Perspectives on Michael Haneke's Cinema.* Eugene, OR: Pickwick Publications.

Orr, John. 2011. "*The White Ribbon* in Michael Haneke's Cinema." In *The Cinema of Michael Haneke: Europe Utopia,* edited by Ben McCann and David Sorfa, 259–64. London: Wallflower Press.

"The Ox-Bow Incident." 1943. Review. *Film Daily,* May 10 [83 (89)], 6.

Parvulescu, Anca. 2010. *Laughter: Notes on a Passion.* Cambridge, MA: MIT Press.

Pasolini, Pier Paolo. 1988. *Heretical Empiricism.* Edited and translated by Ben Lawton and Louise K. Barnett. Bloomington: Indiana University Press.

Patton, Paul, ed. 1996. *Deleuze: A Critical Reader.* Oxford: Blackwell Publishers.

Petrie, Duncan, ed. 1992. *Screening Europe: Image and Identity in Contemporary European Cinema.* London: BFI Publishing.

Petrov, Peter. 2005. "The Freeze of Historicity in Thaw Cinema" *KinoKulktura* 8. http://www.kinokultura.com/articles/apr05-petrov.html. Accessed July 2, 2014.

Peucker, Brigitte. 2010. "Games Haneke Plays: Reality and Performance." In *A Companion to Michael Haneke,* edited by Roy Grundmann, 130–47. Chichester, West Sussex, GB: Wiley-Blackwell.

Pisters, Patricia. 2003. *The Matrix of Visual Culture: Working with Deleuze in Film Theory.* Stanford, CA: Stanford University Press.

Plantinga, Carl. 2009. *Moving Viewers: American Films and the Spectator's Experience.* Berkeley: University of California Press.

Polan, Dana. 1986a. *Power and Paranoia: History, Narrative, and the American Cinema, 1940–1950.* New York: Columbia University Press.

———. 1986b. "Translator's Introduction." In *Kafka: Toward a Minor Literature,* translated by Dana Polan, xxii–xxix. Minneapolis: University of Minnesota Press.

———. 1994, "Francis Bacon: The Logic of Sensation." In *Gilles Deleuze and the Theater of Philosophy.* Edited by Constantin V. Boundas and Dorothea Olkowski, 229–54. New York: Routledge.

———. 2007. *Scenes of Instruction: The Beginnings of the U.S. Study of Film.* Berkeley: University of California Press.

Ponga, Paula. 2003. "According to Saura." *Carlos Saura: Interviews,* edited by Linda M. Willem, 150–56. Jackson: University Press of Mississippi.

Porton, Richard. 1995. "Mambety's *Hyenas:* Between Anti-Colonialism and the Critique of Modernity." *Iris* 18: 95–103.

Powell, Anna. 2005. *Deleuze and Horror Film.* Edinburgh: Edinburgh University Press.

———. 2012. "A Touch of Terror: Dario Argento and Deleuze's Cinematic Sensorium." In *European Nightmares: Horror Cinema in Europe since 1945,* edited by Patricia Allmer, Emily Brick, and David Huxley, 167–77. London: Wallflower Press.

Price, Brian. 2010. "Bureaucracy and Visual Style." In *A Companion to Michael Haneke,* edited by Roy Grundmann, 301–20. Chichester, West Sussex, GB: Wiley-Blackwell.
Price, Brian, and John David Rhodes, eds. 2010. *On Michael Haneke.* Detroit: Wayne State University Press.
The Pythons. 2002. *Monty Python and the Holy Grail: Screenplay.* London: Methuen.
Rajchman, John. 2010. "Deleuze's Time, or How the Cinematic Changes Out Ideas of Art." In *Afterimages of Gilles Deleuze's Film Philosophy,* edited by D. N. Rodowick, 283–306. Minneapolis: University of Minnesota Press.
Rancière, Jacques. 1994. *The Names of History: On the Poetics of Knowledge.* Translated by Hassan Melehy. Minneapolis: University of Minnesota Press.
———. 2004. *The Politics of Aesthetics: The Distribution of the Sensible.* Translated by Gabriel Rockhill. London: Continuum.
———. 2009. *The Emancipated Spectator.* Translated by Gregory Elliott. London: Verso.
Rapfogel, Jared. 2004. "Taiwan's Poet of Solitude: An Interview with Tsai Ming-liang." *Cineaste* 29(4): 26–29.
Reich, Jacqueline. 2004. *Beyond the Latin Lover: Marcello Mastroianni, Masculinity, and Italian Cinema.* Bloomington: Indiana University Press.
Restivo, Angelo. 2002. *The Cinema of Economic Miracles: Visuality and Modernization in the Italian Art Film.* Durham, NC: Duke University Press.
Rhodes, John David. 2007. "Allegory, *mise-en-scène,* AIDS: Interpreting *Safe.*" In *The Cinema of Todd Haynes: All That Heaven Allows,* edited by James Morrisson, 68–78. London: Wallflower Press.
Rhodes, John David, and Elena Gorfinkel. 2011. "Introduction: The Matter of Places." In *Taking Place: Location and the Moving Image,* edited by John David Rhodes and Elena Gorfinkel, vii–xxix. Minneapolis: University of Minnesota Press.
Rodowick, D. N. 1997. *Gilles Deleuze's Time Machine.* Durham, NC: Duke University Press.
———, ed. 2010a. *Afterimages of Gilles Deleuze's Film Philosophy.* Minneapolis: University of Minnesota Press.
———. 2010b. "The World, Time." In *Afterimages of Gilles Deleuze's Film Philosophy,* edited by D. N. Rodowick, 97–114. Minneapolis: University of Minnesota Press.
Rosen, Philip. 2001. *Change Mummified: Cinema, Historicity, Theory.* Minneapolis: University of Minnesota Press.
Rosenstone, Robert A. 2006. *History on Film/Film on History: History, Concept, Theories and Practice.* Harlow, Essex, GB: Pearson Education Ltd.
———. 2007. "In Praise of the Biopic." In *Lights, Camera, History: Portraying the Past in Film,* edited by Richard Francaviglia and Jerry Rodnitzky, 11–29. College Station, TX: Published for the University of Texas at Arlington by Texas A&M University Press.
Rosellini, Robert. 1992. *My Method: Writings and Interviews.* Edited by Adriano Aprà. Translated by Annapaola Cancognini. New York: Marsilio Publishers.
Rush, N. Orwin. 1979. *The Diversions of a Westerner: With Emphasis upon Owen Wister and Frederic Remington, Books and Libraries.* Amarillo, TX: South Pass Press.
Salazkina, Masha. 2009. "Aleksei Balabanov: *Morphia* (*Morfii,* 2008)." *KinoKultura* 25. http://www.kinokultura.com/2009/25r-morphia-ms.shtml. Accessed July 2, 2014.
Salmi, Hannu, ed. 2011. *Historical Comedy on Screen.* Bristol, GB: Intellect.
Savigliano, Marta E. 1995. *Tango and the Political Economy of Passion.* Boulder, CO: Westview Press.

Schaefer, Claudia. 2001. "Crimes of Passion: Arturo Ripstein's *Profundo Carmesi* and the Terrors of Melodrama." *Latin American Literary Review* 29 (57): 87–103.

Schivelbusch, Wolfgang. 1986. *The Railway Journey: The Industrialization of Time and Space in the 19th Century*. Berkeley: University of California Press.

Schoonover, Karl. 2012. *Brutal Vision: The Neorealist Body in Postwar Cinema*. Minneapolis: University of Minnesota Press.

Schwab, Martin. 2000. "Escape from the Image: Deleuze's Image-Ontology." In *The Brain Is the Screen: Deleuze and the Philosophy of Cinema*, edited by Gregory Flaxman, 109–40. Minneapolis: University of Minnesota Press.

Sharp, Jasper. 2009. "Thirst." *Sight and Sound* 19 (11): 79.

Sharrett, Christopher. 2010. "The World That Is Known: An Interview with Michael Haneke." In *A Companion to Michael Haneke*, edited by Roy Grundmann, 580–90. Chichester, West Sussex, GB: Wiley-Blackwell.

Shaviro, Steven. 1993. *The Cinematic Body*. Minneapolis: University of Minnesota Press.

Shiel, Mark. 2006. *Italian Neorealism: Rebuilding the Cinematic City*. London: Wallflower Press.

Sickels, Robert C. 2008. "Beyond the Blessings of Civilization: John Ford's *Stagecoach* and the Myth of the Western Frontier." In *John Ford in Focus: Essays on the Filmmaker's Life and Work*, edited by Kevin L. Stoehr and Michael C. Connolly, 142–52. Jefferson, NC: McFarland & Company.

Siegel, Michael. 2011. "The Nonplace of Argento: *The Bird with the Crystal Plumage* and Roman Urban History." In *Taking Place: Location and the Moving Image*, edited by John David Rhodes and Elena Gorfinkel, 211–31. Minneapolis: University of Minnesota Press.

Sigal, Pierre André. 1985. "*Brancaleone s'en va-t-aux Croisades;* Satire d'un moyen-âge conventionnel." In *Le Moyen Âge au Cinéma*, edited by François de la Bretèque. Special issue of *Les Cahiers de la Cinémathèque* 42–43: 141–44.

Slotkin, Richard. 1992. *Gunfighter Nation: The Myth of the Frontier in Twentieth-Century America*. New York: Atheneum.

Smyth, J. E., ed. 2012. *Hollywood and the American Historical Film*. London: Palgrave Macmillan.

Sobchack, Vivian, ed. 1996. *The Persistence of History: Cinema, Television, and the Modern Event*. New York: Routledge.

———. 2004. *Carnal Thoughts: Embodiment and Moving Image Culture*. Berkeley: University of California Press.

Sorlin, Pierre. 1980. *The Film in History: Restaging the Past*. Totowa, NJ: Barnes & Noble Books.

Speck, Oliver C. 2010. "The Marriage of Past and Present: Intertextuality in Fassbinder and Haneke." In *Fascinatingly Disturbing: Interdisciplinary Perspectives on Michael Haneke's Cinema*, edited by Alexander D. Ornella and Stefanie Knauss, 169–95. Eugene, OR: Pickwick Publications.

———. 2011. "Thinking the Event: The Virtual in Michael Haneke's Films." In *The Cinema of Michael Haneke: Europe Eutopia*, edited by Ben McCann & David Sorfa, 49–64. London: Wallflower Press.

Sragow, Michael. 2008. *Victor Fleming: An American Movie Master*. New York: Pantheon Books.

Stanfield, Peter. 2001. *Hollywood Westerns and the 1930s: The Lost Trail.* Exeter, Devon, GB: University of Exeter Press.

Steiner, George. 1977. "Introduction." In Walter Benjamin, *The Origin of German Tragic Drama,* 7–24. Translated by John Osborne. London: Verso.

Stepan, Nancy. 1985. "Biology and Degeneration: Races and Proper Places." In *Degeneration: The Dark Side of Progress,* edited by J. Edward Chamberlin and Sander L. Gilman, 97–120. New York: Columbia University Press.

Stewart, Garrett. 2010. "Pre-War Trauma: Haneke's *The White Ribbon.*" *Film Quarterly* 63 (4): 40–47.

Stoehr, Kevin L., and Michael C. Connolly, eds. 2008. *John Ford in Focus: Essays on the Filmmaker's Life and Work.* Jefferson, NC: McFarland & Company.

Sypher, Wylie, ed. 1956. *Comedy: An Essay on Comedy by George Meredith; Laughter by Henri Bergson.* Introduction and appendix by Wylie Sypher. Garden City, NY: Doubleday.

———. 1983. *Comedy: George Meredith's "An Essay on Comedy" and Henri Bergson's "Laughter."* Baltimore, MD: Johns Hopkins University Press.

Taubin, Amy. 2005a. "*An Angel at My Table:* Alone, Naturally." Criterion Collection, posted September 19. http://www.criterion.com/current/posts/771-an-angel-at-my-table-alone-naturally. Accessed July 2, 2014.

———. 2005b. "Model Citizens: Nothing Is Quite What It Seems in *A History of Violence,* Cronenberg's Subversive Version of Homeland Insecurity." *Film Comment* 41 (5): 24–28.

Taylor, Clyde. 2000. "Searching for the Postmodern in African Cinema." In *Symbolic Narratives /African Cinema: Audiences, Theory and the Moving Image,* edited by June Givanni, 136–45. London: BFI Publishing.

Tentori, Antonio. 1997. *Dario Argento: Sensualità dell'omocidio.* Alessandria: Edizione Falsopiano.

Thakur, Gautam Basu. 2007. "Re-reading Michael Haneke's *La Pianiste:* Schizo-Politics and the Critique of Consumer Culture." *New Cinemas: Journal of Contemporary Film* 5 (2): 139–52.

Thomas, Greg. 2011. "Hyenas in the Enchanted Brothel: 'The Naked Truth' in Djibril Diop Mambéty." *Black Camera: An International Film Journal* 2 (2): 8–25.

Thoret, Jean-Baptiste. 2002. *Dario Argento: Magicien de la peur.* Paris: Cahiers du cinéma.

Tomkins, Jane. 1992. *West of Everything: The Inner Life of Westerns.* Oxford: Oxford University Press.

Torlasco, Domietta. 2008. *The Time of the Crime: Phenomenology, Psychoanalysis, Italian Film.* Stanford, CA: Stanford University Press.

Trevor-Roper, Hugh. 1985. "The Invention of Tradition: The Highland Tradition of Scotland." *The Invention of Tradition,* edited by Eric Hobsbawm and Terence Ranger, 15–41. Cambridge: Cambridge University Press.

Ukadike, Nwachukwu Frank. 1994. *Black African Cinema.* Berkeley: University of California Press.

———. 1999. "The Hyena's Last Laugh: A Conversation with Djibril Diop Mambety," *Transition* 78 8 (2): 136–53. [Online version: http://newsreel.org/articles/mambety.htm.]

———. n.d. "Hyenas." *California Newsreel.* http://newsreel.org/video/Hyenas.

Uraizee, Joy F. 2006. "Subverting the Status Quo in Sénégal: Djibril Diôp Mabety's *Hyenas* and the Politics of Liberation." *Literature/Film Quarterly* 34 (4): 313–22.

Usai, Paolo Cherchi. 2001. *The Death of Cinema: History, Cultural Memory and the Digital Dark Age*. London: BFI Publishing.

Utz, Richard, and Jesse G. Swan, eds. 2005. *Postmodern Medievalisms*. Cambridge: D.S. Brewer.

Vasudevan, Ravi S. 2006. "Nationhood, Authenticity, and Realism in Indian Cinema: The Double Take of Modernism in Ray." In *Apu and After*, edited by Moinak Biswas, 80–115. Oxford: Seagull Books.

Verhoeff, Nanna. 2006. *The West in Early Cinema: After the Beginning*. Amsterdam: Amsterdam University Press.

Villani, Vivien. 2008. *Dario Argento*. Rome: Gremese Editore.

"The Virginian." 1929. Review of Victor Fleming film. *Film Daily*, December 29 [1 (75)], 8.

"The Virginian." 1946. Review of Stuart Gilmore film. *Variety*, January 30. Reprinted in *Variety Film Reviews 1907–1980*, vol. 7: *1943–1948*. New York: Garland Publishing, Inc., 1983.

Virilio, Paul. 1989. *War and Cinema: The Logistics of Perception*. Translated by Patrick Camiller. London: Verso.

———. 1991. *Lost Dimension*. Translated by Daniel Mosherberg. New York: Semiotext(e).

———. 1995. *The Art of the Motor*. Translated by Julie Rose. Minneapolis: University of Minnesota Press.

———. 1997. *Open Sky*. Translated by Julie Rose. London and New York: Verso.

———. 2006. *Speed and Politics*. Translated by Mark Polizzotti. Los Angeles: Semiotext(e).

Wang, Shujen, and Chris Fujiwara. 2006. "'My Films Reflect My Living Situation': An Interview with Tsai Ming-liang on Film Spaces, Audiences, and Distribution." *Positions: Asia Critique* 14 (1): 219–41.

Warren, Charles. 2010. "The Unknown Piano Teacher." In *A Companion to Michael Haneke*, edited by Roy Grundmann, 495–510. Chichester, West Sussex, GB: Wiley-Blackwell.

Wheatley, Catherine. 2009a. *Michael Haneke's Cinema: The Ethic of the Image*. New York: Berghan Books.

———. 2009b. "Unexpected Tenderness." *Sight and Sound* 19 (12): 18–19. http://old.bfi.org.uk/sightandsound/feature/49581. Accessed July 2, 2014.

White, Frederick H. 2008. "Of Freaks and Men: Aleksei Balabanov's Critique of Degenerate Post-Soviet Society." *Studies in Russian and Soviet Cinema* 2 (3): 281–97.

White, Hayden. 1973. *Metahistory: The Historical Imagination in Nineteenth-Century Europe*. Baltimore, MD: Johns Hopkins University Press.

———. 1978. *Tropics of Discourse: Essays in Cultural Criticism*. Baltimore, MD: Johns Hopkins University Press.

———. 1987. *The Content of the Form: Narrative Discourse and Historical Representation*. Baltimore, MD: Johns Hopkins University Press.

———. 1988. "Historiography and Historiophoty." *American Historical Review* 93 (5): 1193–99.

———. 1994. "Foreword: Rancière's Revisionism." In *The Names of History: On the Poetics of Knowledge*, translated by Hassan Melehy, vii–xx. Minneapolis: University of Minnesota Press.

Whitt, Patrick Pond. Review of Chomet's *"The Illusionist* (Two-disc Blue-ray Combo)." http://www.amazon.com/review/RN53H4HU3G19N. Accessed July 2, 2014.

Willem, Linda M., ed. *Carlos Saura: Interviews.* Jackson: University Press of Mississippi, 2003.

Williams, James S. 2010. "Aberrations of Beauty: Violence and Cinematic Resistance in Haneke's *The White Ribbon.*" *Film Quarterly* 64 (3): 48–55.

Williams, Linda. 1995. "Film Bodies: Gender, Genre, and Excess." In *Film Genre Reader III*, edited by Barry Keith Grant, 140–158. Austin: University of Texas Press.

———. 1999. *Hard Core: Power, Pleasure, and the Frenzy of the Visible.* Expanded ed. Berkeley: University of California Press.

Wister, Owen. 1902. *The Virginian: A Horseman of the Plains,* with paintings by Fredric Remington and drawings by Charles M. Russell. New York: Macmillan Publishing Co., Inc.

Wood, Robin. 2009. "'Do I Disgust You?' or, Tirez pas sur *La Pianiste.*" *CineAction* 59: 55–61.

Wyke, Maria. 1997. *Projecting the Past: Ancient Rome, Cinema, and History.* New York: Routledge.

Yardley, Jonathan. 2007. "Broadening the Western's Horizons." *Washington Post,* April 7, C1.

Zielinski, Siegfried. 2006. *Deep Time of the Media: Toward an Archaeology of Hearing and Seeing by Technical Means.* Cambridge, MA: MIT Press.

Zola, Émile. 2004. *Thérèse Raquin.* Translated by Robin Buss. London: Penguin Books.

Zourabichvili, François. 1996. "Six Notes on the Percept (On the Relation between the Clinical and the Critical)." In *Deleuze: A Critical Reader,* edited by Paul Patton, 188–216. Oxford: Blackwell Publishers.

INDEX

Page numbers in italics indicate photographs and illustrations.

À la recherche du temps perdu (Proust), xv–xvi
Abel, Richard, xiii
academic study of film, xi
Acquarello, 181
action-image: and American westerns, 8; and biopics, 132; and crisis of the movement-image, 2–3, 4–5; and *Deep Red*, 51; as described, 32; and *Destry Rides Again*, 14, 16; and Hollywood films, 1; and horror cinema, 33–35; and *Hyenas*, 171; and *The Illusionist*, 216; and *My Name Is Nobody*, 25; and naturalism, 52; and *The Organizer*, 108; and *The Ox-Bow Incident*, 18; and *The Rise of Louis XIV*, 133; and *Stagecoach*, 11–12; and *The Stendhal Syndrome*, 40
Adorno, Theodor, 226
The Adversary (1970), xxix, 194–96, *195*; Chaudhuri on, 196
aesthetics of counter history, xix, xxvi; and horror, 36; and humor, 72; and surrealism, 37–38
affection-images, 2–3, 10–11, 33, 52
affective images, xxiii
Agamben, Giorgio, 168
Aguirre: The Wrath of God (1972), 26
allegory: and "becoming minoritarian," 164–65; Benjamin on, xiii–xiv, xxx–xxxi, 245–46; and *Brancalone's Army*, 99; and *Carry On Up the Khyber*, 73; and counter-historical thinking, xx; and crisis of the movement-image, xxiv–xxv; and *Deep Crimson*, 53, 59; and global neorealism, 191; and Haneke's films, 218; and horror cinema, 36; and *Hyenas*, 171–73, 175, 177; and *The Illusionist*, 211; and Italian film comedy, 93; and *Meek's Cutoff*, 26; and minoritarian cinematic forms, xxvii; and *Morphia*, 245–46; and *Of Freaks and Men*, 236; and *The Ox-Bow Incident*, 17; and *The Rise of Louis XIV*, 135, 137; and *Stagecoach*, 12; and *The Stendhal Syndrome*, 40, 42–43; and *What Time Is It There?*, 113–22
Althusser, Louis, xii
Altman, Rick, 178
Amad, xiii
American cinema, 5
anarchic film, 81–82
Andalusian Dog, 37–38
Andreotti, Giulio, 2
Andrews, Dana, 17
An Angel at My Table (1990), 128, 140–45, *142*; and minority culture, *142*, *143*, 145
animal imagery, 38, 87–88, 173–75
animation, 210–17

Annales school, xi–xii
antiheroes, 95
antiquarianism, 11
Anti-Semitism, 97–99
Antonioni, Michelangelo: and crime film, 219; and horror cinema, 33, 46–47; and Italian film comedy, 92, 94; and minoritarian cinema, 181; and neorealism, 193–94; and time-image, xvii; and use of gesture, 114; and *What Time Is It There?*, 114
Aparajito (1956), xxix, 191, 193
Aprà, Adriano, 135
Apu Sansar (1959), xxix, 191
Apu trilogy, 188, 191
The Arcades Project (2002), 135
Arcades Project (Benjamin), xxx, 245–46
Argentina, xxvi, 146–50, 151, 153, 155, 157–58
Argento, Dario: and counter-history concept, xxii; and *Deep Red*, 45–51; and digitalization, 43–44, 45; and Hitchcock's films, 36; and sensation, 47; and *The Stendhal Syndrome*, 38–44
Arnold, Matthew, 143
Arrival of a Train at La Ciotat (1896), 236
Artaud, Antonin: and counter-history concept, xv; and dissociative force of cinema, 250; and falsifying narration, xxviii–xxx; and horror cinema, 37; and raw cinema, 38; and theater of cruelty, 243; and "thought without image," 72
Arthurian legend, 80–88
aural technologies, ix–x
authoritarianism, 219
autobiography, 141, 145
avant-garde cinema, 35, 37, 45, 198, 249

Bacon, Francis, 41
Bakjwi (*Thirst*, 2009), xxiv, 33, 61–69, 68
Balabanov, Aleksey, xxii, xxx, 188, 232–40, 240–46
Balázs, Béla, xi
Balzac, Honoré de, 35
banality, 192–93
Bancroft, George, 13
Bannerjee, Karuna, 192

Barboni, Enzo, 21
baroque, 41; and Stendhal Syndrome, 41–42, 187
Barton, David, 120, 121
Bazin, André, xi, xiii, 90, 240
Beaty, Bart, 204, 207
Beckett, Samuel, xvi
becoming as concept, xvii–xviii, 71, 113, 125–27, 186, 232
"becoming minoritarian," 162–64
becoming woman, 141; in *An Angel at My Table*, 144–45; in *The Tango Lesson*, 158–62
"Becoming-Fluid" (Herzog), xx
Bellamy, Madge, 9
Bell'Antonio, Il (1960), 93
Bello, Maria, 203
Benjamin, Walter: on allegorizing, xxx–xxxi; and baroque, 41; and forms of allegorizing, 245–46; and Haneke's films, 218; and horror cinema, 36; and international impact of cinema, xi; and minoritarian cinema, 125, 134–35, 137, 163, 171; and reevaluation of historicizing, xiii–xiv
Bergman, Ingmar, 100–101
Bergson, Henri, xvii, 3, 104, 114, 211
Berressem, Hanjo, 121–22
Bertolucci, Bernardo, 92
Bichevin, Leonid, 241
Bicycle Thieves (1948), 90
Bierstadt, Albert, 11
Big Deal on Madonna Street (1958), 92
Bini, Patrizia, 93
biopics: and *An Angel at My Table*, 140–45; as counter-history, 127–28, 128–32; and *Il divo*, 2; and *The Illusionist*, 216–17; and *The Rise of Louis XIV*, 133–40
The Birth of a Nation (1915), 1, 5
Biswas, Moinak, 190–91
Black Girl (Sembène), 164–65
Blasetti, Alessandro, 89
Blier, Bernard, 107
Blood of the Beasts (1949), 38
Blow-Up (1966), 47
Blue Velvet (1986), 202
Bob le flambeur (1956), 92

bodies, xxi–xxiii, xxv, xxvii; and cinematic, 134; deformed, 101–102; exhausted, 114; and imperialism, 78–79; in minoritarian forms, 168–69; in naturalism, 35–36; and the phallus, 78–79, 82, 87; and sensation, 44; and vampire bodies, 67–68
Bolognini, Mauro, 93; and *Il bell'Antonio*, 93
Borges, Jorge Luis, 126, 156
Boudu Saved from Drowning (1932), 107
bourgeois culture, 226
Boyer, Charles, 53, 55, 59–60
Brancaleone at the Crusades (1970), xxv, 95
Brancaleone's Army (1966), xxv, 74, 95–105, 98, 106
Brat (*Brother*, 1997), 235
Brat 2 (*Brother 2*, 1997), 235
Bread, Love and Dreams (1953), 91
Bread, Love and Jealousy (1954), 91
Bresson, Robert, 33, 250
Brother (1997), 235
Brother 2 (1997), 235
Brownlow, Kevin, 5–6
Brunetta, Gian Piero, 92, 105
Brutal Vision (2012), 90
Buck-Morss, Susan, 137
Buenos Aires, Argentina, 153
Buffalo Bill, 11
Buffalo Livestock Corporation, 6
Bulgakov, Mikhail, 241, 245
Bull, Charles Edward, 8
Buñuel, Luis, xvi, 35, 37, 53
Burgoyne, Robert, xix–xx
burlesque: and *Carry On Up the Khyber*, 73, 77; and crisis of the movement-image, 4; and *Destry Rides Again*, 14–16; and *The Hole*, 179; and *My Name Is Nobody*, 21, 25
The Butcher's Revolt (Artaud), 44

Cabiria (Burgoyne), xx
Cacho, Daniel Giménez, 53
Calamai, Clara, 48, 51
Calcutta trilogy, 193–94
Camerini, Mario, 89
The Camp at Thiaroye (1988), xxvi, 128, 164–70, *169*; and minoritarian expression, 168–69, *169*
Campion, Jane, xxii, 128, 140, 141–42

Canova, Gianni, 41
The Canterbury Tales (Chaucer), 87
caper films, 92, 93
capitalism, 10, 139, 171–72, 176
Cardinale, Claudia, 92
Cargo 200 (2007), 235
caricature: and *Brancalone's Army*, 96, 100; and *Deep Crimson*, 58; and *Eighteenth Brumaire of Louis Napoleon*, 75; and *Hyenas*, 174; and *The Illusionist*, 212; and Italian film comedy, 93, 96; and *Monte Python and the Holy Grail*, 81–82, 84; and *The Organizer*, 106; and *The Rise of Louis XIV*, 136. *See also* stereotypes
Carlyle, Thomas, 130
Carnal Thoughts (Sobchack), xix
Carné, Marcel, 64
Carradine, John, 11
Carry On Up the Khyber (1968), xxv, 73, 77–80, *80*
Castro, Donald, 148
Catholic Church, 59, 102
Cavell, Stanley, 240
censorship, 36, 79, 89
C'era una volta il West (1968), 8, 21, 203
Certeau, Michel de, xii, xiii
Chandra, Barun, 197
Chang, Grace, 179, 181, 183
Chaplin, Charlie, 73, 107, 214
Chaudhuri, Supriya, 194, 196
The Cheese and the Worms (Ginzburg), xii
Chen Shiang-chyi, 116–21
Chiang Kai-shek, 121
chivalry: and *Brancaleone's Army*, 96, 98, 100; and *Monty Python and the Holy Grail*, 80–81, 84; and westerns, 7, 10, 11–14
Chomet, Sylvain, xxii, 188, 214–16
choreography, 6, 8
Christian Democratic Party (Italy), 91
Christianity, 66–67
chronology, 83
Cinema (Godard and Ishaghpour 2005), ix
Cinema (journal), 189
Cinema 1: The Movement-Image (Deleuze): and Eurocentrism, 35; and the future of cinema, 248–49; and historicizing

through cinema, xiv, 131–32; on liquid perception, 182–83; and the movement-image, xvi, 1, 4; and naturalism, 52; on neorealism, 212–13; and powers of the false, 214–15; and writing cinema history, 200

Cinema 2: The Time-Image (Deleuze): and the affection-image, 33; and Eurocentrism, 35; and the future of cinema, xxxi, 248–49; and historicizing through cinema, xiv; and modes of historicizing, 25; and the time-image, xvii, xxxi, 132, 233

cinema of poetry, 46

cinematic movement, 183. See also movement-image

cinematicism, 211

Civil War, 9, 13

class divisions, 12

cliché: and Argento's films, 45; and "becoming minoritarian," 162–63; and counter-historical thinking, xv, xx; and *Deep Red*, 46, 50; and *The Great War*, 110–11; and *A History of Violence*, 202–203, 208–209; and *The Hole*, 179, 183; and humor, xxiv–xxv; and *The Illusionist*, 212, 217; and Italian film comedy, 91; and *Meek's Cutoff*, 28; and minoritarian consciousness, 125; and Monicelli's films, 94; and *Monty Python and the Holy Grail*, 81; and neorealism, xxiv, 190; and *The Organizer*, 108; and *The Piano Teacher*, 225, 232; and *The Stendhal Syndrome*, 41; and "thinking images," 33–34; and *What Time Is It There?*, 75

clock time, 113–22

Clues, Myths, and the Historical Method (Ginzburg), xii

Colbert, Jean-Batiste, 136–37

Cold War, xii, xxiii

collective action, 107

collective memory, 162

colonialism: and *An Angel at My Table*, 140, 145; and "becoming minoritarian," 164; and biopic, 130; and *The Camp at Thiaroye*, 165, 167–68, 170; and *Carry On Up the Khyber*, 73, 77–80; and *Deep Crimson*, 57, 59; and neorealism, 189; and *The Tango Lesson*, 161; and *Tangos: The Exile of Gardel*, 146; and *What Time Is It There?*, 121

comedy: counter-historical use of, xxiv–xxv; history and humor, 75–77; Italian film comedy, 89–93; low comedy, 111–12; and surrealism, 73; and *Thirst*, 61; and types of counter-historicizing, 71–72. See also tragicomedy

Comedy (Sypher), 70

Comencini, Luigi, 91

commedia all'italiana, xxv, 89–93, 94–95, 101, 112

commercial cinemas, xxiii, xxiv

commodity fetishism, 134

Company Limited (1972), xxix, 196–97

computer technology. See digital technology and media

Condee, Nancy, 235, 240

Conestoga wagons, 6

The Content of the Form (White), xiii, xix

contingency, 126

Continuavano a chiamarlo Trinità (1971), 21

continuity, xxviii

Cooper, James Fenimore, 7

Copes, Juan Carlos, 154

counter-revolution, 75

A Country Doctor's Notebook (Bulgakov), 241, 245

The Covered Wagon (1923), xxiii, 1, 5–8, 9, 12; and nation building, 8; and western large form, 5–6

Crawford, Broderick, 93

Creative Evolution (Bergson), 3

crime films: and biopics, 129; and *Deep Red*, 46–48; and *A History of Violence*, 198–209; and horror cinema, 33–36; and Italian film comedy, 92; and *Monty Python and the Holy Grail*, 86, 88; and *Morphia*, 245; and *Of Freaks and Men*, 235, 238; and *The Piano Teacher*, 228; and rethinking of historicizing, xii–xiii; and *Stagecoach*, 11; and *The Stendhal Syndrome*, 40; and *The White Ribbon*, 219–21, 224

criollos, 146

Cronenberg, David, xxii, xxix, 188, 198–209, 246

cruelty: and Artaud's films, xxiv, xxx; and comedy, 72; and *Deep Crimson,* 52–53, 53–55, 60–61; and *Deep Red,* 48; and Deleuze's philosophy of difference, 188; and Haneke's films, 217–19; and horror and naturalism, 32; and horror cinema, 34; and *Hyenas,* 170–74, 177; and Italian film comedy, 89; and Monicelli's films, 105; and *Monty Python and the Holy Grail,* 86; and *Morphia,* 243; and *Of Freaks and Men,* 238–39; and *The Piano Teacher,* 224–25, 227–28, 230, 232; and *The Stendhal Syndrome,* 39–41, 44; and *Thirst,* 63, 66–68; and *The White Ribbon,* 220–21, 223–24
Crusades, 86, 96, 98–103
Cruze, James, xxiii, 1, 6
crystal images, xxix, 179–80
Curtis, Antonio De (Toto), 91–92
Curtiz, Michael, 11

Dalí, Salvador, 37
dance: and *Brancaleone at the Crusades,* 103; and comedy, 71; and *The Hole,* 178–79, 181–84; and *Hyenas,* 176; and *The Illusionist,* 214; and "invention of a people," xxvi; and minoritarian cinema, 128; and *Monty Python and the Holy Grail,* 82; and *Tango,* 153–58; and *The Tango Lesson,* 158–62; and *Tangos: The Exile of Gardel,* 146–53
Dapkunaite, Ingeborg, 243
Darwell, Jane, 17
Das Passagen-Werk (Benjamin), xiii
Dassin, Jules, 92
Dead Man (1995), 26
Debord, Guy, 38
The Decameron (Boccaccio), 87
deconstructionists, 34
Deep Crimson (1996), xxiv, 33, 46, 52–61, 54; and femininity, 57; and history, 56, 57, 59
Deep Red (1975), xxiv, 33, 38–39, 45–51, 47
degeneracy, 235
Del Río, Elena, xix, 76, 159, 162
Deleuze, Cinema and National Identity (Martin-Jones), xx, 35, 123–24, 201

Deleuze, Gilles: and the action-image, 25; and allegorizing, xxx; and anarchic and surreal comedy, 81–82, 88; and *An Angel at My Table,* 141, 145; on Artaud, 38; and "becoming minoritarian," 162–64; and biopic as counter-history, 131–32; and bodily expression, 146; and *The Camp at Thiaroye,* 168; and cinema of belief, 105; and comedy, 70; and counter-history concept, xiv–xviii, xxi–xxii, xxiii–xxxi; and crisis of the action-image, 108; and deterritorialization, 151–52, 159; and electronic "automata," 249; and *The Great War,* 111–12; and Haneke's films, 218–19; and history and humor, xxv, 75–76; and *A History of Violence,* 199–201, 205–206, 207–208; and horror cinema, 38–39, 40–42, 46, 51, 60–61; and *Hyenas,* 172; and "idiosyncratic surrealism," 54; and *The Illusionist,* 210–11, 216; and Italian film comedy, 90; on masochism, 225, 228–30; and *Meeks Cutoff,* 30–31; and mental image, 20; and minoritarian cinema, xxvi–xxvii, 123–28, 176; and *Morphia,* 240, 241–42, 243; and Murray's "digital baroque," 249–50; and musicals, 178–84; and naturalism, 32–36, 52, 59, 64, 67; and neorealism, xxiv, 190, 192–94, 196, 197; and *Of Freaks and Men,* 233; and philosophy of difference, 185–88; and *The Piano Teacher,* 225, 227–29, 230–31; and *The Rise of Louis XIV,* 133–35, 139; and *Tango,* 158; taxonomy of images and signs, 3; and temporality, xxvii–xxviii; and theories of history, 250–51; and "thought without image," 72–73; and time-image, xiv, 33; and types of counter-historicizing, 71–72; and *What Time Is It There?,* 113, 114, 118, 120, 121–22; and *The White Ribbon,* 221–22
Deleuze and World Cinemas (Martin-Jones), xx, 35
DeMille, Cecil B., 11
Dentist on the Job (1961), 82
Derrida, Jacques, xii
Destry Rides Again (1939), xxiii, 1, 14–16

Det sjunde inseglet (1957), 100–101
deterritorialization: and *An Angel at My Table*, 141; and "becoming minoritarian," 163–64; and Deleuze's philosophy of difference, 187; and global neorealism, 192, 196; and minoritarian cinema, 123, 127–28; and *The Tango Lesson*, 159; *Tangos: The Exile of Gardel*, 149, 151–53
Devi, Chunibala, 192
The Devils (1971), 83
Devine, Andy, 11
dictatorship, 75, 153
Die Klavierspielerin (Jelinek), 224
Diescépolo, Armando, 147
Diescépolo, Enrique Santos, 147
Dietrich, Marlene, 15
difference, xxii
Difference and Repetition (Deleuze), xiv, xviii, 72, 76, 124–26, 199
Digital Baroque (Murray), 36, 249–50
digital technology and media: and Argento's films, 39, 43–45; and counter-historical thinking, xx; and electronic "automata," 249; and the future of cinema, xxxi, 247–50; and horror cinema, 36; and *The Illusionist*, 217; and *Morphia*, 246; and realism, 247; and surrealism, 43–44
Dirty War (Argentina), 148
Discépolo, Armando, 147
Discépolo, Enrique Santos, 150
Divorce Italian Style (1961), 93
documentary mode, xiii
Dodge City (1939), 11
Don Camillo novels (Guareschi), 91
Donen, Stanley, 179
Dong (1998), 128
Donlevy, Brian, 16
Dos Passos, John, 189
dreams, 104, 204–205
Dreiser, Theodore, 52
Dreyer, Carl Theodor, 33, 129–30
Drukarova, Dinara, 233
The Drum (Korda), 77
Du rififi chez les hommes (1955), 92
Duck, You Sucker (1971), 21
Dulac, Germaine, 37

Dürrenmatt, Friedrich, 171, 172
Dyer, Richard, 178

economic imperialism, 176
effective history: and *Carry On Up the Khyber*, 74; and comedy, 71; described, xvii; Foucault on, xxv; and *A History of Violence*, 199; and minoritarian consciousness, 127; and *The Organizer*, 109; and rethinking of historicizing, xii; and *The Rise of Louis XIV*, 133
Egurrola, Julieta, 55–56
The Eighteenth Brumaire of Louis Bonaparte (Marx), 75
Eisenstein, Sergei, xi, xvi, 4, 106
El exilio de Gardel: Tangos (1985), 128
embodiment, 134
empire films, 77, 79
Encompasser, 13
Enlightenment, 130
epic form, 4, 5–6, 8–11
epistemological crisis, xxiv
Erlanger, Philippe, 136
eschatology, xxviii
Etcheverry, Michel, 149–50
ethnic conflict, 8–9
Euro-cinema, xx–xxi
experimental film forms, x

Fabrizi, Aldo, 94
Falcón, Ada, 147
falsifying narration, xvii–xxx, 63, 186, 188, 199–200, 209, 210–17, 245
family melodrama, 198–209
fantasy, 104
farce: and *Carry On Up the Khyber*, 73–74, 77; and "effective history," xxv; and Italian film comedy, 95, 96; and minoritarian consciousness, 127; and types of counter-historicizing, 71
fascism: and biopic, 129–30; and *Brancalone's Army*, 99; and *The Camp at Thiaroye*, 165, 167; and counter-historical thinking, xxi; and *Deep Red*, 48–49; impact on cinematic style, xxiii–xxiv; and Italian comedy, 89–90; and Monicelli's films, 94; and neoreal-

ism, 189; and rethinking of historicizing, xii
Fassbinder, Rainer Werner, 44
Fellini, Federico, xvii, 91, 92, 93, 95
femininity, 158–62
Ferguson, Karen, 142
Ferrari, Marco, 35
fetishism, 228
Feuer, Jane, 178
Feyder, Jacques, 64
fiction mode, xiii
film noir, 18
Flaxman, Gregory, xxxi, 124, 186
Flores, Esteban, 146–47
The Fold (Deleuze), xxx, 187
folklore, 96
Fonda, Henry, 7, 17, 18, 20, 21
For Ever Mozart (1996), 247
Ford, Francis, 17
Ford, John, xvi, xxii–xxiii, 1, 11–14; and *The Iron Horse*, 8–11; as reborn popular form, 11; and *Stagecoach*, 12–15
Foucault, Michel: and anarchic and surreal comedy, 88–89; and *Brancaleone's Army*, 100; and comedy, 70; and "concerted carnival" view of history, 22; and "effective history," xii, xvii, xxv, 71, 74, 109–10, 127, 133, 199; and history and humor, 75–76; and monumental history, 21; and *Of Freaks and Men*, 236; and types of counter-historicizing, 71–72
The Fountainhead (1949), 204
Fouquet, Nicolas, 137
The Four Feathers (Korda), 77
The 400 Blows (1959), 114, 117–18
Four Steps in the Clouds (1942), 89
Fox, Kerry, 142
Frame, Janet, 140–45
Franju, Georges, 38
Frederick the Great, 130
Free France, 167
French cinema, 129
French colonialism, 167
French New Wave, 2, 132
Friedel, Christian, 221
Frisky (1954), 91
frontier spaces, 5–14

functionalism, 25
Funny Games (1997), 44
Furman, Rosa, 56

Gallagher, Tag, 136–38
Gallardo, Juan Luis, 154
Gance, Abel, xvi, 4, 129–30
Gardel, Carlos, 147–51, 153
Garden of Eden, 27
Gassman, Vittorio, 92, 95, 110, 111
Gately, Millie, 28
gender issues: and *Destry Rides Again*, 15–16; gender violence, 155–56; gendered politics, 158–62; and *Meek's Cutoff*, 27–28; and *The Ox-Bow Incident*, 17, 18
genre films, 91–92
German New Wave, 132
Germi, Pietro, 93
Gertsman, Yuri, 243
gesture, 114
Ghatak, Ritwik, 197
Gilliam, Terry, 82
Ginzburg, Carlo, xii–xiii, xviii, 71
Girardot, Annie, 107, 225
The Girl with a Pistol (1968), 94
Giù la testa (1971), 21
Gladiator (Burgoyne), xx
Godard, Jean-Luc, ix, xiv, xvii, xx–xxi, 247, 250
Goethe, Johann Wolfgang von, 227
Goncourt, Edmund de, 34–35
Goncourt, Jules de, 34–35
gothic images, 51
Grace, W. G., 81
Gramsci, Antonio, xii, 189
The Great Dictator (1940), 73
The Great Train Robbery (1903), 8
The Great War (1959), xxv, 74, 95, 106, 110–13
Greenwood, Bruce, 26
Gregory (pope), 102
Griffith, D. W., xvi, 1, 4
Grimm's Fairy Tales, 143
Gruault, Jean, 136
Grundmann, Roy, 221–22, 225
Gruz 200 (2007), 235
Guareschi, Giovanni, 91

Guattari, Félix: and "becoming minoritarian," 162–64; and "becoming woman," 141; and deterritorialization, 159; and *Meek's Cutoff*, 30–31; and minoritarian consciousness, 123–24; and theories of history, 250–51
Guha, Ranajit, xii
Gunning, Tom, 247, 248
Gupta, Uma Das, 192

Hale, Alan, 6, 7
Haneke, Michael: and falsifying character of cinema, 188, 240; and *Morphia*, 246; and *The Piano Teacher*, 224–32; and *The Stendhal Syndrome*, 44; and violence and pedagogy, 217–19; and *The White Ribbon*, 219–24
Hansen, Miriam, xiii
Harris, Ed, 205–206
Hawks, Howard, 25
Hawtrey, Charles, 77
Hayes, Heidi, 203
Haynes, Todd, 133
Heavenly Creatures (1994), 140
Hemmings, David, 46–47
Henderson, Shirley, 28
Herder, Johann Gottfried, 130
heroism and hero figures: and American westerns, 5, 7, 10; and biopic, 129; and *Brancaleone's Army*, 96, 100; and crisis of the movement-image, 4, 33; and *Deep Crimson*, 53; and *Destry Rides Again*, 14–16; and *The Great War*, 111–12; and *A History of Violence*, 199, 205–206; and Italian film comedy, 90; and Monicelli's films, 95; and *Monty Python and the Holy Grail*, 81, 84; and *The Organizer*, 108–109; and *The Ox-Bow Incident*, 17, 18–19; and *The Piano Teacher*, 230; and *Stagecoach*, 13; and *Tangos: The Exile of Gardel*, 148
Herzog, Amy, xix–xx, 178, 183
Herzog, Werner, 26
Hill, Terence, 21
Hiroshima Mon Amour (1959), 114, 117
Histoire(s) du cinéma (Godard), xxi

historicity: and biopic, 130, 131–32; and counter-historical thinking, xvi–xix, xxi; and crisis of the movement-image, xxiv–xxvi, 1, 4–5; and Deleuze's philosophy of difference, 187; and *A History of Violence*, 199; and horror cinema, 33–36; and *The Illusionist*, 216; and minoritarian consciousness, 124–28; and *Monte Python and the Holy Grail*, 88; and *Morphia*, 240; and *My Name Is Nobody*, 21–22, 25; and *Of Freaks and Men*, 232–33, 235; and *The Organizer*, 109–10; and repetition, 112; and rethinking of historicizing, xii–xiv; and *The Rise of Louis XIV*, 133, 139; and *Thirst*, 63, 69; and visual technologies, x; and *What Time Is It There?*, 119, 121; and *The White Ribbon*, 224
historiography, 86
historiophoty, xiii
The History of Sexuality (Foucault), 236
A History of Violence (2005), xxix, 188; and falsifying narration, 201, 205–206; and the time-image, 209, 209; and undecideability, 208–209
History on Film/Film on History (Rosenstone), xix
Hitchcock, Alfred, xvi, 20, 34–36, 46
Hoberman, J., 26–27, 202, 205
The Hole (1998), xx, xxvii, 114, 128; and crystal image, 178–80; dehumanized landscapes in, 181; and eclectic form, 179; and liquidity, 181; and the musical, 178–84
Hollywood cinema, xx, xxii–xxiii, 1
Holmes, Ashton, 203
Holocaust, xii, 49
Homer, 22
horror cinema: and Argento's films, 38–44; and *Deep Crimson*, 52–61; and *Deep Red*, 45–51; and digital media, xx; and naturalism, 32–38; and neorealism, xxiv, 35–36, 54; and *Thirst*, 61–69
Hughes, Mary Beth, 17
humor, xxv, 71–72, 91. *See also* comedy
Huppert, Isabelle, 225
Hurt, William, 207

Hyenas (1992), xxvi, 128, 170–78, 175, 177; the role of animals in, 173–75; as satiric allegory, 172; women in, 173
hyperrealism, 35, 54

I compagni (1963), 74, 105–109; and tragicomedy, 108–109; and workers' struggles, 106–108
I soliti ignoti (1958), 92
Idylls of the King (Tennyson), 143
Il bell'Antonio (1960), 93
Il bidone (1955), 93
Il cappello a tre punte (1935), 89
Il deserto rosso (1964), 46
Il divo: La spettacolare vita di Giulio Andreotti (2008), 2
Il fantasma dell'opera (1998), 38
Il formaggio e i vermi (Ginzburg), xii
Il mio nome è Nessuno (1973), 20–25, 24
The Illusionist (2010), xxix–xxx, 188, 210–17, 215; and animation, 188; and false and true images, 215
I'm Not There (2007), 133
immigrants, 10
imperialism, 74, 77–80
impulse-image: and *Deep Crimson*, 54, 60; and *Deep Red*, 46, 51; and horror genre, 32–38; and naturalism, 32–36, 52; and *Thirst*, 64, 67
In Search of Lost Time (Proust), xv–xvi
"incompossibility," 186–87
Incrocci, Agenore, 96
Indian cinema, xiii
industrialization, 9
informatics, xxxi
interdisciplinary methodology, xii
Internet, ix
intertextuality, 100
Intolerance (1916), 1
The Iron Horse (1924), xxiii, 1, 5, 8–11, 11–12; and the melting pot, 10–11; and organic composition, 11; and the railroad, 9–10
irrationality, 85. *See also* surrealism
Italian cinema: and Fascism, 48–49; and film comedy, 89–93; and neorealism, 188, 189–90, 190–91, 193–94; and silent film, 129; and westerns, xxiii, 20–25

Jacobi, Ernst, 220–21
James, Sidney, 77
Jana Aranya (1976), 196–97
Jannings, Emil, 130
Jarmusch, Jim, 26
Jelinek, Elfriede, 224
Jewishness, 49
Jones, Alan, 40
Jour de fête (1949), 215
Jourdan, Raymond, 136
Joyce, James, xvi
just war theory, 110

Kaarsholm, xiii
Kafka, Franz, xxvi, 162–63, 245
Kafka: Toward a Minor Literature (Deleuze and Guattari), xiv, 124, 162–63
Kelly, Gene, 179
Keogh, Alexia, 142
Kermode, Frank, 152
Kerrigan, J. Warren, 6–7
Khruschev Thaw, 232–33
Khyber Pass, 77–80
Kierkegaard, Søren, 30
kilts, 79–80
Kim Hae-suk, 63
Kim Ok-bin, 64
Koc, Aysegul, 120
Kohler, Fred, 10
Korda, Zoltan, 77
Koven, Mikel J., 40, 46, 50, 92
Kracauer, Siegfried, xi, xiii
Kretschmann, Thomas, 40
Kubrick, Stanley, xxii, 2, 110
Kung Fu, 61
Kurosawa, Akira, 194

La grande guerra (1959), xxv, 74, 95, 106, 110–13; the Great War in, 108; and Kubrick, 110; repetition in, 112
La Passion de Jeanne d'Arc (1928), 129
La pianiste (2001), 188, 218, 224–32
La prise de pouvoir par Louis XIV, 128

La ragazza con la pistola (1968), 94
La sindrome di Stendhal (1996), xxiv, 33, 38–44, 42
La Strada (1954), 93
Laclau, Ernesto, xii
Ladri di biciclette (1948), 90
The Ladykillers (1955), 92
Lamarque, Libertad, 147
Lamarre, Thomas, 210–11, 213, 215, 216
Lambroso, Cesare, 235
landscape: and American westerns, 6, 10–11; and *An Angel at My Table*, 143; and *Brancaleone's Army*, 96, 99–100; and *The Camp at Thiaroye*, 165; and *Carry On Up the Khyber*, 77; and counter-historical thinking, xx, xxii–xxiii; and crisis of the movement-image, 4, 32; and *Deep Crimson*, 61; and *Deep Red*, 46–47; and Deleuze's philosophy of difference, 187; and global neorealism, 191, 193, 194, 196; and *A History of Violence*, 202; and *The Hole*, 181–82; and horror genre, 35; and *Hyenas*, 171, 175; and *The Illusionist*, 212, 213, 216; and Italian film comedy, 89; and *Morphia*, 240–41, 245; and *My Name Is Nobody*, 23; and naturalism, 52; and *The Organizer*, 106; and *The Ox-Bow Incident*, 19; and *The Rise of Louis XIV*, 135, 137; and *Stagecoach*, 12, 13; and *The Stendhal Syndrome*, 39; and *Thirst*, 69; and *What Time Is It There?*, 113, 114; and *The White Ribbon*, 220
Lang, Fritz, xvi
Language, Counter-Memory, Practice (Foucault), xvii
L'armata Brancaleone (1966), xxv, 74, 95–105, 106
L'Arrivée d'un train à La Ciotat (1896), 236
Larroca, Angelo, 154, 156–57
L'avventura (1960), 245
Le Rouge et le noir (Stendhal), 39
Le Sang des bêtes (1949), 38
Léaud, Jean-Pierre, 117–18, 121
Lee Kang-sheng, 115, 180
Leibniz, Gottfried Wilhelm, 126, 186–87
Leone, Sergio, 21, 203
Les Quatres cents coup (1959), 114
Les vacances de Monsieur Hulot (1953), 215

Levin, Harry, 76
Lewis, Jerry, 179
Lim, Bliss Cua, 64
Lincoln, Abraham, 8, 9, 11
Lindsay, Vachel, xi
linear time, 113–22
liquid movement, 183
The Logic of Sense (Deleuze), xiv, 38, 76, 113, 199
Lollobrigida, Gina, 91
London, Jack, 52
Loren, Sophia, 91
Losey, Joseph, xvii
low comedy, 111–12
Lowenstein, Adam, xix–xx, 34, 60, 198
Lusted, David, 8
Lynch, David, 202
lynching, 18

MacBean, James Roy, 139
Mackendrick, Alexander, 92
Maestro, Mia, 154
Magherini, Graziella, 39
magical thinking, 88, 104
Magimel, Benoit, 226
Magnani, Anna, 94
Maizani, Azucena, 147
Makovetskii, Sergei, 233
Mambéty, Djibril Diop, xxii, xxvi, 128, 163, 170–72, 175–77
Mamoulian, Rouben, 133
Manzur, Gregorio, 149–50
Marshall, George, xxiii, 1
Marshall, Tully, 7
Martin du Gard, Roger, 167
Martin-Jones, David, xx, 35, 123–24, 201
Marx, Karl, 70, 75, 79, 112; on repetition, 75
Marxism, xii, 83–84
masochism, 224–30, 234
Masochism: Coldness and Cruelty (1989), 225, 228–30
masquerade, 127
Mastroianni, Marcello, 92, 94, 107, 108–109
Materassi Sisters (1944), 89
Matter and Memory (Bergson), 3
Maura, Glauce, 49
Mayer, Sophie, 160

medievalism, 86–87
Meek, Donald, 11
Meek's Cutoff (2010), xxiii, 25–31, 29; and chance, 30; and territoriality, 30; uncertainty, 28–29
Melki, Claude, 150
melodrama: and allegory, xxx; and American westerns, 7; and *An Angel at My Table*, 145; and biopic, 129–30; and *Carry On Up the Khyber*, 74; and counter-historical thinking, xxiii; and *Deep Crimson*, 54, 59; and *A History of Violence*, 198, 199, 202; and humor, xxiv–xxv; and *Hyenas*, 173, 177; and *The Illusionist*, 216; and Italian film comedy, 89, 91; and *Meek's Cutoff*, 25; and *Morphia*, 244; and naturalism, 52; and *The Organizer*, 108; and *The Rise of Louis XIV*, 139; and *Tango*, 153; and *What Time Is It There?*, 120
Melville, Jean-Pierre, 92
memorialization, xii
memory: and *Brancaleone's Army*, 96, 100; and *The Camp at Thiaroye*, 165, 166, 170; and cinematic storytelling, xxvi; and comedy, 76; and counter-historical thinking, xii, xxix–xxxi; and *Deep Crimson*, 59; and *Deep Red*, 48; and *A History of Violence*, 200–201, 207; and horror cinema, 37; and *Hyenas*, 173; and *The Illusionist*, 216–17; and Italian film comedy, 105; and minoritarian cinema, 123–24; and *Morphia*, 245; and *My Name is Nobody*, 22, 23, 25; and neorealism, 188–90, 190–97; and powers of the false, 185–88; and *The Stendhal Syndrome*, 39, 44; and *Tango*, 153, 158; and *The Tango Lesson*, 162; and *Tangos: The Exile of Gardel*, 149–50, 151; and the time-image, xvii, 250; and *What Time Is It There?*, 114, 116, 117; and *The White Ribbon*, 225
Merchant, Veronica, 57
Méril, Macha, 49
Metahistory (White), xiii, xviii–xix
The Metamorphosis (Ovid), 88
metaphysics, 186
Mexican culture, 53–54, 57, 59–61
Mi chiamavono Trinità (1970), 21

Middle Ages, 74, 95–105, 100
The Middleman (1976), xxix, 196–97
milonguitas, 147–48
Minnelli, Vincente, 179
minoritarian cinematic forms: and *An Angel at My Table*, 140–45; and "becoming minoritarian," 162–64; and biopics, 128–32; and *The Camp at Thiaroye*, 164–70; and counter-historicizing, 123–28; and *The Hole*, 178–84; and *Hyenas*, 170–78; and minoritarian literature, 163; and minoritarian pedagogy, 146–53; and politics of exile, 153–58; and *The Rise of Louis XIV*, 132–40; and *The Tango Lesson*, 158–62
Miracle in Milan (1951), 91
mise-en-scène, 63, 109, 135, 191, 244
Mitchel, Thomas, 11
Miti, emblemi, spie: morfologia e storia (Ginzburg), xii
Mix, Tom, 7, 15
mock epics, 96
Modern Times (1936), 214
modernism and modernity: and Argento's films, 45; and *Brancalone's Army*, 96; and counter-historical thinking, xv–xvi, xxii; and *Deep Red*, 47; and global neorealism, 190; and *The Hole*, 178; and *The Illusionist*, 214; and Italian film comedy, 89, 91; and Monicelli's films, 94; and neorealism, 189; and *Of Freaks and Men*, 235–36; and rethinking of historicizing, xii; and *The Rise of Louis XIV*, 134–37; and *What Time Is It There?*, 119
Mon oncle (1958), 214–15, 215
Monicelli, Mario, xxv, 74, 91, 92, 94–96, 105; history and myth in, 100; and intertextuality, 96, 104; and Jews, 99
monstrosity, 102–103; and industrial action, 107–108
montage, 5, 106, 109
Monty Python and the Holy Grail (1975), xxv, 74, 80–89, 83, 84, 101; and historians, 86
monumental cinema: and American westerns, 8, 10–11; and biopics, 129–32; and *Carry On Up the Khyber*, 74; and crisis of the movement-image, 1, 4; and *Destry Rides Again*, 16; and *The Great War*, 110–

11; humor contrasted with, 72; and *Meek's Cutoff*, 26; and minoritarian cinema, 124; and *My Name Is Nobody*, 20–21, 25; and Nietzsche's historicizing scheme, 76; and *The Rise of Louis XIV*, 134
monumental history, xxvii, 21, 59, 111, 130–31
morality, 32–33, 186, 207
Moravia, Alberto, 136–37
Morgan, Harry, 17
Morphia (2008), xxx, 188, 232, 235, 240–46, 242
Mortensen, Viggo, 200–201
Mouffe, Chantal, xii
movement-image: and American westerns, 5–11; and Artaud's "raw cinema," 38; and biopic, 130, 131; and counter-historical thinking, xxi–xxii, xxiii; and "crisis of the movement image," 1–5; and *Deep Crimson*, 60; and *Deep Red*, 45; and *Destry Rides Again*, 14–16; exemplars of, xvi; and *A History of Violence*, 199–201, 205, 207–208; and *The Hole*, 183; and horror genre, 35–36; and *The Illusionist*, 210, 212, 217; and *Meek's Cutoff*, 25–31; and minoritarian consciousness, 123–24, 127; and *My Name Is Nobody*, 20–25; and naturalism, 32–33, 52; and *The Ox-Bow Incident*, 16–20; and philosophy of difference, 187–88; and *Stagecoach*, 11–14
Mr. Hulot's Holiday (1953), 215
Mukherjee, Pradip, 196–97
Münsterberg, Hugo, xi
Murnau, F. W., xvi, 4
Murphy, David, 167–68
Murray, Tim, 36, 249–50
music and musicals, 86–87, 106, 146–50, 178–80, 244–45
Musser, Charles, xiii
My Name Is Nobody (1973), xxiii, 20–25, 24; and history as style, 22–23; memory in, 20–22
My Name Is Trinity (1970), 21
myth, xxvii, 96

Nabucco (Verdi), 157
Nagisa, Ōshima, 33
Napoléon (1927), 129
Napoleon III (Louis Napoleon), 75, 79
Narova, Cecilia, 153–54
nation building, 5
national identity, xx–xxi; and American railroads, 8–11; and *Destry Rides Again*, 16; and *The Iron Horse*, 10–11; and national media, xx–xxi; and wartime propaganda, 18
nationalism, 219
Native Americans, 6, 8, 26–28, 30
naturalism: and Argento's films, 38–44; and *Deep Crimson*, 52–61; and *Deep Red*, 45–51; Deleuze on, 32; and the impulse-image, 32–36, 32–38, 52; and *Thirst*, 61–69
Naveira, Gustavo, 161
Nazism, 220
Nebbia, Carlos, 154
Nehru, Jawaharlal, 191
neocolonialism, 146, 164, 171, 176
neorealism: Bazin on, 89–90; Biswas on, 190; and *Deep Crimson*, 54; Deleuze on, xxiv; and Fascism, 189; and horror genre, xxiii–xxiv, 35–36; and Italian film comedy, 89–91, 95; in Italy, 189; and movement-image, 2; and *The Organizer*, 106, 108; origins of, 188–90; and post-World War II cinema, 89; and Ray's films, xxix, 190–97; Rossellini and, 188; and suffering bodies, 90; and transnational, 190–91; and *The White Ribbon*, 222
Neptune's Daughter (1949), 179
Nevolina, Anzhelika, 234
New Zealand culture, 140, 141, 145
Newman, Kathleen, 150
Ni Na bian ji dian (2001), 74
Nicolodi, Daria, 46
Nietzsche, Friedrich: and becoming, xvii; and comedy, 70, 71; and Deleuze's time-image, xvii–xviii; and falsifying narration, xxviii–xxix; and historical repetition, 112; and history and humor, 75–76; and *A History of Violence*, 208; and minoritarian cinema, 127; and monumental history, 4, 21; and theater of history, 218
nihilism, xxix

nonlinear time, 88
nonsense, 88–89

O'Brien, George, 9
Odysseus, 22
Odyssey (Homer), 22
Of Freaks and Men (1998), xxx, 188, 232–40, 239
Oldboy (2003), 61
"On Uses and Disadvantages of History for Life" (Nietzsche), 76
Once Upon a Time in the West (1968), 8, 21, 203
Once Were Warriors (1994), 140
Open City (1945), 89, 90, 188
Opera (1987), 38–39
operaismo, 105
operatic character, 25
optical drama, 120
optical-sound image, 124
organic representation, 18
The Organizer (1963), xxv, 74, 95, 105–10
The Origin of German Tragic Drama (Benjamin), xiii, xxx, 171, 245–46
Orozco, Regina, 53
Otherness, 28, 68
Ovid, 88
The Ox-Bow Incident (1943), xxiii, 1, 16–20, 19; evolution of western, 17–18
Ozu, Yasujiro, 121

Pagni, Eros, 46
Paisan (1946), 90
Pane, amore, e fantasia (1953), 91
Pane, amore e gelosia (1954), 91
panoramic landscape, 6, 10
parable: and Haneke's films, 218; and *Hyenas*, 171; and Italian film comedy, 93; and *My Name Is Nobody*, 24; and *The Organizer*, 109; and *The Rise of Louis XIV*, 138
Paredes, Marisa, 56
Park Chan-wook, xxiv, 35, 61–69
Park In-hwan, 62
parody: and *Brancalone's Army*, 96, 98, 100; and *Carry On Up the Khyber*, 73, 79; and *Deep Crimson*, 52–53, 59–60; and "effective history," xxv; and *The Great War*, 110; and history and humor, 76–77; and *A History of Violence*, 202, 205; and *Hyenas*, 172; and Italian film comedy, 91–93, 95; and minoritarian consciousness, 127; and *Monte Python and the Holy Grail*, 80, 84–87; and *My Name Is Nobody*, 21, 25; and *Once Upon a Time in the West*, 21, 22; and *The Rise of Louis XIV*, 134; and *Thirst*, 63; and types of counter-historicizing, 71; use in counter-history, 70, 71
Pascal, Blaise, 30
Pasolini, Pier Paolo, xvii, 92–93, 127, 218
The Passion of Joan of Arc (1928), 129
Pather Panchali (1955), xxix, 191, 192
Paths of Glory (1957), 2, 110
patriarchy, 162
patriotism, 110, 111
Patton, Will, 26
Peckinpah, Sam, 21
pedagogy: and biopics, 132; and *Brancalone's Army*, 100; and *The Camp at Thiaroye*, xxvi, 164–70; and counter-historical thinking, xxi; and cultural impact of cinema, xi; and global neorealism, 197; and Haneke's films, 217–19; and *Hyenas*, 176–77; and minoritarian cinema, 125, 128; and *The Organizer*, 109; and *The Piano Teacher*, 224–32; and rationale for counter-history though film, xi; and *The Rise of Louis XIV*, 133–40, 136; and storytelling through cinema, xxvi; and *The Tango Lesson*, 159, 162; and *Tangos: The Exile of Gardel*, 146–53; and *The White Ribbon*, 224
Peeping Tom (1960), 44, 47
Perón, Evita, 148
Perón, Juan, 148
Peronism, 150
perspective, 134
Petrie, xxi
Petrov, Peter, 232–33
The Phantom of the Opera (1998), 38
The Piano Player (Jelinek), 224
The Piano Teacher (2001), xxx, 224–32, 231
Pisters, Patricia, xix, 46
poetry, 104, 146–47
Poggioli, Fernando Maria, 89

Polan, Dana, 17, 135
political corruption, 173
political repression, 148–49
popular cinema, xix–xx, 92–93
pornography, 36, 224, 233–35, 238–39
Porton, Richard, 171
positivists, 34
"possible worlds" concept, 126
postcolonialism, xii, xxvi, 121
postmodernity, xii, xviii, 119, 138
poststructuralism, xii, xxvi
postwar world, 20–25, 25–31, 240
Potter, Sally, xxii, 128, 158–62
Powell, Michael, 44, 46, 214
powerlessness of thought, xv, 71–72
powers of the false, xvii, xxvii–xxix, 186–88, 209–10, 217, 239, 243
Pratidwandi (1972), 194–96, 195
Pribytiye poyezda (1996), 236
Price, Brian, 222
Profondo rosso (1975), xxiv, 33, 38–39, 45–51, 47
Profundo carmesi (1996), xxiv, 33, 46, 52–61, 54
Prokhorov, Vadim, 233
propaganda, 18
prostitution, 12, 146–47, 171–72, 196, 238
Protestantism, 219
Proust, Marcel, xv–xvi
psychoanalysis, 39, 49, 225
punctum, 37–38

Quattro passi fra le nuvole (1942), 89
Queen Christina (1933), 133
Querelle (1982), 44
quest motif, 87–88, 96, 99–100
Quinn, Anthony, 17
Quiroga, Rosita, 147, 148

race issues, 18, 166, 168–69
railroads, 8–11
Rajchman, John, xviii, 250
Rancière, Jacques, xix, 34, 105, 139
raw cinema, 38
Ray, Satyajit, xxii, xxix, 188–89, 190–97
realism: and *Deep Crimson*, 54–55; evolution of, 190–91; and idle time, 192; and Italian film comedy, 90; and naturalism, 34–35; and *The White Ribbon*, 220
The Red and the Black (Stendhal), 39
Red Desert (1964), 46, 193
The Red Shoes (1948), 214
Reich, Jacqueline, 92–93, 95
Reichardt, Kelly, xxiii, 26
religion and religious themes: and affection-image, 33; and Artaud's "raw cinema," 38; and biopic, 129; and *Brancalone's Army*, 96, 99–100, 102, 103; and counter-historical thinking, xviii; and cultural impact of cinema, xi; and *Deep Crimson*, 53, 57, 59–60; and *Monte Python and the Holy Grail*, 81–82, 86, 88; and *The Ox-Bow Incident*, 18; and *The Stendhal Syndrome*, 39; and *Thirst*, 62–63, 66–69
Remembrance of Things Past (Proust), xv–xvi
Renoir, Jean, xvi, 4, 107
repetition, xxii, 212–13, 218–19
Resnais, Alain, 114, 117, 250
revenge motif: and *Brancalone's Army*, 104; and *A History of Violence*, 201; and *Hyenas*, 171–74, 176; and Monicelli's films, 94; and *My Name Is Nobody*, 22; and *The Ox-Bow Incident*, 18; and Park's films, 61; and *Stagecoach*, 13
revisionist westerns, 26
rhizomatic model of expression, xxi, 48, 51, 163, 208
Rhodes, John David, xxx, 222
Rififi (1955), 92
Ripstein, Arturo, xxii, xxiv, 35, 52–61; and idiosyncratic surrealism, 53–54; and Mexican history, 56, 57, 59
The Rise of Louis XIV (1966 [TV]), 128, 133–40, 138; and modernity, 135; as spectacle, 138; and television, 135
Risi, Dino, 91
Risorgimento, 189
Rivarola, Carlos, 153–54
road films, 55
Rodriguez, Rosi, 147
Roma, città aperta (1945), 89–90
Romains, Jules, 167
Romance in Double Bass (1911), 243

romantic comedy, 89
romanticism, 232
Rome, Open City (1945), 89–90
Rondeaux, Ron, 26–27
Roosevelt, Theodore, 7
Roper, Hugh Trevor, 79
Rosen, Philip, xiii
Rosenstone, Robert, x, xiii, xix, 128–29
Rossellini, Roberto: and biopic, 128; and Italian cinema, 92; and neorealism, 188; and post-World War II cinema, 89; and *The Rise of Louis XIV*, 133–40; and time-image, xvii
Rough Riders, 7
Russell, Ken, 83
Russian Revolution, 241, 245
"Russian Train Arriving," 236, 237

sadism/sadomasochism, 221, 225, 228–30, 234
Said, Edward, xii
Salas, Fabián, 161
Salazkina, Masha, 241, 245
Salmi, Hannu, xix–xx
Salo (1975), 218
San Martino, José de, 149–50, 153
Sandrelli, Stefania, 101
Sargeson, Frank, 143–44
satire: and *Brancalone's Army*, 96, 102; and *Deep Crimson*, 53; and *Eighteenth Brumaire of Louis Napoleon*, 75–76; and *The Great War*, 110; and *Hyenas*, 171–72; and Italian film comedy, 89, 91–92, 95, 96; and *Monte Python and the Holy Grail*, 88; and *The Rise of Louis XIV*, 134
Saura, Carlos, xxii, 128, 153, 154
Savigliano, Marta E., 146–49
The Scarlet Empress (1934), 133
Scarpelli, Furio, 96
Schaefer, Claudia, 57
Schifrin, Lalo, 153
Schivelbusch, Wolfgang, 8, 213–14
schizophrenia, 141, 144–45
"The Scholar Gipsy" (Arnold), 143
Schoonover, Karl, xix, xxiii–xxiv, 41, 50, 90
science fiction, xx, 63, 179

Scorsese, Martin, 205
Seduced and Abandoned (1964), 93
Seemabaddha (1974), 196–97
Sembène, Ousmane, xxvi, 128, 163, 164–65, 168
Sen, Mrinal, 197
Senegal, 171
sensationalism, 44
sense and nonsense, 72
sentimentality, 212
The Seventh Seal (1957), 100–101
sexuality and sexual themes: and *Carry On Up the Khyber*, 77–80; and *Deep Crimson*, 53; and *A History of Violence*, 206–207; and *Morphia*, 242–43; and *Of Freaks and Men*, 234–38
Shaviro, Steven, xiii, 126
Shin Ha-kyun, 63
Shocking Representations (Lowenstein), xx
Sica, Vittorio De, 91
silent films, 129
Simon, Michel, 107
Simondon, Gilbert, 211
small form, 4, 11, 14–16, 25, 73
Sobchack, Vivian, xiii, xix
social justice, 13
social realism: and *Deep Red*, 51; and global neorealism, 191; and *Of Freaks and Men*, 235; and *The Organizer*, 105, 108; and *The Ox-Bow Incident*, 17, 20
Solá, Miguel Ángel, 153
Solanas, Fernando E., xxii, 128, 147–49, 151–52, 153, 158
Sollima, Sergio, 21
Song Kang-ho, 62
Sordi, Alberto, 94, 110, 111
Sorelle Materassi (1944), 89
Sorrentino, Paolo, 2
Spaak, Catherine, 98
spaghetti western, 8, 21, 91, 201
Spanish Civil War, 153, 155
special effects, xx. *See also* digital technology and media
spectacle: and American westerns, 6, 10; and Argento's films, 43–44; and biopic, 130; and *Brancalone's Army*, 103; and *Carry On Up the Khyber*, 73, 78, 80; and *A History of*

Violence, 201; and *The Hole,* 179, 181, 183; and horror cinema, 36; and *Meek's Cutoff,* 25; and minoritarian consciousness, 124, 128; and Nietzsche's historicizing scheme, 76; and *The Piano Teacher,* 225, 229; and *The Rise of Louis XIV,* 133–40; and *Tango,* 153, 158; and *The Tango Lesson,* 159; and *Tangos: The Exile of Gardel,* 148–49

spectatorship: and cinematic realism, 248; and counter-historical thinking, xix, xxii; and global neorealism, 192; and Haneke's films, xxx, 217–19; and horror cinema, 36–37; and *The Illusionist,* 211; and *Meek's Cutoff,* 27; and *Morphia,* 244; and *The Rise of Louis XIV,* 139; and *What Time Is It There?,* 117

Spinoza, Baruch, 185–86

Spivak, Gayatri Chakravorty, xii

Stagecoach (1939), xxiii, 1, 11–14, *14;* and Civil War, 13; and the Depression, 12; and John Wayne, 13

Steiner, George, 41

Stendhal (Marie-Henri Beyle), 39

The Stendhal Syndrome (1996), xxiv, 33, 38–44, *42*

stereotypes: and *Carry On Up the Khyber,* 77; and *Deep Red,* 48; and Italian film comedy, 91; and Monicelli's films, 94; and *Monte Python and the Holy Grail,* 87; and *The Organizer,* 106. See also caricature

Sternberg, Josef von, 4, 133

Stewart, Garrett, 224

Stewart, James, 15

Stivaletti, Sergio, 44

Stroheim, Erich von, 35

Subaltern Studies Group, xii

suicide, 62, 68, 165, 238

Sukhorukov, Viktor, 233

supernaturalism, 61–69

surrealism: and Argento's films, 38; and comedy, 73; and counter-historical thinking, xv, xx; and *Deep Crimson,* 53–54, 56–57, 60–61; and digital technology, 43–44; and Haneke's films, 219; and *A History of Violence,* 202; and horror cinema, xxiv, 37; and *Hyenas,* 171; and Italian film comedy, 89; and *Meek's Cutoff,* 26; and *Monte Python and the Holy Grail,* 81; and naturalism, 32

Suspiria (1977), 38

Syberberg, Hans-Jürgen, xvii

Sypher, Wylie, 70

Tagore, Sharmila, 197

Taipei, 121

Tamahori, Lee, 140

Tango (1998), xxvi, 128, 153–58, *156, 157;* as minority form, 157–58; violence and torture in, 156

The Tango Lesson (1997), xxvi, 128, 158–62, *161*

Tangos: The Exile of Gardel (1985), xxvi, 128, 146–53, *152;* and colonial past, 146–48; deterritorialization in, 151; life of exiles in, 149–50

tanguedia, 149, 150–52, *152*

Tarantino, Quentin, 61

Tati, Jacques, xxix–xxx, 188, 211–13, 214–17, *215*

Taxi Driver (1976), 205

Taylor, Clyde, 172

technological advance, ix, xi, xviii, 43, 45, 247–48

teleology, xxviii, 4, 5

television: and *An Angel at My Table,* 140; and Argento's films, 43, 45–46; and biopics, 128–29; and historical events, ix; and *The Hole,* 180; and horror cinema, 36; and *The Illusionist,* 211; and minoritarian cinema, 127; and *Morphia,* 246; and *The Rise of Louis XIV,* 135, 139

temporality, xxvii–xxviii, 36, 86–87, 88, 96. See also time-image

Tennyson, Alfred, 143

theater of cruelty. See cruelty

theatricality, 135, 170–78

Thérèse Raquin (Zola), 63–64, 66–68

thinking image: and biopic, 132; and crisis of the movement-image, xxiv; and horror genre, 34; and minoritarian consciousness, 127; and thought without image, 71–72

Thirst (2009), xxiv, 33, 61–69, *68;* and body politics, 62; and impulse-image, 67; and religion, 63–64; and vampirism, 61, 68
Thomas, Gerald, 77–80
Thomson, Fred, 7
thought without image, 72
A Thousand Plateaus (Deleuze and Guattari), 123, 162
Threads and Traces (Ginzburg), xviii
Three-Cornered Hat (1935), 89
Thriller (1979), 159
time-image: and affection-image, 33; and biopic, 131–32; and Chronos, 113; and counter-historical thinking, xxi–xxii; and crisis of the movement-image, 1; and Deleuze's philosophy of difference, 187; and digital media, xxxi; and the future of cinema, 248–50; and global neorealism, 192, 196; and *A History of Violence,* 199–200, 208–209; and *The Hole,* 183; and *The Illusionist,* 210–11, 213, 216; and minoritarian consciousness, 123, 125, 127; Murray on, 249–50; and *Of Freaks and Men,* 233; origin of concept, xvi–xvii; and "powers of the false," xxvii–xxviii; and *The Stendhal Syndrome,* 40; and *What Time Is It There?,* 114; and *The White Ribbon,* 222
Tognazzi, Ugo, 94
Torlasco, Domietta, 219, 245
Torrence, Ernest, 7
Totò, 94
tragicomedy: and *commedia all'italiana,* xxv; and *The Great War,* 110–11; and *Hyenas,* 171; and *The Organizer,* 105–106, 108, 109–10; and *Tango,* 153; and *Tangos: The Exile of Gardel,* 147; and *Thirst,* 69; tragedy's relationship to comedy, 70; and *What Time Is It There?,* 114
trains, 9–10, 213–14
transience, 192–93
transnational context of film: and biopic, 129; and counter-historical thinking, xx; and cultural impact of cinema, xi; and Deleuze's philosophy of difference, 188; and *A History of Violence,* 207; and *The Hole,* 179, 182; and horror genre, 35; and neorealism, 188; and Park's films, 61–62; and rethinking of historicizing, xii; and *Tangos: The Exile of Gardel,* 149
travesty, 87
Trevor, Claire, 11
trickster figures, 23
Trinity Is Still My Name (1971), 21
The Triplets of Belleville (2003), 212
Trofim (1996), xxx, 188, 235–36, 237, 239
Tropics of Discourse (White), xiii, xix
Truffaut, François, 114, 117–18
truthful narration, 186
Tsai Ming-liang, xx, xxii, xxvii, 122, 128, 178–84

Ukadike, Nwachukwu Frank, 168, 171, 173–74, 176
Un Chien andalou (1929), 37
Union Pacific (1939), 11
Union Pacific Railroad, 9
Ursprung des deutschen Trauerspiels (Benjamin), xiii
Uruguay, 151

Valentino, Rudolph, 148
Valerii, Tonino, xxiii, 21
vampirism, 61–69
Vasudevan, Ravi, 193
Verdi, Giuseppe, 157
Verga, Giovanni, 189
Verón, Pablo, 159
Vertinsky, Alexander, 241
Vertov, Dziga, xi
Vichy regime, 167
vigilante justice, 16–20, *19*
Vigo, Jean, 37
The Village Voice, 26
violence: and *Brancalone's Army,* 98; and *The Camp at Thiaroye,* 167, 170; and *Carry On Up the Khyber,* 73; and *Deep Crimson,* 52–54, 58–61; and *Deep Red,* 45–51; and Haneke's films, xxx, 217–19; and *A History of Violence,* 198–209; and *Hyenas,* 172, 176; and the impulse-image, 52; and Italian film comedy, 90, 93; and *Monte Python and the Holy Grail,* 81, 86–87; and naturalism, 52; and *Of Freaks*

and Men, 238; and *The Organizer*, 110; and *The Piano Teacher*, 225, 228, 230; and *The Stendhal Syndrome*, 40; and *Tango*, 154–58; and *Tangos: The Exile of Gardel*, 149; and *Thirst*, 61–67; and *The White Ribbon*, 219–24
The Virginian, 15
Virilio, Paul, xxi
The Visit (Dürrenmatt), 171, 172
visual technologies, ix–x; in *Stendhal Syndrome*, 39–40. *See also* digital technology and media
Vitti, Monica, 94
Volonté, Gian Maria, 97
voyeurism, 229–30, 234

Wagner, George, 11
wartime propaganda, 18
water symbolism, 115–16
Wayne, John, 7, 13, 14
Welles, Orson, xvii
Wellman, William, xxiii, 1, 16
Wertmüller, Lina, 91, 95
westerns, xxii–xxiii, 1–31, 207
What Is Philosophy? (Deleuze and Guattari), xiv, 126, 151, 250
What Time Is It There? (2001), xxvii, 74, 113–22, 117, 120; bodily exhaustion in, 11; and clock time, 116; mourning in, 115
White, Frederick, 235
White, Hayden, xiii, xviii–xix
The White Ribbon (*Das weisse Band*, 2009), xxx, 188, 218, 219–24, 223; childhood in, 222; and powers of the false, 222
"white telephone" films, 89
Whitehead, Alfred North, 126
The Wild Bunch (1969), 21
Wild West shows, 6
Williams, Esther, xx
Williams, Linda, 44
Williams, Michelle, 26
Wilson, Lois, 7–8
Winninger, Charles, 16
witchcraft motif, 81, 84, 85, 101, 103
World Bank, 171
The World of Apu (1959), xxix, 191
World War I, 2, 74, 110–13, 224
World War II, xii, xxiii, 1, 12, 89, 164–70

Yang Kuei-mei, 180

Zachanassian, Claire, 172
Zavattini, Cesare, 189
Zola, Émile, 35, 52, 63–64, 66–68

MARCIA LANDY is Distinguished Professor in English/Film Studies with a secondary appointment in the French and Italian Department at the University of Pittsburgh. Her books include *Fascism in Film: The Italian Commercial Cinema 1931–1943* (1986); *British Genres: Cinema and Society, 1930–1960* (1991); *Imitations of Life: A Reader on Film and Television Melodrama* (1991); *Film Politics, and Gramsci* (1994); *Cinematic Uses of the Past* (1996); *The Folklore of Consensus: Theatricality and Spectacle in the Italian Cinema, 1930–1943* (1998); *Italian Film* (2000); *Stars: The Film Reader* (2004; with Lucy Fischer); *Monty Python's Flying Circus* (2005); and *Stardom, Italian Style: Screen Performance and Personality in Italian Cinema* (IUP, 2008). Her essays have appeared in *Screen, Quarterly Review of Film and Video, boundary 2, Post Script, Rethinking Marxism, Journal of Romance Studies, Cinema Journal, Jump Cut, KinoKultura,* and in many anthologies.

www.ingramcontent.com/pod-product-compliance
Lightning Source LLC
Chambersburg PA
CBHW050431240426
43661CB00055B/2339